In the Footsteps of Peter Ellis

Architect of Oriel Chambers and 16 Cook Street, Liverpool

Robert Ainsworth and Graham Jones

Liverpool History Society, 2013

First published 2013 by the Liverpool History Society.

The images on the front cover and the facing page to chapter 10 are courtesy of the Mitchell Library, Glasgow. Those on the facing pages to chapters 1 and 2 are courtesy of the Athenaeum. That on the facing page to chapter 9 is courtesy of Colin Wilkinson at The Bluecoat Press. Images on facing pages to the remaining chapters are courtesy of the Liverpool Record Office (LRO). The origins of images within chapters are identified in the captions. All modern photographs are by Graham Jones.

The Society regrets if any part of this book inadvertently breaches copyright held by any other person or body with regard to either images or quotations. The views expressed in this book are those of the individual authors and are not necessarily those of the LHS. Addresses for internet site references were correct at the date of publication.

The Liverpool History Society is a registered charity, no. 1093736, and was founded on 18th February 2001. It publishes an annual Journal to which members and non-members are encouraged to contribute articles, and provides the Journal and several newsletters each year to its members. Talks are held once a month on eight months of the year with invited speakers offering subjects on a wide range of subjects concerning the history of Liverpool and its environs. Further details can be found on the Society's website - *www.liverpoolhistorysociety.org.uk*
and the Society can be contacted at - *enquiries@liverpoolhistorysociety.org.uk*

Designed and typeset by Matthew Duddington - *www.matthewduddington.com*
Main text in Adobe Garamond Pro. Titles and captions to images in Gill Sans.

Printed in China by WKT.

ISBN 978-0-9559428-3-9

Dedicated to the memory of

Rob Ainsworth, 1955-2012

who enthusiastically researched this book with me
but whose death denied him the opportunity
of seeing its publication.

From Rob and me
With best wishes
Graham

Graham Jones
The Athenaeum
2013

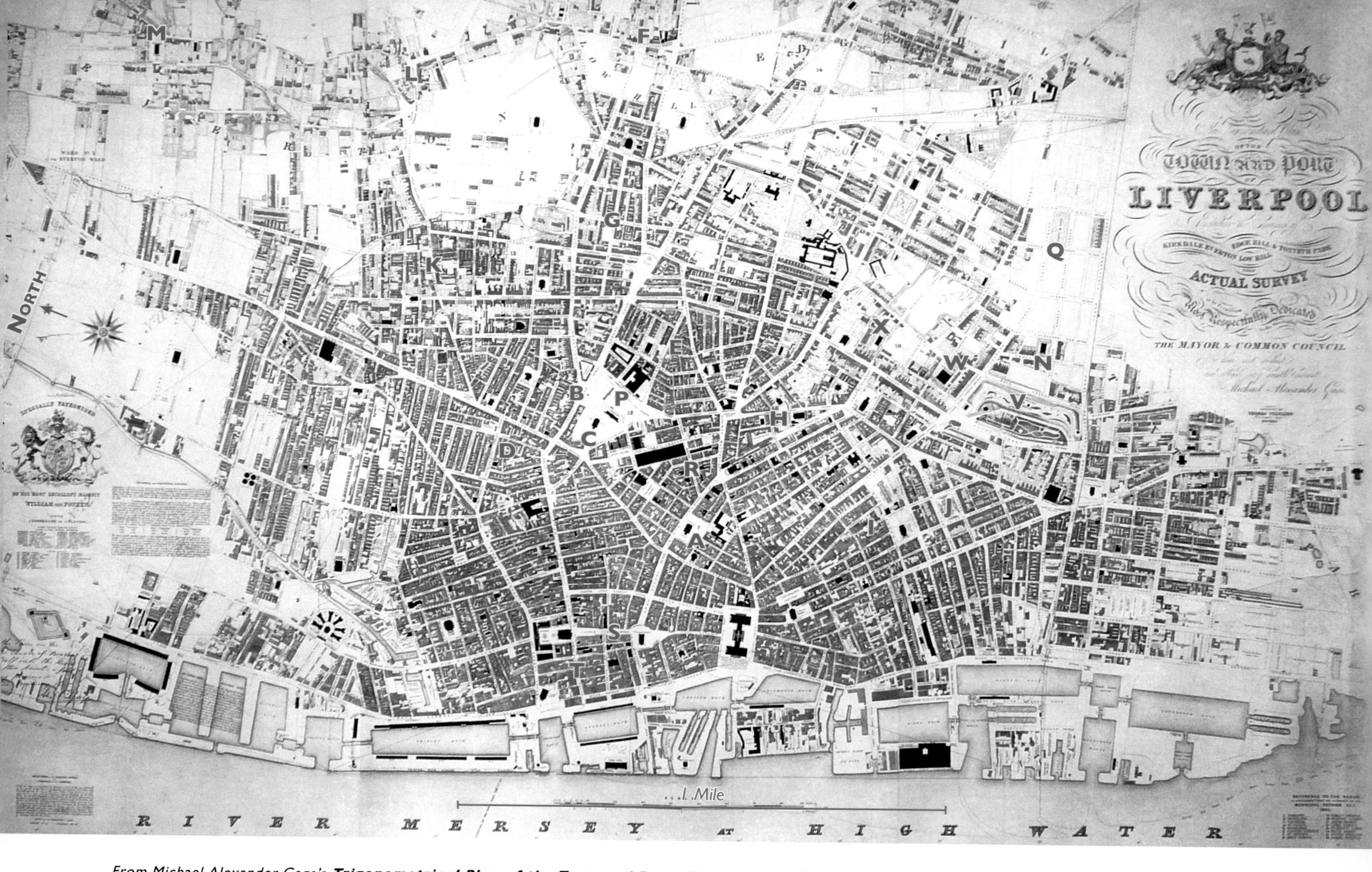

From Michael Alexander Gage's ***Trigonometrical Plan of the Town and Port of Liverpool***, 1835, oriented approximately to the east.

A St Peter, Church Street.
B Shaw's Brow.
C St John, Haymarket.
D Primrose Hill.
E Gloucester Street.
F Low Hill.
G Finch Street.
H Renshaw Street.
I Kent Square.
J Great George Square.
K Richmond Row.
L Everton Village.
M St George, Everton.
N St Bride, Percy Street.
P Site of St George's Hall.
Q Sandon Street and Falkner Square.
R Clayton Square.
S Castle Street, Cook Street and Orange Court.
T Water Street and site of Oriel Chambers.
V St James' Cemetery.
W Hope Street.
X St Philip, Hardman Street.

In the Footsteps of Peter Ellis

Architect of Oriel Chambers and 16 Cook Street, Liverpool

Preface

In 2009 I began researching the history of some of the buildings which stand in Water Street and the surrounding streets, or which stood there many years ago, together with a selection of their occupants. This was with a view to creating a series of articles, under the general title '*Walking on Water Street*', for offering to the Liverpool Record Office (LRO). One of those articles began to take shape on the subject of Oriel Chambers.

In April 2011 Cynthia Stonall, the librarian for the Liverpool History Society, invited me to join her and two of her colleagues for lunch. One of her friends was Rob Ainsworth, and by the end of that lunch Rob and I realised that we shared a mutual interest in discovering more about Peter Ellis, and that in both cases our curiosity had been aroused by reading Quentin Hughes' wonderful book *Seaport.* I told Rob that I had inherited my mother's copy of the 1993 Bluecoat Press reprint, and Rob delighted me with the story of how – much to his mother's surprise – he had used several months of paper-round wages to purchase an original 1964 hard-back copy.

Rob showed immediate interest in what I was preparing and began to undertake some of his own research. Then, in an e-mail in August 2011, he told me that his mother's maiden name was Ellis and that '*five of my Mum's brothers fought in the Spanish Civil War. They then went on to fight in the Second World War. I was surprised they felt so strongly about Fascism that they fought against Franco. I now know where I got my battling streak from.*' With the information that Rob had an Ellis connection it seemed a delightful idea for us to combine our interests and continue to research Peter Ellis together.

Little did I realise how rapidly, with Rob's enthusiasm, my research would develop into the possibility of a book. Where I had concentrated on the Liverpool directories and the vast collection of archive material at the LRO for information on Peter Ellis, Rob commenced an on-line search of the *Liverpool Mercury* and soon identified a dozen fascinating references of which I had been unaware, and which led me to follow up these leads in the LRO's archives. His results also prompted me to begin my own extensive search of the *Mercury*, an undertaking which was to prove immensely productive. Rob showed me around the library of the Athenaeum where for several years he had been a proprietor, and thus opened up another rich source of material for our book. He also identified the site of Peter and Mary's grave at Toxteth Cemetery which we subsequently visited together.

Then, in late November 2011, Rob was suddenly admitted to hospital. A few weeks later a bewildered Rob, family and friends were told by surgeons that he had three days to live, and he began to put his affairs in order and to make his farewells. It was therefore nothing short of a miracle that another consultant heard of the case and, from his experience of having operated on Rob ten years earlier, knew that there was the possibility of a surgical intervention. Within a few hours, an operating theatre which had become available because of the lead-up to Christmas was commandeered, and the subsequent combination of wonderful teamwork at the Royal Liverpool University Hospital, his surgeon's magnificent skill and Rob's all-important *battling streak* proved triumphant. Christmas Day 2011 was one for particular celebration, and Rob was considered well enough to be discharged in mid-January 2012.

Over the next few months, along with all the other things that Rob again entered into with all his customary enthusiasm and commitment, he steadily continued his research for our book. Throughout that period however he was suffering recurring bouts of pain, and the e-mails that he sent me quite frequently were composed in the small hours of the morning when, unable to sleep, he sat at his computer, distracted himself with work, and continued to search for new evidence about Peter Ellis. On the last day that I saw him in July before he went into hospital for a second time, he handed me, with great excitement, a document we had requested from a Glasgow library. Although unknown to us at the time, it was to be his final contribution, and it is this patent diagram that I have selected for the front cover of our book.

Sadly, a second surgeon's miracle proved not to be possible and, with Rob's passing from this life on 4th August 2012, I lost a great friend and co-researcher with whom I had worked all too briefly.

I continued the research for a further six months and although, by force of circumstance, our story is in my words, many aspects of Peter's career in the pages that follow are here only because of Rob's dedicated research throughout those sleepless, pain-filled nights.

Graham Jones
2013

Acknowledgements

Permission was kindly given by Roger Hull at the Liverpool Record Office (LRO) for me to reproduce material from their extensive collections of art work, maps, books and photographs. Much of my later research was carried out at the LRO's temporary accommodation at their Archive Satellite Service at Sandhills following the closure of the old Central Library building on William Brown Street in preparation for refurbishment. These were difficult times for the staff, with material stored in several dispersed locations, and they responded magnificently to every one of my requests for items to be retrieved. On more than one occasion, their enthusiastic support for our research presented me with unexpected material which I have gratefully incorporated, of which an 1888 Letters of Administration reference discovered by Kevin Roach is one example. Through the facilities made available by the Liverpool Libraries Information Services, free access was obtained to both *ancestryinstitution.com* and the British Library on-line archive of 19th century British Newspapers. The latter enabled me to carry out a selective OCR search of the *Liverpool Mercury* and this proved to be a crucial source of information for the book.

In 1797 a prospectus entitled '*Outlines of a plan for a combined Library and Newsroom,*' indicated that a building was being designed to have '*within reach a valuable repository of books in every department of useful knowledge,*' and to '*furnish the room with all the best maps that can be procured.*' The result was the Athenaeum, originally on Church Street, and its popularity was such that the membership limit was soon increased to 500. Several early members find mention in our book, whilst James Picton, who was a contemporary of Peter Ellis, by virtue of his excellent and comprehensive *Memorials of Liverpool*, and Quentin Hughes, through his pioneering book *Seaport*, are both quoted extensively. The Athenaeum continues to flourish today as a unique private source for investigating Liverpool's history, complementing that of the LRO, and it is thanks to the inspiration of the founder members that valuable material exists in its library for incorporating into our account of Peter Ellis and the Liverpool in which he lived and worked. The ability to make frequent inspections of the comprehensive collection of *Gore's Liverpool Directories* proved to be of major benefit, and the Athenaeum's Library Sub-Committee kindly granted me permission to incorporate copies of many of its items, particularly art work and maps. I am most grateful to the immense help provided to me by the librarians, Joan Hanford and Vincent Roper, who so often have been essential guides to finding my way around the Athenaeum's wonderful collections. On several occasions they kindly brought to my attention items of which I was unaware, the 1801 population survey being but one example.

It is a measure of the fundamental importance of these primary sources of material that, of the approximately 190 archive images in this book, over 80 are from the LRO and over 50 from the Athenaeum, whilst use has been made of over 70 of the several hundred relevant references in the *Liverpool Mercury*, with a number appearing as images. Other libraries which also provided us with valuable archive material are Birkenhead Central Library, Mitchell Library (Glasgow), Sefton Local History Unit and Sheffield Central Library.

Valuable use has also made been made of the *Lancashire OnLine Parish Clerk Project* database which proved to have important BMD information which is missing from other sources, particularly concerning several of Peter's siblings.

It will become apparent, from the many chapter references and the captions to images, that many other people, publishers and websites have also kindly allowed reproduction of their material. To them I offer my grateful thanks, with particular mention of the following.

The Blue Plaques Team at English Heritage provided a copy of their 1999 report which had led to the plaque being placed at Falkner Square and which also included reference material which I was able to follow up. Iain Jackson, lecturer at the School of Architecture, University of Liverpool, drew my attention to the Quentin Hughes Archive at the Sydney Jones Library, material from which I subsequently incorporated in several chapters by courtesy of Maureen Watry, Head of Special Collections and Archives. Over and above permission to quote frequently from his excellent *Pevsner Guide* on Liverpool (© Yale University Press), Joseph Sharples kindly provided several key references and interpretations which are included in a number of chapters; drawing my attention to the Corporation Lease Registers was of particular importance. Colin Wilkinson at The Bluecoat Press e-mailed a unique 1880s view of Water Street from his extensive personal collection, many photographs from which appear on his interesting website. It was a flash of inspiration that prompted my wife, Martha, to search for Peter Ellis in *The London Gazette*, the result of which led to a considerable portion of chapter 10.

This account of Peter would have had considerably less depth had Rob and I not received such generous help and support from so many people.

Colleagues at the Liverpool History Society enthusiastically supported our suggestion that the book could be an LHS publication and I am grateful for the encouragement that they subsequently have shown, including proof-reading. Ron Jones, the Society's Journal and newsletter editor, kindly supplied the vital solution to our dilemma when neither of the two English printers that we approached felt able to quote, and I extend my particular thanks to our printers, WKT, in China. Ron also provided an interesting ca. 1950 photograph of 16 Cook Street showing it in context with its neighbours.

Last, but very much not least, I would like to express my grateful thanks to our book designer, Matthew Duddington, who worked on the layout with immense thoughtfulness and creativity. He also patiently coped with the countless occasions that I requested amendments to the text and when I asked for new material to be added at a late stage to chapters that had already been carefully set out. I am delighted with the result, and I know that Rob also would have been immensely pleased.

Graham Jones
Liverpool History Society
2013

Introduction

Although Peter Ellis is now known in architectural circles the world over as a pioneer in the method of construction of office buildings which later would lead to American skyscrapers, this is not a book on architecture.

It is the history of Peter himself, the story of a man born 1st August 1805 at Shaw's Brow, and who died 20th October 1884 at Falkner Square, having lived to see the town of Liverpool become a city.

It is perhaps a book for the many people who came to know of Peter Ellis through the account of his work by Quentin Hughes in his marvellous book *Seaport* ('*every town needs this kind of poem*' had written one reviewer), and who were saddened to learn that the design of Oriel Chambers was so ahead of its time that Peter was ridiculed by the architectural press of the day and that his career may have suffered badly as a consequence. Our account of Peter's life suggests that this concern can be laid to rest.

Our story traces Peter's upbringing and his marriage to Mary, and identifies a number of their relations; it looks at the various stages of his career, and revisits the places where he lived and worked to see how they have changed between his time there and the present day; it identifies several other buildings for which he was the architect – both before and after his two famous offices – and illustrates other professional matters with which Peter was concerned as a valuer, surveyor and civil engineer. And, in the very last year of Peter's life, we will discover an intriguing entry in *Gore's Liverpool Directory*.

Mid-afternoon in January 2012. 16 Cook Street faces north and its upper floors are making the best of reflected sunlight from the opposite building, aided considerably by Peter Ellis's large windows.

The Water Street entrance to Oriel Chambers, October 2010.

The plaques either side of the doorway read:-

on the left hand side: 'Oriel Chambers 1864. Peter Ellis Architect. Pioneer in the use of prefrabricated structural units in cast iron.'

and on the right hand side: 'Oriel Chambers 1960. David Brock Architect. War Damaged in May 1941. Reinstated by Melville Curlender.'

MILL PLACE
ALE PORTER
AND SPIRITS

Chapter 1

From Shaw's Brow to Primrose Hill

The Liverpool directories do not reveal the existence of Peter Ellis until 1834 when he was nearly 30 years old, and when his father – Peter Ellis senior – had retired and passed the Renshaw Street business on to Peter junior. His father is first listed in 1810 at Primrose Hill where courts were being constructed for the rapidly growing population of Liverpool, and several years after Peter junior had been born. Much had happened in the Ellis household in those formative 30 years which prepared Peter for the independent world of work and for marriage in 1836. He had grown up in the midst of the building sites with which his father was involved, and he had mourned the loss of four siblings. So let us take a step back in time before the directories knew either Peter or his father, to the close of the 18th century and to his parents' marriage. [1] From record number 64 in the register for St Peter's Church in 1795 we learn that:-

> *'Peter Ellis of the parish of Liverpool Joiner and Ann Appleton of the Same Parish Spinster were married in this Church by Banns this twelfth Day of April in the Year One Thousand Seven Hundred and ninety five'.*

1,1. From the 1795 marriage register of St Peter's Church. Image courtesy of the Liverpool Record Office (LRO), microfilm ref. 283 PET 3/5.

No. 64 Peter Ellis of the Parish of Liverpool Joiner
and Ann Appleton of the Same Parish Spinster
were married in this Church by Banns this twelfth Day of April in the Year
One Thousand Seven Hundred and Ninety five by me R Blayney Curate
This Marriage was solemnized between Us { Peter Ellis / Ann Appleton
In the Presence of { Thomas Powell / Anne Humphreys

Peter and Ann's records show that they were living on Shaw's Brow in 1800, and that Ann's parents were Robert and Ann Appleton of Prescot. Who Peter's parents were has not been confirmed but a joiner, George Ellis, is recorded in *Gore's Directory* for 1790 and 1796 and in an 1801 census at Mill Place, Shaw's Brow. On Michael Gage's highly detailed 1835 '*trigonometrical plan*' of Liverpool (fig. 1,2), Mill Place and the neighbouring Mill Lane can be seen running north from the junction of Islington and Shaw's Brow (re-named William Brown Street decades later).

Peter and Ann's first daughter (Ann, 1796) and first son (Robert, 1798) were baptised at St Mary the Virgin, Prescot, where Ann had herself been baptised in 1773. Childbirth in those days was extremely hazardous and she perhaps had returned each time to the safety of her parent's home for her confinements.

Then, five years into their marriage, with the family crowded into a '*back house*' on Shaw's Brow and under the watchful gaze of several beautiful smock mills (fig. 1,3), Ann gave birth to another son, Peter Ellis, on 12th November 1800, named after his father and baptised at St. Peter's on 28th December 1800 (fig. 1,4). [2]

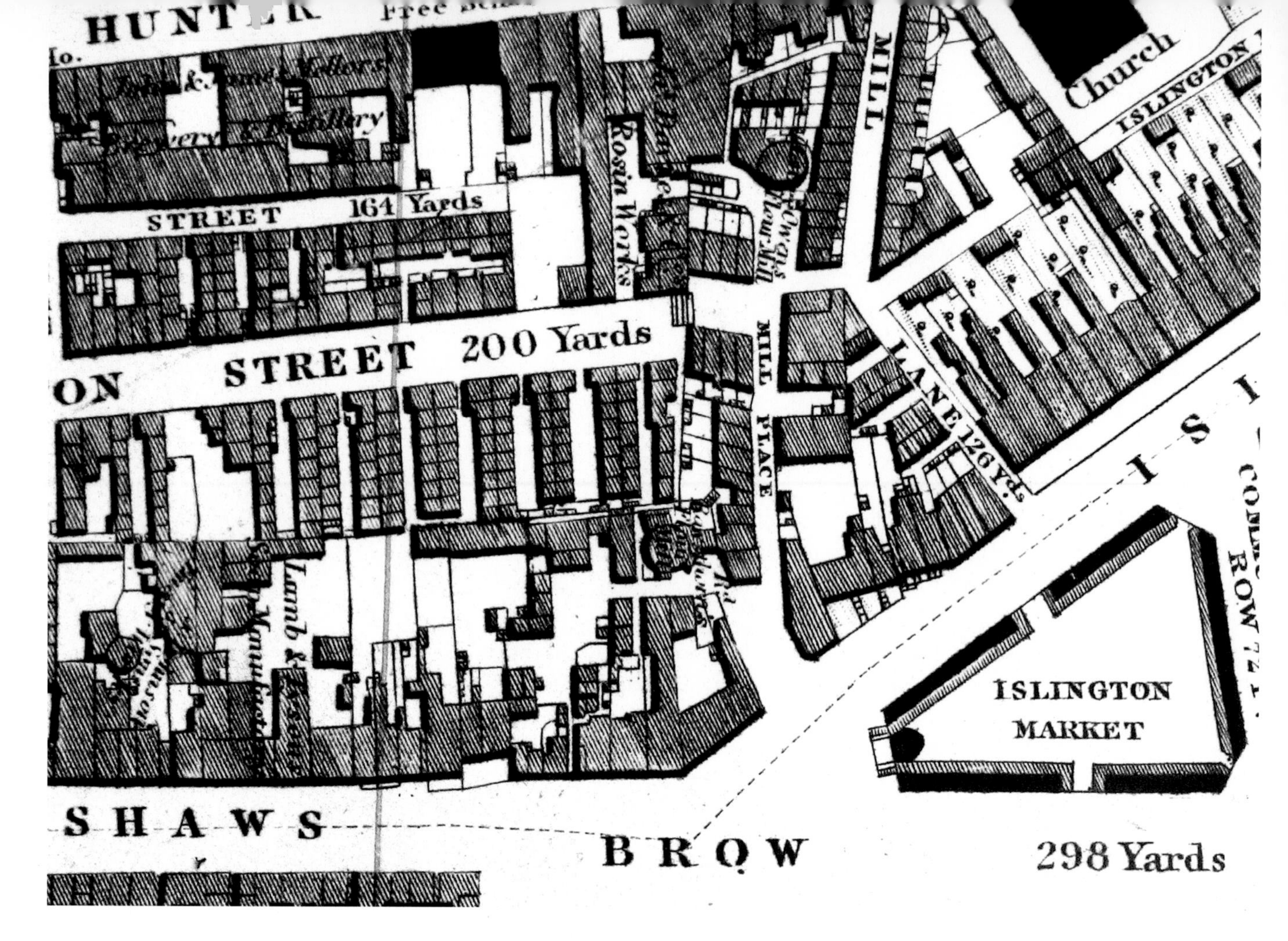

1,2. The Shaw's Brow detail from Michael Gage's trigonometrical plan. Survey completed October 1835, published March 1836.

Two flour mills – Rawsthorn's and Owen's – stood in Mill Place, whilst a third was further west (the circle above the 'H' of 'SHAWS').

The location of this area within the town is identified on the map on p. iv by the letter B.

Private collection.

The WINDMILL, in Mill Place, top of Shaw's Brow, 1828.

1,3. Mill Place, from the Brierley collection. Image courtesy of the Athenaeum.

Novr. 12 Peter S of Peter and Ann Ellis Joiner Shaws Brow 28

1,4. From the 1800 christening register for St. Peter's Church.
Image courtesy of the LRO, microfilm ref. 283 PET 1/6.

This record, however, presented a problem which had become apparent during earlier research. Quentin Hughes' account had given the dates for Peter Ellis the architect as 1804-1884, but a search on *ancestryinstitution.com* in 2011 had failed to identify a Peter Ellis born in 1804 in Liverpool. A wider search plus or minus 2 years had provided only a Peter Ellis born to a John and Jane Ellis on 16th January 1806 and baptised on 31st January at St Nicholas, together with a time-line claiming to link this Peter to a Peter Ellis recorded in the 1881 census with the information *'Residence, 40 Falkner Sq. (occupation Architect)'*. Whilst the 1881 record was clearly correct, the link to an 1806 birth record presented a puzzle. Why should Peter Ellis the joiner have passed on the family business to Peter junior if they were not father and son?

Although the search of the baptism records at St Peter's, where Peter Ellis the joiner and Ann Appleton had been married, and the identification of the birth of their son in 1800 appeared to have solved the problem, a subsequent examination of the census records produced a further puzzle.

The collector for the census in March 1841 had written down Peter's age as 35 whereas, if Peter Ellis the architect had been born in November 1800, it should have been 40. There were similar apparent anomalies in 1851 where Peter was recorded as 45 years old, in 1861 as 55, and in 1871 as 65 years old, all pointing to a birth between March 1805 and March 1806. Since Peter presumably had known his correct age, and if Peter Ellis the architect was indeed the son of John and Jane Ellis, what had become of the Peter Ellis born in 1800?

And, sadly, the discovery was made that he had died at Shaw's Brow. Having perhaps taken baby Peter to the merriment of Folly Fair [3] during his first Easter, and then having celebrated his first birthday on November 12th 1801, a heartbroken Peter and Ann Ellis found themselves watching his interment fourteen days later. It was a year in which the records suggest that many infants died, as the neighbouring entries to that of Peter's bear witness (fig. 1,5).

1,5. Record 385 for 26th November 1801 from the burial register for St Peter's Church, together with two neighbouring records showing deaths at the ages of one day and three and a half years. The same page includes deaths at two, four, seven and eleven months.
Image courtesy of the LRO, microfilm ref. 283 PET 1/6.

383 25 Townshend S of Sarah Hinde Spinster Elliot Hill 1 Day
384 25 Ellen D of David Hughes Tabr. New Bird Street 3½ yr
385 26 Peter S of Peter Ellis Joiner Shaws Brow 1 yr

However, with the church of St John, Haymarket, being the more local for Peter and Ann (fig. 1,8), the records for the period around 1804 for that church were checked and revealed that a second son was born to them, again named Peter Ellis, and baptised there on 1st September 1805. The *Lancashire Online Parish Clerk Project* database confirms this information, where the editor has interpreted a birth date of 1st May 1805 (fig. 1,6). However, the somewhat ambiguous handwriting for all the non-July births (fig. 1,7) suggests August 1st 1805 as Peter's birth date (the others have been entered in the database as August 5th, 19th and 25th), the month being abbreviated and written with an old-fashioned capital '*a*', the complete entry reading:-

The birth year for Peter Ellis the architect-to-be was thus 1805 and the subsequent census records remain consistent whichever month is correct, as in either case his birth falls within the March 1805 – March 1806 timescale. Why this record is absent on the *Ancestry* database, why Peter's correct 1881 census record has been linked to a different Peter Ellis, and how the information supplied to Quentin Hughes came to be provided incorrectly all remain puzzles.

We therefore arrive at the realisation that, had the original baby Peter survived, the Peter Ellis who was destined to become the architect would not only have ended up with a different name but, as the third son and unlikely to share in the family business,

*aug^st^ 1st*　　*Peter s. of Peter & Ann Ellis*　　*Joiner*　　*Shaw*['s] *Brow*　　*1st*

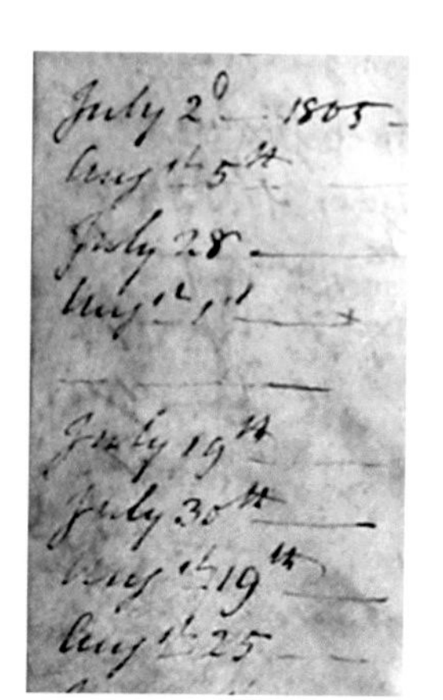
July 2d 1805
Aug 5th
July 28
Aug 1st
July 19th
July 30th
Aug 19th
Aug 25

Above: 1,6. Christening records for St John, Haymarket, for 1805 showing the record for Peter Ellis and for three earlier entries, the first record reading 'Sepr 1st' in the final column (for the baptism date).

Left: 1,7. A detail from the first column of the records for July and August births and a blank line for a 'Native of Africa aged 18 years' (of unknown birth date). The August records, including that for Peter Ellis (fourth down), show the characteristic style in which 'August' was written in an abbreviated form.

Images courtesy of the LRO, microfilm ref. 283 JOH 1/1.

he may well have pursued a wholly different career. Liverpool would never have had Oriel Chambers or 16 Cook Street, and even Chicago may have developed differently. So when next you walk up William Brown Street and mount the steps of the Walker Art Gallery (fig. 1,10), perhaps give a thought to the little Peter Ellis that died in 1801, for you are treading where he lived to see but one spring and one summer on Shaw's Brow, and that same autumn died there.

A South View of ST JOHN'S CHURCH, Liverpool, 1830.

Right: 1,8. St John, Haymarket, viewed from St John's Lane, with the smock mill in Mill Place in the distance. James Picton gave St John's a disappointing 0 out 10: 'Making every allowance for the period of its erection, it would be scarcely possible to rate the design too low' (Memorials, 2nd edition, 1875, vol. II, p. 188).

The church was consecrated in 1783 on a portion of what had been the 'Great Heath' (fig. 1,13). Peter Ellis was baptised there and perhaps held it in greater respect and affection. In the following century it fell victim to being considered an 'ugly' obstruction to the west view of St George's Hall.

Image courtesy of the Athenaeum, from the Brierley collection.

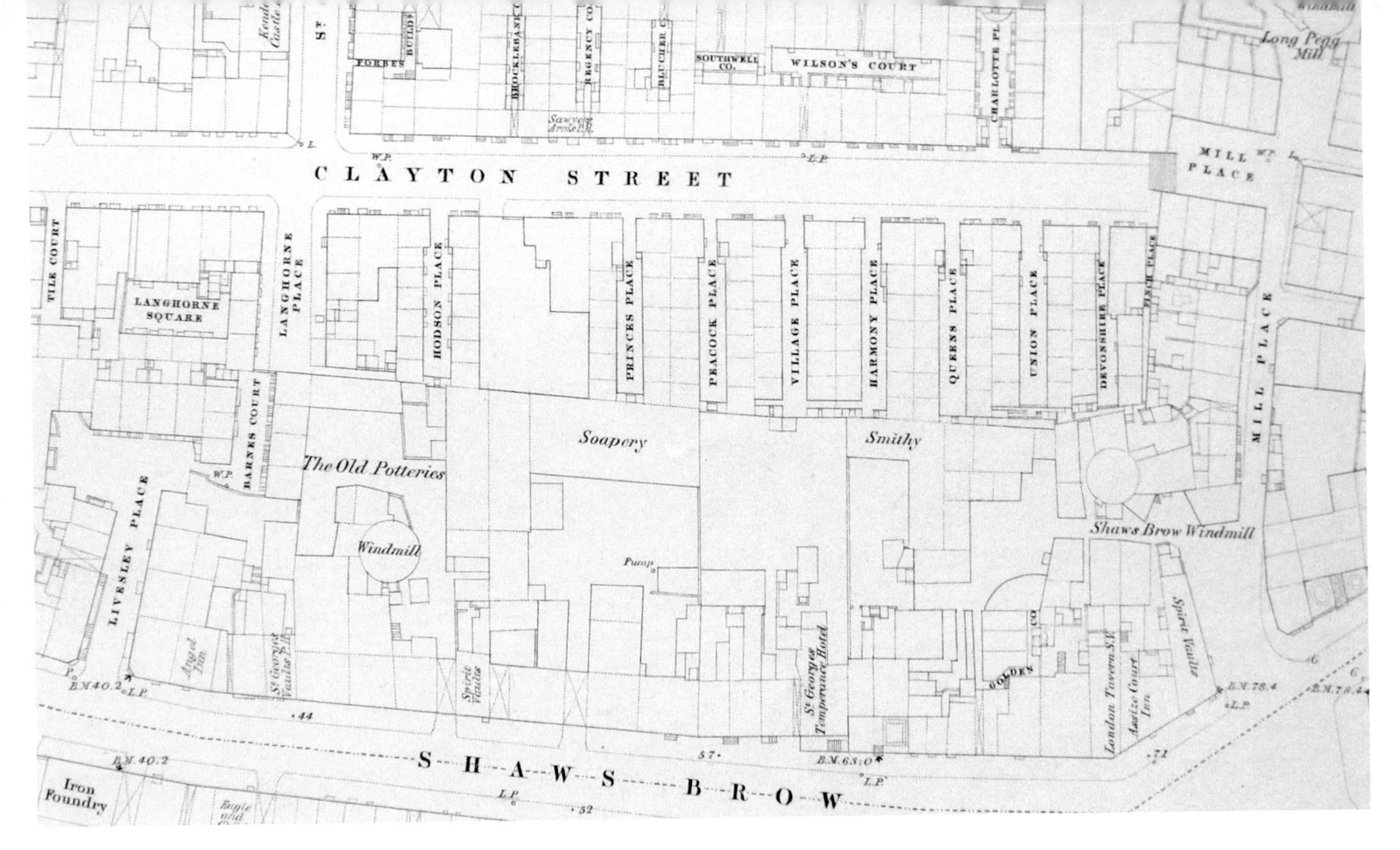

1,9. A detail from the O.S. map for 1848.

Image courtesy of the Athenaeum.

The mill in the pictures by James Brierley is marked on this map as 'Shaw's Brow Windmill'. The second is shown to the west, by the Old Potteries.

The third mill at the northern end of Mill Place, which on Michael Gage's 1835 map is marked as 'Owen's Flour Mill', by 1848 had become 'Long Pegg Mill'.

1,10. The steps of the Walker Art Gallery mark approximately where Mill Place once ran.

1,11. Mill Lane still exists today between the Walker Art Gallery and the County Sessions House.

1,12. Shaw's Brow ca. 1850 by W G Herdman.
By 1850 the Shaw's Brow mill was derelict, the victim of a fire, and was the last of the three to be demolished.
The whole of the area at Mill Place was subsequently flattened to make way briefly for a wholesale vegetable market before finally providing the site for the Walker Art Gallery.
Image courtesy of the LRO, ref. Herdman Collection 1461.

With the information that Peter Ellis the architect-to-be, born ten years into the marriage of Peter and Ann, was baptised at St John, Haymarket, the *Lancashire Online Parish Clerk Project* website was used to search for other siblings.

Peter Ellis senior had made his first appearance in *Gore's Directory* in 1810 as '*joiner and flour dealer, 19 Primrose hill*'. Primrose Hill had itself first appeared as a new street in the 1807 directory as '*Primrose hill, Johnson street*' but was subsequently redefined as '*Primrose hill, Fontenoy street*', suggesting that the town developers had altered their original plans of running it across Trueman Street and North Street (compare figs. 1,14 and 1,15).

It was at Primrose Hill that William Ellis was born to Peter and Ann on 6th October 1807, and at St John's that he was christened on 8th November 1807 (LRO microfilm ref. 283 JOH 1/1), indicating that the family had moved to Primrose Hill at the very start of its existence. And so, in the autumn of 1807 Peter Ellis, the architect-to-be, at the age of two found himself growing up with an 11 year old sister, a 9 year old brother and a new baby brother.

If it had ever known primroses, this delightfully named location – seen on earlier maps, including that of Charles Eyes, to have been the southern edge of open fields – was soon destined to lose all memory of its former existence as it was transformed into the access route to a cluster of courts, the majority of which were complete by 1813. The naming of some of the courts hints that Peter Ellis senior may have been a leading figure in the overall building works, choosing to live where the construction was taking place, because two of the courts were named *Ellis court* and *Appleton court*, perhaps as a mark of respect to his and Ann's parents. A third was subsequently named *Mary Ann court*. Various church records show that the name was a popular one at the time, including more than one Mary Ann Ellis, and we will meet another Mary Ann later, although not an Ellis.

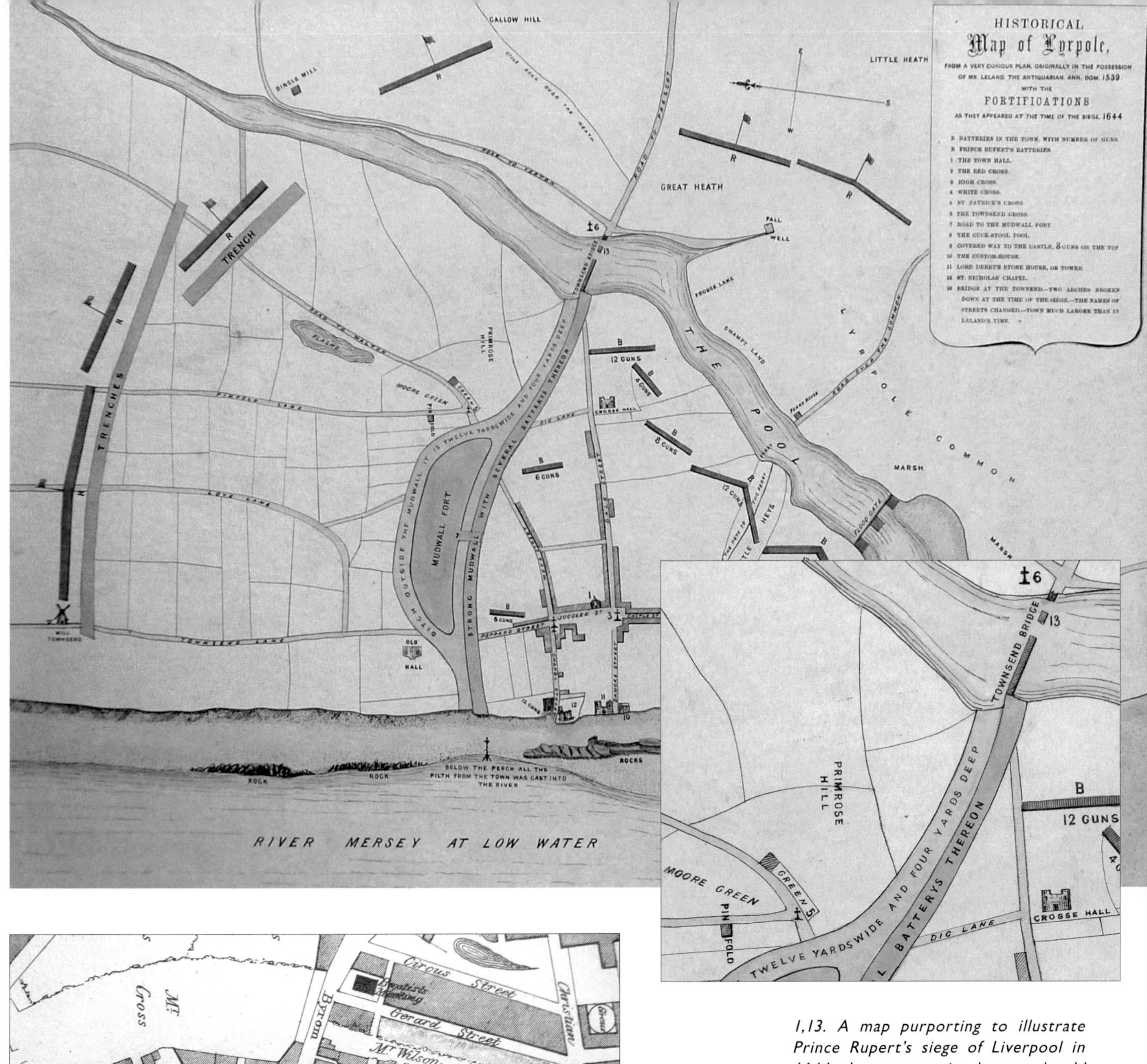

1,13. A map purporting to illustrate Prince Rupert's siege of Liverpool in 1644, drawn centuries later and sold by Adam Bowker ca. 1870. The map suggests that the name Primrose Hill was already in existence by then.

Image courtesy of the Athenaeum.

1,14. A detail from Charles Eyes' map of 1796, reissued as a lithograph by L Syers and sold by Adam Bowker ca. 1870, showing the fields of the Cross family, the windmills in Mill Place, and two of the four mills (bottom right hand corner) that existed along a route that would be developed in the following century as Hotham Street.

Image courtesy of the Athenaeum.

Several of the other courts appear to have been named after the surnames of tradespeople that could have been involved with the construction: Richard Arthur, listed as a stone mason; Benjamin Bennett, builder; John Duckworth, bricklayer, subsequently joiner; several Harrisons, listed as a painter, a plasterer and as joiners; and Richard Hunter, plumber and glazier. *Hadwen court*, however, may have been so named in recognition of Isaac and Joseph Hadwen for having provided the means to undertake the whole enterprise;[4] it subsequently found itself converted, possibly through a misunderstanding, into *Hawden court*. The remainder were *Primrose court* (initially *Primrose place*), *Reece place* and *Cross court*. Although there was an Edward Cross, painter, and a John Cross, bricklayer, the most likely candidate for this naming is the previous owner of the land not only at Primrose Hill but also between Shaw's Brow and Hunter Street. James Stonehouse subsequently wrote that:-

'The Crosse family held large plots of ground in and about Liverpool. In Byrom Street they possessed a considerable portion of it. The land from Dale street corner to Addison street belonged to Mr. Crosse, and it was through this field (about 1801) that the "New Crossehall street" was formed, since entitled "Great Crosshall street".'[5]

In 1828 Charles Okill drew up a plan of *'The Ancient Pool of Liverpool as it appeared previous to the year 1670 at high water'* for the benefit of the Corporation (fig. 1,16).[6] It showed the stream which fed the Pool surfacing to the north of what was then the *Townsend Bridge* (Town's End Bridge) at the eastern end of Dale Street, a field labelled *Shaw* (from which Shaw's Brow would derive its name),

1,15. A detail from Michael Gage's plan of 1835 showing the development around Primrose Hill. The location of this area within the town is identified on the map on p. iv by the letter D. Private collection.

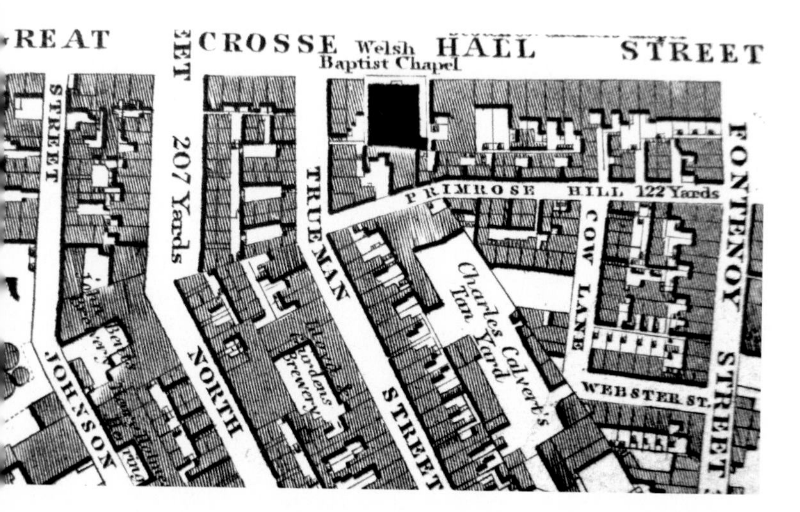

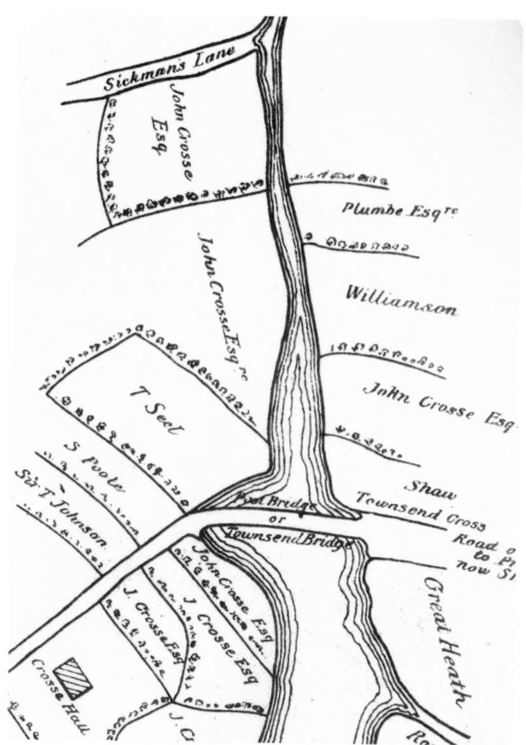

1,16. A detail from Charles Okill's map of 1828 showing the development of the town in 1670. Image courtesy of the Historic Society of Lancashire and Cheshire.

fields bearing the names *Johnson*, *Poole* and *Seel* (upon which Johnson, North and Trueman Streets would be built), Crosse Hall on the southern side of Dale Street, and *Sickmans Lane* bordering the northern edge of one of the many fields in the possession of John Crosse. Stonehouse's quotation above continues:-

> *Addison street occupied the site of a country lane, running to Bevington lane; this locality, in the time of Elizabeth, was called "Sick Man's lane", from the fact that when a virulent plague was raging, numbers of persons were accommodated in temporary receptacles therein, and who were buried in the vicinity if they fell victims to those dreadful visitations... In making some excavations of late years for the sewers, quantities of human bones were discovered by the navvies, who sold them by the bushel to the marine store dealers, until stopped by the authorities.'*

Primrose Hill and its courts were thus positively surrounded by places rich in historical interest. Although for several years these courts managed a brief acknowledgement in the directories as part of the street index which preceded the alphabetical directory, they never ranked of sufficient importance to produce occupant listings of their own (in a section called the *numerical directory* when it was introduced in 1839). After all, *Gore's Directory* had made it perfectly clear on each year's title page that the listings were for 'Merchants, Traders and *Principal Inhabitants*' and, sadly, most residents of the courts were never classified as principal enough. The courts themselves, however, did manage to secure two other lasting pieces of evidence of their existence, for the detailed Ordnance Survey map of 1848 revealed their individual positions, whilst a series of three watercolours attributed to William Herdman provide the 21st century visitor with a guided tour of the area as it was 150 years ago.

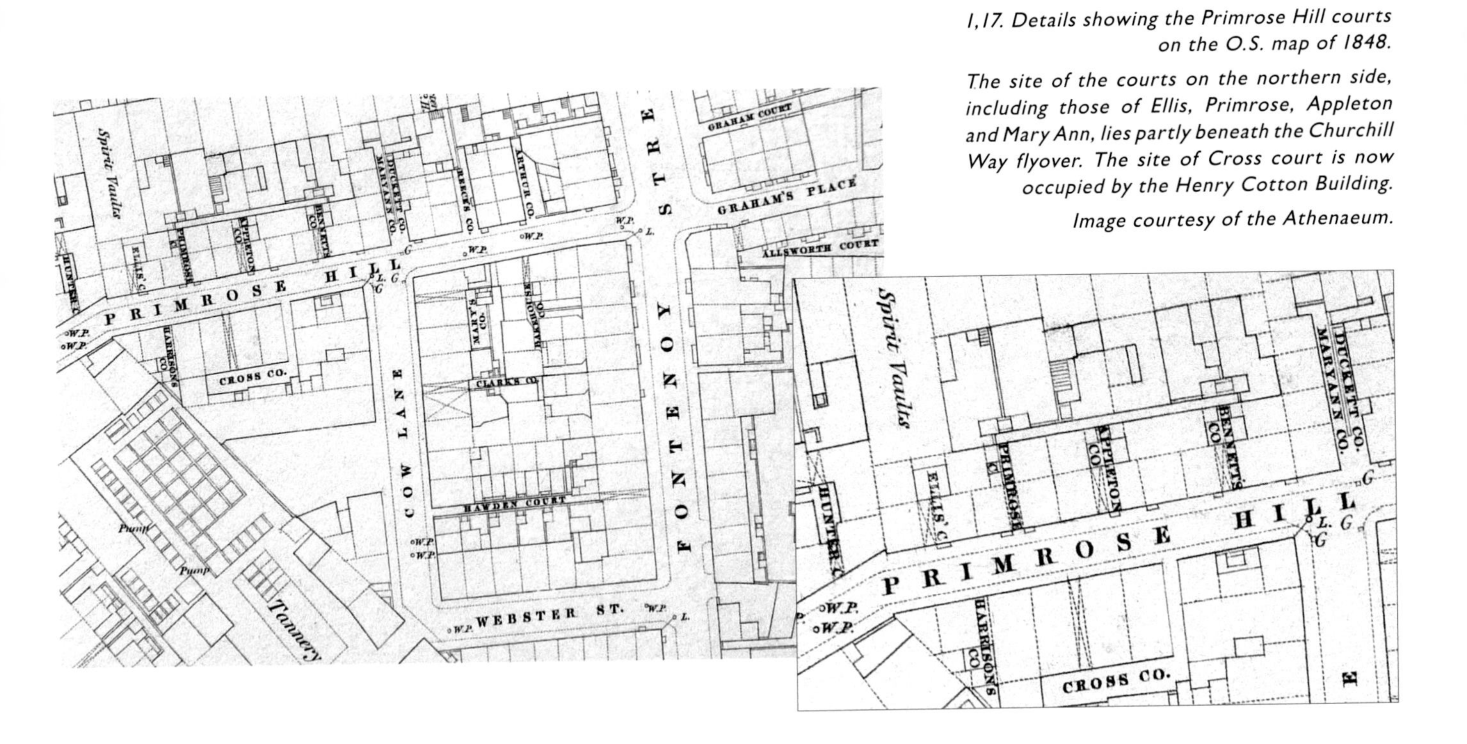

I,17. Details showing the Primrose Hill courts on the O.S. map of 1848.

The site of the courts on the northern side, including those of Ellis, Primrose, Appleton and Mary Ann, lies partly beneath the Churchill Way flyover. The site of Cross court is now occupied by the Henry Cotton Building.

Image courtesy of the Athenaeum.

1,18. Webster Street in 1863, looking west from Fontenoy Street with Cow Lane curving to the right in the distance. Image courtesy of the LRO, ref. Herdman Collection 732.

The views are along Webster Street from Fontenoy Street towards Cow Lane, along Cow Lane from Webster Street towards Primrose Hill, and along Primrose Hill itself from Fontenoy Street. In the scene along Cow Lane there is a distant glimpse of Mary Ann court disappearing northwards towards the rear of property on Great Crosshall Street.

1,19. Cow Lane in 1863, looking north with Mary Ann court in the distance. Image courtesy of the LRO, ref. Herdman Collection 766.

1,20. Primrose Hill in 1863, looking west from Fontenoy Street. Image courtesy of the LRO, ref. Herdman Collection 461.

The courts were swept away in the city's 20th century clearances, and those on the northern side now predominantly lie beneath a section of the Churchill Way North flyover across Byrom Street. Although Peter Ellis the architect-to-be was still a youngster when the family left Primrose Hill and may have retained only the vaguest childhood memories, he might well have listened many years later to his parent's recollections, and pondered upon the construction of the courts [7] with their lack of adequate ventilation and light when it came for him to design Oriel Chambers.

1,21. July 2011, looking west from the Fontenoy Street seating area. The Henry Cotton building marks where Cross court once stood. Cow Lane now exists between the statue and the Henry Cotton Building entrance.

1,22. Looking east from the junction with Trueman Street, with the Henry Cotton Building to the right.

1,23. Looking east, at the side of the Churchill Way flyover, with the beds of shrubs marking where access would have been gained to the courts.

References and notes to Chapter 1

1 Wikipedia suggests that Ellis is both a first name and a surname of Welsh original spelling, and the Oxford Names Companion suggests that the name in Wales is a derivative of *elus* (kindly, benevolent). However Peter's parents were married at St Peter's Church and his grave is in a Church of England part of Toxteth Cemetery, and it has not been established whether Peter's more distant ancestors came originally from Wales. In *The Welsh Builder on Merseyside* by J R Jones, although Ellis does not appear as a surname, it occurs four times as a first name (Ellis Davies, Ellis Evans, Ellis Jones and Ellis Owen), and in 1841 the first Ellis Ellis (albeit a shoemaker) finds a mention in the Liverpool directories.

Belchem and MacRaild in *Liverpool 800, Culture, Character & History,* Ed. John Belchem, Liverpool University Press, p. 345, quote the words of R W Jones in a paper presented in 1901 about Welsh 'non-assertiveness':- *"It was, rather, along paths less noteworthy that they trod their way to positions and affluence, their trend being mainly towards the timber, stone, slate and other quiet home trades which catered for every day comfort of their neighbours."* Certainly the Ellis name had become well established in Liverpool before the end of the 18th century and the directories show that several Ellis families were becoming involved in the building trade in the early 19th century.

2 Ann's history is unambiguous. The *Lancashire OnLine Parish Clerk Project* website gives Ann's details as: born 11th September 1773; baptised 3rd October at St Mary the Virgin, Prescot; daughter of Ann and Robert Appleton, Prescot; Robert's occupation Joyner [sic]. Their children, Ann (born 14th August 1796; baptised 11th September 1796; daughter of Ann and Peter Ellis, occupation Joiner) and Robert (born 8th July 1798; baptised 5th August 1798; son of Ann and Peter Ellis, occupation Joiner) were baptised at the same church. It is even possible that her parents are the Robert and Ann Appleton who are shown as being married in the parish of Rainford on 19th November 1771.

However, the choice of George Ellis the joiner as the father of Peter Ellis the joiner relies solely upon the evidence of his being at Mill Place, Shaw's Brow in the 1790 and 1796 directories and still being there in the 1801 census (when Peter and Ann are shown as living on Shaw's Brow for the birth of their third child). Another possibility is a John Ellis who is listed in 1790 and 1796 as a painter in North Street and who is perhaps the same John that is listed in 1800 and 1803 as a joiner in Byrom Street.

The 1790 directory included the '*Names of the Streets, Lanes, &c. within the Liberties of Liverpool, with the number of persons in each; Taken by M. Simmons, from October 13th, 1789, to January 13th, 1790.*' Shaw's Brow is listed with 76 dwellings and 374 people, whilst Mill Place is shown with 14 dwellings and 65 people.

The Athenaeum possesses a large handwritten book, *An Account of the Population of Liverpool Taken in pursuance of An Act of Parliament March 1801.* The lists provide the names of the principal occupants of each dwelling, whether the properties were front houses, back houses or cellars, and the numbers of families, males, and females, and those in a trade. On page 259 for Mill Place, George Ellis is listed at a very crowded front house property containing two families, comprising eight males and six females, with only one person in a trade. On page 263 for Shaw's Brow, Peter Ellis is listed at a crowded back house property containing one family, comprising five males and two females, with two of the occupants in a trade. An analysis of aspects of this survey is provided by P Laxton,

Liverpool in 1801: A Manuscript Return for the First National Census of Population, *Transactions of the Historic Society of Lancashire & Cheshire*, 130, 1980, p. 73.

Ann Ellis might have chosen to travel to Prescot for her first two births for very good reason. The hazards to mother and child are exemplified by the history of James Picton, a contemporary of Peter Ellis the architect. He was the sole survivor of his mother's four children, whilst she died giving birth to the fourth.

3 Folly Fair was held each Easter Monday and Tuesday from about 1780 – 1818 on a triangle of land which is shown on Gage's 1835 map as having become Islington Market (and now occupied by the Steble fountain). It contained merry-go-rounds, swing-boats, temporary theatres, gingerbread booths and other stalls, and was the scene of great merry-making. Its location there had followed the closure of the original *Gibson's Folly* situated further east and which had given rise to the name.

4 As will be seen in the next chapter, Peter Ellis subsequently moved his family to Gloucester Street. At that time this was crossed by Duncan St East, later renamed Hotham Street. James Picton (*Memorials*, vol. II, p. 195), mentions that *'On the line of Hotham Street, hard by, formerly stood four windmills. One of these, the site of which is absorbed by the railway, belonged to Joseph Hadwen, a member of the Society of Friends, who, somewhere about 1810, took down the mill and erected a charity school on the site.'* The four mills are shown on Charles Eyes' map of 1796 (of which two can be seen on the detail herein). Picton also mentions (vol. I, p. 396) that, during a financial panic and a run on the banks which had begun in 1825, the bank of Joseph Hadwen was forced to suspend payment in 1826. The Corporation Lease Register for 4th July 1801 (LRO ref. 352 CLE/CON 3/5) shows that Isaac and Joseph Hadwen (at that time respectively silversmith and grocer) obtained a lease for a large portion of land on which a series of streets had been laid out but which at that stage lacked names. Three times in the lease the clerk carefully left a space for the un-named streets using the phrase *'intended to be called street'*. This area surrounded Gloucester Street and Duncan Street East, and in 1817 a portion of the lease is confirmed as being re-granted to the Duncan Street School. The remaining land was re-granted to a large number of other people, including three plots to John Kilshaw (1813, 1828 and 1829), a builder whose significance for this story will become apparent in chapter 3.

5 James Stonehouse, *The Streets of Liverpool*, Edward Howell, 1869, p. 42; reprinted for Liverpool Libraries and Information Services, 2002.

6 R. Stewart-Brown, The Pool of Liverpool, *Transactions of the Historic Society of Lancashire and Cheshire*, 82, 1930, map facing p. 96.

7 Rob Ainsworth, James Newlands (1813-1871). Britain's & Liverpool's First Borough Engineer, *Journal of the Liverpool History Society*, 2012, p. 62. The whole of the 1863 report by James Newlands can be seen at www.archive.org/details/reporttohealthco00liverich where some details of the Primrose Hill courts are listed in Table 11, p. 208 of that pdf file. For a brief analysis of Liverpool's courts see Joseph Sharples, *Liverpool. Pevsner Architectural Guides*, Yale University Press, 2004, p. 8.

Chapter 2

From Gloucester Street to Low Hill

Four years after the Ellis family's arrival at Primrose Hill, and with construction of the courts well advanced (half of them had entered *Gore's* 1811 street listing), although the 1811 directory lists the family as still there, the record of the birth of John Ellis to Peter and Ann shows that they must have moved during that year, for John was born on 20th August 1811 and baptised on 15th September 1811, also at St John, Haymarket, where the entry reads *'John s. of Peter and Ann Ellis, joiner, Gloucester Street'* (LRO microfilm ref. 283 JOH 1/1). The next directory, that for 1813, indicates that Peter Ellis senior, entered as joiner and flour dealer in the earlier directories, had by then discontinued his involvement with the flour trade. Charles Ellis perhaps was a relative, being listed in the directories between 1790 and 1811 as a flour dealer with a flour warehouse at 1 Old Ropery, off Fenwick Street.

When Peter's family arrived at Gloucester Street in 1811 it must have been at the very earliest stages of construction for, a century later, it was Charles Hand's understanding that, *'Gloucester Street, although projected in 1802, was not built upon until 1814.'* [1]

Thus Peter Ellis senior appears to have moved there in order to be on site and fully involved in the development from the outset, just as he had done at Primrose Hill. By 1824, shortly after the Ellis family had departed, *Baines' Directory* shows the street as being numbered from 1 to 94, whilst Michael Gage's 1835 plan (fig. 2,1) shows that it had been constructed east-west from Copperas Hill to Lime Street.

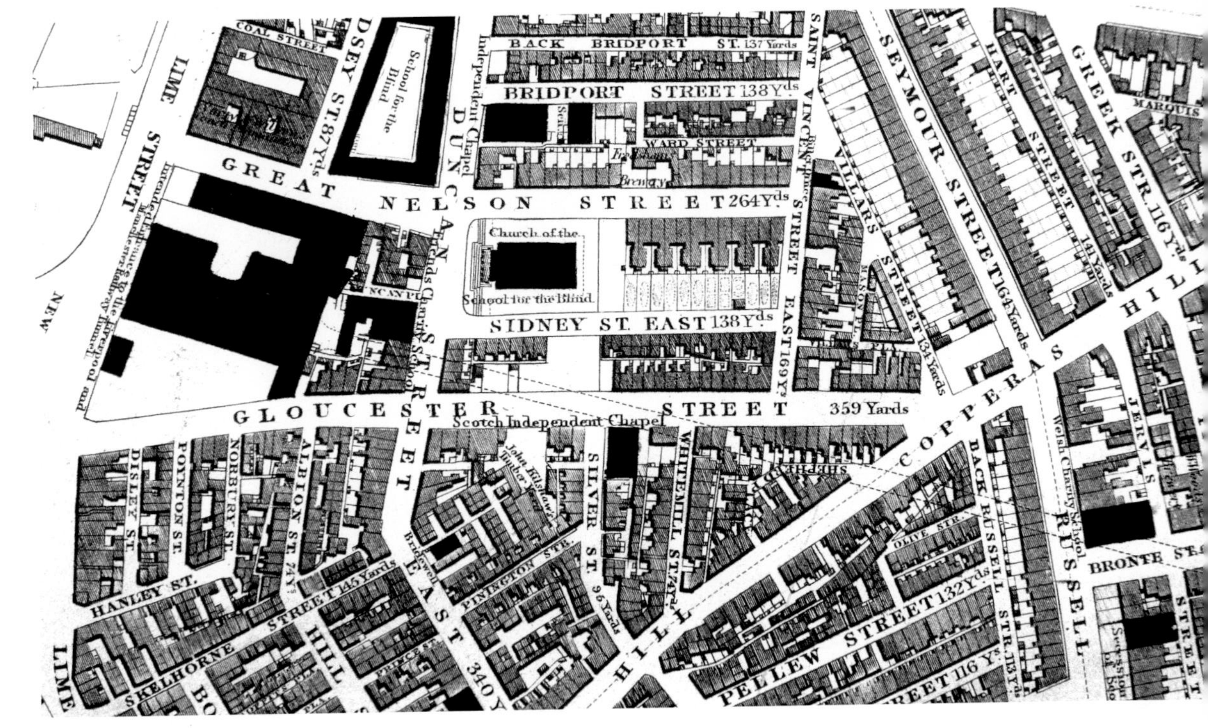

2,1. A detail from Gage's plan showing the development of Gloucester Street by 1835 with the 'Intended Entrance to the Liverpool and Manchester Railway Tunnel' marked on Lime Street.

The location of this area within the town is identified on the map on p. iv by the letter E.

Private collection.

Opposite right: 2,3. A detail from the O.S. map of 1848 with partial revision to 1864. Image courtesy of Digital Archives.

This seems to have been a period during which the names initially given to streets were susceptible to subsequent alteration. Thus, on Troughton's map of 1807, Gloucester Street is labelled as Gloucester Place, whilst the location which would eventually become Gloucester Place, some distance away at Low Hill, is labelled Gloucester Row; Troughton's map also shows the spirited attempt that had been made by someone in authority to change the well-established name of Copperas Hill into Elliot Hill, but the residents seemingly rebelled and so the name was changed back again. Thus, whilst the 1810 directory listed it as *'Gloucester Street, Elliott Hill'* (with two 't's this time), the 1811 directory altered it to *'Gloucester Street, Copperas Hill.'*

This was also in the days when buildings were still numbered consecutively up the left hand side of the street (starting from the end nearest the Town Hall) and then returned down the right hand side. Whenever new buildings were added much of the street had to get renumbered, and the postman presumably found himself needing to deliver by knowledge of people's names rather than through use of their ever-changing addresses.

In 1822 the Liverpool and Manchester Railway Company had been promoted by Henry Booth and, following the successful passing of the Liverpool and Manchester Railway Act in 1826, this was eventually to have fatal consequences for Gloucester Street and neighbouring streets. The 1848 O.S. map (fig. 2,2) and directories in the 1850s indicate that Gloucester Street was already beginning to lose properties on its northern side, whilst the O.S. map with revisions to 1864 (fig. 2,3) shows just how much the station had begun to be enlarged. The street found itself seriously obliged to realign itself around the unwelcome intrusion which would eventually all but obliterate it, and several Herdman paintings in the mid 1860s (figs. 2,4 - 2,6) show the demolition in progress. St Simon's Church was just one of a vast swathe of buildings that were removed to make way for later expansions of Lime Street station.

2,2. A detail from the O.S. map of 1848. Image courtesy of the Athenaeum.

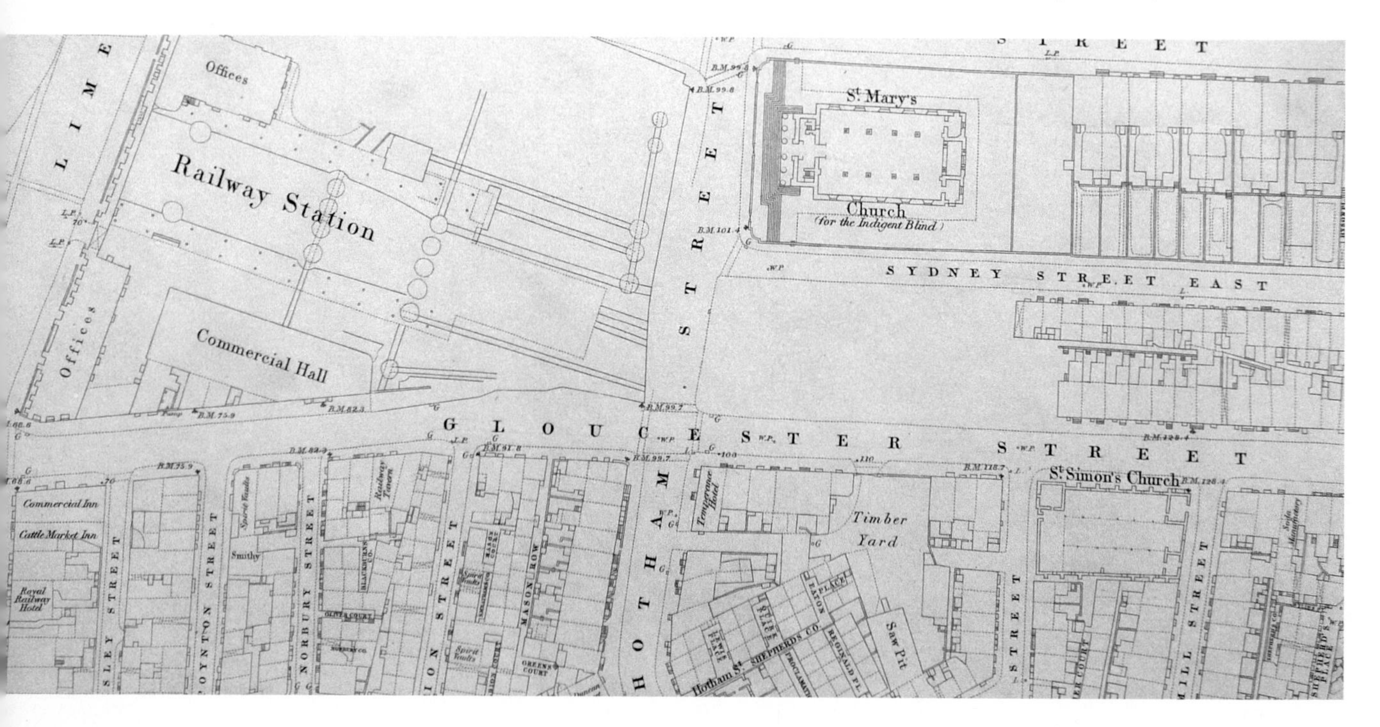

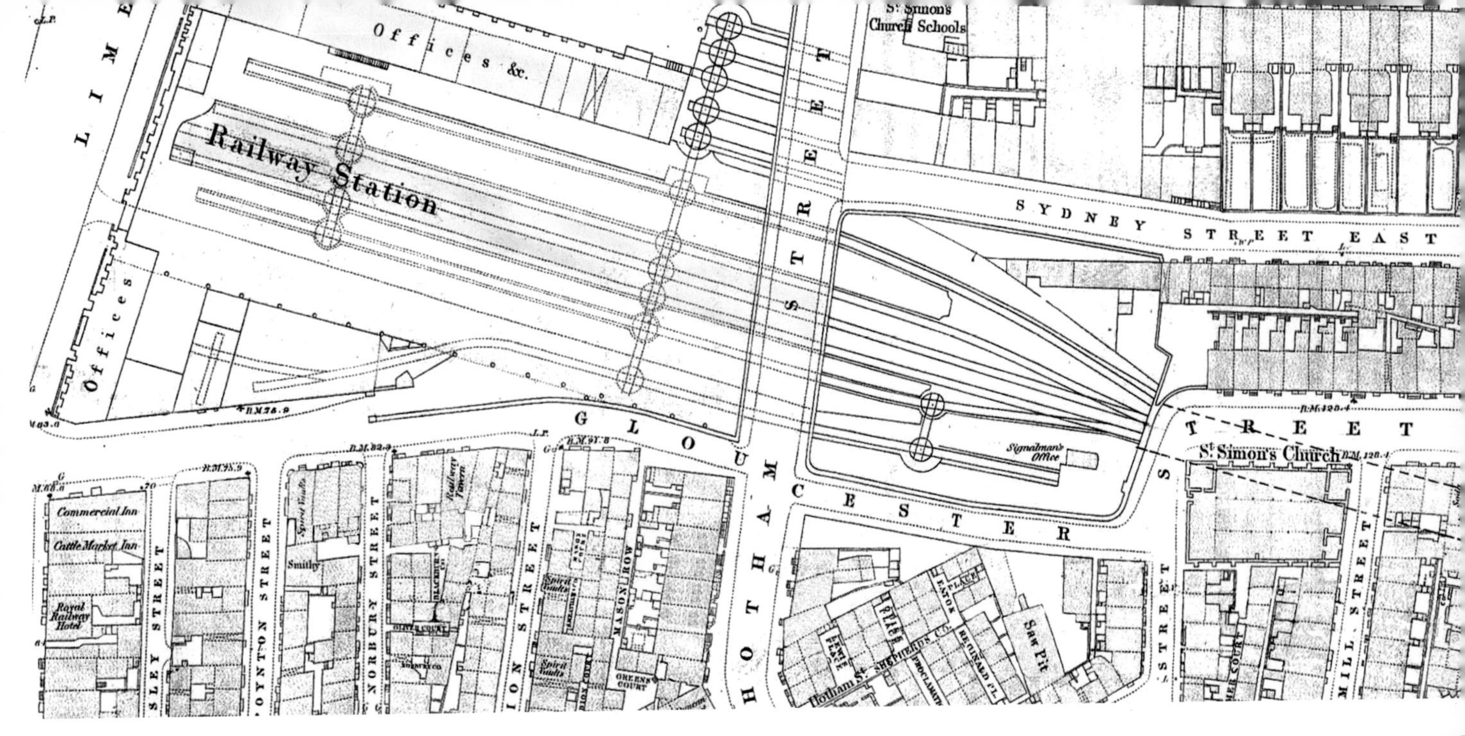

Above left: 2,4. A watercolour entitled 'Gloucester Street, N. side, looking eastwards, shewing St. Simon's Church in course of demolition, 1865.' Comparison of the view with the O.S. map with revisions to 1864 (fig. 2,3) indicates that the continuing realignment of Gloucester Street had placed it to the south of the church by the time of Herdman's painting.

Built on the site of the Scotch Chapel shown on Michael Gage's plan (fig. 2,1), St Simon's had only been completed and consecrated in 1848, oblivious of what was so soon to befall it. A replacement was constructed in 1866 further east near the junction of Gloucester Street and St Vincent Street East.

Image courtesy of the LRO, ref. Herdman Collection 556.

Above right: 2,5. A view from a few yards beyond the junction with Hotham Street and labelled 'Gloucester Street (old), looking Westwards, 1865, shewing excavations for the extension of the Station.' The 1848 O.S. map identifies the building to the left of the station arch as 'Commercial Hall', destined to suffer the same fate as St Simon's Church when the second station arch was built.

Image courtesy of the LRO, ref. Herdman Collection 481.

2,6. Looking west towards Lime Street in a watercolour described as 'Gloucester Street, N. side, and corner of Hotham Street, 1865.'

Image courtesy of the LRO, ref. Herdman Collection 555.

A picture in the *Illustrated London News* shows Gloucester Street providing a grand approach to the station in 1870, flanked by the newly completed London and North-Western Hotel (fig. 2,7). Peter Ellis would have been 65 years old when the hotel arrived and over the years he would have watched the street altering almost completely from his teenage recollections. The station was subsequently enlarged yet again and the street briefly sought survival by stealing the route of Skelhorne Street. Soon however the Gloucester Street name was returned to the original location with its western end having been reduced to little more than a route into the station from Lime Street, and Mawdsley's maps from 1872 – 1879 show the transformation in progress.[2] By the early 20th century Gloucester Street had become defined by an archway into the station, and the scene was captured in two evocative paintings by Allan Tankard in 1948 and 1959,[3] a detail from the former of which is reproduced here (fig. 2,8).

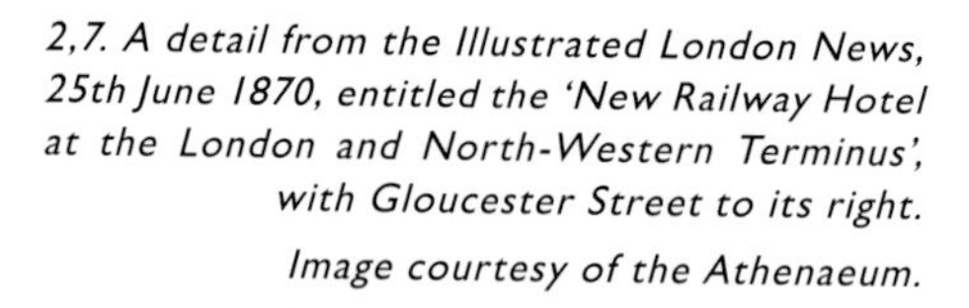

2,7. A detail from the Illustrated London News, 25th June 1870, entitled the 'New Railway Hotel at the London and North-Western Terminus', with Gloucester Street to its right. Image courtesy of the Athenaeum.

2,8. A detail from Allan Tankard's view of Lime Street Station in 1948. By the mid-20th century Gloucester Street existed as little more than a taxi-rank entrance to the station, whilst by 2011 it had vanished completely following redevelopment. Image courtesy of the LRO, ref. Binns Collection C198.

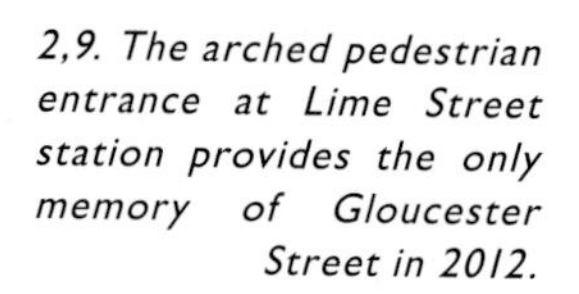

2,9. The arched pedestrian entrance at Lime Street station provides the only memory of Gloucester Street in 2012.

It is uncertain whether Peter Ellis senior built his own house in Gloucester Street on his own lease, or whether initially he constructed houses with other builders under their leases (John Kilshaw being a likely colleague), because the Corporation Lease Register shows only one lease there in his own name, and that was not until 1820. The lease (entered on the register on 18th May 1820, LRO ref. 352 CLE/CON 3/6) reads:

> *'All that piece or parcel of Land situate and being on the North Side of Gloucester Street in Liverpool bounded on the East by a House now or late belonging to Matthew Roberts on the North in part by Villers Place and in other part by Mason's Place and on the West by a House belonging to Mr. John Hicks Containing in front to Gloucester Street aforesaid 33 feet and running in rear or depth backwards on the East Side 56 feet and on the West Side 60 feet and being in breadth at the back or North End 31 feet 10 inches.'*

The lease was in the names of Peter Ellis senior's three youngest sons, William (then 12 years old), John (8) and Thomas (5) (fig. 2,10). The lease also shows that in 1857 it was re-granted to John Ellis (as survivor of the three), and John's lease (entered in the register on 28th September 1857, LRO ref. 352 CLE/CON 3/10) shows that by then it comprised *'All that piece or parcel of land with the two messuages or dwelling houses thereon erected situate on the north side of and being Nos. 31 and 33 Gloucester Street and the cottages in rear thereof...,'* with dimensions closely relating to those of the 1820 lease.

Lives and Years | Ages
William Ellis aged 12
John Ellis aged 8
Thomas Ellis aged 5
Sons of Peter Ellis the Lessee
42 Years

2,10. The names entered on the lease as 'Sons of Peter Ellis the Lessee' on 18th May 1820 for a building plot in Gloucester Street.

Image courtesy of the LRO.

In 1851 John also received a re-grant of another Gloucester Street property. This lease was entered in the register on 17th May 1851 (LRO ref. 352 CLE/CON 3/9; having taken possession in 1847) for:

> *'All that piece or parcel of Land with the messuage or dwellinghouse and buildings thereon erected situate on the South side of Gloucester Street bounded on the South by Copperas hill on the East by premises leased to Ann Yates and on the West by premises leased to the Trustees of Ann Nelson and containing in front to Gloucester Street aforesaid 15 feet 6 inches and to Copperas hill aforesaid 14 feet 10 inches and running in depth backwards on the East side thereof 48 feet 5 inches and on the west side thereof 48 feet.'*

With these various descriptions and a detail from Gage's 1835 plan (fig. 2,11) it becomes possible to identify the properties as being amongst those near to the junction of Gloucester Street and Copperas Hill and which faced each other across the section of Gloucester Street where the dimension *'359 Yards'* is shown.

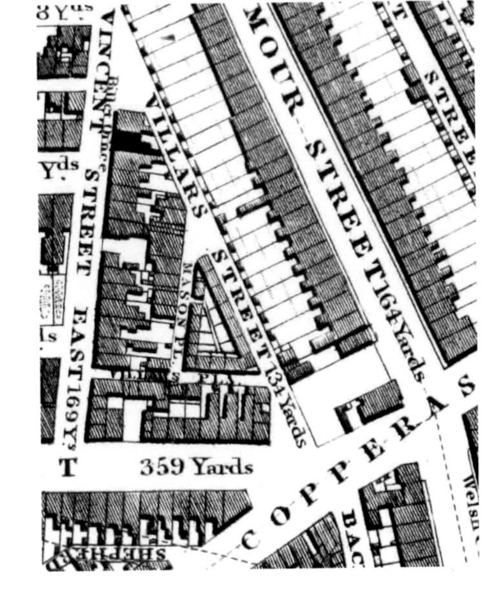

2,11. The eastern end of Gloucester Street in 1835 (a detail from fig. 2,1). The north and south sides of the street at '359 yards' include properties which Peter Ellis senior had built and which were inherited by his son, John Ellis.

Private collection.

Subsequent additions to these leases confirm that what soon happened to St Simon's Church as a result of the expansion of Lime Street Station (fig. 2,4) also happened to John's properties. On 22nd May 1867 the Corporation register shows that his lease of 1857 passed to *'Nominees of L & N. W. Rway Co. Site for St. Simon's Ch.'* Thus the 1865 directory lists nos. 25 – 41 Gloucester Street as being between St Vincent Street East and Villars Street, whilst the 1867 directory confirms that the new St Simon's church had replaced nos. 25 – 35. Then on 26th April 1882 John's lease of 1851 was *'sold (with other land) to L & N W Ry Co (1873 & 1875 Acts),'* ending the Ellis family's connection with Gloucester Street.

A map from the 1930s shows how different the area had become by the 20th century (fig. 2,12). The residual western section of Gloucester Street is between the *'E'* and *'S'* of *'Lime Str'* and forms the station approach. The relocated St Simon's Church is shown on the short un-named eastern section (between the *'A'* of *'East'* in St Vincent Street East and where Villars Street joins Copperas Hill). Today this church has also vanished and, along with the Ellis properties and the southern half of St Vincent Street East, the whole site is now part of the car park for the Liner Hotel on Lord Nelson Street.

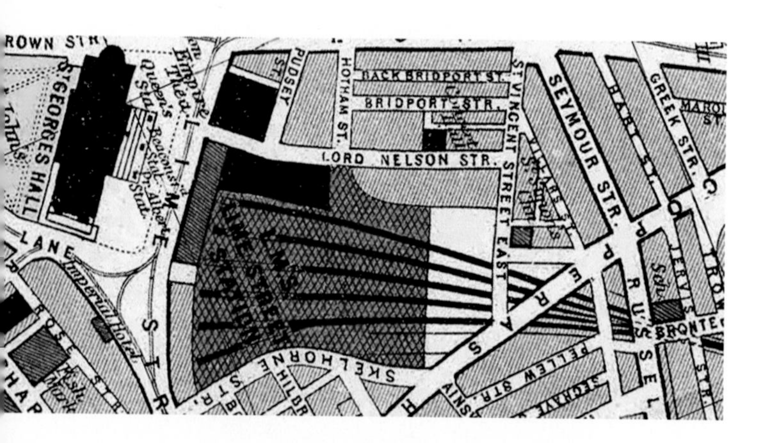

2,12. A detail from a Bartholomew's Town Plan showing the fate of Gloucester Street prior to the 2nd World War. Private collection. Image courtesy of Harper Collins.

Baines' Directory of 1824 shows that Peter Ellis senior had moved again, for the entry now reads *'joiner & builder, 10 Gloucester place, Low hill'* (is it mere coincidence that the move was from one Gloucester to another?). [4] Both Primrose Hill and Gloucester Street had been at the very earliest stages of development when the family had first moved there whereas, according to James Picton, *'Phythian Street and Gloucester Place leading eastward from Low Hill, were laid out in 1811-13, with moderate-sized houses standing in gardens.'* [5] Thus by the early 1820s Peter Ellis senior had apparently progressed sufficiently in the world to move his family to a home well away from his new area of work at Finch Street (see later). Low Hill was at that stage still on the very fringes of the expanding town, and Herdman's scene in 1790 showing Low Hill before the arrival of the new streets (fig. 2,13) is romantically different to the scene today (fig. 2,14).

The view from Low Hill in the days long before the builders had begun to move in, and copied from an original by *'the late Mr McMorland taken about 1790'*, would have been little changed by the time Ann Ellis journeyed to and from Prescot later that decade for the births of her first daughter and son. W G Herdman wrote that the scene:-

> *'commences on the left with the Old Red Lion Inn, at the foot of which is seen the old road to Prescot. The spire of St Thomas's Church, and one of the old Mills on Copperas Hill, are next seen. The near square building in the foreground is the Old Well, situated in the ground between Harper Street and Low Hill. This was a noted well of excellent water, and supplied the neighbourhood, free of charge, for a considerable distance. It will be remembered by many now living, as it remained until about 1828.'* [6]

2,13. 'Liverpool from Low Hill' ca. 1790, copied by W G Herdman from a scene looking west by McMorland. Private collection.

By 1931 Michael O'Mahony was commenting that

> *'Whatever Low Hill looks like to-day, it doesn't look like a place with a past; and yet its story can be traced to a time anterior to the Danish occupation in England... The air being pure and salubrious, roses once flourished luxuriously round the thatched eaves of the Low Hill cottages. Indeed, up to 1820, and long after, where modernity now spells itself so emphatically in Low Wood Street and Holborn Street, stretched the green vistas of Stringfellow's Nursery. Building on the hill came slowly, though a large stone quarry, open to Prescot-street, stood on the spot where the bridewell is erected. Near the northern side of this delf was a small building shaped like a summer-house, called "Rats' Castle"... Harper Street commemorates Mr. Harper, whose house stood in a large garden opposite Phythian Street. Close to his garden was a deep well which was at one time open to the public. The inmates of Low Hill Workhouse used, by crossing through a passage cut in the rock from the opposite side of the street, to draw water from this well.'* [7]

2,14. Liverpool from Low Hill in 2012, looking west from Holborn Street, corresponding to the position and direction in fig. 2,13.

2,15. An undated watercolour entitled 'Harrison's "Rats' Castle" or "Rats' Tower", Low Hill.' Image courtesy of the LRO, ref. Herdman Collection 1414. [8]

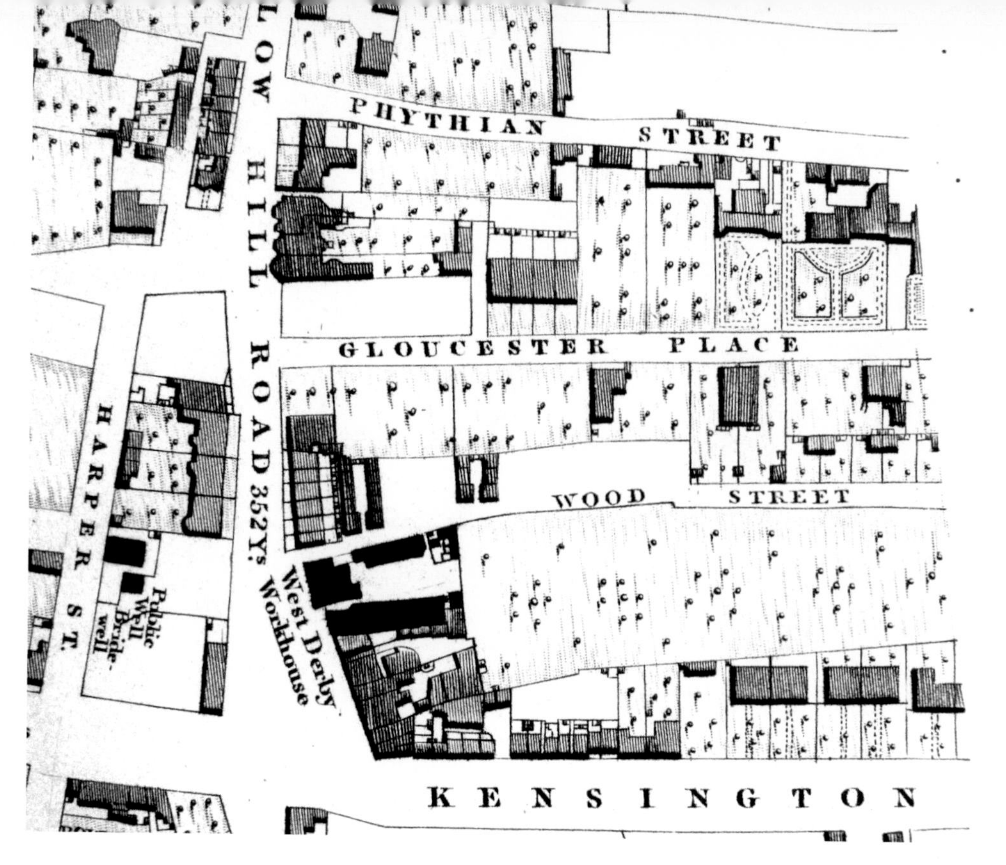

2,16. A detail from the edge of Michael Gage's plan of 1835 showing Wood Street, Gloucester Place and Phythian Street running east from Low Hill, the West Derby Workhouse and the site of the Public Well on Harper Street.

The location of this area within the town is identified on the map on p. iv by the letter F.

Private collection.

A combination of Michael Gage's plan of the area around Gloucester Place in 1835 (fig. 2,16) and a number of Herdman paintings provides some indication of the extent of the development of the southern end of Low Hill in the days that Peter Ellis was living there. Turning right out of Gloucester Place, Peter would have seen that a number of ancient cottages had survived (figs. 2,17 and 2,18) and modern property at the junction of Erskine Street had arrived (fig. 2,19). Of the first cottage (fig. 2,17), W G Herdman wrote that, '*This was an old stone house, which stood on the east side of Low Hill, near Phythian Street. It is supposed to have been built about 1680. It had large grounds at the back, which the inhabitants used for drying clothes in.*'[9] The second cottage (fig. 2,18) stood on the opposite side, at the northern end of the row of houses shown to the left of the '*W*' of '*Low*' in fig. 2,16. The picture is dated 1856 and the sign on the right, '*This Land to be Sold*', was ominous for this ancient remnant of Low Hill. It survived until 1864 when it is shown in another Herdman painting in a half-demolished state.[10] At the junction with Erskine Street (fig. 2,19, looking east towards the '*ILL*' of '*Low Hill*' in fig. 2,16) the house on the extreme left of the scene and to the rear of the lamppost was the southern member of the terrace of six of which the cottage in fig. 2,18 was at the northern end. The properties with bay windows facing Erskine Street are also shown on Michael Gage's plan. Erskine Street was laid out in 1812 and was named after Thomas Erskine, a famous barrister of the time.

2,17. A cottage near Phythian Street in 1828.
Image courtesy of the LRO, ref. Herdman Collection 1413A.

2,18. Entitled 'Low Hill, old cottage opposite Phythian Street, 1856.'

Image courtesy of the LRO, ref. Herdman Collection 452B.

2,19. A view of Low Hill at its junction with Erskine Street in 1867 with Harper Street disappearing to the right.

Image courtesy of the LRO, ref. Herdman Collection 97.

2,20. 'Riding the Liberties' at Low Hill in 1821 by W G Herdman.
Image courtesy of the LRO. [11]

2,21. James Brierley's view of the West Derby Workhouse (which Herdman refers to as the Poor House).
Image courtesy of the Athenaeum.

Turning left out of Gloucester Place would have led Peter past a row of cottages on the north side of Wood Street and the West Derby Workhouse (Poor House) on the south side (figs. 2,20 and 2,21) to the Coach and Horses (fig. 2,22) which is marked on Horwood's map of 1803. Of his view of Low Hill in 1821 (fig. 2,20), W G Herdman wrote that:

'The Plate represents the old Poor House of the township of West Derby, with the cottages which, at the date of the sketch, 1821, stood at its north side. The drawing was taken by the author, whilst witnessing the ceremony of "Riding the Liberties of the Town." It was then the custom of the major, (carrying his wand,) the corporate body, and a numerous cavalcade of gentlemen, to ride round the boundaries of the town, stopping at Low-hill to lunch.' [11]

2,22. A detail from a William Herdman watercolour. Although dated 1850, the view must be somewhat earlier than this because the 1848 O.S. map (fig. 2,24) shows Holborn Street in existence and already lined with houses.
Image courtesy of the LRO, ref. Herdman Collection 610.

2,23. The same location in 1867 as the view in fig. 2,22. Image courtesy of the LRO, ref. Herdman Collection 795.

By the early 1820s Peter Ellis, then a late teenager and living a matter of a few yards away from the ceremony, might well have been given the opportunity to watch this annual event. After the brandy, rum and wine that accompanied the lunch had been ceremoniously disposed of, it is perhaps questionable how conscientiously the remaining Liberties were ridden, [12] and the excuse for a lavish lunch at Low Hill died out after 1835 when the town boundaries were extended. James Brierley produced a closer view of the Workhouse in 1830 (fig. 2,21), and it is interesting to compare the interpretations of the building by the two artists. A painting by William Herdman (one of W G Herdman's sons) some years later (fig. 2,22) shows the south side of Low Hill as far as its boundary at 2 Low Hill, the premises of Samuel Lunt, for many years a tailor and proprietor of a beer house. Outside his shop two flights of steps approach each other but lead only to a window, pointing back to a time when the shop had been split into two dwellings (as suggested by the number of properties there in fig. 2,16). With Kensington seen disappearing to the right, this is a period immediately prior to the arrival of Holborn Street which is shown on the 1848 O.S. map (fig. 2,24) and which had first appeared in the directories a year earlier. Its arrival caused the demolition of the properties south of the Workhouse [13] and the construction of a new Coach and Horses (fig. 2,23) which for a period of time was renamed the Low Hill Coffee House before reverting to its original name. [14] The building to the right of the Coffee House which had been Samuel Lunt's appears to have survived but with modifications: the earlier steps have gone and a doorway has reappeared.

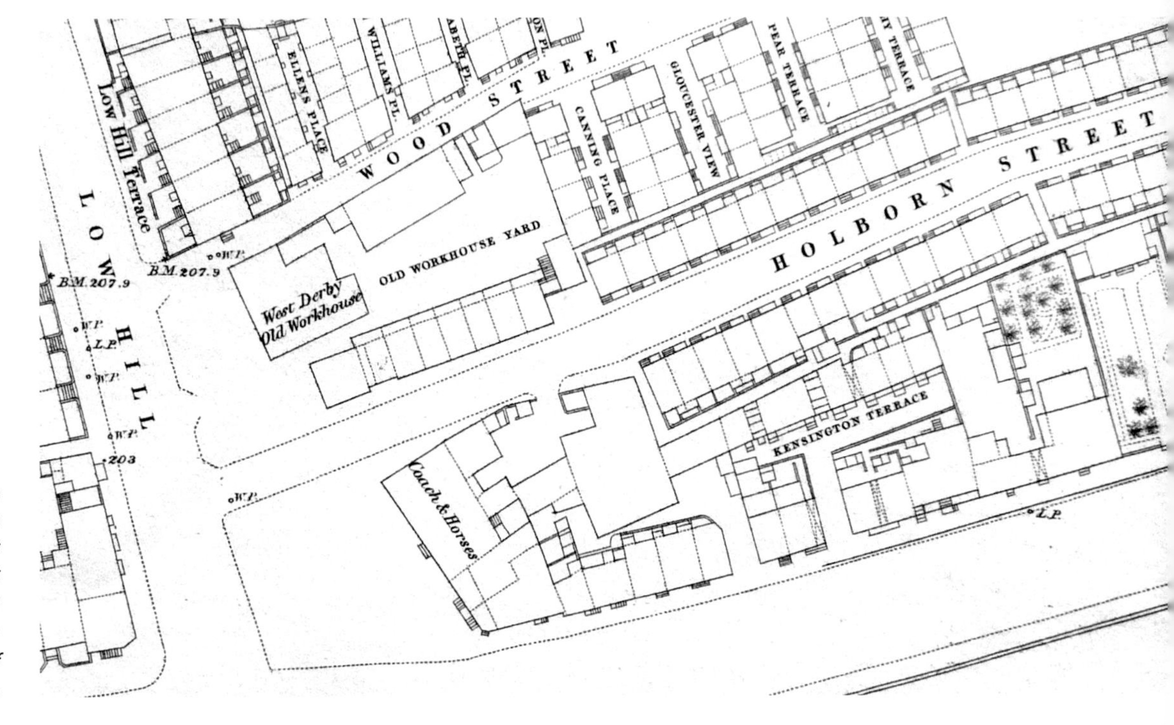

2,24. A detail from the 1848 O.S. map showing the arrival of Holborn Street shortly before the West Derby Workhouse was demolished.

Image courtesy of the Athenaeum.

2,25. Looking east to the Low Hill / Kensington junction in 2012, with Holborn Street in the centre of the view (from where fig. 2,14 was taken).

Although *Baines' Directory* of 1824 was the first to indicate that the Ellis family had moved to Gloucester Place, the Liverpool Record Office has two Lancashire Deeds dated 4th November 1822 which identify precisely when Peter Ellis senior acquired their house. [15] They name the previous owner of the lease as William Williams, a Liverpool bricklayer, who had in turn acquired the land and premises from Peter Robinson, a slater and plasterer from Liverpool, in 1814. William Williams is shown in the directories as living at Warren Street in 1813 where he continued to be until 1821 after which he is listed at Seymour Street. These two streets were situated on either side of Copperas Hill, a matter of yards from Peter Ellis senior's property in Gloucester Street. Peter would therefore have become aware of the property by knowing William as a fellow member of the building trade in that area. The property at Gloucester Place was shown as '*bounded on the East by Land now or late of Thomas Plumbe Esquire on the West by Land sold and surrendered to John Alderson and on the North by Land late of Miss Phythian and on the South by Gloucester Row*'.

The directories from 1813 show that John Alderson, '*oil merchant, lamp and wax candle manufacturer, 10 Gloucester place*', had been an existing tenant when Williams took on the lease and that his family continued to live there until the Ellis family arrived. Mrs Elizabeth Phythian was listed at Low Hill in the 1800 and 1803 directories and was a member of the family which is remembered by the street of that name. The directories also indicate that Gloucester Row became Gloucester Place from 1813 onwards.

Although Michael Gage's plan (fig. 2,16) does not show the eastern end of Gloucester Place, two other detailed maps for 1835 (fig. 2,27) and 1848 (fig. 2,26) do extend that far. Together with the directories it then becomes possible to establish that the Ellis property was the one at the very end of the row on the north side. [16] In 1835 there was still a vacant plot of land to the left of the home of the Ellis family, and the directories suggest that the owner of the plot, John Alderson (according to the lease), had died in 1822 or soon after. The executors of John's estate (or a subsequent purchaser) must have chosen to leave it undeveloped until 1848 when the O.S. map shows that a terrace had appeared next to what had been the Ellis home together with terraces immediately north on Phythian Street.

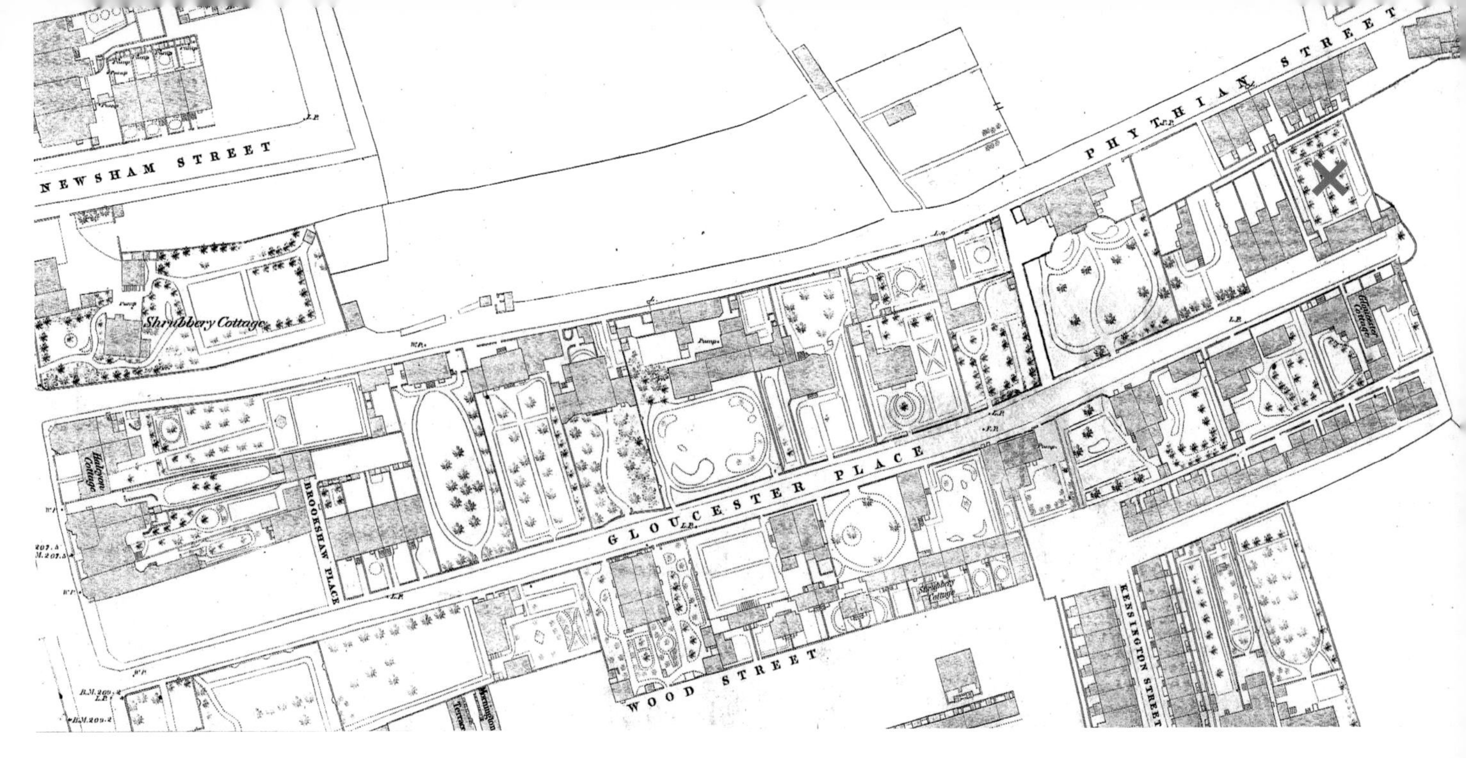

*2,26. Gloucester Place on the 1848 O.S. map. What had been the Ellis property is marked '**X**'.*
Image courtesy of Digital Archives.

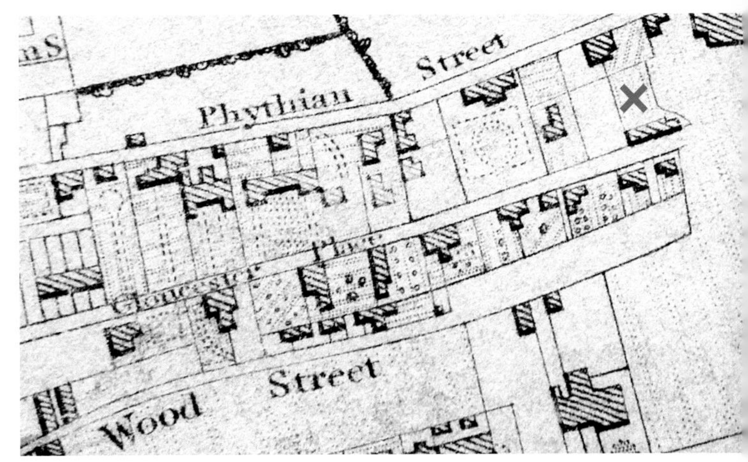

*2,27. Gloucester Place as shown on Jonathan Bennison's map of 1835. The Ellis property is marked '**X**'.*
Image courtesy of the Athenaeum.

Writing in the early 1870s, James Picton continued his comments quoted earlier, [5] regarding the laying out of Phythian Street and Gloucester Place in 1811-13, with the reflection that '*After the lapse of nearly sixty years, their quiet semi-rural appearance is almost altogether destroyed,*' and one wonders what Peter might have thought in his later years as he saw the changes inexorably taking place there. As with Gloucester Street, so too with Gloucester Place: surviving until the late 20th century in the form of two short western and eastern ends, with redevelopment down the centre section, Gloucester Place has now also disappeared. A photograph taken in 2012 (fig. 2,25) from the same vantage point as the 1867 painting (fig. 2,23) shows Holborn Street in the centre of the view, completely transformed with modern housing, and only the building that was once the Coach and Horses living on in the form of a business premises. To the far left the new buildings mark where Wood Street and Gloucester Place used to join Low Hill. What is left of Gloucester Place in the 21st century has been renamed Gilmartin Grove. To find out more about what life was like and who the residents were in the Low Hill area as it grew in the 19th century after Peter had departed, Fred Forrest's article concerning the development of Phythian Street provides a detailed account. [17]

2,28. An advertisement in Gore's 1835 directory showing Peter McQuie's premises at the junction of Covent Garden and Water Street. He remained at this building until 1863 when something of singular importance happened to it.

Image courtesy of Birkenhead Reference Library.

PETER M'QUIE,
Commission Merchant,
1, COVENT-GARDEN, WATER-STREET.

AGENT TO THE MANUFACTURERS FOR THE SALE OF
SCOTCH LINENS,
Dundee SALT and CORN SACKS; SAIL CANVASS, SACKING, TARPAULING, HAMMOCKING, BUNTING, PARCELLING, OSNABURGS, SHEETINGS, DUCKS, DOWLAS, DRILLS, DIAPERS, LINEN THREAD, WOOL SHEETING,
Cotton, Coffee, Bread and Mending BAGGING, HESSIANS, TWINES, LINES, and NETS, of all sorts; HEMP, FLAX, TOW, MATS;
Atkinson's Patent Stockton SAIL CLOTH;
White and Rock SALT; COALS, CANNEL, SLACK; RUTHVEN'S PATENT and other PRESSES, for Letter Copying, with Bound BOOKS, &c. replete;
SEAL and LITHOGRAPHIC PRESSES; GERMAN STONES;
Portable Improved
PRINTING PRESSES and FIRE ENGINES;
Composition Metal LETTERS; PRESS FURNISHINGS.
STEAM-PACKETS Supplied with Genuine
RUSHY PARK COALS.
Also, BEDDING, TABLE LINEN, MATTRESSES, HAIR SEATING, and CABIN FURNITURE, of every description.

—— Lewis, master mariner, 15, Horatio street
—— Lister, gentleman, 5, Rodney street
—— Margaret, boarding house, 4, Harford street
—— Peter, builder, 11, Gloucester place, Lowhill
—— —— shop, 45, Finch street
—— Ralph, victualler, 9, South Union street
—— Robert, joiner and builder, 45, Finch street

In 1824, soon after the Ellis family had settled in at Gloucester Place, Peter Robinson McQuie is shown in *Baines' Directory* as also arriving at Low Hill, having moved from Upper Pitt Street. With so few houses existing along Low Hill at that time it was sufficient for the postman merely to know to deliver to *'Mr McQuie, Low Hill'*, for it is not until 1843 that *Gore's Directory* first lists the McQuie's house as no. 22, on the east side of the road between Wood Street and Gloucester Place. Living a matter of a few yards apart, it will become apparent later that the two families must have become well acquainted, for their sons – Peter Ellis the architect and Peter B McQuie the accountant – are found to be sharing offices together at two different locations in the 1850s and 1860s. In addition, for a period of almost 30 years, the office of Peter McQuie senior was located in the building at the junction of Water Street and Covent Garden (fig. 2,28) that, significantly for Peter Ellis the architect, would come to be replaced by Oriel Chambers.

2,29. A section from Gore's Directory for 1827 showing the shop of Peter Ellis senior and Robert Ellis at Finch Street, and Lewis Ellis as a master mariner.

Image courtesy of Sefton Local History Unit.

Although the Ellis household had moved to Gloucester Place in 1822, in 1825 Robert Ellis, Peter and Ann's eldest son, appeared in *Gore's Directory* as having premises at Finch Street as a builder and joiner. In 1827-1829 he and Peter Ellis senior are shown as sharing the premises as a shop (fig. 2,29). Indeed, during the period 1825-1837 the directories suggest that Finch Street became an important location for a variety of other potential Ellis relations: Ellis & Sowerby, seminary (1835-1837); Edward B Ellis, book keeper (1837); Elizabeth Ellis (1829, no occupation given); Ellen Ellis, dressmaker (1835) and lodging house (1837); Lewis Ellis, master mariner (1834-1835); and William Ellis, silk mercer and haberdasher (1825). [18]

On 24th February 1824 '*Robert Ellis of Liverpool Joiner*' is shown in the Corporation register as having taken a building lease for land in Finch Street (LRO ref. 352 CLE/CON 3/6). It was for:-

> '*All that Piece or Parcel of Land situate and being on the South side of Finch Street and West side of Gildart Street in Liverpool Bounded on the South side by a back Street of Five yards wide and on the West by Ground in Lease to Messieurs Foster Stanistreet & Eden Containing in front to Finch Street 28 Yards 1 Foot and running in depth from thence along Gildart Street and on the West side severally 25 yards and being in breadth at the back to the front of the said Back Street 27 1/2 Yards.*'

The site is shown on Michael Gage's plan (fig. 2,30) as the whole of the eastern half of the land bounded by Audley Street, Finch Street, Gildart Street and Percy Street North (the '*back street*' in the lease). The western half being already in lease to a Foster consortium (see p. 45 regarding the Fosters), Gage's plan shows the various properties that Robert constructed, one of which will have been his shop, together with what appears to be a substantial builder's yard. Robert nominated his three youngest brothers for the standard lease of '*three lives & 21 years*'. [19] By then William, John and Thomas were respectively 16, 12 and 8 years old. John, as we have seen, lived on to inherit property in Gloucester Street (fig. 2,11).

In the 21st century Percy Street North (later renamed Prudhoe Street) no longer exists and all Robert's property has vanished.

Then, in the Corporation register for 7th December 1824, '*Peter Ellis of Liverpool Joiner*' (Peter Ellis senior) is shown as taking a lease on land close to that of Robert's (LRO ref. 352 CLE/CON 3/7). The entry reads:-

> '*All that piece or parcel of Land situate and being on the East side of Audley Street in Liverpool Bounded on the North by an intended Street of Five Yards wide on the South by another intended Street and at the Back or East by a Common Passage of Six feet wide containing in front to Audley Street and at the Back severally 94 feet 6 Inches and running in depth backwards on the North side 78 and on the South side 77 feet 6 Inches.*'

This is shown on Gage's plan as comprising the western half of the land bounded by Audley Street, Percy Street North, Gildart Street and Ilford Street (being the other '*intended street*').

From the plan it can be seen that Peter created a group of properties with an intriguingly symmetrical central area, and Joseph Sharples has kindly provided an interpretation of the appearance on the later and more detailed 1848 O.S. map (fig. 2.31).

Oposite left: 2,30. A detail from Michael Gage's plan showing the development of Finch Street in 1835. The location of this area within the town is identified on the map on p. iv by the letter G. Private collection.

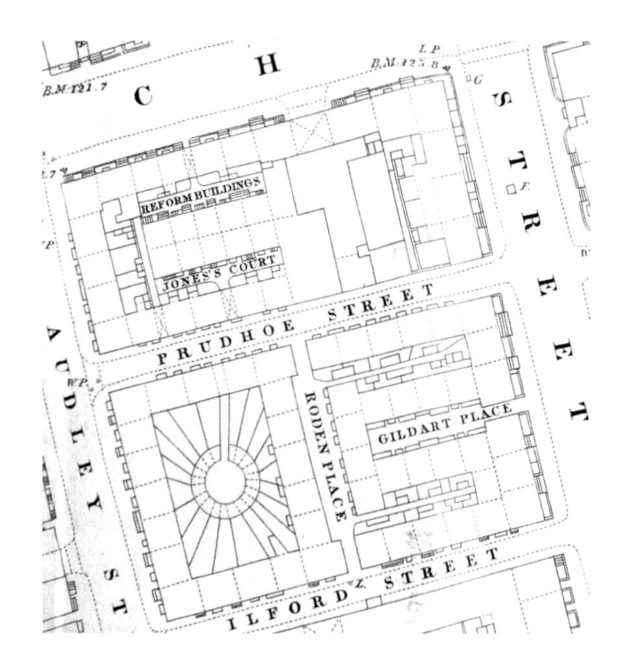

2,31. A detail from the 1848 O.S. map.

The properties built by Peter Ellis senior are surrounded by Audley, Ilford and Prudhoe Streets and Roden Place.

The buildings constructed by Robert Ellis comprise the eastern half of the block north of Prudhoe Street (i.e. excluding the Reform Buildings and Jones's Court). By this stage Percy Street North had been renamed Prudhoe Street.

Image courtesy of the Athenaeum.

> *'The houses round the perimeter seem little bigger than court houses, but they are evidently superior to the extent that on three sides of the block they face the street, and each house has its own wedge-shaped back yard or garden. At the end of each yard there seems to be a small outbuilding – Wash house? Privy? Coal store? All three combined? – forming a ring in the middle of the block. A tunnel-like passage from the street on the north side gives access to the circular open space enclosed by these outbuildings. This access would be necessary for emptying the privies or delivering coal. The whole arrangement is like one side of a terraced street wrapped round a square plot and joined at the ends.'* [20]

Much of the Finch Street area that was constructed by other builders comprised conventional court dwellings, of which the neighbouring Gildart Place is an example. Peter Ellis senior had clearly decided upon an imaginative departure from that tradition and one wonders how much Peter Ellis junior, about to leave his teenage years behind, played a part in the design. Just as with Robert's property, all these houses have long since been demolished, the lease indicating that the site was taken over by Owen Owen in 1896 along with other land facing it in Audley Street (today T J Hughes).

With the construction at Audley Street in progress, if not already completed, in 1826 Peter Ellis junior looked forward to the celebration of reaching his 21st birthday. And yet the year was to prove a sad one for the family. The columns of the *Liverpool Mercury* on 10th March 1826 carried the briefest notification of a death two weeks earlier. '*On Monday, the 27th ult. after a lingering illness, Ann, only daughter of Mr Peter Ellis, builder, Gloucester-place.*' The first-born of the marriage of Peter Ellis senior and Ann Appleton, her death at their home at the age of 29 must have been heartbreaking for the whole family. Unknown to them, the deaths of two of Peter's younger brothers, William and Thomas, would follow within a few years.

What was required two centuries ago in order to become recognised as a qualified architect is not clear. John Foster senior (1759-1827), for example, had no formal training but managed to end up as Corporation Architect, apparently consulting experts in areas outside his competence. His son, John Foster junior (1786-1846), went on a Grand Tour for five years, studied Greek ruins, and ended up being the architect for many of Liverpool's most notable buildings. James Picton started out on his career as a self-taught quantity surveyor.

How Peter Ellis became a recognised architect with the inspiration to design Oriel Chambers and 16 Cook Street is unknown. Certainly he could have developed all the constructional skills he would have needed whilst growing up and working alongside his father, and interestingly Peter Ellis senior finally described himself as *'architect and builder'* in the 1832 directory shortly before retiring. But was his father also a skilled artist and draughtsman, or might those skills have been developed elsewhere?

It is intriguing therefore to speculate that Peter learned some of his drawing techniques from James Sherriff, the surveyor whose maps of 1816-1826 (figs. 2,32) show such delightful details of the countryside surrounding Liverpool. Four of the maps, each traditionally oriented to the east, have surviving examples and are unusual for focusing not upon their use in planning a route but as social maps in which they name a whole variety of residents (perhaps subscribers) together with notable buildings. They cover the surrounding countryside as far away as Ormskirk and Crosby to the north, Hale and Widnes to the south, and St. Helens to the east, and provide a memory of some of the evocative place names along the Mersey's shoreline. [21]

2,32. Sections from James Sherriff's map of 1823. Images courtesy of the Athenaeum.

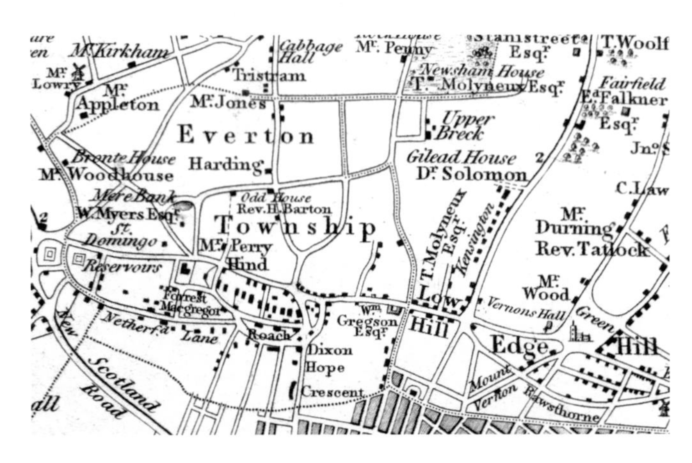

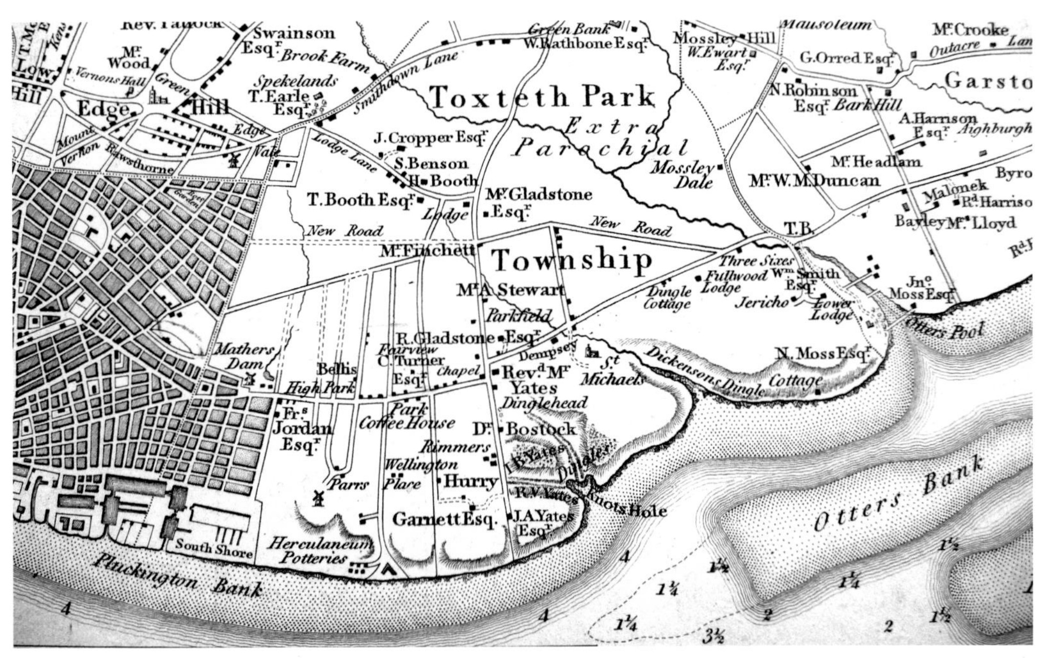

Over the period that the directories and leases show Peter Ellis senior as sharing a workshop in Finch Street, and where Peter Ellis junior would have been involved in the building work in progress in nearby Audley Street, James Sherriff lived in Finch Street and was listed not only as a land surveyor but also as a drawing master (fig. 2,33). In an age when women so frequently remained invisible in the directories until a male was no longer present at the address, the Sherriff household was delightfully unusual in listing husband, wife and daughter. Sherriff Street in Everton was probably named after him. It appears with that spelling on the 1848 O.S. map, in the numerical section of *McCorquodale's Directory* for 1848, and in the first two *Gore's Directories* which showed its arrival (in the 1843 and 1845 street lists). Some official, presumably armed with a dictionary but unaware of the historical association, subsequently stole the second '*r*' and it became Sheriff Street. Like the second '*r*' and much of Everton, the street has long since vanished.

Sherriff James, surveyor & drawing master, 68, Finch street
——— Mrs. and Miss, teachers, 68, Finch street

2,33. From Gore's 1829 directory.
Image courtesy of the Athenaeum.

In 1868 Finch Street was renamed Blandford Street and in 1892 it was renamed yet again, this time to Kempston Street by which it remains known today. Now a mere shadow of its former self, in the years that Peter Ellis and James Sherriff were there they would have been working in a vibrant community. *Baines' Directory* shows that several dozen properties already existed by 1824, whilst *Gore's* 1839 directory (the first to follow Baines' example of providing a numerical index of inhabitants in each street) lists well over 100 dwellings and shows that a diverse mix of trades and professions had arrived.

Later directories indicate that the street became a strong focus for joiners and related trades, and an 1870 water-colour attributed to William Herdman shows the junction of Falkland Street and Finch Street (by then renamed Blandford Street) with a joiner displaying his board outside his premises at Belle Vue, and where his front garden was doubling up as a timber yard (figs. 2,34 and 2,35). Herdman chose one of the few buildings on Finch Street that was not part of a terrace or court but he misread the joiner's name. The directories throughout the period consistently list an Adam Amos, joiner and builder, at this location. Adam had lived at this house before the street had its name changed from Finch to Blandford, having taken out a Corporation lease on 14th November 1857 (LRO ref. 352 CLE/CON 3/10), and he was still there in 1892 to witness the street suffering yet another name change.

2,34. A detail from the 1848 O.S. map which allows the precise location of Herdman's scene in fig. 2,35 to be identified. This junction no longer exists.
Image courtesy of the Athenaeum.

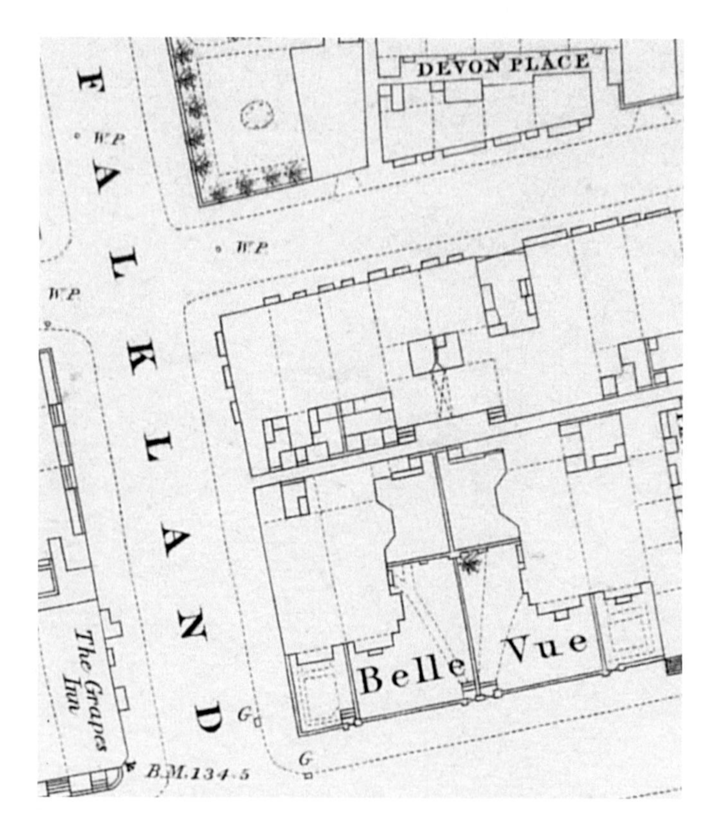

2,35. A scene in 1870 at the junction of Falkland Street and Blandford Street (previously Finch Street). In the distance in Herdman's view can be seen the Presbyterian Chapel which then existed on the north side of Islington.

Image courtesy of the LRO, ref. Herdman Collection 103.

2,36. A photograph by the City Engineer's Department showing nos. 88 to 76 Kempston Street.

Image courtesy of the LRO, ref. Photographs & Small Prints: Streets and Districts: Kempston Street.

In 1926 a member of the City Engineer's Department visited Kempston Street to provide a record of the south side between Falkland Street and Gildart Street (backing onto what is shown as Mill Street East on fig. 2,30). On the photograph (fig. 2,36), looking west towards Gildart Street, can be seen (left to right) the premises of Jacob Cohen, wood carver (ground floor) and Solomon Glassar, cabinet maker at no. 88; next door at no. 86 at an open first floor window Jacob Sorenson can be seen at work as an upholsterer; then at no. 84 one of its occupants, Ben Nelson (french polisher) or L Richards (upholsterer), is chatting to a passer-by; the photograph terminates further down the street at St Mary Magdalene Church (completed around 1860 and therefore not on Gage's 1835 map). Kelly's 1926 directory shows the remarkable concentration of overlapping trades that then existed all along Kempston Street, part of which is reproduced here to accompany the photograph (fig. 2,37). Had the Ellis builders still been alive in 1926, they would surely have felt a strong connection with many of these craftspeople. However a comprehensive demolition of Kempston Street was completed by 1970 and, returning there today, the Ellis family would be unable to make any sense of what they would see around them.

Gildart st
56 Grossman Abraham cabinet makers' requisites
66 Rosenberg Louis cabinet maker
St. Mary Magdalene Church
76 James Miss Elizabeth caretaker
78 Crugman David french polisher
80 Isbovitch Hyman wood carver
80 Blankstone Saul cabinet maker
82 Levy Hyman cabinet maker
84 Richards L. & Son upholsterers
84 Nelson Ben french polisher
86 Sorenson Jacob upholsterer
88 Glassar Soloman cabinet maker
88 Cohen Jacob Alexander wood carver
92 Mathieson Frank cabinet maker
92 Abrahams Ephraim cabinet maker
92 Bosman Charles cabinet maker
92 Stone Folly cabinet maker
92 Daniels Sol french polisher
92 Ginsburg Harry wood carver
92 Tipping James wood turner
Falkland st

2,37. A section of the list for the south side of Kempston Street from Kelly's directory for 1926.

Image courtesy of the Athenaeum.

References and Notes to Chapter 2

1 C R Hand, *Olde Liverpoole & Its Charter*, Hand & Co, 1907, p. 107 (reprinted by the Book Clearance Centre, Liverpool).

2 The Liverpool directories were frequently made available with a Mawdsley map (Mawdsley's by then having become the publishers of the *Gore's Directories*), and the copies at the Athenaeum show Gloucester Street's continuing battle for survival. In 1878 it made a spirited attempt to take over the route of Skelhorne Street but in 1879 Skelhorne Street reasserted its brief loss of identity, and from then on it was the entrance to Lime Street Station that was re-established as the location for Gloucester Street's western end. One of the residents of Gloucester Street – born there in 1832, and possibly in an Ellis-built house – was John Hulley, founder of the modern Olympic movement and organiser of its first festivals in Liverpool in the 1860s (see Liverpool History Society newsletter 34 which can viewed on its website).

Ron Jones has also pointed out that Frank Hornby (*'Inventor of the world's most famous toy'*) was born at 77 Copperas Hill in 1863 and, ironically (as the inventor of Hornby trains), one of the platforms at Lime Street Station is on the site of his birthplace.

3 Allan Tankard, *Lime Street 1948* (LRO ref. Binns Collection C198) and *Lime Street 1959* (LRO ref. Local Collection 511). Reproductions of these paintings can also be seen in Kay Parrott's book, *A Portrait of Liverpool, The Paintings of Allan P Tankard*, The Bluecoat Press, 2006. The 1959 painting captures *'Professor Codman's'* famous Punch and Judy show, a scene which many Liverpool people will still recall.

4 J A Picton, *Memorials of Liverpool*, G G Walmsley (Liverpool), 2nd edition, 1875, vol. I, p. 267, notes that Prince William, subsequently Duke of Gloucester, had taken up residence at St Domingo House in Everton in 1803, where he then resided for three years having been appointed commander of forces in the district. The names for Gloucester Street and Place, and briefly for other locations in Everton and Edge Hill, appear to be in recognition of this.

The 2nd edition of the *Memorials* (vol. I, historical; vol. II, topographical) can be downloaded from the internet as pdf files thanks to the University of Toronto (visit the Liverpool History Society website and go to *'on-line books'*). James Picton's frequently less than enthusiastic comments on so many buildings designed by other architects are disappointing aspects of an otherwise excellent and unparalleled history of Liverpool from which this book draws many valuable quotations.

5 J A Picton, *op. cit.*, vol. II, p. 426.

6 W G Herdman, *Pictorial Relics of Ancient Liverpool*, 1856, p. 84 with reference to plate 37 (which is an un-tinted version of fig. 2,13). LRO ref. Hf 942.7214 HER (1856).

7 Michael O'Mahony, *Ways and Byeways of Liverpool*, Daily Post, 1931, p. 17 (using James Stonehouse, *Streets of Liverpool*). James Picton (*op. cit.*, vol. I, p. 5) suggests that *'Low'* is a corruption of the Anglo-Saxon word for a tumulus or grave-mound. *'As these tumuli were usually erected on eminences, the hill and the mound became associated together under the same name...*

in the names Low Hill and Brownlow Hill, we preserve the faint memory of the interment of chief men of our own race, more than twelve hundred years since.'

In contrast, W G Herdman (*Pictorial Relics*, 1843, p. 98) suggests that the name was formerly Law-hill and derives '*from its being without the boundary of the borough, and also from its being a place of refuge for tradesmen not burgesses, who were occasionally not suffered to carry on any business in the town, freemen alone having that privilege by charter.*'

8 '*There once lived a curious person at Low-hill who had peculiar tastes. He built a place which was called "Rat's Castle". It stood on the brink of a delf, the site of which is now occupied by the Prescot-street Bridewell. This person used to try experiments with food, such as cooking spiders, blackbeetles, rats, cats, mice, and other things not in common use; and, it is said, was wont to play off tricks upon unsuspecting strangers by placing banquets before them that were quite unexpected and unprecedented in the nature and condition of the food.*' Quotation from *Recollections of Old Liverpool by a Nonagenarian*, J F Hughes, 1863, p. 80 (reprinted by the Dodo Press). The story was recited by the unidentified Nonagenarian to James Stonehouse and subsequently repeated in Stonehouse's own book, *The Streets of Liverpool*, Edward Howell, 1869, p. 107.

9 W G Herdman, *Pictorial Relics of Ancient Liverpool*, 1878, vol. II, text on p. 21 with regard to the same view (in monochrome) in plate 46. LRO ref. Hf 942.7214 HER (1878 (2)).

10 Albion Terrace, immediately to the left of the lamp-post in fig. 2,18, had arrived by the time the 1848 Ordnance Survey was carried out. It had required the demolition of one of the middle houses in the Low Hill terrace of six properties shown opposite Phythian Street in fig. 2,16. Another Herdman painting dated 1864 (LRO ref. Herdman Collection 747) portrays the cottage in a half-demolished state; upon the margin of that painting has been written '*Site of Sadler Street*'. In the 20th century both Albion Terrace and Sadler Street met the same fate as the cottages they had replaced. Clearly a building much loved by the Herdmans, the LRO possesses at least two other views of it, referenced as Herdman Collection 437 and 545B. The latter also appears in Kay Parrott, *Pictorial Liverpool, The Art of WG & William Herdman*, The Bluecoat Press, 2005 in which the view in 1855 contains a glimpse down Albion Terrace. James Stonehouse, *op. cit.*, p. 108, wrote of Halcyon Cottage, which also clung onto its existence near the Phythian Street junction, that it was '*erected by a sea captain, who so called it after the name of the ship in which he had "ploughed the salt ocean".*' By 1867 it too had vanished, replaced by the Chemist and Broker's premises shown in fig. 2,19.

11 W G Herdman, *Pictorial Relics of Ancient Liverpool*, 1843, text p. 98 for plate 44. LRO ref. Hf 942.7214 HER (1843).

12 See accounts by Picton, *op. cit.*, vol. II, p. 425, and O'Mahony, *op. cit.*, p. 18. James Picton indicated that '*a spacious tent was wont to be pitched and a pleasant collation spread therein*' (the tent is on the left in Herdman's picture). He also reproduced a copy of the tavern bill for 1800 and suggested that after lunch, '*the company usually dispersed, leaving the southern boundaries to chance or fate.*'

13 The Workhouse was taken down about 1850 following the formation of the West Derby Union and the building of a new workhouse in Mill Lane, Everton, which was first listed in the directories in 1843.

14 The 27th June and 25th July 1888 editions of the *Liverpool Citizen*, in a series entitled '*Old Liverpool Snuggeries*', carried extensive reminiscences of the Low Hill Coffee House which had a '*large banqueting room in which many sumptuous feasts were held*' and an '*old signboard of a coach and horses over the door*'. The Coffee House reverted to being known as the Coach and Horses, and the LRO has a photograph of the scene in 1948 (LRO ref. Photographs & Small Prints: Streets and Districts: Low Hill) and a painting of it in 1950 by Allan Tankard (LRO ref. Binns Coll. C256, also reproduced by Kay Parrott, *A Portrait of Liverpool*, *op. cit.*, 2006).

15 920 LAN 1/58 is entitled, '*West Derby. 1822. Mr William Williams to Mr Peter Ellis. Copy. Surrender of Premises in Gloucester Place in West Derby.*' The preamble reads, '*The Halmote Court of Bamber Gascoyne Esquire Lord of the Manor of West Derby in the County of Lancaster especially held at Lowhill within the said Manor on Monday the fourth day of November in the third year of the Reign of our Sovereign Lord George the Fourth by the Grace of God of the United Kingdom of Great Britain and Ireland King Defender of the Faith and in the year of our Lord one thousand eight hundred and twenty two before John Shaw Leigh of Liverpool in the said County Gentleman Deputy Steward of the said Manor.*'

The document opens by referring to the surrender of land and premises in 1814 by Peter Robinson, a slater and plasterer of Liverpool, to William Williams, a Liverpool bricklayer, for a consideration of £315. The process involved Robinson first surrendering the land and premises to the Lord of the Manor through his Steward, followed by a re-grant to Williams in order for him to become the new leaseholder. It continues by indicating that in 1822 William Williams then '*...surrendered to Peter Ellis of Liverpool aforesaid Joiner at or for the price or sum of Three hundred and seventy pounds... All that piece or parcel of land situate lying and being near Lowhill within the Manor of West Derby aforesaid and on the North side of and adjoining a new Street or Road of eight yards wide called Gloucester Row containing in front and in breadth at the back thereof severally twenty yards or thereabouts and running in rear or depth backwards on the East and West sides severally thirty yards or thereabouts bounded on the East by Land now or late of Thomas Plumbe Esquire on the West by Land sold and surrendered to John Alderson and on the North by Land late of Miss Phythian and on the South by Gloucester Row aforesaid and which piece of land now describing is of the yearly rent to the Lord of the said Manor and his heirs of One penny and is part of a copyhold Estate late the customary inheritance of Mr John Orme since of William Whitlow afterwards of the said Peter Robinson who sold and surrendered the same to the said William Williams Together with free ingress egress and regress for the Owner and Occupiers of the said piece of Land for the time being through and over a Passage of four feet wide leading out of Gloucester Row Northerly through and over the Premises there sold to Mr Banks and Mr Holden to a Pit of water in order to the proper use of such water in common with others having a right thereto the said Peter Ellis his heirs or assigns bearing and paying a proportionate part of the expense in and about repairing and keeping in good repair the said Road and Passage and together with the Summer house Walls and other Buildings and improvements erected and made upon the said piece of Land and all ways waters watercourses liberties easements privileges profits commodities advantages hereditaments and appurtenances whatsoever to the said piece or parcel of Land and Premises expressed and intended to be hereby surrendered or any part thereof belonging or in any wise appertaining...*'

A second document, 920 LAN 1/71, also dated 4th November 1822 and entitled '*Mr Peter Ellis to Mrs Millett – Copy Surrender of Premises in Gloucester Place In trust to sell for securing £400 and Int[erest]*', indicates that Peter Ellis senior then simultaneously entered into an agreement with Mrs Millett, a Prescot widow, in order to finance the purchase. For historical currency conversions see www.nationalarchives.gov.uk/currency

Having a right of access to the '*Pit of water*' would have been of considerable benefit. Brian White (*Corporation of Liverpool, 1835-1914*, University Press, Liverpool, 1951, p. 11) noted that, '*In 1786 the Council had also obtained powers to supply water; but water supply remained in private hands until 1847, becoming increasingly inadequate as time went on.*' In the days before the arrival of a reliable Corporation water supply it was common for wells to be dug on private land in order to supplement supplies from wells that were accessible to the general public – such as the one on Harper Street (fig. 2,13) and at Gregson's Well (p. 70, fig. 4,16).

16 The terrace towards the west end of Gloucester Place on the 1848 O.S. map (fig. 2,26, to the right of Brookshaw Place) is shown to have been completed between the compiling of the 1827 and 1829 directories. In 1829 the Ellis house became no. 15, the number that it retained until 1841, after which it was no longer listed as an Ellis home.

There were 29 houses in Gloucester Place in 1841, and up to that year the numbering of the houses was continuous (1, 2, 3, 4, 5..., west to east on the north side, returning east to west down the south side). Nos. 1 and 29 were therefore both at the west end of Gloucester Place, but there was no indication in the directory of which house number was the last on the east end of the north side before the numbering began to return down the south side.

In the 1843 edition the numbering had become odd on the north and even on the south, both starting from the west end, but by then Ann Ellis had departed.

The commentary by George T Shaw & Isabella Shaw, *Liverpool's First Directory*, Henry Young & Sons, Liverpool, 1907, p. 18, indicates that this change in the numbering system in Liverpool had commenced around 1838, so the change must have taken several years to reach the Low Hill fringe of the town.

The Table below shows that a majority of occupants were the same in both the 1841 and 1843 directories (all those pairs where the 1841 numbers are not in brackets). This enables a sufficient number of houses to be confidently paired, and the missing pairs to be matched up correctly.

Comparing the two numbering sequences thus indicates that no. 15 in 1841 became no. 31 in 1843, and therefore was the very end house at the eastern end of the north side. Having become no. 31 in 1843 it retained that number until 1847 after which numbers began to increase following the arrival of the adjacent terrace and further development.

The numbering of the 29 properties in Gloucester Place in 1841 and 1843.
The Ellis property was listed in the directories as no. 15 from 1829 to 1841.

North side

1841	1	(2)	3	4	(5)	6	7	8	9	10	11	12	(13)	(14)	(15)
1843	1	3	5	7	9	11	13	15&17	19	21	23	25	27	29	31

West ← Gloucester Place → East

South side

1841	29	28	27	26	(25)	24	23	(22)	(21)	(20)	(19)	18	17	(16)
1843	2	4	6	8	10	12	14	16	18	20	22	24	26	28

17 Fred Forrest, Urban & Socio-Economic Change in Late 19th Century Liverpool – A Case Study, *Journal of the Liverpool History Society*, 2004, p. 20. Fred has also commented that the redbrick building on Harper Street (in the distance beyond the trees in fig. 2,14) '*strongly featured in an episode in Boys from the Blackstuff, Yosser Hughes attempting to build a wall in front of it and Snowy Malone falling to his death from it while attempting to evade the DHSS.*' The series was originally transmitted on BBC2 in 1982. It proved so popular that it was almost immediately rebroadcast on BBC1 for those who still only had 405 line televisions.

18 This William Ellis cannot be Peter Ellis junior's brother since he is listed with his business from 1821, when Peter's brother was only around 14 years old.

However, although Peter's brother died in his mid-20s (which will be covered in a later chapter) and was never listed in the directories, the Athenaeum has a copy of the '*Liverpool Call Book up to May 1831*' which lists the town's freemen. In it appear 13 Ellis names including '*Robert Ellis joiner Finch street*' and '*William Ellis joiner Finch Street*'. William was therefore presumably working at his elder brother's premises.

The name '*Peter Ellis architect Renshaw street*' also appears in the Call Book but seems to refer to Peter Ellis senior. An 1852 Poll Book at the Athenaeum shows an absence of the symbol '*f*' (to indicate '*freeman*') after '*Ellis Peter Falkner sq*' in the *Liverpool Mercury* report of the result of the 1852 parliamentary election (see p. 111).

19 The LRO folder '*Archives. 352 MD. 352 CLE/CON*' provides information on the historical granting of leases. The '*3 lives & 21 years*' lease to Robert in February 1824 and the lease to Peter Ellis senior in December of the same year mark the transition to a new system of standardised lease years. Peter's lease was entered into a different register entitled '*Register F. Leases for 75 Years commencing 1824*', and the names of Peter's children do not appear.

20 Joseph Sharples, e-mail 01-10-12.

21 The references for James Sherriff's maps at the LRO are Hf 912 1816, Hf 912 1823, and Hf 912 1826. The Athenaeum also possesses an 1825 edition. The maps show unusual features that are missing from more conventional maps and which have proved valuable to historians. See for example the chapter, '*Where have all the rivers gone?*', in Jim Moore's entertaining book, *Underground Liverpool*, The Bluecoat Press, 1998. This book also contains interesting accounts of the development of Liverpool's water supplies as the rapidly growing town became unable to meet its needs from wells, and of the development of a comprehensive sewerage system which, in part, aimed to address the situation in Liverpool's insanitary courts (see chapter 1, ref. 7).

Chapter 3

Renshaw Street and leaving home

And so we reach the point where Peter Ellis junior finally climbed onto the stage with his first directory listing in 1834, alphabetically immediately beneath that of his father who had now retired into the happy state of *gentleman* (fig. 3,1). His brother Robert must have been sufficiently well established in his own business by the late 1820s for Peter Ellis senior to set up another branch of the family business at Renshaw Street. It is Peter Ellis junior, the architect who would eventually design Oriel Chambers and 16 Cook Street, that customers would now find in charge of the Renshaw Street premises - previously a shop but now upgraded to an office.

One of John Eyes' maps of 1765 (fig. 3,2) shows a large number of roperies in the area around '*Renshaw's Street*', and routes radiating out of Liverpool from their junction with Ranelagh Street with their early names for Lime Street, Copperas Hill, Brownlow Hill and Mount Pleasant.

—— **Peter, gentleman, 15, Gloucester place, Low hill**
—— **Peter, jun. architect, 15, Gloucester place, Low hill**
———— —— **office, 22, Renshaw street**

3,1. A section from Gore's 1834 directory showing the first entries for both father and son. Image courtesy of Birkenhead Reference Library.

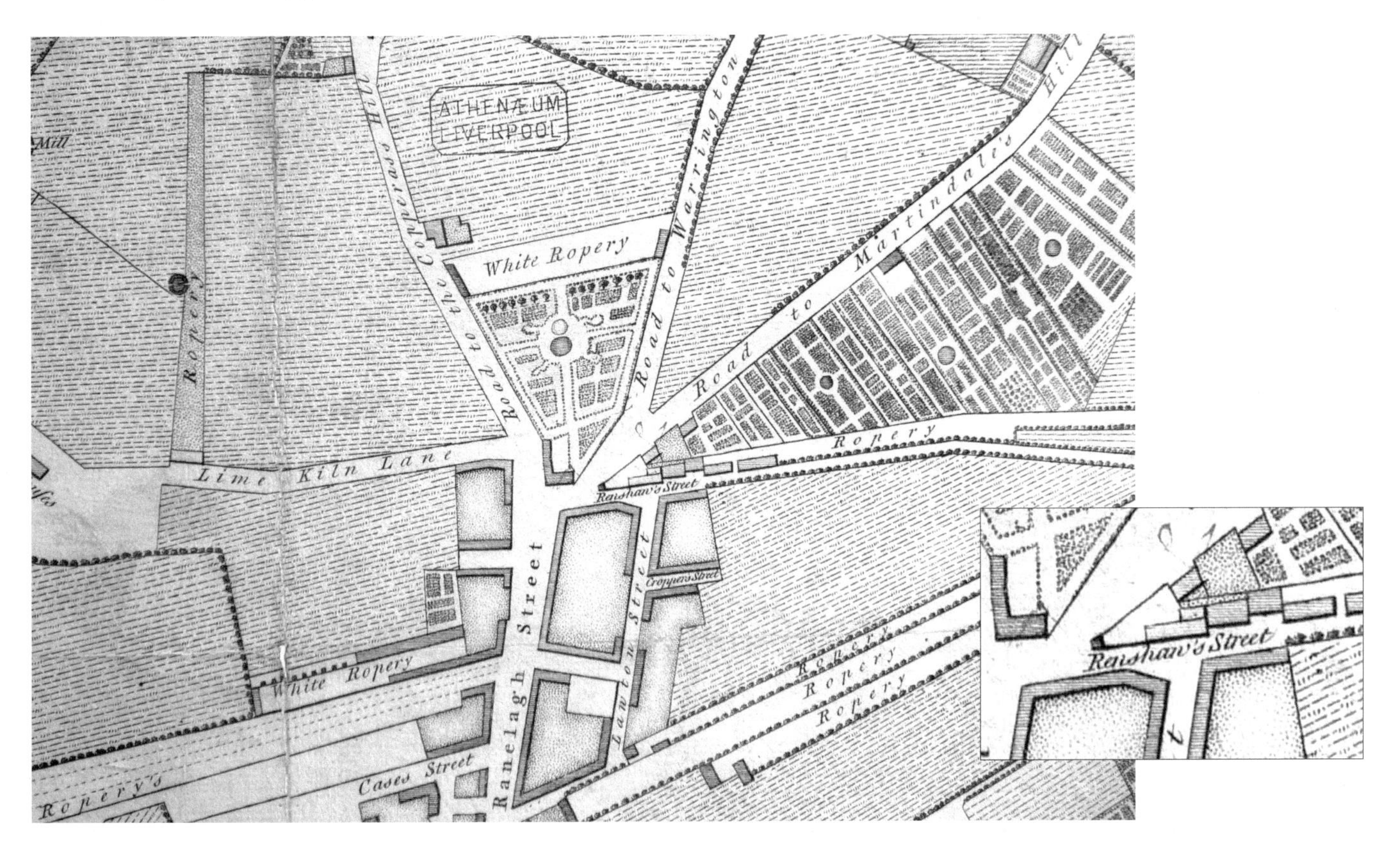

3,2. From one of John Eyes' maps of 1765, oriented to the east (as on the original map). Image courtesy of the Athenaeum.

W G Herdman commented that:-

> *'the line of some of our principal streets, and the sites of many of our public buildings, have been determined more by accident than design or forethought, and that to the ancient rope-walks we are indebted for many of our most valuable thoroughfares,'* [1]

whilst a writer in the early 20th century observed that:-

> *'Where Renshaw Street now stands John Crosbie had a ropery from 1780 to 1793, and in the latter year it was taken over by John and Edward Renshaw, who were well suited to work it because they were agents for the Dublin sailing packets and also brothers-in-law of Edward Grayson, then the leading shipbuilder of the port. They retained the ropery until 1810 when the land was taken for building purposes.'* [2]

Horwood's map of 1803 (fig. 3,3) shows that some buildings had by then arrived at each end of Renshaw Street but that the land opposite Heathfield Street still comprised a number of strips which later would become home to the Unitarian Chapel, the Ellis's shop/office, William Rowlandson's timber yard and Benson Street. Liverpool's decision from about 1838 onwards to begin introducing the *'odd on the left, even on the right'* system of numbering buildings caused the office at 22 Renshaw Street to become no. 45. Michael Gage's plan of 1835 (fig. 3,4) and *Gore's Directory* of 1841 (fig. 3,5) therefore allow the precise location of Peter's first office to be identified as the building (and possibly dog-leg row of buildings) standing between the Unitarian Chapel and William Rowlandson's Timber Yard.

3,3. A detail from Horwood's map of 1803, oriented to the east (as on the original map). The vacant strips of land above the 'W' of 'Renshaw Street' are where the Unitarian Chapel and the Ellis office would later be built.

Image courtesy of the Athenaeum.

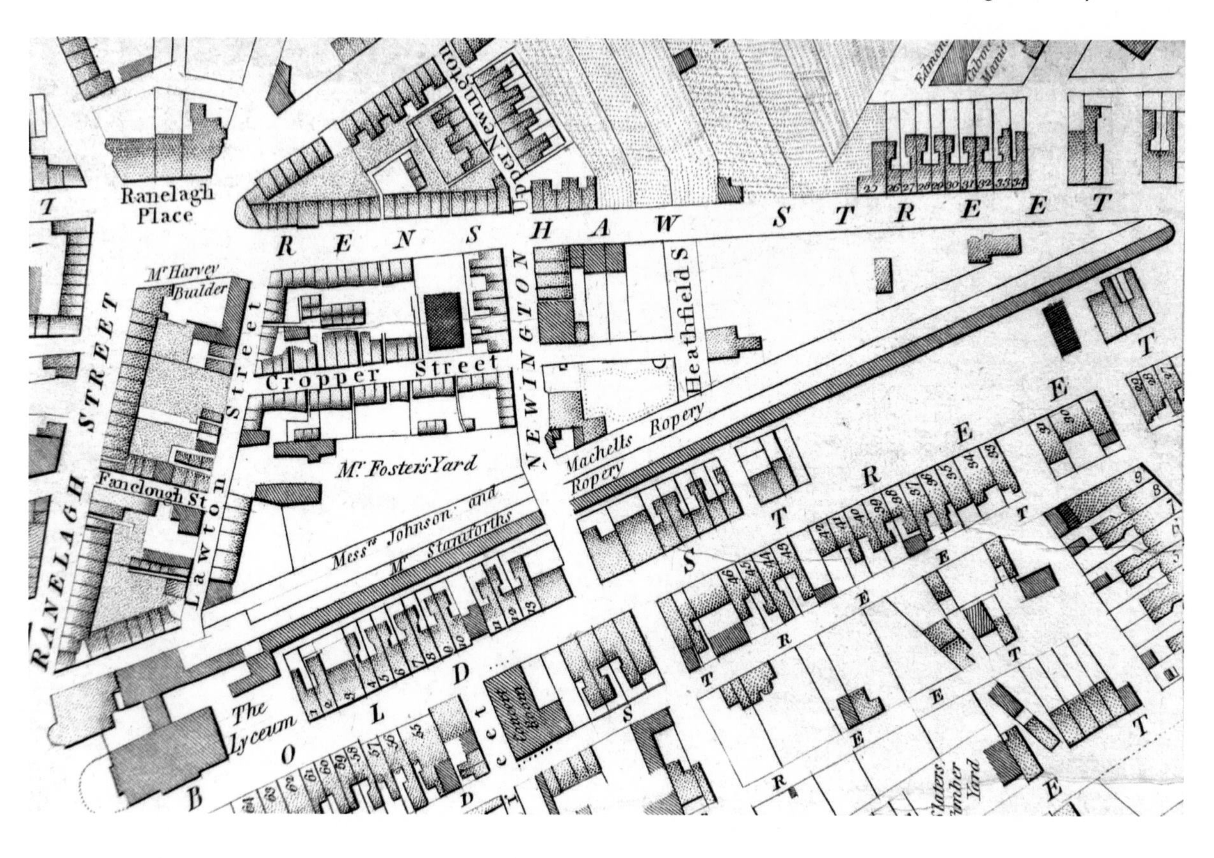

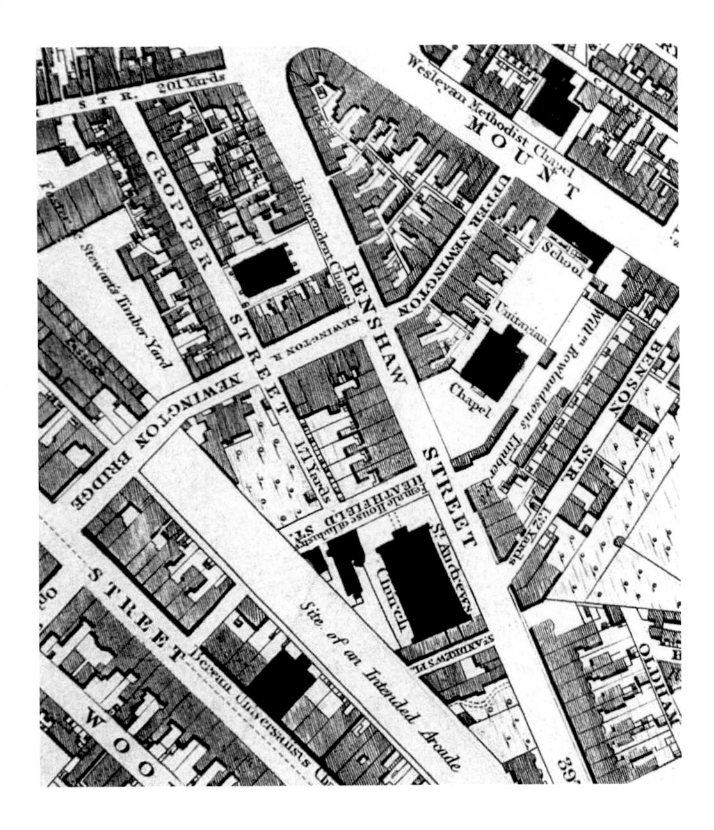

3,4. *A detail from Michael Gage's 1835 plan of Renshaw Street and surrounding area, re-oriented to the north (Gage's original is oriented roughly east, see location H on p. iv). The 'Intended Arcade' later became the Roscoe Arcade. Nearby can also be seen the yard of William Foster and John Stewart.*

Private collection.

3,5. *A section from Gore's 1841 directory, identifying the location of Peter's office between the Chapel and Rowlandson's Timber Yard.*

Image courtesy of Sefton Local History Unit.

43 Webster Sarah
Unitarian Chapel
45 Ellis Peter
47 Rowlandson William
Edwards Richard

The Chapel (fig. 3,6) was completed in 1811, and three of the original subscribers were William Roscoe, Henry Berry, and Thomas Booth (father of Henry Booth of Liverpool and Manchester Railway fame, see p. 16). Asking people today for the names of the engineers who were responsible for the construction of Liverpool's docks and the answers in most cases will stop after the mention of Thomas Steers and Jesse Hartley. However, Henry Berry (1720-1812), originally Steers' clerk, was Liverpool's second dock engineer between 1759 and 1789, and was thus responsible for the construction of the Salthouse, King's and George's docks. [3] One of many religious dissenters at that time, Henry lived just long enough to know of the completion of the Unitarian chapel, but was perhaps too infirm by then to worship in pew no. 23 for which he had subscribed £100. [4]

The street which links Renshaw Street to Great George Street was named after Henry Berry and would have been one of Peter's routes to his office from Sandon Street (his first marital home) via Canning Street and Upper Duke Street. An entertaining report in the *Liverpool Mercury* on 18th December 1840 concerned a court case which hints at Peter's early enthusiasm for large window openings. Peter was summoned to appear before the stipendiary magistrate to answer information provided by Mr. Rishton, surveyor of buildings, charging him with:-

> *'having violated a clause in the building act, in the alteration of a shop window at premises in Berry-street,'* and stating that *'the breadth of the window was 14 feet, and that it had no story post, whereas the act required that every window, the breadth of which exceeded 10 feet, should be supported by a story post.'*

3,6. *Renshaw Street Unitarian Chapel with buildings on Mount Pleasant visible in the background.*

Image courtesy of the LRO. [5]

Peter sent his clerk, Mr. Longrigg, with a letter of explanation, maintaining that the building was quite secure without the storey post, but the magistrate gave Peter a fortnight to put the matter right. Today the street sign includes its Chinese spelling (fig. 3,7).

3,7. The Berry Street sign, a few yards from the beautiful Chinese arch leading to Great George Square (fig. 3,17).

After the 1829 directory, when Peter Ellis senior's shop was listed at Finch Street, sharing with his eldest son Robert, the next directory was in 1832 when his move to Renshaw Street had already taken place, having taken out a building lease for land in Kent Square in 1831. Although Peter Ellis junior's birth, marriage and death records indicate that he was brought up and continued within the Established Church, the proximity of this office to the chapel would almost certainly have meant his becoming familiar with many members of the congregation. So it is just possible that Peter came to know William Roscoe (1753-1831) – another of the subscribers of £100 for a chapel pew – not only by reputation as Liverpool's MP who had voted for the slavery abolition bill of 1807 when Peter was but an infant, but also perhaps by introduction one day when passing each other in Renshaw Street in the final years of Roscoe's life.

1829 saw the repeal of the 1673 Test Act that forbade dissenters from holding office unless Church of England communion had been taken – a repeal brought about in part due to a lengthy petition in 1828 by the members of the Renshaw Street chapel. It thus became possible for William Rathbone V, a member of the congregation, to be elected Mayor of Liverpool for 1837–38 (a statue of him, raised by public subscription after his death, still stands in Sefton Park). Rathbone in his capacity as Mayor laid the foundation stone for St George's Hall, an event which will be seen to be of great significance for Peter in his desire to develop a career as an architect.

The chapel survived for almost 100 years before being replaced by the Central Hall of the Liverpool Wesleyan Mission, opened in 1905 and which exists today in secular hands. [6] The chapel memorial is situated in a garden which is entered from Mount Pleasant (fig. 3,8).

3,8. The entrance to the memorial gardens of the Renshaw Street Chapel.

3,9. Three of the plaques in the memorial gardens of the Renshaw Street Chapel, the one in the distance being for the 1821 Unitarian School.

The circular plaque on the memorial (fig. 3,9) reads:-

'1753 – 1831
William Roscoe MP
Solicitor & Slavery Abolitionist
'Greatest of Liverpool's Citizens'
Buried Here'

The Mount Pleasant Unitarian School, erected in 1821 and which is shown to the rear of the chapel on Michael Gage's plan (fig. 3,4), is also commemorated on a plaque, now badly worn with the passage of time.

Whilst relocating to a shop adjacent to Rowlandson's Timber Yard and a few minutes walk along Berry Street and Nelson Street to the firm's next planned property development seems a sound choice by Peter's father for their joinery business, it was also perhaps uncomfortably close to the Yard of William Foster and John Stewart.

Peter Ellis senior had worked all his life in the building trade throughout a period in Liverpool's history when the Foster family wielded immense power as *'Kings of Liverpool'*.[7] John Foster senior, a very able but extremely ruthless man (for example, removing Charles Eyes from office as Corporation Surveyor),[8] was forced to resign in disgrace in 1824 only after concerns over corruption became overwhelming. His place was then taken by his estranged son, John Foster junior, who continued as Surveyor and Architect to the Corporation until he too resigned in 1836.

So Peter Ellis junior began his career perhaps having been carefully instructed by his father to keep on good terms with the influential Foster empire (and Robert Ellis, for example, had obtained land immediately adjacent to where the *Reform Buildings* and *Jones's Court* were built on land in possession of Foster, Stanistreet and Eden – see pp. 29-30).

As a young architect Peter would perhaps also have been aware that John Foster junior and Charles Cockerell had been companions in an architectural *Grand Tour* some years earlier and, a few years later, would discover that Cockerell was a close friend of the father of Harvey Lonsdale Elmes and was Elmes' mentor when an important competition was announced.

Opposite right: 3,11. Kent Square a century after construction and shortly before the whole area was demolished in 1938. Image courtesy of the LRO, ref. Photographs & Small Prints: Streets and Districts: Kent Square.

Although Peter's first appearance in *Gore's Directory* is in 1834, the Corporation Lease Registers enable us to look back to a period several years earlier when the father and son were building a large number of properties in the area around Kent Square and Great George Square. The register entry for 16th July 1831 shows that Peter Ellis senior had been granted a lease on land in Kent Square on 6th November 1830. From the register details, the houses that he built can be identified on Michael Gage's map as extending along the southern side of the Square (fig. 3,10, between '*Square*' and '*T Pooles' Cooperage*' and as far as the '*Up. S*' of Upper Surrey Street), and it is a development with which Peter Ellis junior, by then 26 years old, would have had a substantial involvement.

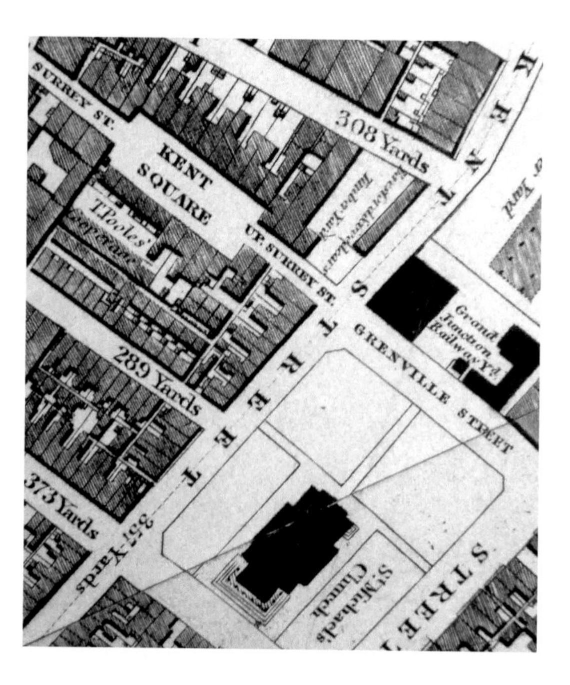

3,10. A detail from Michael Gage's plan, re-oriented to the north, showing properties on the south side of Kent Square and Upper Surrey Street constructed by Peter Ellis senior in the early 1830s (location I on the map on p. iv).

Private collection.

Immediately to the north west of Surrey Street for many years there existed on Lydia Ann Street the famous Fawcett and Preston Iron Foundry, a firm associated with Coalbrookdale in Shropshire. Kent Square and the foundry have long since vanished, but memories of the Square are preserved in a substantial collection of photographs in the Liverpool Record Office from which fig. 3,11 is taken. The photographer was standing in Upper Surrey Street with his back to Grenville Street and looking towards Surrey Street, and the houses built by the Ellis father and son can be seen running down the left hand side of the Square. All the properties were three storeys high plus basement and their flights of steps were mainly in pairs, back to back with each other. Over the years several photographers had found Kent Square a fascinating place and, when it became known that the Square was to be demolished in 1938, Father D'Andria took an evocative series of his own photos in 1937 which he presented the following year.

3,12. A detail from Michael Gage's plan, re-oriented to the north, showing that by 1835 the area around Great George Square, Upper Pitt Street, White Street and Cookson Street had been fully developed.

Private collection.

The register entry for 28th January 1832 shows that Peter Ellis senior took out a further building lease on neighbouring land between Great George Square and White Street (fig. 3,12, along the '*Stre*' of Nelson Street, the '*Upper*' of Upper Pitt Street, and the '*Street*' of White Street). The Corporation's standard covenants included the requirement:-

> *'to build conformably with plan approved by the Finance Com: dwellinghouses only to be built to the Square similar to the rest in the Square. To keep area in good repair. No shop or tavern to be opened.'*

The artist Austin captured a glimpse of the progress of construction at the junction of Upper Pitt Street and White Street (fig. 3,13, looking north west from '*Upper*' in fig. 3,12), showing the latter street in the foreground disappearing off to the right with building materials piled up against the wall and timber slung beneath the cart. This is precisely the view of St Michael's Church that Peter and his father would have seen on the daily visits to supervise construction of their properties, and indicates the way in which timber would have reached their site.

3,13. A view by Austin and published by Fisher, Son & Co in 1832 looking north west from Upper Pitt Street towards St Michael's Church (completed in 1826). White Street disappears off to the right in the foreground. Private collection.

Opposite right: 3,15. Part of the lease granted by the Corporation to 'Peter Ellis the Younger of Liverpool Surveyor' on 20th April 1833 and entered on the register on 25th May.

Image courtesy of the LRO, ref. 352 CLE/CON 3/8.

Although there was a fairly comprehensive demolition of Great George Square in the 1960s, including all the Ellis properties, four houses in a terrace of the larger properties on Nelson Street were permitted to survive and were subsequently renovated (fig. 3,14). Peter Ellis senior's lease required that his buildings were to be '*similar to the rest in the Square*', although according to the map they can be seen to be smaller in depth, and James Picton certainly regarded them as inferior. From the Corporation registers the house on the left hand end of the more substantial Nelson Street terrace (fig. 3,12, above the 'S' of '*Street*') can be identified as the one on which John Ellis (one of Peter's brothers) obtained a lease in 1846 and to which he moved his family in 1857. By then, as part of his inheritance, John already held the lease on the smaller adjoining property which his father had built.

Subsequently an entry in the Register for 25th May 1833 (fig. 3,15) shows that '*Peter Ellis the Younger of Liverpool Surveyor*' obtained a lease for land on the south east side of Great George Square. [9] This was the first lease he obtained in his own name, as his father entered into retirement. Michael Gage's 1835 plan again shows precisely the position of the houses that '*Peter Ellis the Younger*' constructed (fig. 3,12, enclosed by the '*NT*' of Vincent, the '*ST*' of Upper Pitt Street and the '*Street*' of Cookson Street). The covenants required that Peter was:-

> *'Not to erect more than 5 Houses to front Gt George's Square nor more than 6 to Upper Pitt Street nor more than 4 Houses to Cookson Street and to be built conformably to a plan agreed to by the Select Finance Committee on 25th January 1833. Not to alter Elevation without consent. Area to be sunk in front of houses to Gt George's Square of 5 feet wide to be inclosed by Iron Pallisades. Not to suffer land to be used as a Timber Yard. Not to erect any Steam Engine. Not to build Courts or Backhouses. Not to carry on Offensive Trades. No house to be used as an Inn, Tavern or Public House.'*

3,14. Part of a terrace of four renovated properties on the Nelson Street side of Great George Square in 2012 (some of those between the 'LE' of 'Grenville' and the 'S' of 'Nelson Street' in fig. 3,12).

Peter Ellis the Younger of Liverpool Surveyor

All that piece of Land marked with the Letter A on the plan situate on the Southward side of Great Georges Square the Eastward Side of Upper Pitt Street and Northward Side of Cookson Street in Liverpool Containing in front to Great Georges Square including an Area of 4 feet 6 inches in width to Upper Pitt Street 103 feet 6 inches and Containing in front to Upper Pitt Street and at the back thereof including an Area of 5 feet wide to Great George's Square aforesaid severally 126 feet 8 inches and being in front to Cookson Street including the said Area of 4 feet 6 inches to Upper Pitt Street 105 feet 4 inches.

And Also All that other piece of Land marked with the Letter B upon the said Plan situate on the Southward side of Cookson Street and Containing in front thereto and at the back thereof along Land and Premises in Lease to Mr. John Callin severally 20 feet 6 inches and running in depth backwards from Cookson Street on the Eastward side along the said Land and Premises in Lease to the said John Callin and on the Westward side along a Common Passage of 4 feet 6 inches wide severally 45 feet 3 inches With use of Common Passage.

From the 20th of April 1833

75 / 1908

Commenting on the area, James Picton noted that the names of the streets around Great George Square:-

> *'sufficiently indicate the stirring period in its history through which the nation was then passing. It was a time of glorious naval successes. The victories of the Nile, of Camperdown, of Cape St. Vincent, were fresh in memory, and we find their heroes commemorated in the streets of Cornwallis, Nelson, St. Vincent, and Duncan. The statesmen Pitt and Grenville attach their names to the cross-streets; and in the centre Great George Square perpetuates the sense of loyalty which pervaded the nation.'* [10]

He then went on to express dissatisfaction at the development of the area during the Ellis's period of construction:-

> *'The houses in Great George Square were commenced on a high-class scale; but, as I have had more than once occasion to notice, these great expectations too often terminated in disappointment. The scale could not be maintained; and after lying idle for many years, the square had to be completed by houses of an inferior description.'*

If '*inferior*' equates to '*affordable by less than high-class people*' then maybe the Ellis father and son business was merely responding to the needs of the majority of the population of the town. Subsequent records show that the family thought highly enough of what they had built to retain several of the properties, either for personal use or to let. [11]

3,16. The south east side of Great George Square in 1941 after the May Blitz (below the 'NT' of 'Vincent' in fig. 3,12). Peter's constructions, nos. 12-16 , are those with the five doorways on the right hand side of the photograph, no. 16 having been bombed.

Image courtesy of the LRO, ref. Photographs & Small Prints: Streets and Districts: Great George Square.

A scene which includes Peter's properties along St Vincent Street (subsequently renamed Hardy Street) on Great George Square was captured by the WWII photographer W H Tomkinson (fig. 3,16). The year was 1941, it was shortly after the May Blitz and it shows no. 16, Peter's end-of-terrace property, standing in ruins. It had been a boarding house, but the only boarding by then was in order to cover the front door. Further along, no. 13 was still rather hopefully exhibiting a café sign. The same May Blitz destroyed St Michael's Church (fig. 3,13) and part of the Covent Garden side of Oriel Chambers (chapter 12). Nos. 12-16 have the steps up to the front doors and the '*Iron Pallisades*' around the sunken areas which are characteristic of the renovated properties on the opposite side of the Square (fig. 3,14). The frontages of Peter's houses on St Vincent Street and his father's properties on Nelson Street were probably essentially identical, but everything they built was demolished in the late 20th century. Long before that it had become part of Liverpool's Chinese district and today, largely redeveloped, Great George Square is approached from the north east through a beautiful arch in Nelson Street (fig. 3,17).

3,17. The modern route from the site of Peter's office in Renshaw Street to Upper Pitt Street via Berry Street proceeds via this beautiful arch at the north east end of Nelson Street. Pictured in 2012, it is the gateway to the Chinese Quarter.

3,19. The southern end of the west side of Renshaw Street in 1871 in a painting by J Hooper.

Image courtesy of the LRO, ref. Herdman Collection 1362. The two other Hooper paintings of the same period can be found under refs. Herdman Collection 1368 and 1385.

From his front office window on Renshaw Street Peter would have looked out directly down Heathfield Street with a view of St Andrew's Church at the junction (fig. 3,18). Erected in 1815 by John Gladstone, James Picton was somewhat less than ecstatic: '*It was built at a period when ecclesiastical design was at a very low ebb*' (*Memorials*, vol. II, p. 241). The building was sold in 1892 to the Cheshire Lines Railway (its headquarters being at Central Station) and subsequently demolished. Peter remained at his Renshaw Street premises until the mid-1840s and would have watched the street developing. In 1871 a scene was captured in a painting by J Hooper (fig. 3,19). Viewed from St Luke's Place, the left hand side shows the elegant entrance to the Roscoe Arcade ('*Site of an Intended Arcade*' in fig. 3,4), and to its right is a view, looking towards St Andrew's Church, of shops which are shown as already present on an 1848 O.S. map of the area. The LRO has two other scenes by Hooper of Renshaw Street of the same period, and the three pictures show a variety of the premises that Peter would have passed daily on his journey to and from work, many of which survived into the early 20th century.

3,18. Peter's view from his office of St Andrew's Episcopal Church at the junction of Renshaw Street and Heathfield Street.

Image courtesy of the Athenaeum, from the Brierley collection, dated 1830.

From 1857 the directories indicate that the Unitarian Chapel had been allocated no. 45, with the office that had been Peter's being renumbered as no. 47. In the building's very last days, *Gore's Directory* for 1900 shows that it had become sub-divided and was occupied by a picture framer, a slater & plasterer, and a painter (fig. 3,20). Had Peter still been alive no doubt he would have been delighted to see his premises being used by these craftsmen. Also included in the listing is Edward Bowker's fine art shop at no. 27 for a reason that will become apparent in a future chapter.

Although no view of Peter's office has been located, [12] demolition of the area in 1901 in preparation for the Methodist Central Hall was captured by the camera of Richard Brown, a photographer with a delightfully named and thoroughly up to date '*electric light studio*' at 32 Bold Street, in a whole series of evocative scenes of Renshaw Street. [13]

Peter's office was, by then, one of the buildings that had already been demolished between no. 43 (fig. 3,21) and no. 51 (fig. 3,22). In the first scene, Benjamin Hunt's shop awaits its obliteration, whilst on the right of the shop is the entrance to the abandoned Unitarian Chapel. By then the congregation had moved to their new church in Ullet Road, now a Grade I listed building and to which the memorials to William Roscoe and Henry Booth were taken. In the second scene, and under magnification of the original, to the left of the shop a sign pasted to the fence can be seen to read, '*T. Leigh. Glass Merchant. Removed to 52 Wood Street*', whilst above the fence a small square sign reads, '*Geo. Nicholson. Registrar. Births and Deaths. Now Removed to 105 Mount Pleasant.*' Behind the fence is where Peter's office had once stood.

27 Bowker Edward fine art dealer
29 Bowman Thomas K. ironmonger
31 Brown Mrs. Catherine watchmaker
33 Lowe Henry victualler
Upper Newington
35 Ledger John window-blind manufctr
37 Byrom John musical instrument mkr
39 Jaggard & Co. booksellers
43 Hunt Benjamin baby carriage and perambulator manufacturer
Renshaw st. Unitarian Chapel
47 Williams Wm. picture-frame maker
Jones Thomas slater & plasterer
47A Adams James E. painter
49 Cuthbertson John foreign stamp dlr
49A Nicholson George registrar of births and deaths
51 Leigh Thomas glass merchant
53 Corless Martin Thomas picture frame maker
Benson st

3,20. The section of Gore's Directory for Renshaw Street in 1900 showing the properties between Upper Newington and Benson Street, many of which began being demolished the following year to make way for the arrival of the Methodist Central Hall.

Image courtesy of the Athenaeum.

3,21. Nos. 35 – 43 Renshaw Street in March 1901, scheduled for demolition.

Image courtesy of the LRO, reference WG30.

3,22. The vacated property at 51 Renshaw Street in March 1901. Peter's office had been on the left of the view. Image courtesy of the LRO, reference LIC 677, WG37.

The precise site of Peter's office – occupied today by a building in which the ground floor is a casino – can still be identified through its being opposite Heathfield Street (currently clinging onto its existence in the face of redevelopment between its Renshaw Street and Bold Street ends). Standing on the spot where his office was once located and looking around him today, Peter would find almost everything utterly changed. The sole survivor of his time – though only just – at the southern end of Renshaw Street is the ruin of St Luke's Church where, as will be seen, two of Peter's brothers were married. James Picton commented that the church was, *'generally considered the crowning point of Liverpool ecclesiastical architecture,'* but then rather spoilt it by adding that, *'as an original composition, it must be pronounced a failure'* (*Memorials*, vol. II, p. 242). Quentin Hughes more charitably described it as being of *'a rather loveable cardboard Gothic design of the two Fosters, father and son'*, noting also what must have been on the cards in 1964 as part of the Shankland Plan, but from which the city was spared: *'The ruined nave, the fine cast-iron gates and railings and the regular flower-beds of trained ivy may soon go to make way for the elevated motorway...'* [14]

An important event whilst Peter was at Renshaw Street will be mentioned in chapter 5 and, during this period in his early career, archive material enables us now to follow a little of the lives of two of his brothers. Although the directory for 1835 shows members of the Ellis family – Peter senior (and an invisible Ann), Peter junior, John and Robert – still resident at Gloucester Place (fig. 3,23), the three brothers had no doubt become somewhat distracted from concentrating on work and home life with thoughts of their beloved Mary (though fortunately not the same one).

3,23. A section from Gore's Directory for 1835 showing family members at Gloucester Place. By then John Ellis had established his veterinary surgery at Upper Pitt Street, whilst a tailor called Peter Ellis (a possible relation) is shown at White Street, both streets being the sites of property built under Peter Ellis senior's 1832 lease. Image courtesy of the Athenaeum.

—— John, veterinary surgeon, Gloucester place, Low hill
———— surgery, 7, Upper Pitt street
—— John, watch-dial maker, 9, Williamson street
—— Joseph, spirit dealer, 19, Limekiln lane
—— Lewis, master mariner, 68, Finch street
—— Margaret, boarding house, 4, Harford street
—— Mary, straw-hat manufacturer, 55, Whitechapel
—— Michael, carpet and furnishing warehouse, 30, Byrom st
—— Olivia, 5, Rodney street
—— Owen, provision dealer, 45, Standish street
———— shop, 70, Great Crosshall street
—— Peter, gentleman, 15, Gloucester place, Low hill
—— Peter, jun. architect, 15 Gloucester place, Low hill
———— office, 22, Renshaw street
—— Peter, tailor, St. George's terrace, White st. Upper Pitt st
—— Rainford, brickmaker, 1, Boundary street, Kirkdale road
—— Robert, joiner and builder, 15, Gloucester place, Low hill
———— shop, 74, Finch street

The marriage records of St Luke's Church (LRO ref. 283 LUK 3/1) show that:-

> *'Robert Ellis of this Parish, Surveyor, and Mary Georgina Black of this Parish, Spinster, were married in this Church by License with Consent of [blank] this seventh Day of December in the Year One Thousand Eight Hundred and Thirty Six, By me James Aspinall Minister.'*

The directory for 1837 (the next after 1835) shows that Robert and Mary Ellis were by then living at Juvenal Street, an entry that also confirms that Robert had changed from joiner and builder to surveyor. Their marriage was to prove desperately short. In the columns of the *Liverpool Mercury* for 6th April 1838 it is recorded that (following other entries identifying '*Same day*' as referring to 29th March 1838), '*Same day, much lamented aged 22, Mary Georgina, wife of Mr. Robert Ellis, Juvenal-street.*' Mary's death at such a young age and, after no more than 16 months of their happiness together, suggests perhaps a tragic loss during pregnancy.

A little over two years later a report of a second marriage appeared in the 23rd October 1840 edition of the *Liverpool Mercury*, under Marriages, Births and Deaths reading, '*On Tuesday, the 13th instant, at St. Bride's Church, Mr. Robert Ellis to Miss Elizabeth Symonds, both of this town.*' Marriage record no. 302 for St Bride's Church (LRO ref. 283 BRI 3/2) confirms that on 13th Oct 1840, Robert Ellis ('*Condition: Widower. Rank or Profession: Gentleman. Residence at the Time of Marriage: Juvenal Street*') married Elizabeth Symonds ('*Spinster. Great Orford Street*') by licence. Robert's father is given as Peter Ellis ('*Rank or Profession: Builder*', although he had died the previous year), and one of the witnesses was John Ellis.

The *Liverpool Mercury* for 29th September 1843 shows that Robert and a certain Thomas Lewis went on to be:-

> *'elected sub-surveyors, under the district surveyors, for the purpose of carrying out the provisions of the last improvement act relative to buildings in courts. The salary attached to this office is £80 per annum,'*

the appointment being confirmed at the Town Council Proceedings of 6th December (*Mercury*, 8th December 1843). Robert's last definite directory listing shows him as still resident at Juvenal Street in 1849 where he entered himself as gentleman. Neither the remainder of Robert's life nor whether he had children has been discovered, but his unexpected appearance on John Kilshaw's lease supplies the date of his death.

In 1813 John Kilshaw, a joiner, is listed in *Gore's Directory* as living at 15 Gloucester Street with a shop at 3 Silver Street. By then Peter Ellis senior and his family had also arrived at 27 Gloucester Street. John Kilshaw's first of three Corporation leases, dated 15th January 1813 (LRO ref. 352 CLE/CON 3/6),

3,24. A detail taken from the Gloucester Street area on Michael Gage's plan (chapter 2, fig. 2,1) showing John Kilshaw's timber yard which he had prepared for himself in 1813 on a Corporation lease of land. Private collection.

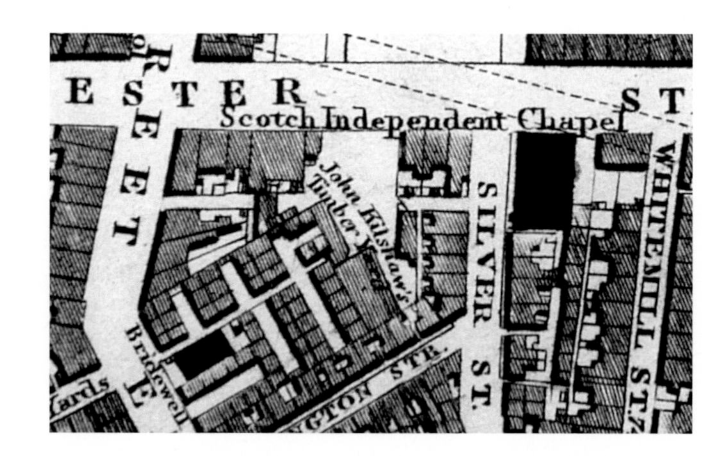

shows it to have been for a number of very substantial pieces of land, with Gloucester Street, Duncan Street, Silver Street, Sidney Street, and '*the late Mr. Skelhorne's ground*' (from whom Skelhorne Street derives its name) all being mentioned. By 1835 his importance was such that his timber yard warranted inclusion on Michael Gage's plan (fig. 3,24), whilst the 1841 census indicates that his eldest child (then 25) had not been born in 1813. Thus when he specified the '*three lives and 21 years*' on his 1813 lease he decided to name the children of three other Liverpool joiners, the youngest being '*Robert Ellis Son of Peter Ellis of Liverpool Joiner*'. Many years later a note was written on the Corporation register against Robert's name: '*Last life died 19 March 1870.*'

Between 1837 and 1841 the directories show Robert and Lewis Ellis as living next door to each other in Juvenal Street, but how Lewis Ellis was related to Peter's family has not been established. Lewis first appears in the 1813 directory as a Captain and in directories from 1821 as a master mariner. Saying farewell to the sea in 1841, and whilst still at Juvenal Street, he tried his hand as a coppersmith and listed himself as being in the firm of Foster and Ellis (with Henry Foster, who had an already well-established business). In the same year the census collector for Juvenal Street recorded Lewis as a brassfounder and that he and his wife, Ellen, had three children, John (20), Ellen (15) and Cornelius (12). By 1843 they had crossed over the water to live in Tranmere, with Lewis now listing himself as brassfounder and coppersmith with his own shop in South John Street (the arrival of steam-powered ferry boats in 1817 having provided a reliable timetabled service for crossing the Mersey). However by 1845, having apparently abandoned that line of business and whilst remaining in Tranmere, he entered himself as gentleman, reverted in 1847 to his earlier description as master mariner, and finally settled for gentleman once more in the 1849 and 1851 directories. Dying in 1861 at the age of 73, the record, whilst showing his abode by then as having been in Wallasey, indicates that he chose to be buried at the '*Church of St George's Everton in the Parish of Walton on the Hill*' (LRO microfilm ref. 283 GEV 4/1). [15]

St George's Church (fig. 3,25) was the first of a trio of Rickman and Cragg iron-framed churches (the others being St Philip's, Hardman Street, and St Michael's in the Hamlet). [16] It was consecrated on 26th October 1814 and the *Liverpool Mercury*'s account two days later included the comment that:-

> *'The church is built in the Gothic Style, and we can only add, that it is considered as one of the handsomest structures of the kind in the kingdom, and does infinite credit to the contractor, John Cragg, Esq. of the Mersey Iron-Foundry. Its length from east to west is 119 feet, by 47 broad, and the height of the tower when completed, will be 96 feet, from which a more extensive and truly picturesque view, both of land and sea, is not to be exceeded in the United Kingdom.'*

3,25. St George's Church Everton in June 2012. Lewis Ellis was buried there in 1861 at a funeral which Peter may well have attended.

Peter perhaps attended Lewis Ellis's burial and it is a church with which Peter would almost certainly have already been familiar from courting days. James Picton refers in several places in his Memorials to the church in disappointingly unflattering terms. '*It would be unfair to the architect to criticise too severely the results of conditions so restricted*' (by Cragg's enthusiasm for the abundant use of cast-iron). [17] '*As an original composition, it is stiff and feeble... The design, both externally and internally, is meagre and thin*'. [18]

Like Oriel Chambers St George's suffered WWII damage and, James Picton's comments notwithstanding, as the world's first cast-iron church, is now also a Grade I listed building. The civil engineering aspects of its iron-work may have influenced Peter Ellis in the design of Oriel Chambers and 16 Cook Street.

Gore's Directory for 1837 indicates that John Ellis, another of Peter's brothers, had also moved away from home. A few months after Robert Ellis and Mary Black had been married at St Luke's, the records for the same church (LRO microfilm 283 LUK 3/1) show that:-

> *'John Ellis of this parish, Veterinary Surgeon, and Mary Stockdale Procter of this parish, Spinster, were Married in this Church by License with Consent of [blank] this twenty fifth day of April in the Year One Thousand Eight hundred and Thirty Seven, By me James Aspinall Minister.'* [19]

For many years John continued the veterinary practice he had established at Upper Pitt Street in a property constructed for him by his father and at which premises he would later begin to advertise his shoeing forge.

On 9th March 1838 the first of six children to be born to John and Mary – a boy and thus, by tradition, also named John – arrived and was baptised on 2nd May (LRO microfilm ref. 283 MIC 2/1) at St Michael's, Upper Pitt Street (fig. 3,13).

How cruel a fate that, only 20 days after the arrival of baby John, Robert's young wife Mary was destined to die, perhaps having been awaiting with great joy the birth of her own first-born. We will meet both John senior and junior and their families again in later chapters.

Ellis Peter, gentleman, 15, Gloucester place, Low hill
—— Peter, jun. architect, 6, Sandon st ; office, 22, Renshaw st

3,26. A section from Gore's Directory for 1837 showing Peter as having left the parental home to begin married life at Sandon Street.
Image courtesy of Sefton Local History Unit.

By 1837 Peter Ellis senior and Ann Ellis (quietly continuing to be his invisible wife as far as the directories are concerned) finally had 15 Gloucester Place to themselves (fig. 3,26), for Peter Ellis the architect had also departed, having married Mary Helen Syers in April 1836. He thus beat his two brothers to the altar by a few months and perhaps had also set the trend for falling in love with girls by the name of Mary.

It becomes appropriate therefore to turn now to look at the background of this Evertonian with whom Peter the architect would share the rest of his life – a period of almost 50 years – initially at Sandon Street and then at Falkner Square.

References and Notes to Chapter 3

1 W G Herdman, *Pictorial Relics of Ancient Liverpool*, G G Walmsley, Liverpool, 1878, vol. II, p. 13. LRO ref. Hf 942.7214 HER (1878 Vol. II).

2 Official Handbook of the Liverpool Chamber of Commerce, *Liverpool: Its Trade and Commerce*, 1918, p. 71.

J A Picton, *Memorials of Liverpool*, G G Walmsley (Liverpool), 2nd edn., 1875, vol. II, p. 372, relates the circumstances whereby a certain Lieutenant Sparling withdrew from his engagement with Miss Anne Renshaw, the insult of which prompted Edward Grayson (Anne's uncle) to brand Sparling as a scoundrel and villain, and the outcome of which was a duel in which Edward Grayson was shot dead.

3 Stanley A Harris, Henry Berry (1720-1812): Liverpool's Second Dock Engineer, *Transactions of the Historic Society of Lancashire and Cheshire*, 89, 1937, p. 91. See also Adrian Jarvis, *The Liverpool Dock Engineers*, Alan Sutton, 1996, p. 11.

4 For historical currency conversions see www.nationalarchives.gov.uk/currency

5 Anne Holt, *Walking Together. A Study in Liverpool Nonconformity, 1688-1938*, George Allen & Unwin, 1938. LRO ref. 288 HOL.

6 Joseph Sharples, *Liverpool. Pevsner Architectural Guides*, Yale University Press, 2004, p. 230. The O.S. map for 1906 shows Central Hall on the site of the Chapel, an arched entrance to a yard that had been William Rowlandson's and, between them, a replacement building standing at the location of Peter's office. The Renshaw Street Chapel congregation moved to the Ullet Road Unitarian Church which was built for them in 1899: see the meeting report of a visit to the church in the Liverpool History Society newsletter 34 which can be viewed on the Society's website.

7 Hugh Hollinghurst, *John Foster and Sons, Kings of Georgian Liverpool*, Liverpool History Society, 2009.

8 R Stewart-Brown, Maps and Plans of Liverpool and District by the Eyes Family of Surveyors, *Transactions of the Historic Society of Lancashire and Cheshire*, 62, 1910, p. 155. Stewart-Brown had some difficulty in deciding for certain how John Eyes and Charles Eyes were related (p. 153).

9 Joseph Sharples (e-mail 29-08-12) kindly provided the key LRO reference 352 CLE/CON 3/8 regarding the grant of the 1833 building lease to '*Peter Ellis the Younger of Liverpool, Surveyor.*' An immensely valuable lead, it prompted a search through all the Corporation Lease Registers and resulted in the discovery of the other leases noted in this book. The leases to Peter Ellis senior in 1831 and 1832 mentioned in this chapter are from the same register.

10 J A Picton, *op. cit.*, p. 287.

11 The directories from 1834 show a long association of John Ellis senior (and later John Ellis junior) with Upper Pitt Street at a house which his father had built (shown in fig. 3,12 above *'Upper'*) and which became his shoeing forge. The Corporation Lease Register for 28th November 1846 also records that on 2nd October 1846 John Ellis senior obtained a lease on property in Great George Square and backing onto White Street and which was adjacent to *'premises leased to Peter Ellis the elder now deceased and now belonging to the said John Ellis and others.'* The lease description together with the directory numbering of Great George Square indicate that these neighbouring properties, the smaller of which was originally built by Peter Ellis senior, were mid way along the Nelson Street side of Great George Square, one on each side of the junction with the terrace which partly survives today and which is shown in fig. 3,14.

In chapter 11 it will be seen that in 1882 Peter Ellis advertised 25 Upper Pitt Street to let (one of the properties he had built in 1833-34). Finally, in 1885, six houses in White Street (which Peter's father had built in 1832-33) and two houses at the junction of Upper Pitt Street and Cookson Street (nos. 25 and 27 Upper Pitt Street which Peter had built) formed part of Peter's estate that was put up for sale. All these houses have long since been demolished.

12 James Stonehouse makes an intriguing comment on p. 80 of his 1869 book *The Streets of Liverpool*, that *'Nearly opposite Heathfield-street there will be noticed a tall thin house that seems as if it had once belonged to a row, but had run away from its neighbours til it stopped for want of breath... A view of it is given in an engraved picture of Liverpool taken from the "Public Walk," which may be met with in the Binns' Collection in the Free Public Library.'* It has not been possible to locate this picture at the LRO, but the isolated position of Peter's office on the 1835 and 1848 maps suggests that it may well have been the one to which Stonehouse referred (an alternative candidate shown mid-way between the *'W'* of *Renshaw* and the *'S'* of *Street* in 1803 (fig. 3,3) is shown on these later maps as no longer in existence – or no longer isolated – by the time Stonehouse made his observation). At the time that Stonehouse would have been gathering material for his book, Peter's former office was occupied by a boot and shoe maker (1867) and then by general drapers (1868), whilst earlier in the decade for several years it had been a beer house.

13 Richard Brown's dozen valuable photographs of Renshaw Street at the turn of the century are listed at the LRO as L.I.C. 677 and 678 (both in watercolour gallery WG37) and in other galleries (WG30 and WG38B). Other views include one of the Cocoa Rooms in the semi-circular Adelaide Building at the junction with Mount Pleasant (ladies rooms and smoke rooms suitably segregated, and with a sign sporting a Liver Bird and *'British Workman Public House Company Ltd'* inscribed around it) and, in stark contrast, a rather depressing view of *'Court no. 3'* which existed between nos. 11 and 15 Renshaw Street.

14 Quentin Hughes, *Seaport. Architecture and Townscape in Liverpool*, Lund Humphries, 1964, p. 87. Reprinted with postscript by The Bluecoat Press, 1993. See also the accompanying engraving of St Luke's on p. 88 of *Seaport*, viewed from the southern end of Renshaw Street, in the foreground of which is depicted a cart carrying timber in a manner similar to that in fig. 3,13.

15 Note that *'the Church of St George's Everton'* was classed as being *'in the Parish of Walton on the Hill.'* It will be seen in a later chapter that Peter's wedding certificate shows his Evertonian bride as being *'of the Parish of Walton on the Hill.'*

That Lewis Ellis and Robert Ellis lived next door to one another for several years suggests a family connection. Since Lewis was recorded as being 73 when he died in 1861, he was born around 1788. In a later chapter we will see that Peter Ellis senior was born around 1765. It seems possible therefore that Lewis was Peter Ellis senior's much younger brother and hence an uncle of Peter Ellis junior.

The 1801 census (chapter 1, ref. 2) indicates that Peter Ellis senior was living in a back house on Shaw's Brow in which there was one family comprising two females and five males, two of whom were in an occupation. The two females would have been Peter's wife Ann and their daughter Ann, and three of the males would have been Peter and their sons Robert and first baby Peter. Was Lewis, at the age of roughly 13, one of the other two? And who was the other male living there and in an occupation?

16 All three churches are covered extensively by Quentin Hughes, *op. cit.*, pp. 138-145.

17 J A Picton, *op. cit.*, p. 74.

18 J A Picton, *op. cit.*, p. 370.

19 J A Picton, *op. cit.*, p. 244, notes that the first incumbent of St Luke's was James Aspinall. He was the author of *Liverpool a Few Years Since, by an Old Stager* (LRO ref. 942.721 ASP, 1852 and also 1869 and 1885 editions), and James Picton describes the Rev. Aspinall's accounts as '*showing a power of developing individual character in its amusing and humorous aspects and of felicitous description of a very rare kind*'. It was this incumbent who thus officiated at both John's marriage and Robert's first marriage. See this Old Stager's chapter 5 for an account of how the Mayor of Liverpool caused offence to Prince William of Gloucester (the book can be viewed on the Liverpool History Society website by going to *On-Line Books, Memoirs and Biographies*).

Chapter 4

The road to Everton Village

Mary Helen Syers was born on the 16th of February 1811 and baptised at St Anne's Church, Richmond, on the 17th of April of the same year (fig. 4,1).

Her parents were listed as William Syers, merchant, and Margaret his wife of Rose Hill, which in those days ran into Richmond Row. William Syers (1778-1833) is listed in *Gore's Directory* for 1811 as '*ship chandler, Rosehill*', with the firm of Syers and Walthew, ship chandlers, having premises near the Salthouse and Duke's docks. William and his bride Margaret Rideing had married in 1799 at St Mary's Church, Walton on the Hill, and Mary Helen grew up with three elder brothers, William, John and Thomas.

In the 1830s William Harper Syers (born 1804) became an appraiser and auctioneer, inherited his father's business in Houghton Street, Clayton Square, married and moved to Low Hill; John Aspinall Syers (born 1805) became a cotton broker, married and later moved to Warwickshire; Thomas Syers (born 1807) became a tailor and draper with a premises in Clayton Square, married and moved briefly to Great Homer Street, but died in his early 30s. Mary Helen's brothers will be mentioned again in other chapters, and one of Thomas's sons will appear many years later at Oriel Chambers.

After early days as a ship chandler, Mary's father became an appraiser and auctioneer, and the family moved home several times within a small radius during Mary's upbringing: Richmond Row, Mansfield Street and Myrtle Street. Richmond Row in the Township of Liverpool led eastwards into Everton Brow in the neighbouring Township of Everton (fig. 4,2).

For several years before Mary Helen was born, William and Margaret Syers had lived in Netherfield Lane (subsequently Netherfield Road) and it was to Everton Village, a few hundred yards away, that the directory shows they had returned by 1829.

Robert Syers was one of William Syers' elder brothers and therefore one of Mary Helen's uncles. In his highly detailed account of *The History of Everton*, published in 1830, he described the positions and occupiers of many of the houses in the village with the aid of maps from 1790 (fig. 4,2) and 1821.

4,1. The record at St Anne's Church, Richmond, for February 1811.

Image courtesy of the LRO, microfilm ref. 283 ANN 1/2 (there is also a second entry, ref. 283 ANN 8/1).

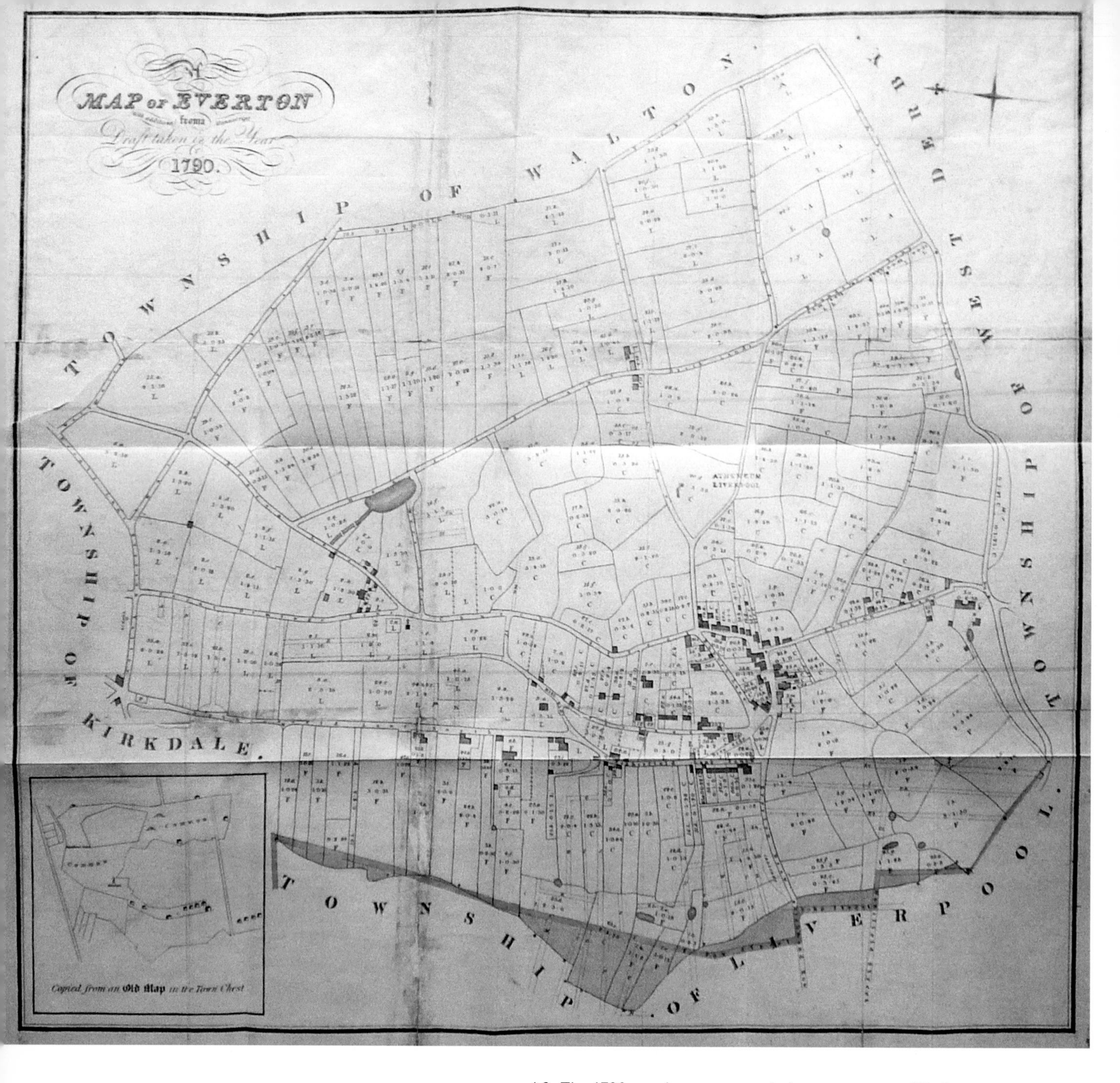

4,2. The 1790 map by an unrecorded surveyor as modified by Robert Syers. The map is conventionally oriented to the east, and Richmond Row enters the Township of Everton through the 'I' and 'V' of 'Liverpool'.

The locations of Richmond Row and Everton Village are identified on the map on p. iv (also oriented to the east) by the letters K and L.

Image courtesy of the Athenaeum.

Below: 4,3. A detail from fig. 4,2. Image courtesy of the LRO, contained in ref. 942.7213 TOF (see later).

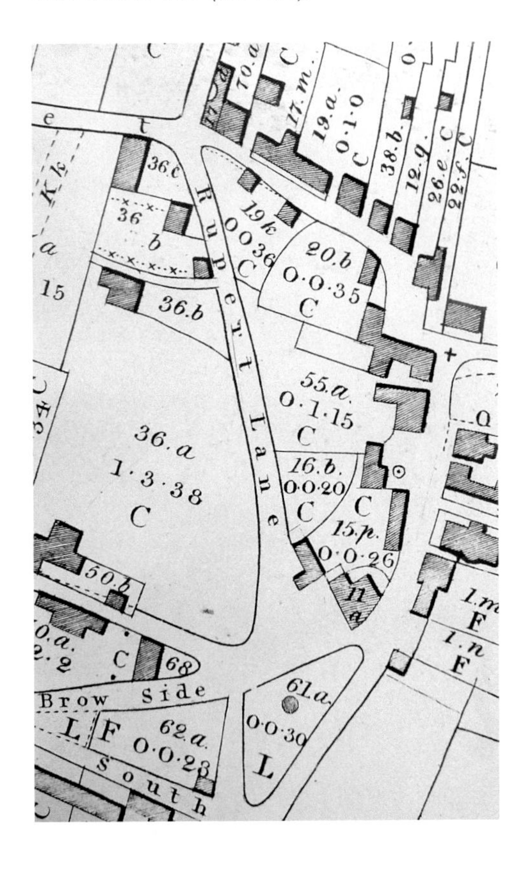

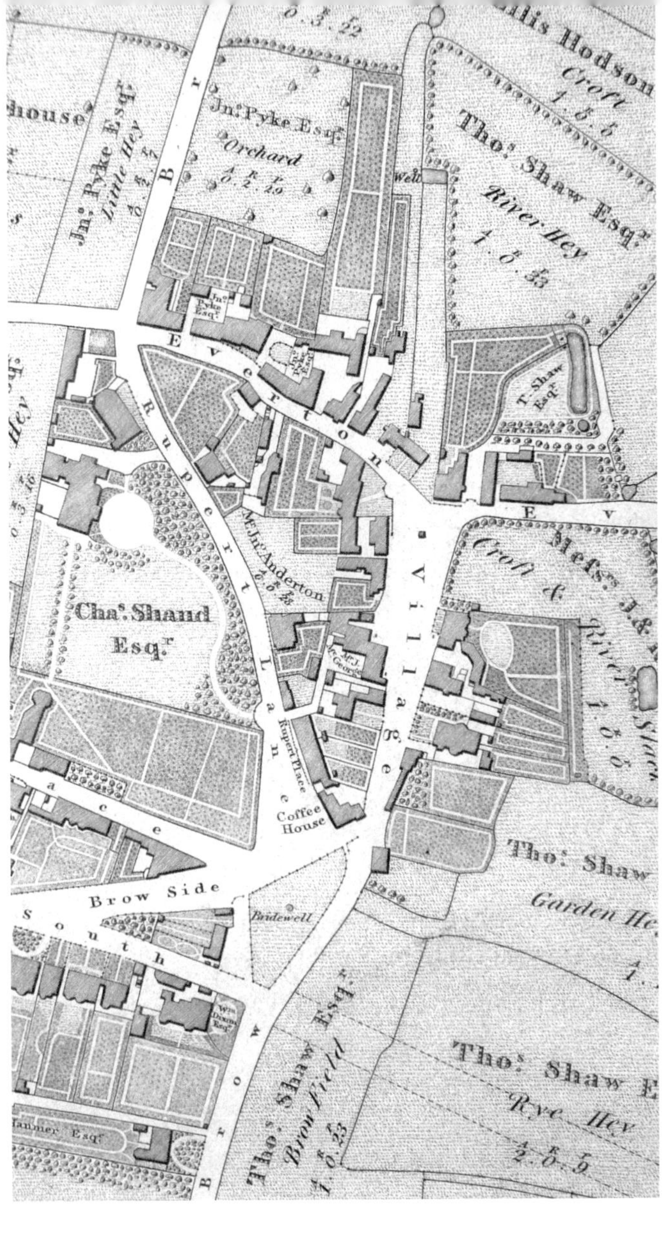

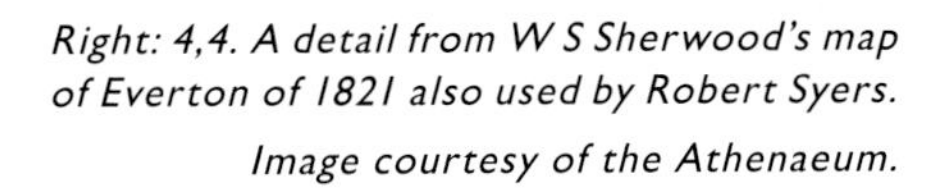
Right: 4,4. A detail from W S Sherwood's map of Everton of 1821 also used by Robert Syers. Image courtesy of the Athenaeum.

Robert used the 1790 map to identify residents' houses in Everton in 1830 by adding a symbol at each location to which he then referred in his narrative. Details from the 1790 map (fig. 4,3) and Sherwood's 1821 map (fig. 4,4) show the centre of the village. On the 1790 map, the site of what would become the home of Mary Helen Syers is marked as '*12.g*' and can be seen at the top right. Other significant buildings towards the bottom, and running right to left, include Rupert's Cottage ('*1.m*'), the Everton coffee-house ('*11.a*'), the Bridewell ('*61.a*') and Mrs Cooper's toffee shop ('*62.a*', just above the '*h*' of '*South*'). The ancient Everton cross (which many years previously had been converted into a sun-dial) is marked on fig. 4,4 in the middle of the road above the '*V*' of '*Village*'. Thomas Shaw's home is shown near this cross, at the junction of Everton Village and Everton Lane (subsequently Everton Road, running off to the right towards Low Hill). At the foot of the map the two diagonal dotted lines mark the proposed route of what would become Shaw Street.

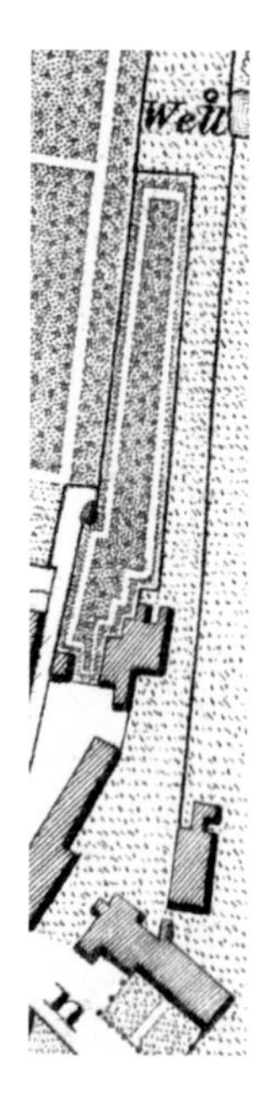

By 1821 the house that subsequently had been built on the plot marked '*12.g*' on the 1790 map had become joined to another house. It is shown above the '*n*' of '*Everton*' in fig. 4,4 and can be seen to possess a well at the end the garden (fig. 4,5). Of this property Robert wrote in 1830 that it:-

'is now the residence of Mr. Wm. Syers, one of a family which has, in some or other of its branches and connexions, been resident in the township for the last fifty years – the individuals of this name (all of one and the same family) at the present moment compose in the aggregate a greater number than that of any other name in the township.' [1]

4,5. From Sherwood's map showing Mary Helen Syers' house as possessing a well towards the end of the garden.

Image courtesy of the Athenaeum.

Opposite right: 4,7. Mrs Cooper's Toffee Shop on Everton Brow in 1828. The site is annotated '62.a' by Robert Syers at the foot of the detail from his map of 1790.

A second view in 1830 is part of the Athenaeum's Brierley Collection. Comparison of all three of Brierley's views suggests either surprisingly frequent modifications to the buildings or a degree of artistic license.

Image courtesy of the LRO, ref. Brierley Collection 73.

Gore's Directory for 1829 lists a mere six Syers names and gives little clue as to the size of this '*aggregate*'. Robert and his brothers and sister were the offspring of a merchant, Robert Syers senior (1743-1783). The family tree for Robert (1774-1838) lists him as having produced nine children, whilst his brother George Syers (1776-1854) had eleven offspring. By the time that Robert published his history, Everton contained the three brothers, their wives, and a total of 19 children that had survived childhood. In addition, Mary Syers (the sister of Robert, George and William), had married in 1796 and, although her subsequent history has not been discovered, her daughter will be the subject of several important appearances in future chapters.

4,6. Everton Brow in 1830 looking east and showing the bridewell ('mere stone-jug') in the centre.

Image courtesy of the LRO, ref. Brierley Collection 74.

The Everton Village of Mary Helen Syers' days is unrecognisable today but fortunately, in addition to the Everton maps used by Robert Syers, several paintings and historical accounts provide some indication of what would have been familiar to Peter during his and Mary's courtship. James Brierley's view of Everton Brow in 1830 shows the bridewell in the centre and Halliday's Coffee Shop to its right (fig. 4,6). Disappearing off to the right is a glimpse of Prince Rupert's Cottage, with a row of cottages disappearing to the left.

In James Brierley's painting of these cottages two years earlier he had included the Cooper's Toffee Shop (fig. 4,7).

Of the various buildings to which Robert Syers refers, he was clearly not enthusiastic for the bridewell which for him was:-

> *'a mere stone-jug or watch-box, a diminutive building, and, as regards its interior, a dark, damp strong-hold, for the temporary reception and incarceration of the unruly, the vicious, and the criminal, that is, until a magistrate's committal consigns such unfortunate human beings to a more fit and congenial place of confinement. This apology for a bridewell ought to be taken down – it is a discredit to the community...'*

Although Molly Bushell's had been the original Everton toffee shop, by 1810 it had become Mrs Cooper's on Everton Brow. Marked '*62.a*' on his 1790 map, Robert Syers thought highly of it:-

> *'The westernmost of these domiciles has long been Mrs. Cooper's manufactory for that luscious compound of sweets, whose excellence is celebrated far and near, under the name of Everton toffee.'*

4,8. An undated painting by Beattie of Cooper's Everton Toffee Shop on Browside undergoing demolition.

Image courtesy of the Athenaeum, from the 'Liverpool Buildings, Box 4B' collection.

The shop underwent demolition in the late 19th century (fig. 4,8).[2]

Robert wrote of the Everton coffee-house at '*11.a*' on his 1790 map that it had been first licensed about 1770 and that William Halliday (for whom he was full of praise) had:-

> *'entered upon the establishment in the year 1803... It is at this house that the public affairs of the township have been long, and still are transacted... The prospect in the north-west of the coffee-house is truly delightful; and in fine weather, on Sundays and holidays, the place is generally crowded.'*

The prospect four miles to the north west would have been of great interest to the coffee-house clientèle in the late 1820s, and what there was to see is indicated on Jonathan Bennison's detailed map of 1835 (fig. 4,9). The foundation stone for the lighthouse that was erected on the site of the old Rock Perch was laid in 1827 whilst Fort Perch Rock (planned decades earlier to protect Liverpool from the French) dates from 1829. These same Evertonians would also have used the vantage point of the coffee-house to train their telescopes upon land at New Brighton acquired by one of their residents, James Atherton (who had been instrumental in the erection of St George's Church), and the map suggests that at that stage there would not have been a lot to view other than Atherton's hotel. New Brighton was one of the places to which the Everton merchants would flee when Liverpool later expanded and swallowed up their mansions.

4,9. A detail from Jonathan Bennison's 1835 map, the first one of sufficient detail to show the Fort and the Rock Lighthouse, and while New Brighton was little more than a street plan.
Image courtesy of the Athenaeum.

In the 21st century a splendid panorama can still be gained from the Rupert Lane Recreation Ground (fig. 4,10) which now covers much of the Everton Village of Mary Helen Syers days, including the site of the coffee-house. The view looks out across the Mersey estuary and beyond Fort Perch Rock to the Burbo Bank wind farm on the horizon. Peter Ellis, whose interest in civil engineering will be seen to have blossomed later in his career, would no doubt have been fascinated by the technology involved in the wind farm which came two centuries later.

4,10. The Mersey estuary viewed from the Rupert Lane Recreation Ground in July 2012. In the distance beyond New Brighton (to the left), Fort Perch Rock (centre of view, at low tide) and the Lighthouse (to its right), can be seen the Burbo Bank wind farm.

Robert Syers wrote with particular enjoyment at his recollection of an incident in 1830 concerning an election held at the Everton coffee-house and involving his brother George Syers, another of Mary Helen Syers' uncles. The rooms during the election proceedings were:-

> *'so crowdedly filled, as to raise alarm in the minds of some, touching the safety of their limbs, and even their lives, should the extraordinary pressure on the floors cause them to give way.'*

In the event, no injuries were sustained and the candidate that George Syers had proposed eventually won a contest which exhibited:-

> *'something of the character of similar affairs occasionally conducted at Liverpool, and the tactics of some experienced electioneerers were called into play.'*

These proceedings at the coffee-house however were unlikely to have resembled a contest within the '*rotten borough*' of Liverpool during 1827 of which James Picton wrote entertainingly (*Memorials*, vol. I, p. 407) and concluded that:-

> *'The whole affair was one of the most extraordinary exhibitions of senseless folly on the one hand, and of shameless greed and corruption on the other, which had ever been witnessed'.*

4,11. Prince Rupert's Cottage when it still looked to be in use and well cared for.
Image courtesy of the LRO. [3]

Robert regarded the cottage which Prince Rupert had used as his headquarters during the 1644 siege of Liverpool (fig. 4,11) as being '*stamped with some celebrity*' despite the '*workmanship and materials being of the rudest class.*' He provided a detailed description of both the outside and inside of the building and observed that, '*From the window of the west gable a beautiful prospect is obtained, quite exhilarating to the tenant,*' and noted that two families occupied this small cottage in 1830. Of the cottage Michael O'Mahony commented a century later that:-

> *'Perched on a rocky escarpment at a corner of the village, the cottage where he planned his battles, while it commanded a prospect of unbroken clearness, had nothing luxurious about it. It was a long, low, thatched house of four rooms in which the kitchen had a tiled floor. Compared to it many a modern cottage given to us by Sir Hugh Rutherford would be a palace. Yet, it was for many a long year an object of public interest, if not veneration. Indeed, its admirers loved it well enough to finally accomplish its destruction. So many paper knives, ornaments, and frames for complimentary addresses were cut from its timbers, that if not taken down in 1845, it would have fallen down.'* [4]

James Stonehouse was more circumspect, however, and trusted that Joseph Mayer (a founder member of the Historic Society of Lancashire and Cheshire and provider of the Mayer Collection for the Liverpool Museum) had the courtesy to wait until the building was indeed pulled down before arranging for various objects to made from its timber, including the case for containing the complimentary address of the Corporation of Liverpool on the occasion of Queen Victoria's visit in 1851. [5]

Michael Gage's plan (fig. 4,12) shows the route that Peter would have taken on his journey from Low Hill to Everton in the early 1830s to visit Mary, passing a number of properties which had survived when the Herdmans came to paint them some years later.

Turning right out of Gloucester Place, Peter's first view would have been along Low Hill Road with Erskine Street entering from his left (fig. 4,13). This watercolour from 1864 provides a view of the house at the top of Erskine Street that can be seen from another angle in chapter 2 (fig. 2,19) and indicates that the house had at that stage survived the new generation of builders.

Passing the three-storey Bedford Terrace (fig. 4,14) Peter would have reached the home of James Plumpton, the owner of large amounts of land in both West Derby and Everton. In 1824 Mr Plumpton had laid out land on the west side of Everton Lane (later Everton Road) for building a row of double-fronted houses, shown on Michael Gage's plan adjacent to Plumpton Street.

In 1825 the Necropolis was opened on a five acre field called Mill Hey that had been purchased from James Plumpton, whilst in 1832 nine acres of land known as '*Plumpton's Hollow*' were leased by him for Thomas Atkins' Zoological Gardens (4,15).

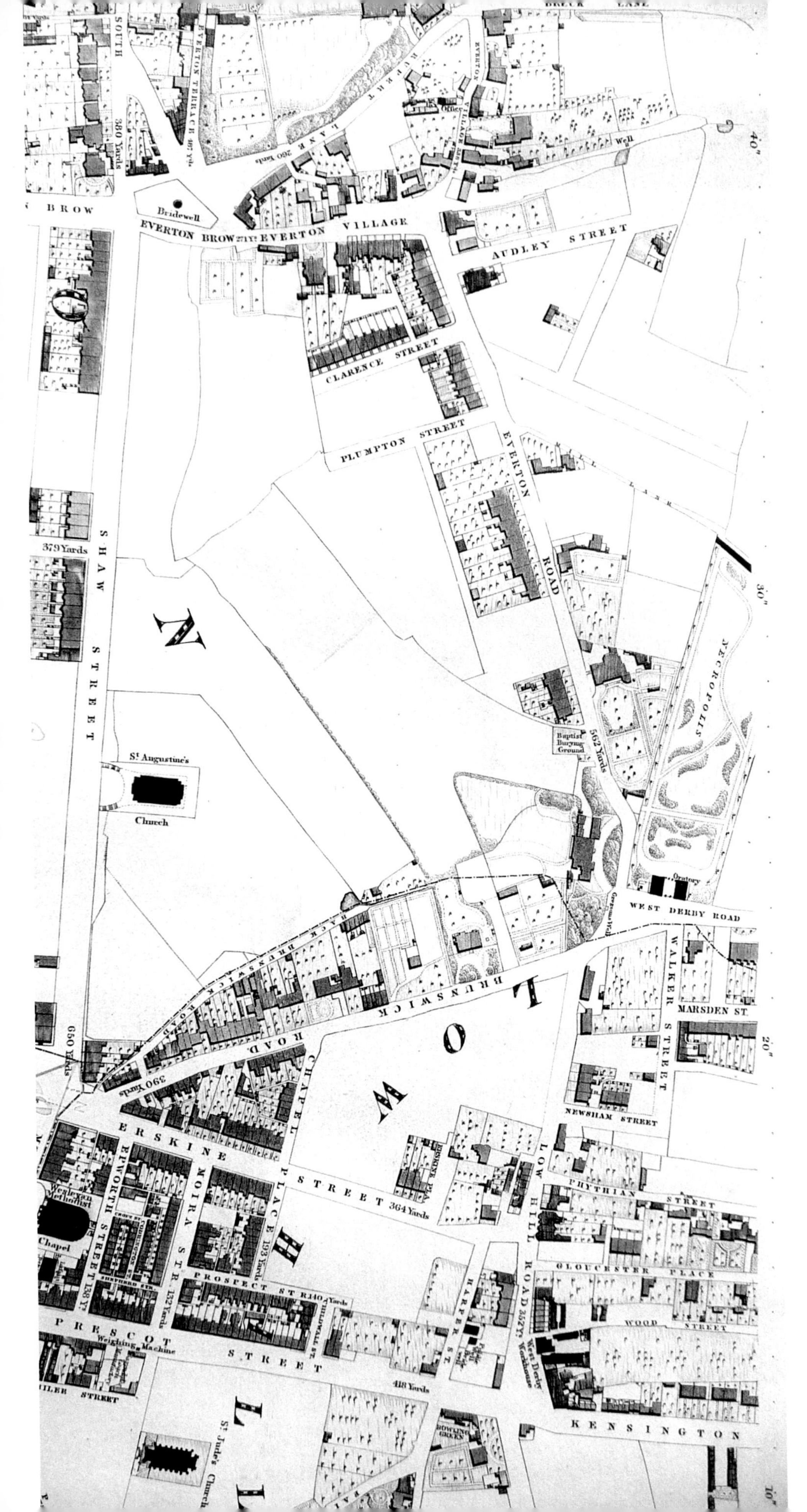

4,12. The route from Gloucester Place to Everton Village on Michael Gage's 1835 plan, re-oriented to the north (a detail from the complete map on p. iv, from F to L).

Private collection.

4,13. The beginning of Peter's route from Low Hill to Everton at the junction with Erskine Street.

Image courtesy of the LRO, ref. Herdman Collection 599.

Below: 4,16. A closer detail from Michael Gage's plan showing the Necropolis, the Baptist Burying Ground on Everton Road and Gregson's Well outside the home that had been William Gregson's. The Zoological Gardens were a few hundred yards along West Derby Road (previously known as Rake Lane).

Private collection.

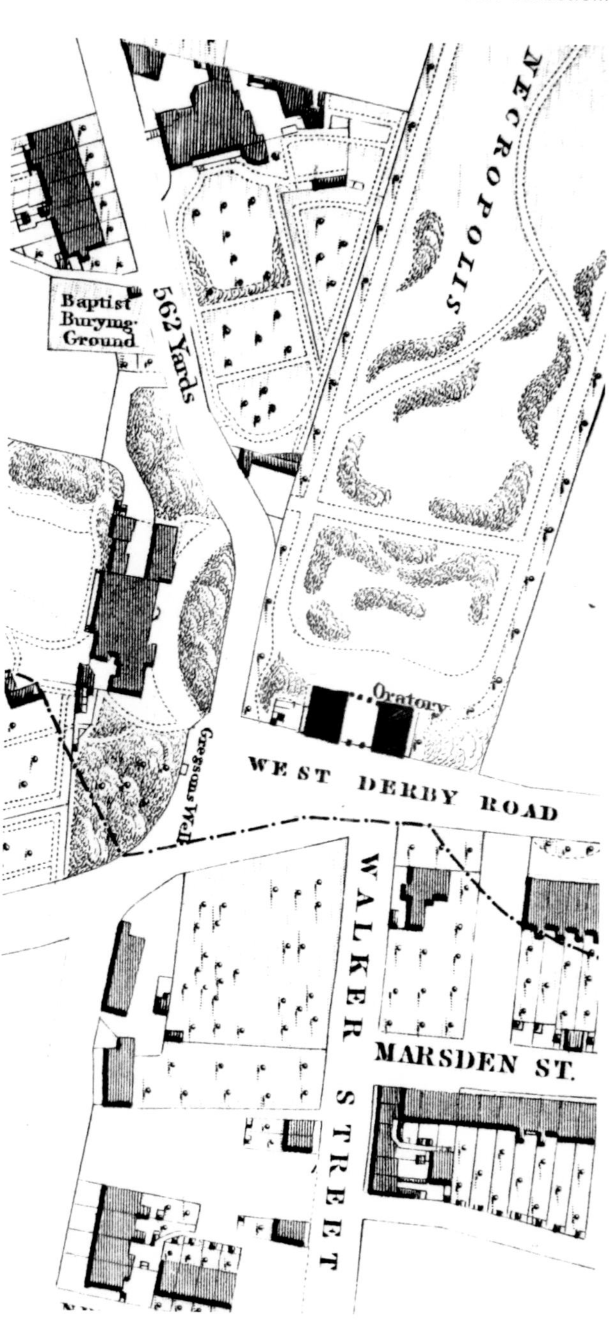

4,14. The view from a short distance along Low Hill having reached Newsham Street on the right.

Mr Plumpton's house shown in the centre of this view is the one standing on its own in fig. 4,16 with the garden extending back to the 'S' of Walker Street.

Bedford Terrace in the foreground is the group of four buildings at the lower left corner of the same map.

Image courtesy of the LRO, ref. Herdman Collection 352.

Opposite right: 4,15. From the O.S. map of 1848 showing the Zoological Gardens on the south side of West Derby Road (running diagonally, top left). Modern-day Boaler Street runs across the site. Opposite, on the north side, and to the west of Boundary Lane were the Strawberry Gardens.

Image courtesy of the Athenaeum.

4,17. W G Herdman's view of Everton House from his 1856 'Pictorial Relics', plate 42.
Image courtesy of the Athenaeum.

Michael Gage's plan does not extend as far as the Zoological Gardens, but Bennison's map of 1835 shows a second Plumpton Street stretching west from the Gardens. At the junction with West Derby Road and Everton Road (fig. 4,16) Peter would have passed Everton House on his left (fig. 4,17).

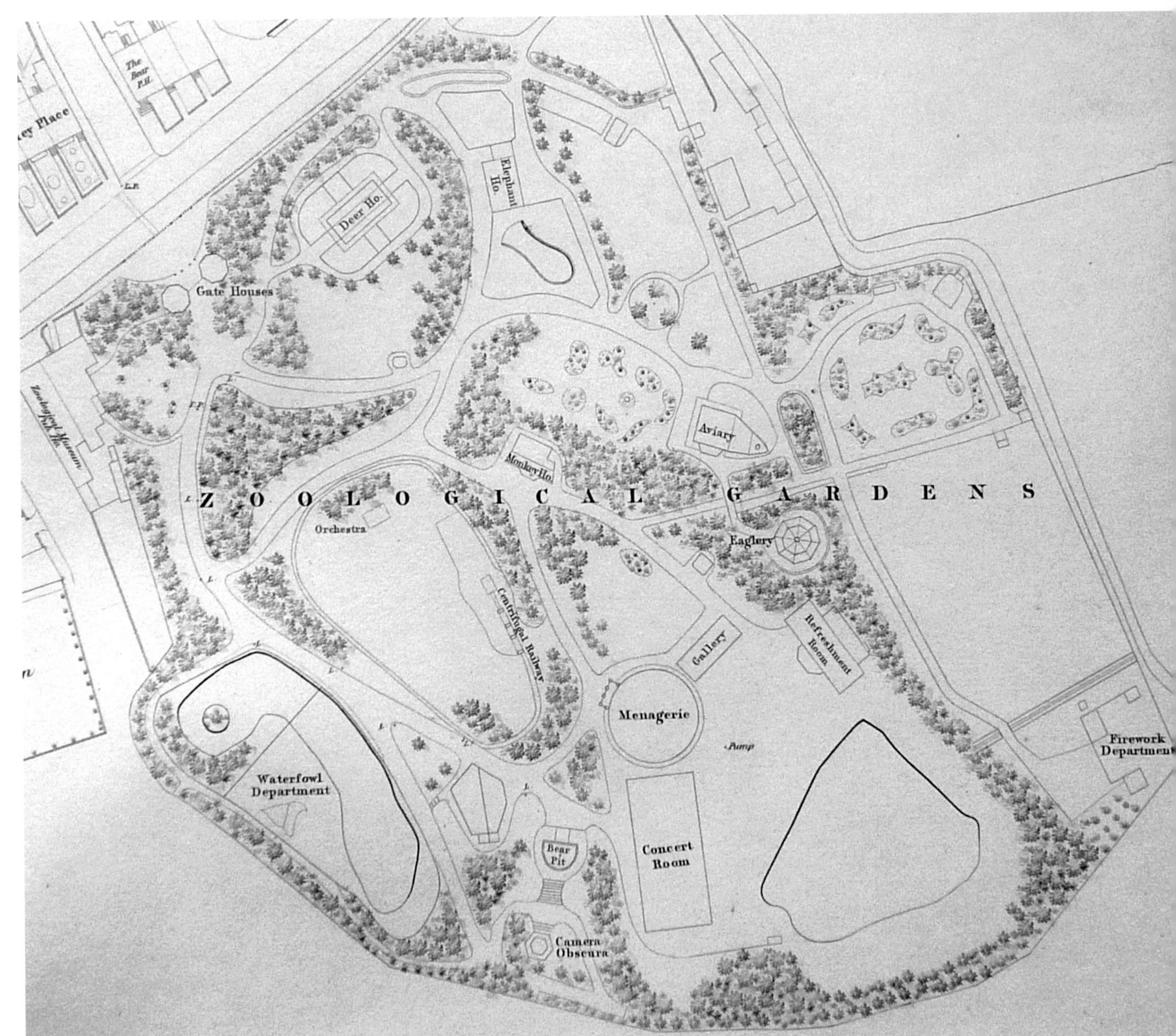

Of the house that William Gregson purchased about 1786, James Picton commented that it was:-

> *'almost rebuilt, and fitted up in a style of magnificence... William Gregson was mayor in 1769... When the alterations were in progress Mr. Gregson fancied the public road came too near the front of his house. The overseers of the highways, willing to oblige so magnificent a personage, consented to alter it, so as to give adequate space in front of the mansion. Hence the awkward curve in the road as it now exists, which it would cost thousands of pounds to make straight.'* [6]

It remained the home of William Gregson until his death in 1800, and W G Herdman remembered that the well, shown to the left of its gates:-

> *'supplied the surrounding inhabitants with excellent water, but in later years it was filled with rubbish and useless. It was taken down about 1842.'* [7]

Everton House, perhaps inevitably, became more popularly known as *Gregson's Well.* When years later the house was also pulled down, two pubs that were subsequently built opposite each other nearby took on its name (see later).

Facing Everton House was the Necropolis which Peter would have passed on his right as he turned into Everton Road (fig. 4,18). The cemetery became necessary because the churchyards elsewhere had become full to overflowing. It was established by the Protestant Dissenters and designed by John Foster (James Picton, *Memorials*, vol. II, p. 348).

On the very edge of the growing town, and still with open fields along Low Hill and Everton Road, the walk or horse ride between the two homes must have been a delightful part of Peter and Mary's courtship. James Picton in his introduction to William Herdman's 1864 *Views* noted that:-

> *'The road from Low Hill to Everton Village in the first quarter of the present century was one of the most beautiful in the environs of the town. Lined on each side with venerable and umbrageous trees and open pastures, the mansion of Mr. Shaw at one end, and [that] of Mr. Gregson at the other, it was a favourite study for the artist and the lover of beautiful scenery.'* [8]

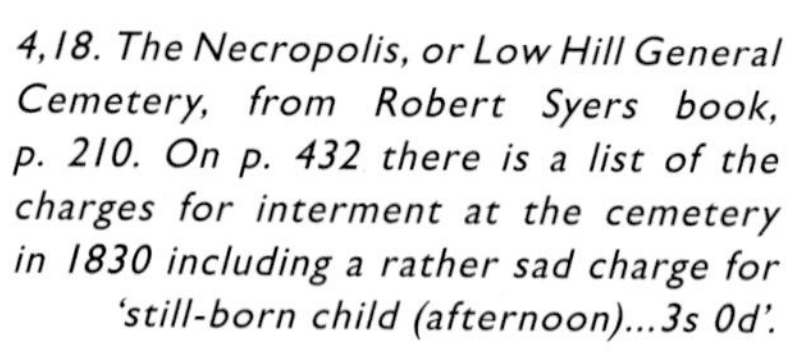

4,18. The Necropolis, or Low Hill General Cemetery, from Robert Syers book, p. 210. On p. 432 there is a list of the charges for interment at the cemetery in 1830 including a rather sad charge for 'still-born child (afternoon)...3s 0d'.

Image courtesy of the LRO, ref. 942.7211 EVE.

In his own *Memorials*, James Picton remembered that a part of the ancient Whitefields of Everton still retained a rural character up to about 1840 and that:-

> *'a footpath branched off from West Derby Road and led to a small house of entertainment with a bowling-green and strawberry garden extending to Boundary Road, along the south side of which ran a stile road forming a beautiful lovers' walk.'*[9]

In 1833, Peter and Mary may well have attended the ceremony of the opening of the Zoological Gardens (figs. 4,19 and 4,20) where, according to James Stonehouse, '*The leading families in Liverpool might have been seen at that time promenading the walks,*' [10] whilst crossing West Derby Road and walking a few yards north would have led them to the Strawberry Gardens.

4,19. The entrance to the Zoological Gardens by W G Herdman, on the occasion of Queen Victoria's visit to Liverpool in 1851. Herdman would have been standing on West Derby Road facing the Gate Houses (top left of fig. 4,15) and would have needed a rather large umbrella to protect his canvas.

Image courtesy of the LRO, ref. 942.7214 HER (1878, vol. II), plate 51.

Although they would have looked forward to their enjoyment of both Gardens, Peter's visits to the Necropolis to tend graves there would have been filled with immense sadness, and whenever Mary Helen Syers accompanied him, she would have been much needed to console him.

The *Lancashire OnLine Parish Clerk Project* website reveals that Peter's sister Ann (aged 29) was buried there on 2nd March 1826, and was followed by two of Peter's brothers, Thomas (aged 14) on 5th June 1829, and William (aged 24) on 3rd June 1832. Ann and Thomas had died whilst still living at home at Gloucester Place. William, dying of apoplexy, is recorded as having been living at Gloucester Street, probably in a house that his father had built.

4,20. A second view of the Zoological Gardens, taken from an unidentified publication and depicted as being on a somewhat sunnier day. The artist had his back to the Camera Obscura (centre bottom of fig. 4,15).

Image courtesy of the LRO, ref. L.I.C. 912.

Today the graves have long gone and the site has become Grant Gardens.

The scene at the junction of Low Hill and Brunswick Road was set to change dramatically after Peter had left Gloucester Place. Fig. 4,21 offers a view looking back along Low Hill Road past James Plumpton's house and Bedford Terrace. Time had moved on from Peter's days at Low Hill, although this scene in 1868 gives little hint of what has happened.

4,21. Looking back along Low Hill Road in 1868, past James Plumpton's house and Bedford Terrace.

Image courtesy of the LRO, ref. Herdman Collection 715.

The ancient building in the foreground bears a sign '*Fire. Police Station*' but seems long ago to have ceased functioning in that capacity. Attached to it can be seen the premises of Abraham Highton, of whom the directories indicate that his career began in 1851 as a tobacconist in Finch Street and progressed via Dansie Street to Low Hill. James Stonehouse noted that by the time of his paper to the Historic Society in 1852, '*Gregson's villa and gardens have disappeared, and are covered by multitudes of small houses.*' [11] These houses were accompanied by two pubs which faced each other across the junction, one in the township of Everton and the other in the township of West Derby (fig. 4,22). Left to right can be seen the original *Gregson's Well* pub that was built on a site close to that of the well, the Necropolis in the background and, adjacent to the entrance to Abraham Highton's premises, a pub on the West Derby side of the junction which had taken on the name '*Gregson's House P.H.*' on the 1848 O.S. map.

Brunswick Road is shown as Mill Lane on Horwood's 1803 map, and as Brunswick Place on some later maps. [12] It was a continuation of Folly Lane which was subsequently renamed Islington. James Picton wrote of Brunswick Road that from 1835 (the time that Peter was preparing to leave Gloucester Place to get married):-

> '*The road, from a quiet rural lane, began to assume the aspect of a leading artery. Shops took the place of front gardens. The villas one by one succumbed to their fate, and a busy commercial thoroughfare had fully established itself about 1860.*' [13]

4,22. A view in 1867 along the boundary of the townships of Everton (on the left) and West Derby (on the right); see fig. 4,2.

Image courtesy of the LRO, ref. Herdman Collection 15.

A photograph from the LRO's collection (fig. 4,24) shows this commercial thoroughfare in 1936 looking east towards the pubs at the junction with Low Hill and before the shops in their turn succumbed to a yet newer version of progress.

Fig. 4,23 shows the junction in 2012 corresponding to that in fig. 4,22. Everton Road disappears off to the left behind the disused Midland Bank, whilst West Derby Road disappears to the right behind the derelict building (the large Higson's pub in the distance in fig. 4,24). The bank marks approximately where the original well had been located, beyond which had been Everton House and to the side of which the pub which was demolished in the late 1970s had stood. The grassed area indicates the site of the Necropolis (now Grant Gardens).

It seems an unkind fate for the second of the two *Gregson's Well* pubs to be abandoned in this forlorn and half-demolished state, a free noticeboard for a multitude of fly-posters, silently awaiting its final obliteration. Adjacent to it once stood the Royal Hippodrome Theatre.

4,23. A view in 2012 of the point where Brunswick Road, entering from the near left, joins Low Hill, corresponding with the view in 1867 (fig. 4,22).

4,24. Brunswick road in 1936 showing the 'busy commercial thoroughfare' to which James Picton referred as having been fully established about 1860.

Image courtesy of the LRO, ref. Photographs & Small Prints: Streets & Districts: Brunswick Road.

Opposite right: 4,27. A painting attributed to William Herdman entitled, 'Everton Village showing old sundial, c. 1820.' The large house on the right was the home of Thomas Shaw (located towards the top right in fig. 4,4).
Image courtesy of the LRO, ref. Herdman Collection 592.

4,25. James Brierley's view entitled 'Cottages, left side of the Road, leading from Low Hill to Everton, 1830.'
Image courtesy of the Athenaeum.

Returning now to the early 1830s, as Peter left Low Hill and entered the township of Everton he would have next passed the Baptist Burying Ground and the adjacent group of five old cottages which are marked on Michael Gage's plan (fig. 4,16) and depicted in a delightful view in 1830 by James Brierley, just as Peter would have known them (fig. 4,25). James Picton wrote of the burial ground in William Herdman's 1864 *Views* that:-

> *'the first Baptist Chapel near Liverpool was erected in a quiet rural lane leading from Low Hill to Everton, about the latter end of the seventeenth century. The chapel has long since disappeared, but the small enclosure of its burial ground still exists, or very recently did so, hemmed round by the advanced tide of population which has surrounded it and flowed far beyond.'* [14]

4,26. A scene by James Brierley entitled 'A view from Everton Road, near Liverpool, 1829.'
Image courtesy of the LRO, ref. Brierley Collection 71.

Still further along Everton Road, Peter would have arrived at the outskirts of Everton Village, captured in 1829 in another of James Brierley's splendid views (fig. 4,26: he was famous for his occasional out-of-scale figures, in this case including a diminutive horse and its rider).

Arriving in Everton Village, and with Robert Syers having located Mary Helen Syers' home as being a few yards beyond the junction with Everton Road, the house can be identified in two views of the village, the first from W G Herdman's 1856 *Pictorial Relics* (plate 38, a detail of which faces the opening to this chapter) and the second by William Herdman (fig. 4,27). Mary's house stands in the background behind the smaller of the two trees and joined to a slightly lower house to its right. [15]

Of the view of the village, Charles Hand wrote that it shows:-

> *'Everton Village early in 1820. On the extreme left stands Molly Bushell's House, the original Everton Toffee Shop, next some cottages and the Old Ivy Public House, with horse-steps in front, such as are now very seldom seen, except at very old country houses. Then comes one of the old Everton 'mansions', and a portion of the residence of Thomas Shaw, Esq. In the foreground is the noted 'Everton Cross' which was a round stone pillar, about four feet in height, surmounted by a sun-dial, and standing on a square pedestal or base, consisting of three stone steps. The Cross, as Everton increased in population, ultimately became a nuisance; standing as it did almost in the centre of the roadway, it became the cause of constant collisions by vehicles and pedestrians, especially after dark, when oil lamps only shed faint rays around and gas lights were not in use. Many applications for its removal were made to the authorities, but to no purpose; the Evertonians loved their Cross, and would not hear of its abolition, and the authorities shrunk from their task. At length, one dark and stormy winter's night in 1820 – when all Everton was at rest – two bold spirits, armed with crowbar, pickaxe and spade, approached the ancient gathering place... and made short work of its destruction. In the course of two or three hours every stone was safely locked up in the Round House on Everton Brow, and the place where it had stood being carefully raked and smoothed over, it appeared as if the Cross – raised doubtless by pious hands on some remarkable occasion long forgotten – had never existed. When morning dawned, the consternation was extreme. From house to house – then few in number – ran the news that the Father of Lies had taken it away during the storm of the previous night. And so the report spread through Liverpool in the year 1820, that the Devil had run away with the Cross at Everton; and it was not until many years afterwards that it became known that the abductor of Everton Cross was the late Sir William Shaw, the surveyor of the high roads of the township.'* [16]

Stories of the disappearance of the Cross were probably still being embellished during Peter and Mary's courtship, and maybe Peter made it an excuse (if excuse were needed) to hold her protectively close every time they passed the spot where it had stood – a matter of a few yards from Mary's home.

And if during their courting days Mary had told Peter of the Evertonian pastime of fashioning keepsakes from pieces of timber surreptitiously removed from Rupert's Cottage, who knows what a skilful young man from Low Hill might have been prompted to make for her.

The corresponding view in 2012 to that in fig. 4,27 is shown in fig. 4,28. [17] If Mary and Peter had returned to Everton Village a decade after they were married in order to see how things were changing they would have discovered that Rupert's Cottage had gone, that Mary's house was a Post Office and that her garden had become Hodgson Place (4,29).

4,28. Everton Village in 2012 (corresponding to the location in fig. 4,27), looking towards where Mary Helen Syers' house had once stood.

The gates leading to the Rupert Lane Recreation Ground mark the site of Molly Bushell's Toffee Shop referred to by Charles Hand.

On the extreme right the Liverpool Provincial Grand Hall stands on the site of Thomas Shaw's house.

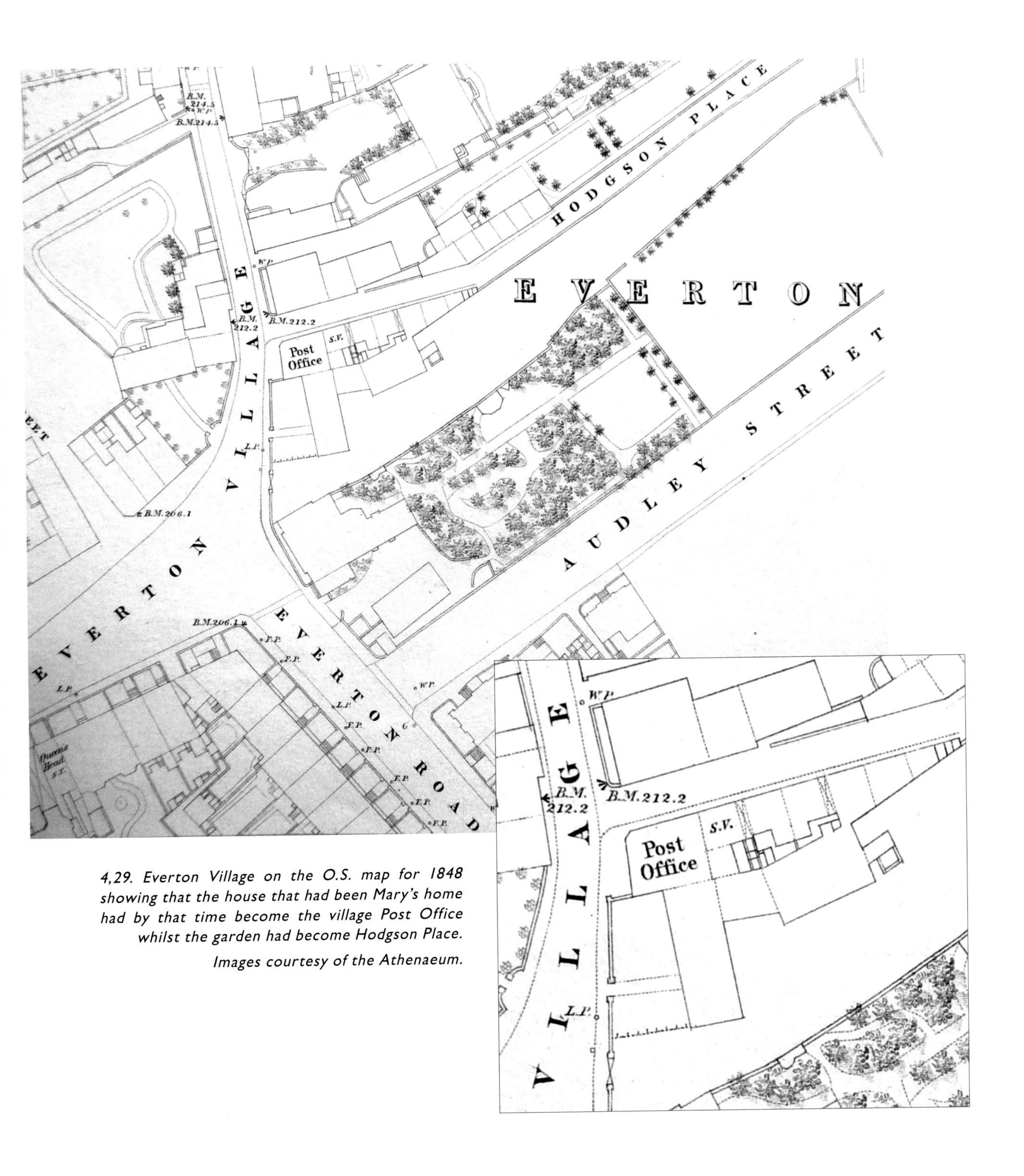

4,29. Everton Village on the O.S. map for 1848 showing that the house that had been Mary's home had by that time become the village Post Office whilst the garden had become Hodgson Place.

Images courtesy of the Athenaeum.

4,30. St George's Church and the Everton mansions in an 1819 engraving, before the merchants fled to more distant places including James Atherton's New Brighton. Image courtesy of the Athenaeum.

The Everton hillside before the merchants' mansions eventually succumbed to the devouring needs of an expanding Liverpool was captured in a view which appears as a decorative addition to Sherwood's map to which Robert Syers had referred (fig. 4,30).

The engraving, '*by Thos. Dixon, Caxton, Liverpool, 1819*', must have been one of the last produced by the Caxton Printing Office, which at that date was located on Bolton Street which ran off Skelhorne Street. James Picton wrote at considerable length on the history of the firm and of the fire in January 1821 '*which destroyed the entire building and its contents, of the value of £36,000. After this disastrous event, the business was removed to London.*' [18]

Everton eventually underwent a rebuilding programme in which a famous Welsh family by the name of Elias played a dominant role, and eventually it housed an entirely new population.

J R Jones wrote that:-

> *'Everton was a picturesque village when these three brothers began their building operations. Owen Elias, in his early years, lived in Water Street and his daughter used to walk through country lanes until she reached the top of what is now Brunswick Road, and climbed over a style through fields to the 'Dog and Gun,' where the little private school which she attended was held.'* [19]

By the 1870s James Picton was writing that:-

> *'Everton is the Goshen of the Cambrian race. Its modern development is almost entirely the work of Welsh builders... Everton is now inhabited by the working classes, and it may be said to their honour that there is no part of the town more orderly, more free from beggary and squalid poverty than this district.'* [20]

Evertonians with long memories will recall just how steep were the streets going up the Everton hillside, and Ivy Ireland wrote of those streets as they were in 1938:-

'In the early history of Liverpool, Everton is described as a pleasant outlying village on the hilltop where wealthy merchants from the port of Liverpool made their country homes in an atmosphere of peaceful retirement. Were those fortunate people to return to Everton today, they would find scarcely one tree or a blade of grass to remind them of their former rural home. The hill is still in evidence, but only as a homeward struggle for many a weary mother pushing her perambulator or carrying a heavy baby. The hill is covered with houses as closely packed as architecture will permit, and its skyline bristles with chimney pots. Some of the streets seem to run almost perpendicularly upwards if one looks at them from below and one could easily imagine that a baby, falling from its doorstep at the top house, would roll all the way down the street without stopping. The houses in these streets are built step-wise, each one a little higher than the other, and seen from a distance they appear to cling with giddy insecurity to the steep side of the slope.' [21]

Today the bridewell (fig. 4,31), held in such low opinion by Robert Syers, and St George's Church are almost the only original landmarks which enable visitors to locate themselves within the Everton Village of Peter and Mary's days. [22]

Both are now listed buildings, and the bridewell is an important symbol for supporters of Everton Football Club. Nicknamed *The Toffees*, the club was founded in 1878, an event which Peter and Mary lived to see. Peter would have approved of the club's 1930s motto:-

'Nothing but the best is good enough'.

4,31. The Everton bridewell in 2012, looking from the point where Shaw Street becomes Netherfield Road.

References and Notes to Chapter 4

1 Robert Syers, *The History of Everton*, G & J Robinson, Castle Street, and D Marples, Lord Street, Liverpool, 1830, p. 200. The book can be downloaded from the internet as a pdf file, thanks to the University of Toronto (visit the Liverpool History Society website under '*on-line books*'). First appearing in the directories in 1800 as a merchant in Drury Lane, Robert was subsequently listed in 1805 at Netherfield Lane and in 1807 at Everton Town. For the remainder of his career his office was in Chorley Street, residing between 1810 and 1824 at Roscommon Street, and between 1825 and 1827 at Richmond Row. In 1832 he retired and in 1838 he died. His brother George Syers was for many years a surveyor in customs.

Whether the original map of ca. 1790, of which Robert made a copy and then added his symbols, has survived is uncertain, and Ronald Stewart-Brown (Maps and Plans of Liverpool and District by the Eyes Family of Surveyors, *Transactions of the Historic Society of Lancashire and Cheshire*, 62, 1910, p. 165) speculated that it was a Charles Eyes' map.

Robert's *History of Everton* was very much enjoyed by James Picton when he came to write his own history nearly half a century later, whilst George also received several appreciative comments. He wrote of Robert that he '*presents us with an entire survey of the state of the township, made by himself in 1829, in which almost every inhabitant of the least note is distinguished by a most Boswellian minuteness of portraiture, and a naïveté which is racy and amusing in the highest degree... a work to which I must express my obligations for the fulness and completeness of its details, throwing a light on the condition of the district, at and immediately before his time, which is to be met with nowhere else, and which is seldom to be found in works of much higher pretension.*' (*Memorials*, vol. II, pp. 339 and 367).

It was customary in those days to dedicate books to some noble or other, and Robert Syers – who was proud to be an Everton copyholder – dedicated his book to the Marquis of Salisbury who, through marriage, had recently got his hands on the '*Manors of Everton, &c. &c. &c.*' Both Robert Syers and James Stonehouse (ref. 5) provide detailed accounts of how changes in ownership of the land at Everton came about.

The LRO also has a copy of an extraordinary book entitled '*The Liverpool Repository of Literature, Philosophy, and Commerce. By an Association of Literary Gentlemen.*' It began life as the 12 monthly issues which have been bound together as volume 1 in 1826, and almost all the contributors apparently decided that it would be more fun to use pseudonyms ('*The Hermit*', '*Juventus*', '*Hal the Etcher*', '*Josephus*', '*The Ghost of Tim Bobbin*', for example). The catalogue of a '*Collection of Liverpool Prints and Documents*' issued by the Liverpool Public Library in 1908 identifies Robert Syers as the contributor '*Iron Mask*' who, in that 1826 volume, submitted a series of articles on Liverpool streets, beginning with the letter B (Blundell, Bold, Bolton, Bridewell, Bridge), presumably with the intention of continuing alphabetically in future years.

Although the LRO possesses no subsequent volumes, and it is therefore uncertain whether *Iron Mask's* perambulation through the alphabet ever continued, Robert might be considered to have been the forerunner of a variety of later publications on Liverpool lanes and streets by the likes of Stonehouse, Picton, Reilly and O'Mahony.

2 The agitated and entertaining exchanges in the 1926 *Liverpool Echo* as to the site of the original Everton Toffee Shop have been gathered together in a collection assembled by the Liverpool Library under the title, *Everton Toffee Shop. Molly Bushell, Everton Village, John Cooper, Brow Side, 1926* (LRO ref. 942.7213 TOF). It is also in this collection of papers that photographic details of the 1790 and 1821 maps may be found to which Robert Syers referred (the 1790 map which he included in his book has been removed from the LRO copy).

3 The view is taken from Robert Syers, *op cit.*, p. 46. Another view of Prince Rupert's cottage some years later when it was approaching the end of its life appears in W G Herdman's 1843 edition of his *Pictorial Relics of Ancient Liverpool*, plate 42, and a conjectural internal view during its use in the Civil War is in his 1878 edition, vol. II, plate 63.

4 Michael O'Mahony, *Liverpool Ways and Byeways*, Daily Post, 1931, p. 151.

5 James Stonehouse, Historical Notes, Respecting the Township and Village of Everton, *Transactions of the Historic Society of Lancashire and Cheshire*, 4, 1852, p. 73. '*The rafters were of oak, and two beams are at this date* [1852] *to be seen in the yard of Mr. Jones of Everton, plasterer, who purchased the materials when the cottage was taken down, and serve as uprights for a timber rack. From its timber also, Mr. Joseph Mayer, F.S.A., caused a vase to be made, which was presented by the Society in 1848 to Lord Albert D. Conyngham, now Lord Londesborough, and a case for containing the address of the Corporation of Liverpool on the occasion of Her Majesty's visit in 1851.*' The paper also contains a drawing by W G Herdman of '*The battery mound at the back of Prince Rupert's cottage*' (facing p. 71).

6 J A Picton, *Memorials of Liverpool*, G G Walmsley (Liverpool), 2nd edn., 1875, vol. II, p. 348.

7 W G Herdman, *Pictorial Relics of Ancient Liverpool*, 1856, p. 101, with reference to plate 42. LRO ref. Hf 942.7214 HER 1856, of which the Athenaeum copy is shown in fig. 4,17.

8 William Herdman, *Views in Modern Liverpool*, 1864; text by James Picton, p. xv. LRO ref. Hf 942.7214 HER (1864).

9 J A Picton, *op. cit.*, vol. II, p. 381 (the location appears always to have been called Boundary Lane).

10 James Stonehouse, *The Streets of Liverpool*, Edward Howell, 1869, p. 117. Reprinted for Liverpool Libraries and Information Services, 2002. Stonehouse provides an extensive account of the Zoological Gardens.

W G Herdman in the text on p. 34 of his 1878 *Pictorial Relics*, vol. II, from which fig. 4,19 is taken, commented that '*The day will be long memorable as a thoroughly wet day. The Queen, during her visit, had to pass the gardens on her way from Croxteth; in honour of the occasion Mr. Atkins erected a magnificent triumphal arch, from the top of which, and swinging across the road were placed living eagles, parrots, and other birds.*

Here they remained throughout the day, as seen in the Plate. It is said that the severity of the weather caused the death of most of them. No vestige of this once popular place of resort now remains. Its locality may be understood by our explaining that Boaler Street runs through the centre of the gardens.'

11 James Stonehouse, Historical Notes, *op. cit.*, p. 76.

12 James Stonehouse, *Streets, op. cit.*, p. 106, recounts a story of the origin of Brunswick Road's name: '*The change from Mill-lane arose in this wise. If the story is not true it is well told. About [1820] a young lady, having strong proclivities towards the reigning dynasty, observed that the painter who was re-inscribing the names of the streets had left his ladder against the house in which she resided while he went to his dinner. She availed herself of the opportunity of his absence to rub out "Old Mill-lane" and chalk up "Brunswick-place." On his return, seeing the latter name boldly written, he considered that that was the title he had to inscribe, and accordingly "followed his copy".*'

13 J A Picton, *op. cit.*, vol. II, p. 423. See also James Stonehouse in a continuation of ref. 12.

14 William Herdman, *Views, op. cit.*; text by James Picton, p. 16, with reference to the Baptist Burial Ground. By the time that William Herdman came to publish his *Views* in 1864 the Baptist Chapel was located at the junction of Hope Street and Myrtle Street, opposite the building which would subsequently become the shoeing forge of Peter's nephew, John Ellis.

15 An advertisement in *Gore's* 1865 directory for Everton Toffee ('*Manufactured only by R. H. Wignall, late of the original toffee shop, who is grandson of Molly Bushell*') shows a scene based on fig. 4,27. A copy of the advertisement accompanies several interesting views of the other (Browside) shop which are included in reference 2. Mary Helen Syers' home was in the area known as the '*Straits of the Village*', and Herdman's *Relics*, 1878, vol. II, plate 50 (2) shows a view of the Straits.

16 C R Hand, *Olde Liverpoole & Its Charter*, 1907, p. 123. Available as a reprint with its many interesting advertisements. Charles Hand clearly drew his commentary from *Recollections of Old Liverpool by a Nonagenarian*, 1863, chapter VIII (dictated to James Stonehouse by an unidentified source, and also available as a reprint). The nonagenarian was a friend of one of those who removed the cross, for he recounted to Stonehouse that, *"My old friend, who many a time chuckled over his feat, and who told me of his doings, said that for many years he feared to tell the truth about it, so indignant were many of the inhabitants who knew that its disappearance could not have been attributed to satanic agency. My friend used to say that he had hard work to preserve his gravity when listening to the various versions that were prevalent of the circumstance."*

17 For the scene at the junction of Village Street and Everton Road in the 1960s see Ken Rogers, *The Lost Tribe of Everton & Scottie Road*, Trinity Mirror Media, 2010, p. 156.

18 J A Picton, *op cit.*, vol. II, pp. 200-204.

19 J R Jones, *The Welsh Builder on Merseyside*, 1946, p. 31. Privately published, and printed by Hugh Evans & Sons, The Brythron Press, 9 Hackins Hey. The Oxford Names Companion notes that *Elias* is a variation of *Ellis*.

20 J A Picton, *op. cit.*, vol. II, p. 353.

21 Ivy A Ireland, *Margaret Beavan of Liverpool*, Henry Young & Sons, 1938, p. 239, in her chapter recounting Margaret Beavan's unsuccessful attempt to win the Everton seat in the 1929 Parliamentary Election.

An example of the houses that were '*as closely packed as architecture will permit,*' is shown in Quentin Hughes' book *Seaport*, p. 122, whilst some of the houses that '*cling with giddy insecurity to the steep side of the slope*' can be seen on the cover of Ken Rogers' book, *op. cit.* A popular picture showing three young lads climbing the steep street, it also features in the opening chapter of Jim Moore's *Underground Liverpool*, The Bluecoat Press, 1998. This latter book also contains a nostalgic view of a group of infants playing in the Everton terraces, and Colin Wilkinson has confirmed that this ca. 1960 photograph by Karl Hughes is of Havelock Street, long since gone (see *The Streets of Liverpool*, The Bluecoat Press, 2011, p.11, and commentary on the facing page).

22 Retracing Peter's footsteps between Low Hill and Everton in 2012 I was struck by the engaging response of a variety of residents whenever I was spotted with my camera, several occasions of which come to mind.

No sooner had I begun to photograph the disused Midland Bank on the junction of Brunswick Road and Everton Road than a man leapt out of his parked car and began to show me the precise site of Everton House and where the Gregson's Well pub had once stood, and told me of the current plans to develop the site where the remnant of the other pub on the opposite corner still stands. He had grown up near there and the fate of the place clearly mattered dearly to him. A little way down Everton Road, the sight of my showing interest in the derelict mansion at the junction with Plumpton Street brought forth a man from a neighbouring building who told me about the mansion's less neglected days, and how he used to go there. Further on, having explored the Rupert Lane Recreation Ground, I entered a grassy enclosure where two men were sunbathing next to the bridewell. As soon as my camera appeared, one of them began to tell me with evident pride of the significance of the building, proceeded to recite his club's motto in Evertonian Latin, and was then perhaps amused that (as a south Liverpool lad) I had not a clue what he was saying.

On another occasion, having photographed views towards New Brighton, I called in at May Duncan's Restaurant & Bar on Heyworth Street (Church Street in Mary Helen Syers' day). Greeted warmly by the staff, I was shown an aerial photograph of their '*Little House on the Prairie*' as the pub became affectionately known after the bulldozers came and demolished everything around them, leaving this mid-1870s pub in splendid isolation on the edge of the park. They were delighted that I had a copy of Freddy O'Connor's *Liverpool. It All came Tumbling Down*, and said, "*If you come back tomorrow we'll bring in some more books about Everton.*" So I did, and later in the day found myself calling at the *Echo* office to purchase my own copy of Ken Rogers' *The Lost Tribe of Everton & Scottie Road*.

Having grown up in Aigburth many years ago, Everton had always been a foreign country. Those various conversations made tracing Peter's footsteps all the more memorable, and provided me with a delightful reminder that a proud and enthusiastic remnant of the *Lost Tribe* lives on.

Chapter 5

Marriage, Sandon Street and the designs for St George's Hall

The Corporation Lease Register for 18th July 1835 shows that *'Peter Ellis of Liverpool Builder'* was granted a lease on 4th March of that year for three houses and land in Chatham Street (fig. 5,1). Since Peter Ellis senior is shown in *Gore's Directory* for 1834 as *'gentleman'* (i.e. retired), this lease refers to his son. The special covenants are recorded as being:-

> *'To keep area inclosed with Iron Pallisades. Not to carry on Offensive Trades. Nor build any Steam Engine. Nor open Warehouse Doors to Chatham Street. Nor build to exceed 60 feet in height. Nor alter Elevation without consent. Nor build Courts or Backhouses. Nor build other than 7 yards Dwellinghouses to Chatham Street. To flag Foot Walk to Chatham Street.'*

Chatham Street was renamed Sandon Street later in 1835 and is shown as such on Michael Gage's plan (fig. 5,2). It was to 6 Sandon Street, the middle one of the three houses to the south of Howard Street (fig. 5,3), that Peter brought his bride in 1836, and it was on the adjacent land to the south that he eventually built a further two houses of seven yards width to complete a terrace of five. As the housing development in Sandon Street progressed and infilling took place, their home became no. 14. By 1845 nos. 18 and 20 (which Peter built) and a neighbouring building at the junction with Canning Street (no. 22) are all listed in the directory as being occupied.

5,1. Part of the lease granted by the Corporation to 'Peter Ellis of Liverpool Builder' on 4th March 1835 and entered on the register on 18th July 1835.
Image courtesy of the LRO, ref. 352 CLE/CON 3/8.

LESSEE.	DESCRIPTION of PREMISES.
Peter Ellis of Liverpool Builder (now Sandon St) from 4th. March 1835	All that piece or parcel of Land with the three several Messuages or Dwellinghouses thereon erected situate on the Westward side of Chatham Street Containing in front thereto and at the back thereof along a Street of 5 Yards wide severally 64 feet and running in depth backwards from Chatham Street on the Northward Side along a Street of 10 Yards wide and on the Southward Side along Land in Lease to the Executors of Edward Falkner deceased severally 90 feet including an Area to the front of Chatham Street of 6 feet wide

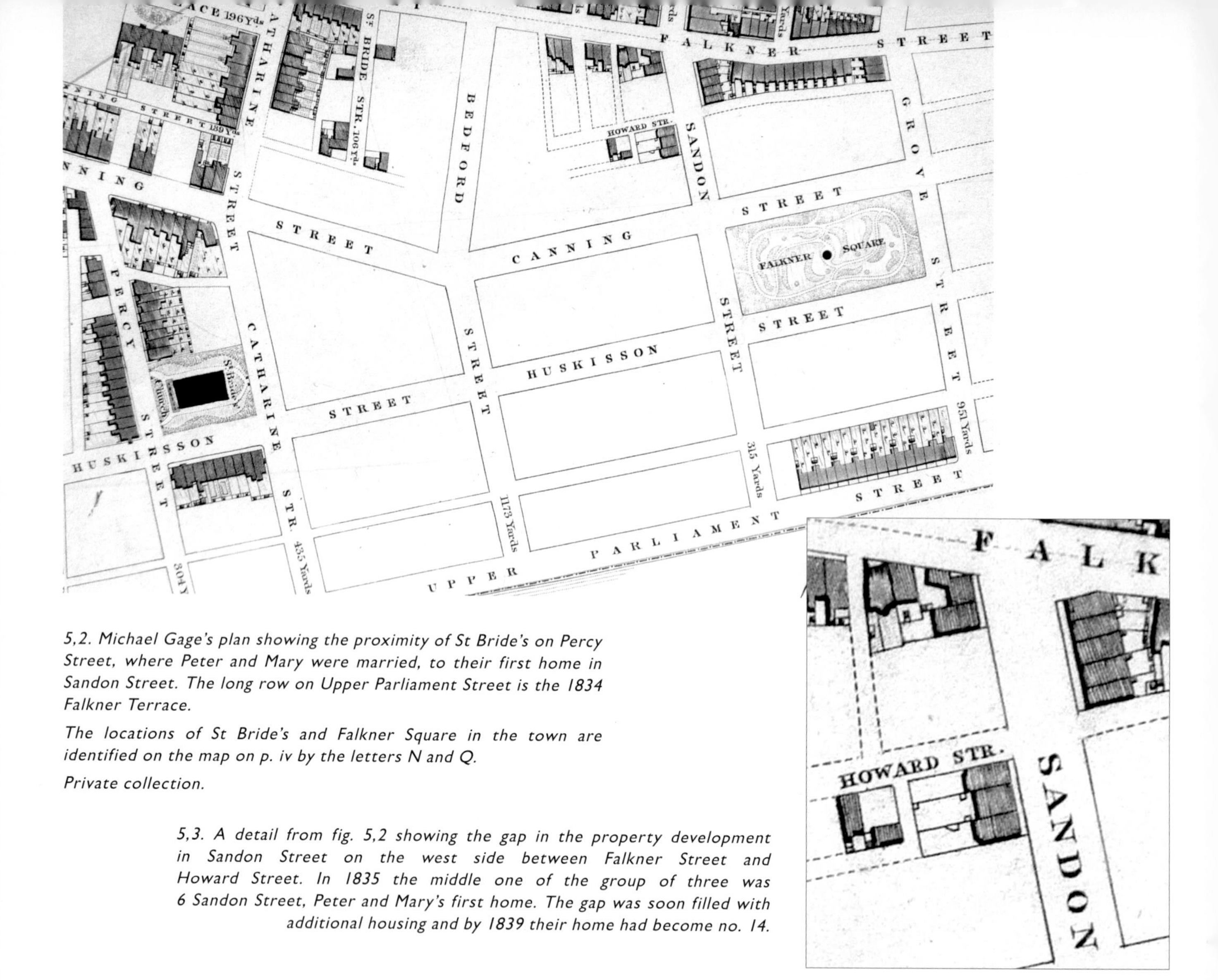

5,2. *Michael Gage's plan showing the proximity of St Bride's on Percy Street, where Peter and Mary were married, to their first home in Sandon Street. The long row on Upper Parliament Street is the 1834 Falkner Terrace.*

The locations of St Bride's and Falkner Square in the town are identified on the map on p. iv by the letters N and Q.

Private collection.

5,3. *A detail from fig. 5,2 showing the gap in the property development in Sandon Street on the west side between Falkner Street and Howard Street. In 1835 the middle one of the group of three was 6 Sandon Street, Peter and Mary's first home. The gap was soon filled with additional housing and by 1839 their home had become no. 14.*

Peter disposed of his leases on all the properties at nos. 12-20 in three stages between 1841 and 1872. Of the original Sandon Street properties, nos. 2-20 on the west side and nos. 1-7 on the east side have all been demolished, but nos. 9-15 (fig. 5,4) which faced Peter's properties and nos. 24-34 (south of Huskisson Street) do survive and give some indication of the common three-storey-plus-basement style in which the whole street was developed, and in which Peter and Mary began their married life. It was a construction pattern with which Peter was familiar from his work at Great George Square (p. 50, fig. 3,16).

Mary Helen Syers (by then 25 years of age) and Peter Ellis (30) were married on 28th April 1836 at St Bride's, a proprietary church in Percy Street which had been consecrated by the Bishop of Chester on 29th December 1830 (figs. 5,5 and 5,6). The church and the street came into existence following the closure of the original church of the same name and in a street of the same name in London in 1828 (further details can be found in the LRO ring-binder under 283 BRI). Both appeared for the first time on maps in 1831, whilst the street index in *Gore's Directory* for 1832 indecisively lists

5,4. *The sun shines through the trees in Sandon Street onto nos. 9-15 after heavy rain in September 2012, viewed from the junction with Back Falkner Street South (shown as Back Canning Street in fig. 6,5 on p. 106).*

5,5. *James Brierley's view of St Bride's in 1831 prior to the arrival of the neighbouring Percy Street terrace.*

Image courtesy of the LRO, ref. Brierley Coll. 2.

the street as both '*Percy Street, Canning Street*' and '*Percy Street, Upper Parliament Street*', since it could be approached from either direction. True to form, James Picton was disappointed with the building:-

> *'The name of the patron saint calls up visions of Wren's beautiful steeple in Fleet Street, with its graceful gradation of forms in the ascending scale. Let no such expectations be cherished, for be it known our St. Bride's, despairing of successful rivalry, does not boast a steeple at all.'* [1]

5,6. *St Bride's in 2012 viewed from the southern of the two Percy Street entrances. James Picton's comments not withstanding, for Joseph Sharples it is 'The best surviving Neoclassical church in the city.'* [2]

5,7. A 1950 photograph from the City Engineer and Surveyor's Improvements Department. See also Joseph Sharples' commentary and modern photograph of Percy Street. [2]

Image courtesy of the LRO, ref. Photographs & Small Prints: Streets and Districts: Percy Street.

Handsome terraces of houses were soon under construction along the street. Some residents had already started to be listed there in *Gore's Directory* for 1834 and the list was essentially complete in time for the following edition which was published late in 1835 (and which contained an extensive advertisement for Michael Gage's *Trigonometrical Plan* with various testimonials including, from Lord Brougham, "*Mr Gage's survey... is the finest thing I ever saw*"). Several years later, proprietors of the church included William Brown, MP and merchant, and William Inman, the steamship owner. [3]

A photograph from the City Engineer and Surveyor's Improvements Department in the mid-20th century entitled '*Greek Revival Houses*' shows the buildings on the odd-numbered (east) side of Percy Street running northwards from the northern of the two pairs of gates of St Bride's (fig. 5,7). Unlike many areas in Liverpool which Peter had known and which subsequently vanished, this scene would still have been familiar to him had he revisited the street today.

Page 57

St Bride's Church

MARRIAGES solemnized in the Parish of Liverpool
in the County of Lancashire in the Year 1836

Peter Ellis of the Parish
Liverpool Architect
and Mary Helen Syers of the Parish
of Walton on the Hill Spinster
were married in this Church by Licence with Consent,
this twenty eighth Day of
April in the Year One Thousand eight hundred and thirty six
By me C. W. ...

This Marriage was solemnized between us { Peter Ellis. Mary Helen Syers
In the Presence of { Thomas Syers. Mary Ann Kelshall
No. 169

The priest who completed the record of solemnisation at Peter and Mary's wedding had sufficiently careless handwriting that several of the details are ambiguous (fig. 5,8). For the person whose job it was to copy the information into an ancestry database over a century and a half later, Peter would appear to have married '*May Helena Lyers*' (whilst in the 1861 census the apparently deaf collector, who also used '*ditto*' for her surname, managed to enter her first names onto his form as '*Martha Ellin*').

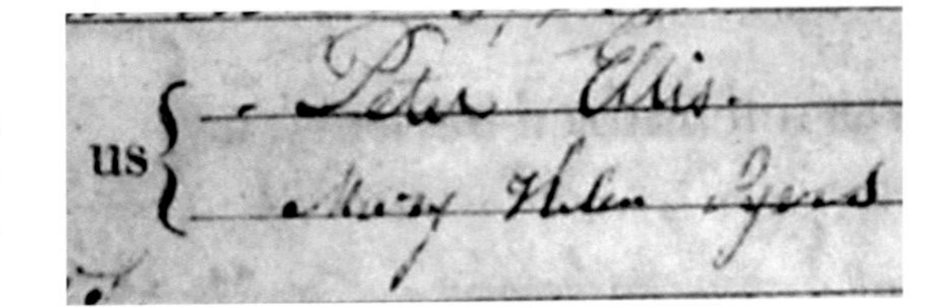

5,8. The certificate of Peter and Mary's marriage at St Bride's, and a detail showing Peter and Mary's signatures. Images courtesy of the LRO, microfilm ref. 283 BRI 3/1.

It may be significant that the marriage took place at St Bride's Church - the parish church for 6 Sandon Street – rather than at Mary's church in Everton (Mary being shown on the marriage certificate simply as '*of the Parish of Walton on the Hill*'). From probate records it is known that Mary's father, William Syers, the appraiser and auctioneer, had died in 1833 (although hopefully he had known Peter well enough to have been able to appraise his suitability as a future son-in-law). Margaret Syers, Mary's mother, appears in the directories for 1834 and 1835 as '*Mrs William Syers*', living at Breck Lane, [4] but she is not listed in the 1837 directory, and it seems possible therefore that Margaret had also died before Mary and Peter had been united.

Following their father's death, 1834 is the first year that two of Mary's brothers are listed: William as an appraiser and auctioneer (inheriting his father's business), and John as a cotton broker, both living at home with their mother. William was married in December 1834 at St Mary's, Everton, whilst John was married in December 1835 at St George's, Everton. Their younger brother, Thomas, had already been listed in the 1829 directory as a tailor and draper, living at home. Although he had moved to Great Homer Street by 1832 (where his first son, Llewellyn, was born), he is shown as having returned to Breck Lane by 1834.

The witnesses to Peter and Mary's marriage were Mary's brother, Thomas, and Mary Ann Kelshall. Mary Syers (the sister of Robert, George and William Syers, see p. 64) had married John Kelshall in 1796, and their daughter, Mary Ann Kelshall, was therefore a cousin of Mary Helen Syers. Both Thomas and Mary Ann will re-appear in a later chapter, and it is a tempting thought that Mary Ann's appearance as a witness might be because she was the person who introduced Peter to Mary Helen Syers.

Three years into Peter and Mary's marriage, and whilst his office was still at Renshaw Street, Peter became aware of the announcement in *The Times* of March 1839 that there was to be a competition for a new concert hall in Liverpool which was to be called St George's Hall. The foundation stone had already been laid in the previous June by William Rathbone V, and Peter became one of the 75 competitors who submitted designs. [5] Following the Committee's announcement in July 1839 that Harvey Lonsdale Elmes had won, Peter prepared a book of his '*Rejected Designs*' (fig. 5,9) for presentation in October of that year to the Hall's subscribers (presumably a selection, for there were over 450 of them) in order that they might have:-

> *'an opportunity of examining my labours more conveniently, and more at leisure, than would be possible from the Designs themselves.'*

The Liverpool Record Office has a copy of that publication with its five drawings and accompanying commentary (the two drawings not reproduced here are the '*Plan of Upper Part of Great Hall*' and the '*Section of Gallery or Corridor*'), and the preface continues with a puzzling sentence:-

> *'I most distinctly disclaim the imputation (which possibly may occur to some) that I am prompted by any feeling of dissatisfaction with the decision of the Committee: for, whatever my private opinion may be of the discretion of their selection, neither I nor any other competitor have any right to complain, the choice having been made, as I am fully persuaded, not only without partiality, but without motive.'*

5,9. The title page of Peter's book.
Image courtesy of the LRO, ref. Hf 942.7213 GEO (Ellis).

REJECTED

DESIGNS

FOR THE INTENDED

ST. GEORGE'S HALL,

LIVERPOOL.

BY P. ELLIS, ARCHITECT.

"Tre cose in ciascuana fabrica deono considerarsi, senza lequali niuno edificio meriterà esser lodato: e queste sono, l'utile ò commodità,—la perpetuità,—e la bellezza."—PALLADIO.

LIVERPOOL:
MITCHELL, HEATON, AND MITCHELL, PRINTERS, DUKE STREET.
1839.

In the same month that Elmes' success at winning the St George's Concert Hall competition was made known, a second competition for an Assize Court was announced, and Elmes went on to win that as well. Elmes' subsequent design for a combined building underwent several revisions, with other architects becoming involved, and he died before seeing the building completed. Neil Sturrock has examined the background to the competitions,[6] and his analysis may throw some light on the reason for Peter's preface comments.

However, in a tone perhaps prompted by the wording of that preface, on 10th January 1840 the *Liverpool Mercury* carried an ambiguously worded '*fancy sketch*' paragraph regarding his plans:-

> '*Mr Ellis's Design For The Intended St. George's Hall. – This gentleman, upon whose design for our intended now suit* [sic] *of public rooms, the choice of the committee did not fall, has, at a great expense, published the ground plan, elevations, and prospective view of the buildings, according to his fancy sketch, and the publication cannot fail to gratify the friends of that gentleman, by proving to them that his claims to their estimation as an artist and architect are of no ordinary kind. As Mr. Ellis is a native of Liverpool, this specimen of his skill will be enhanced in interest.*'

As Adrian Jarvis notes, it was Robert Rawlinson in the 1840s who '*solved the structural problem of the huge brick arch ceiling of St George's Hall which the architect had conceived but could not build.*'[7] In 1933 the Liverpool Central Library put together paperwork concerning St George's Hall, and tucked away within that collection is a letter from William Wordley to Robert Rawlinson in 1863 regarding this brick arched ceiling. The opening and concluding sections read:-

5,10. A view of John Foster junior's 1836 neo-classical façade to Lime Street Station, published by Lacey, Stationer, 100 Bold St as No. 9 in the series 'Liverpool Localities'. Private collection.

> '*I have read the proof you were good enough to send me, and return it with one or two alterations. There seems a good deal of misunderstanding about the real place of merit or demerit due in connection with St George's Hall... As to who was or was not consulted by Mr. Elmes, either as to the construction, or the Architectural design of any part of his work, I am not now required to speak, although I could correct many misstatements, but now will only say that if all claims are to be allowed there would be little credit left for* ~~~~~~~~~'.

At this point William Wordley made an attempt to rub out the name he had written, overwrote it with a wavy line, and instead concluded the sentence with, '*he to whom credit is really due.*'[8] Whether this was also a reference to the original design is uncertain.

Returning to Peter's own design, his summary of the Committee's principal instructions notes their requirement that the design should be '*of the Grecian or Roman character*', whilst later he refers to the approach from Lime Street which involved Foster's 1836 façade for the Station (fig. 5,10).

Opposite right: 5,11. A lithograph from Peter's publication showing the Principal Floor. For his lithographer Peter chose John McGahey, who at that time had an office at 23 Lord Street.

Image courtesy of the LRO, ref. Hf 942.7213 GEO (Ellis).

Peter's description of his design makes fascinating reading. He notes that the '*instructions furnished to the architects by the Committee were very clear and precise*', lists their principal points and then explains how his designs meet the requirements. In the representative samples below, taken from his detailed commentary, Peter speaks to us from all those years ago of what might have been.

One of the Committee's proposals was that:-

> *'A Concert Room must be provided for an audience of five hundred persons; and it is desirable, if possible, that this room should be so arranged as to admit of its being laid open to the Great Hall when required.'*

Peter questioned what had been meant by '*being laid open,*' and wondered whether:-

> *'If by this is meant that the rooms should be so arranged that, the partition dividing them being removed, they should together form a handsome whole, it is, in other words, asking for a moveable partition of perhaps an area of three thousand feet.'* [9]

He judged this to be either impracticable or fraught with the risk of '*utter destruction of the due circulation and equable distribution of Sound,*' together with other issues that included its '*unseemly, unarchitectural appearance.*' Peter addressed the requirement that:-

> *'The Lobbies must be spacious, and the utmost possible facilities given for ingress and egress, and for the convenience of carriages taking up or setting down, for which purpose a Colonnade or other external covered way, to some extent, is considered desirable.'*

Thus for his Ground Plan he wrote that:-

> *'I have devoted the whole of this Floor to what may be called the business of the Concern. I have formed three spacious Public Entrances, on the South; the principal one, in the centre, under a double portico, the advanced inter-columniation of sufficient width and height for a carriage drive. By this arrangement, perfect protection from the weather will be obtained to all alighting from carriages, and convenient also to those who walk. The two side Porticoes are also suitable for either. The porticoes will afford ample protection from the weather; the upper loggie or Terraces not being so high as to allow the rain to beat in.'*

Explanation of this part of the plan continued with mention of a range of rooms including those for the stewards, secretaries and receivers, the house-keeper's apartments, the kitchens and the refectory. He proposed warming the Hall with hot water '*as being efficient, safe and economical*', and noted that in his design:-

> *'No part of the Building is below the surface of the Ground, which would be advantageous in respect of ventilation, light, and drainage, and consequent wholeness and freedom from damp.'*

Those were conditions which the town's court-dwellers could only ever dream of, and Peter perhaps quietly reflected upon this as he brought to mind faint childhood memories of Primrose Hill.

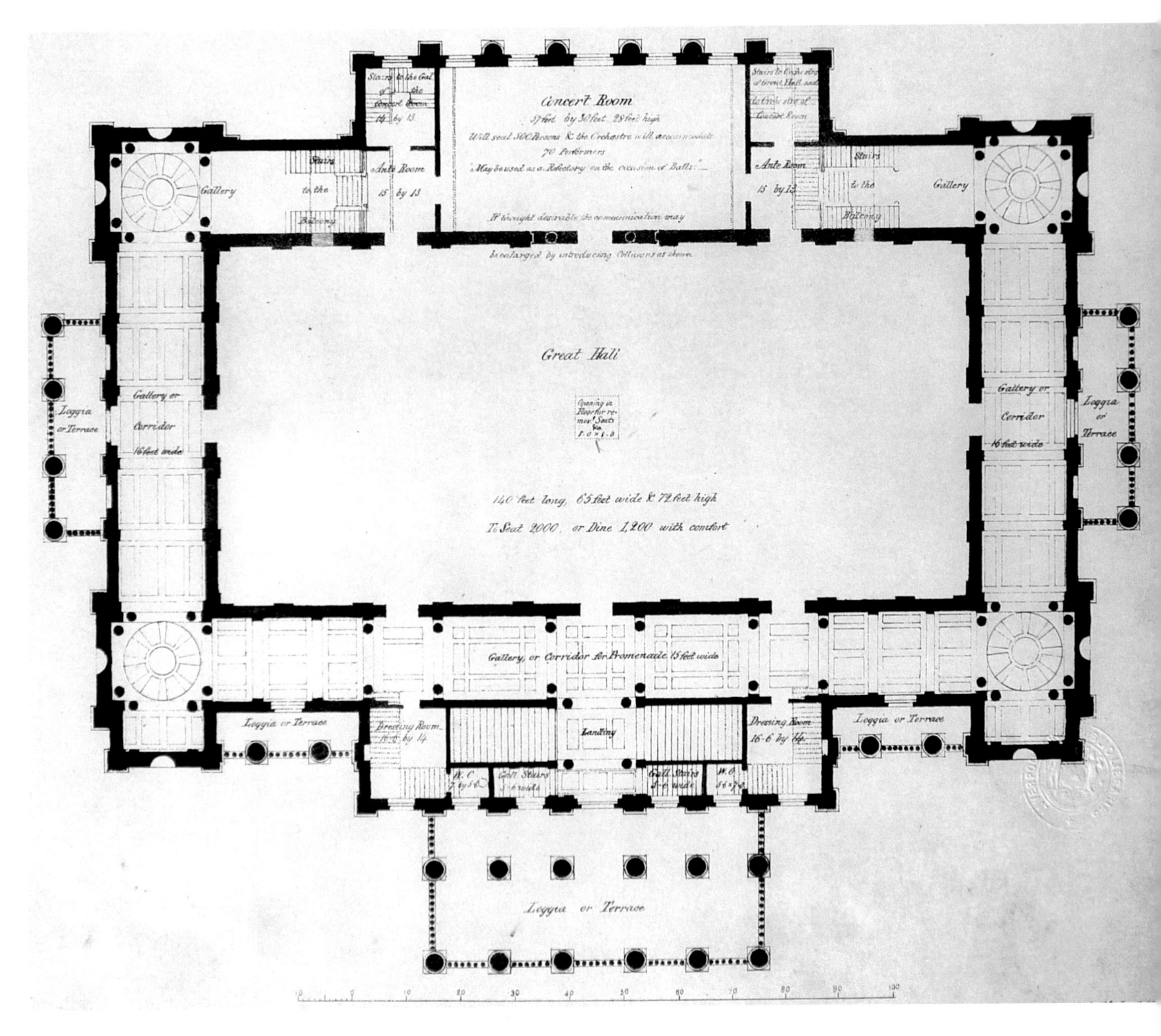

Peter introduced his description of the Principal Floor (fig. 5,11) with the observation that:-

'The Stairs meet at a spacious Landing, leading to an ample Gallery or Corridor. Instead of making this merely a passage of communication, I have formed a Gallery, lighted from above, spacious, lofty, and handsomely decorated; - a suitable communication with the Great Hall, and to which it forms a perfect adjunct as a promenade, &c. This Gallery would also be admirably suited to the purpose of a permanent Museum or Gallery of Art, much wanted, and indeed recently much talked of, in Liverpool... and in a manner greatly surpassing any provincial town in the kingdom...'

Several other issues were covered, and Peter's plan provided for eight entrances to the Great Hall (which measured 140 feet long, 65 feet wide and 72 feet high, surrounded by a handsome balcony) and, over the adjacent Concert Room, space to '*accommodate 570 Musicians, allowing space for a stupendous Organ*' (the instructions having required space for 400 musicians). Peter's design stands in contrast with Joseph Sharples' description of the entrance to Elmes' Hall (sentiments which echo those of James Picton, *Memorials*, vol. II, p. 184):

> '*The main entrance, central behind the E portico, is the least satisfactory part of Elmes's plan. Instead of a spacious and dignified vestibule, it leads into a corridor running N-S to the courts at each end. A matching corridor runs along the W side. Crossing the corridor and entering the Concert Hall brings further disappointment, because the entrance is on the short rather than the long axis.*'[10]

The section through the building (fig. 5,12) was drawn from the point of view of '*the spectator supposed to be on the level of the principal floor*', whilst the south east perspective (fig. 5,13) showed '*the South or Principal Front. Under the advanced columns is the Drive – affording a perfect shelter.*' Although the St George's Hall which was eventually built ended up facing east towards Lime Street Station, the Committee had originally requested that '*the principal front should be to the south*', and that is therefore what Peter's design addressed. In his preface Peter wrote that:-

> '*In respect of the cost, I have, as I believe, kept within the limits named, of which my calculations are to me satisfactory; but of course much of this would depend on the manner in which the Plans might be carried into effect.*

The buildings would occupy less space than the land granted, especially in length, which would greatly improve the East and West approaches, – that at Lime Street being rather narrow. The Portico extends beyond the allotment, which is frequently done, and in this case, the space being so very great, would not be attended with the most remote shadow of inconvenience.'

Peter also kept within the requirement that '*the cost of the building is not to exceed £30,000*', and it is interesting that the final cost of the Hall designed by Elmes, albeit incorporating the later Assize Court, was approximately £300,000.

It is perhaps an indication of how proud Peter was of his work that, even after his submission was unsuccessful, he was prepared to pay for publication of his designs and for the publication to be made available to a number of subscribers.

Peter's life having begun in a home on Shaw's Brow, a mere hundred yards from the site of the Hall, working on his designs must have been immensely exciting and perhaps quite emotional. On the left in fig. 5,13 (and more obvious on the much larger original) Peter had faintly sketched the windmill on Shaw's Brow.

By then 34 years old, and with Mary smiling with approval and offering ideas and encouragement at each stage, the failure to secure the winning entry must have been hugely disappointing for them both. Had he won it, however, Peter's career would almost certainly have developed along very different lines.

Losing that competition was perhaps the price he was called upon to pay in order that he would design more modest buildings for the town's community – a school, a dispensary, a chapel – as well as the office buildings for which he is now so widely known.

Opposite left: 5,12. A section through the middle of the building. Image courtesy of the LRO.

5,13. The perspective from the south east. Image courtesy of the LRO.

Peter's *Rejected Designs* bears the date 1st October 1839, and the book must have been one of the very last compositions that he had the opportunity to show his father, for the Births, Marriages and Deaths column of the *Liverpool Mercury* for Friday 11th October 1839 recorded in the briefest of terms:-

> *'On Sunday last, at his residence, Gloucester-place, Low-hill, aged 74, Mr. Peter Ellis.'* [11]

The name of Peter Ellis senior, for several years *gentleman*, thus disappeared from the directories, and 1841 was the only year in which Peter's mother, Ann Ellis, still living at Gloucester Place, Low Hill, received a listing there in her own right. After an absence from the 1843 directory, Ann reappeared in 1845 at Prescot Street where she was living close to a possible relative, Elizabeth Ellis (living at Moira Street, running off Prescot Street), and where she is recorded as dying in 1846 in similarly brief terms (*Mercury*, 20th February 1846):-

> *'Feb. 14, at her residence, Prescot-street, aged 73, Ann, relict of the late Mr. Peter Ellis.'*

Four years into his marriage and perhaps prompted by his father's death the previous year, the loss of his sister and three of his brothers at early ages, and the recent death of one of Mary's brothers (of which more in a later chapter), Peter wrote his will and signed it on 3rd November 1840. He bequeathed:-

> *'the whole of my property of whatsoever kind unto John A. Syers of Liverpool Cotton Broker and John Ellis of Liverpool Veterinary Surgeon upon trust'*

Mary's and Peter's brothers were required to see to Mary's future wishes and needs if he was to die before her. The residue of his estate was to go '*to my Brothers Robert and John in equal shares or to their children.*'

Although he was destined to outlive both John Aspinall Syers and John Ellis, Peter never revised this will. The witnesses to Peter's signature were Cornelius Sherlock and Edward Davies. Cornelius (1823-1888) had grown up a few doors away from Peter in Gloucester Place and by the age of 17 was already articled to him, and it seems likely that Edward also began his career with Peter. In its obituary of Cornelius Sherlock the *Liverpool Citizen* for 28th January 1888 (LRO microfilm) recorded that:-

> *'On entering business life Mr. C. Sherlock was articled to Mr. Peter Ellis, many years one of the foremost architects and valuers in this city, whose death took place only a comparatively short time ago,'* and went on to mention (regarding the valuing of land and property) that *'he was associated sometimes as colleague, at others as opponent, with the leading local experts, many of whom have predeceased him. Amongst the latter may be called to mind his first instructor, Mr. Peter Ellis...'*

When they witnessed Peter's will, both Cornelius and Edward were waiting to complete their training, but in the 1851 directory they are shown as sharing an architects' office together in King Street. [12] Other valuable information would have been lost had Peter produced a later version and disposed of the original, and these aspects will be covered in later chapters along with parts of Mary's own will.

And so in the 1840s, perhaps sharing with his brothers in a small inheritance from his father, and with possible additional financial assistance as a result of his mother's move to a smaller home, Peter took the first steps in his plan to transfer his office a few hundred yards from Renshaw Street to Clayton Square, and to move himself and Mary an even shorter distance to a new home.

5,15. Looking south west across the junction of Canning Street and Sandon Street in August 2011.

On 1st April 1843 Peter obtained a Corporation lease on a piece of land on the corner of Canning Street and Falkner Square (fig. 5,14), proceeded to build what became 78 Canning Street, and rented it out. The Corporation register shows that in 1865 the lease was re-granted to Maxwell Hyslop. He had already been renting the property for over a decade, and the directory for that year confirms that the property extended from Falkner Square to Back Sandon Street (the un-named '*Back Street of 7 yards in width*' in Peter's lease). Maxwell Hyslop's new lease also shows that after the '*Usual Covenants*' an additional requirement was added:-

> '*To the payment of One Guinea p. Ann. for the privilege of using the Garden in the Square*'

because, although his main windows looked onto the Square, his front door was in Canning Street. The house remained 78 Canning Street until the 1960s but was subsequently divided in two and is now nos. 78 and 80. In the view looking south west at the junction of Canning Street and Sandon Street (fig. 5,15), the two-storey building in the foreground is now 80 Canning Street which extends to the right and has its front door there. The additional front door for what is now no. 78 is further to its right. The three-storey building with the English Heritage blue plaque above the entrance is 40 Falkner Square, with the entrance to 39 Falkner Square further to the left.

With the lease for the land upon which he built 78 Canning Street having been secured in 1843, the following year Peter obtained a lease on the neighbouring piece of land to the south and commenced building what was to become the home in which he and Mary would reside for the rest of their lives together.

5,14. Part of the lease granted by the Corporation to 'Peter Ellis of Liverpool Architect' on 1st April 1843 and entered on the register on 16th September of that year for land upon which he built 78 Canning Street.

Image courtesy of the LRO, ref. 352 CLE/CON 3/9.

Peter Ellis of Liverpool Architect From 1st April 1843	All that piece of Land situate on the West side of Falkner Square and South side of Canning Street Bounded on the West side by a Back Street of 7 yards in width and on the South side by Land leased to the executors of Edward Falkner Esquire deceased containing in front to Falkner Square (inclusive of an Area of 5 feet 8 inches in width to the front of Canning Street) 40 feet 3 inches and at the back or West side thereof (inclusive of the said Area) 40 feet 2 inches and running in depth (inclusive of an Area of 22 feet 5 inches in width to the front of Falkner Square) on the North side thereof 136 feet 2 inches and on the South side thereof 136 feet 5 inches XC

References and Notes to Chapter 5

1 J A Picton, *Memorials of Liverpool*, G G Walmsley (Liverpool), 2nd edn., 1875, vol. II, p. 261.

2 Joseph Sharples, *Liverpool. Pevsner Architectural Guides*, Yale University Press, 2004, p. 240.

3 Miscellaneous Papers from St Bride's Church, LRO ref. 283 BRI 16/2.

4 Many of Liverpool's roads began life as lanes. Breck Lane became Breck Road, Everton Lane became Everton Road, while Netherfield Lane became Netherfield Road. Not infrequently names were completely changed at a later date: Mill Lane on Horwood's map of 1803 had already become Brunswick Road by 1835 on Gage's map, whilst Rake Lane on Sherwood's map of 1829 later became West Derby Road.

5 The *Liverpool Post and Mercury*, Sept. 13th 1927, quoting from a book by Robert Rawlinson, reported that 75 sets of plans had been submitted for the St George's Hall design and 86 sets of plans for the subsequent Assize Courts design. It is not known whether Peter contributed plans to the second competition.

6 Neil S Sturrock, in a chapter from an electronic book abstracted at:
www.victorianweb.org/art/architecture/elmes/ns2.html

Dr Sturrock has indicated by e-mail that he is revising some of the now suspect '*verbal tradition*' that he drew upon for his chapter. See the 2012 *Journal of the Liverpool History Society*, p. 45, for Neil Sturrock's article on the ventilation system for St George's Hall which made it the world's first air-conditioned building. The article also includes Elmes' perspective of the '*Forum*' for which one face was to be Foster's Lime Street Station façade (fig. 5,10).

7 Adrian Jarvis, *The Liverpool Dock Engineers*, Alan Sutton, 1996, p. 97.

8 Liverpool Library, *St George's Hall, Liverpool. Collection of illustrations, photographs, newspaper cuttings, &c*, 1933. LRO reference 942.7213 GEO. This also contains the cutting from the *Liverpool Post and Mercury* report cited in ref. 5 above. One of the current St George's Hall display posters describes Rawlinson's roof design. William Henry Wordley is mentioned in a *Mercury* report on 7th April 1854 of the Town Council Proceedings concerning '*a recommendation that the salary of Mr W. H. Wordley, architectural draughtsman at St. George's-hall, be increased from £240 to £280 per annum.*' In later years he was a partner in the firm of Gee and Wordley.

9 At first sight the omission of '*square*' (as in '*an area of three thousand feet*') seems to be a mistake. Several other 19th century sources indicate however that this was common practice.

10 Joseph Sharples, *op. cit.*, p. 54. However, both commentaries are otherwise enthusiastic about Elmes' building that continues to be regarded as a masterpiece of which Liverpool is rightly proud.

11 Dying in 1839 at the age of 74, Peter Ellis senior was therefore born about 1765, a year before John Gore's very first Liverpool directory. His baptism record has not been located in Lancashire or Welsh church records, and there is only one ancestry record for marriages of potential Ellis fathers backwards from 1765 that might rival George Ellis as Peter's possible father.

Although no Ellis names are listed in the four directories between 1866 and 1872 (the first being Edward Ellis, a grocer, in Peter Street in 1874), the *Lancashire Online Parish Clerk Project* shows that a William Ellis (grocer of Neston) married Sarah Morris (spinster of Liverpool) at St George's, Derby Square, in 1765. One of Peter and Ann's sons was called William.

In 1884, the year in which Peter Ellis the architect died, the directory listed over 300 Ellis names.

12 Cornelius Sherlock was born on 3rd January 1823 and baptised '*in the Church of St George Everton in the Parish of Walton on the Hill*', where his baptism certificate (LRO microfilm ref. 283 GEV 2/1) shows that the family was living in Gloucester Place. Indeed, the directories show that his father, Thomas Sherlock, clerk in customs, was one of the earliest arrivals, being listed there from 1805 when it was still known by its original name of Gloucester Row.

In 1813 his home first received a number – 3 Gloucester Place – which enables its position to be identified on fig. 2,26 (chapter 2) as the house with the carriageway entrance above the '*L*' of '*Gloucester*', a few doors from what had been the Ellis home. By the time that Cornelius was 22 and old enough to have his own directory entry in 1845 he was listed as still at the family home.

Edward Davies was first listed as an architect in the 1849 directory, living at 17 Phythian Street where a William Ellis is also listed (although who this particular William Ellis was has not been determined). Details of the earlier life of Edward Davies have not been established and, although the directory list for '*Davies*' was extensive, a possible father, Charles Davies, a wholesale bookseller and stationer, is listed in the 1839 directory at 2 Erskine Street, a few hundred yards from Gloucester Place.

Elevation Canning Str^t

Chapter 6

Falkner Square and Clayton Square

When Peter and Mary first planned to move the few yards from 14 Sandon Street to Falkner Square in the early 1840s, although the Square had been laid out for several years, there was scarcely a single property built around it. Over a century and a half later a sign stands in the now mature garden (fig. 6,1) and part of the commentary reads:-

'Falkner Square was named after Edward Falkner of Fairfield... In 1797 England was rumoured to be under threat of invasion by the French. Falkner reacted quickly. It is said that within 24 hours he mustered a fighting force of 1,000 men ready to repel the threatened invasion. When news reached the shores of France, the French leaders were amazed that such a force could be assembled in so short a time, and the threat was withdrawn. In later years Falkner and his family decided to invest in land and property. Land was purchased outside the city centre and around 1830 Falkner Square was completed. Although the houses were of a handsome design many stood empty for years. The Square was located too far out of town and up a considerable incline when the mode of transport was horse and carriage. It soon became known as "Falkner's Folly".'

6,1. The garden in Falkner Square in Spring 2012 looking towards 40 Falkner Square and adjoining properties.

James Stonehouse attributes the nickname *Falkner's Folly* to the neighbouring Falkner Terrace on Upper Parliament Street (chapter 5, fig. 5,2), dating from 1834 and which stood for a long time in a skeleton state because of its similar distance from the town centre. [1]

A copy of a Charles Eyes' map of 1796 (fig. 6,2) shows Crabtree Lane, the fields of a *'Mr Faulkner'*,[2] and the stone quarry where the Anglican cathedral now stands. Disappearing off to the left at the foot of Crabtree Lane is an early stage in the development of Hope Street prior to its extension to the right across the top of the quarry. To the right of Crabtree Lane are also shown the several fields of *'Mr Blackburn'*, upon which Blackburne House was built. The line at the right hand edge of the map marks what would eventually become the route of Upper Parliament Street, and indicates the boundary with Toxteth Park.

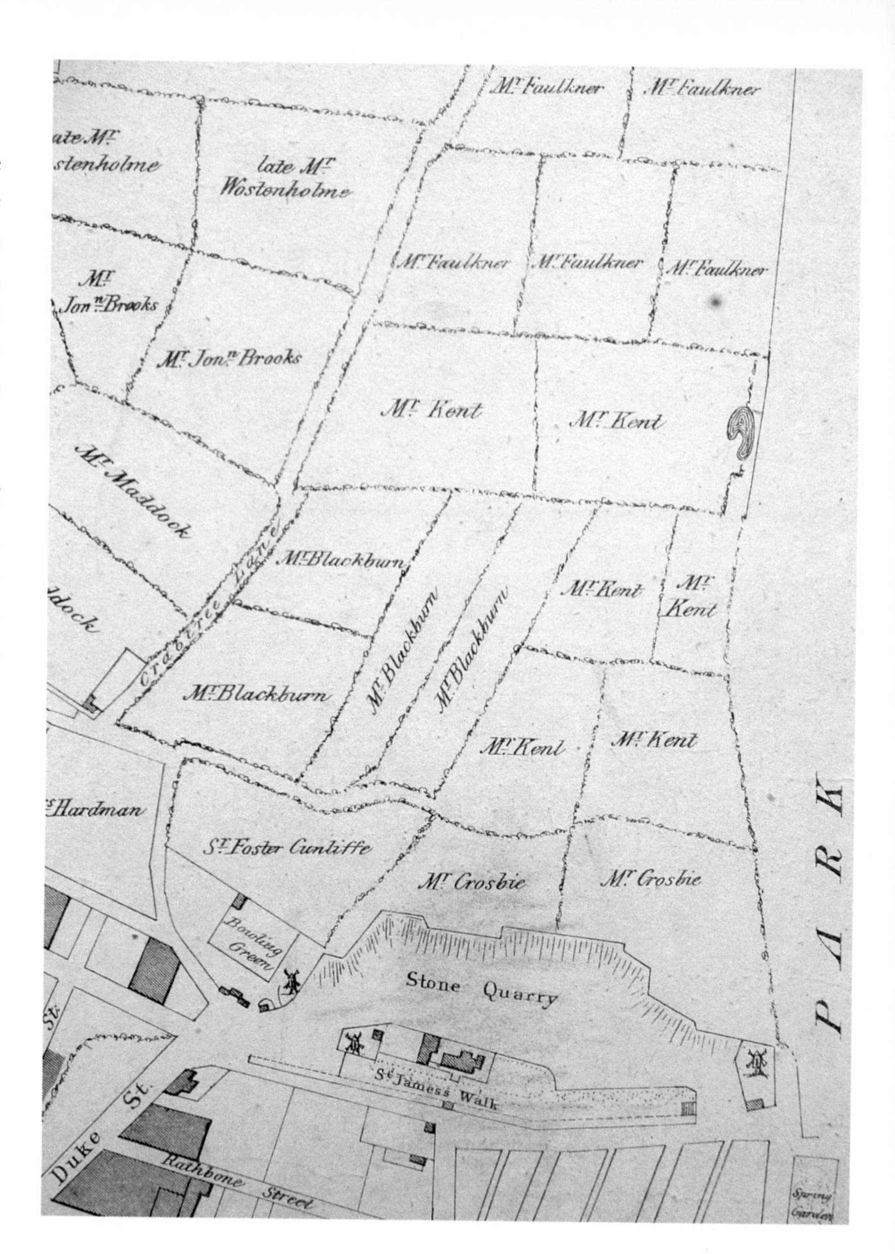

6,2. A section from a copy of Charles Eyes' map of 1796, oriented to the east (as in the original). Image courtesy of the Athenaeum.

A map published in 1831 for *The Stranger in Liverpool* (fig. 6,3) shows how the streets were subsequently laid out across the southern part of the Mosslake Fields, with Chatham Street running from Abercromby Square across Crabtree Lane, Canning Street and Huskisson Street to Upper Parliament Street. Michael Gage's plan (chapter 5, fig. 5,2) shows that by late 1835 Crabtree Lane had become Falkner Street and the section of Chatham Street between Falkner Street and Upper Parliament Street had been renamed Sandon Street.

Having obtained a lease on land in 1843 upon which he built 78 Canning Street (chapter 5), in the following year Peter secured another lease on land adjoining it (fig. 6,4) and built the home to which he and Mary subsequently moved.

Opposite right: 6,3. A detail from Thomas Kaye's map for the 1831 edition of the 'Stranger in Liverpool', reoriented to the north. Image courtesy of the LRO, ref. Binns Collection, vol. 9, Hf 942.7204.

Peter Ellis
of Liverpool
Architect

From 2d November 1844

All that piece of Land situate on the West side of Sandon Street bounded on the West side by a back Street of 7 yards in width on the North by Premises leased to the Lessee and on the South by Premises leased to The Reverend John Houghton containing in front to Sandon Street 23 feet 8 inches and at the back or West side 26 feet 9 inches and running in depth backwards on the North and South sides severally (inclusive of an area of 22 feet 3 inches in width to the front of Sandon Street) 135 feet 3 inches

6,4. *Part of the lease granted by the Corporation to 'Peter Ellis of Liverpool Architect' on 2nd November 1844 and entered on the register on 2nd January 1845 for the land upon which he built 40 Falkner Square.*

Image courtesy of the LRO, ref. 352 CLE CON 3/9.

A description of the house appeared in the *Liverpool Mercury* (14th July 1885) following Peter's death in 1884 when it was advertised for sale as the first of several lots:-

> *'The house was designed by the late Mr. Peter Ellis, of Liverpool, architect and surveyor, for his own private residence, and was occupied by him until his death in October last. The house is substantially built and highly finished, and contains on the basement a kitchen, larder, cellars, washhouse, &c.; on the ground floor, two entertaining rooms, housekeeper's room, kitchen, scullery, &c.; on the first floor, a library, two bedrooms, and a dressing room, &c.; and on the second floor, two bedrooms and two dressing rooms. The tenure is leasehold under the Corporation of Liverpool for a term of 75 years from 2nd November, 1844, at a peppercorn rent.'*

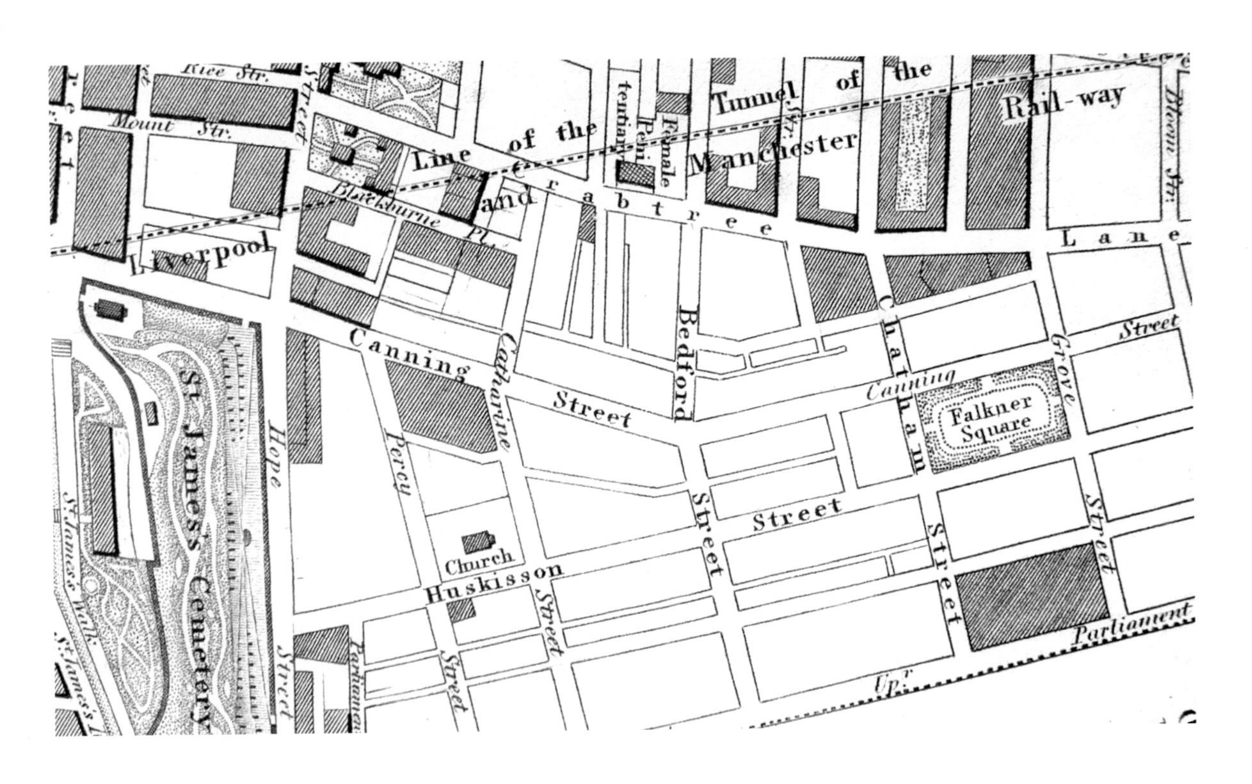

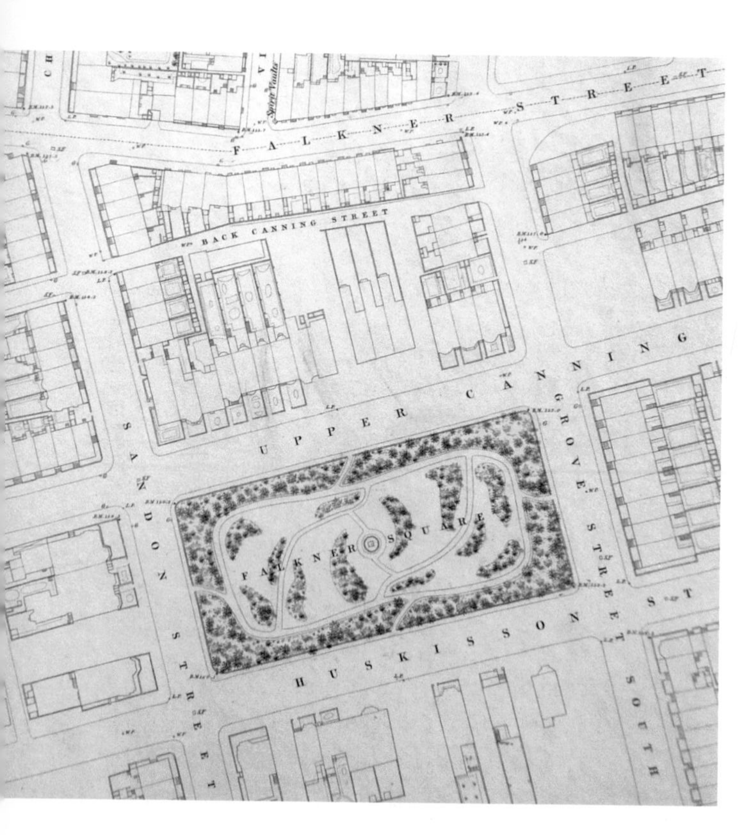

6,5. A detail from the left hand edge of sheet 36 of the 1848 O.S. map showing two completed terraces on the north west side of Sandon Street, each of five properties, respectively nos. 2-10 and 12-20 (nos. 18 and 20 being those built by Peter), and gaps in the housing development around Falkner Square.

Image courtesy of the Athenaeum.

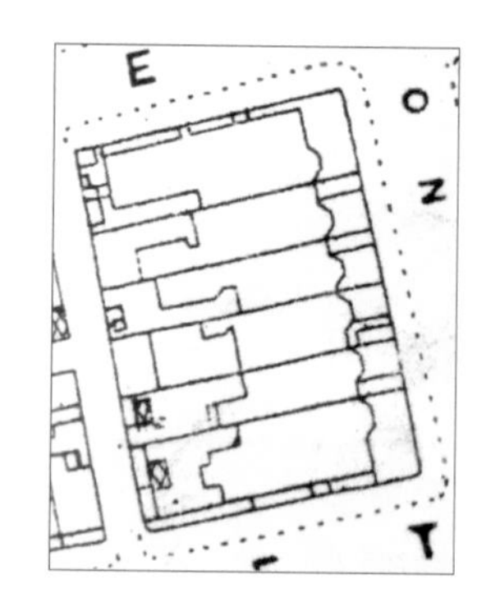

6,6. A detail from the 1890 O.S. map showing the completed properties along the west side of Falkner Square. The street to the rear of the properties is Back Sandon Street (the un-named 'back street of 7 yards in width' in Peter's 1843 and 1844 leases).

Image courtesy of the LRO.

The Corporation register shows that following Mary's death in 1888 the property was re-granted in June 1889 to Emma Sumners (who, along with Henry Sumners, will be mentioned again in a future chapter). Although the alphabetical section of the 1845 directory indicates that there were a few early arrivals to the Square that year (including the splendidly symmetrical Algernon Frederick Jones, gentleman, and Frederick Algernon Jones, merchant), the first directory to have a numerical section for the Square was not until 1847, and the O.S. map for 1848 shows it still in an incomplete state (fig. 6,5).

When the Corporation leases for Falkner Square were made available, it had been decided that the properties with front doors directly onto the Square would be given Falkner Square numbers rather than street numbers, and that the numbering would proceed clockwise from the western end of Upper Canning Street, down Grove Street, along Huskisson Street, and back up Sandon Street. 78 Canning Street is shown to the left of the '*D*' in fig. 6,5 and it was the adjacent plot of land to the south upon which Peter built their home. It was thus allocated the very last number in the Falkner Square sequence. However, quite how many properties the various developers were allowed to build appears not to have been settled at an early stage, and their house did not become unambiguously no. 40 until 1853. [3]

A detail from the 1890 O.S. map (fig. 6,6) shows the six properties that were eventually built on the west of the Square namely, from south to north, 53 Huskisson Street, nos. 37-40 Falkner Square and 78 Canning Street (today nos. 78 & 80 Canning Street). It confirms the accidental absence of a dividing line on the 1848 O.S. map between the houses that eventually were nos. 39 & 40 Falkner Square.

6,7. 40 Falkner Square viewed from the garden in April 2012, with its front door and English Heritage blue plaque central to the photograph, and the ground and first floor bay windows to their left. The two-storey building to its right has its front door on Canning Street.

The main bedroom of Peter and Mary's home looked out upon the Falkner Square garden (fig. 6,7) and they would have had pleasure watching it developing and maturing. The entrance to the garden (fig. 6,8) is almost opposite no. 40. In his guided tour around the area surrounding Falkner Square, James Picton wrote that:-

'Ascending Canning Street, we enter the best-built and most respectable quarter of what may be called intramural Liverpool. The district between Falkner Street and Parliament Street was the last portion of Mosslake Fields laid out for building, and was completed between 1835 and 1855, with spacious avenues and high-class houses. Nearly the whole of the land belongs to the corporate estate, and is let on building leases for seventy five years.' [4]

James Picton was well known for his criticism of the work of other architects and was characteristically unimpressed by the design of the buildings in Falkner Square:-

'Of course, in a region so recently peopled there can be nothing of interest derived from antiquity. Everything is comparatively raw and fresh. There is none of that "distance" which "lends enchantment to the view"... The houses are commodious, though not distinguished by any special architectural taste. For the most part they are only two storeys in height, which imparts to the general aspect a somewhat undignified effect.' [5]

6,8. The gate into the Falkner Square garden in August 2011, looking in the opposite direction to fig. 6,1.

Writing in 1921, Charles Reilly was somewhat more enthusiastic. In a chapter entitled *A Liverpool Bloomsbury* he commented that:-

> *'Falkner Square is a strong contrast to Abercromby Square. It is much gayer and brighter, the houses are smaller and less regular. You can even imagine an actress living there without loss of self-respect. Indeed, I have known one. Some of the houses have trellis verandas, and most being in stone or plaster are painted light colours. At the corner of Sandon Street is a very beautiful house.'* [6]

A decade after Charles Reilly's comments, Michael O'Mahony recalled that:-

> *'When the frozen flashes in Crown Street were to skaters what Sefton Meadows is today, when Canning Street was a rope-walk, Sandon Terrace a bowling green, and when because of its April fragrance an old path winding out from it towards the country was called Crabtree Lane, there was no mention of Falkner Square... Falkner Square with its enclosed central garden and shaded walks might be regarded as the last of the squares and the first of the parks, and a park it really was when its gates were first opened... 'More like London than any other part of Liverpool' is not an infrequent remark about Falkner Square, but while it has a resemblance to certain quiet areas to be found in Hampstead or Regents Park, nowhere else in Liverpool is there such definite evidence of a feature of the social life which prevailed at the time it was erected... It was the age of the horse. Every merchant rode to business; consequently with the houses in the square were built adjoining stables, and if houses of its kind were provided with wine-cellars and not with bathrooms, it was at the time not considered an inequality.'* [7]

Peter's horse would surely have been well chosen for him by his younger brother John, and over the years it would also have been kept well shod and cared for at John's veterinary practice and shoeing forge in Upper Pitt Street, and subsequently by John's eldest son. Peter died two years before the first motor car (the '*Benz Patent-Motorwagen*') was unveiled to the public, and horse-drawn trams were not converted to electricity in Liverpool until 1898.

The lease registers showing that Peter had secured land upon which he built nos. 18 and 20 Sandon Street, 78 Canning Street and 40 Falkner Square, suggest that he perhaps consciously repeated his father's early preference for living '*on site*' as a new development first began to take shape. Joseph Sharples, outlining the development of the Square, mentions that:-

> *'Drawings for No. 29 are signed by William Culshaw, 1845. Was he responsible for the whole S elevation and therefore probably those on the N and W too, or did his drawings conform to an overall elevation by another?'* [8]

The 24th October 1884 *Daily Post* account of Peter's funeral noted that he was '*frequently associated with the late Mr. William Culshaw*', and so it seems possible that Peter and William were also associated in some way with the design and construction of other Falkner Square houses, although Joseph Sharples has perhaps expressed caution. [9]

The census records indicate that Peter and Mary routinely had servants living with them in their homes at both Sandon Street and Falkner Square. In 1841 at Sandon Street they employed Mary McLean (25) and Susannah Parks (15) (roles unspecified).

Having moved to Falkner Square by 1847, they are shown in the 1851 census as employing Jane Roberts (26), a domestic cook.

In 1861 Alice McGinnis (34) was a waitress, Louisa Howell (28) was a cook and Margaret Oakley (24) was a housemaid.

In 1871 Jane Unsworth (31), Catharine Copeland (40) and Ann Jane Bailey (25) were listed as servants, whilst in 1881 Jane Unsworth (41, born in Widnes) was still there, along with Grace Johnston (41, born in Workington, Cumbria) and Caroline Clarke (23, born in London) as other servants.

In 1888, for her faithful service, Jane Unsworth would find herself mentioned as a beneficiary in the will of Mary Helen Ellis.

Turning now from Falkner Square to Peter's place of business, in the 1845 directory he can be seen to be in the process of moving his office from 45 Renshaw Street (as listed in the alphabetical section of the directory) to 3 Clayton Square (as listed in the architects & surveyors section).

James Picton commented that Clayton Square (taking its name from the Clayton family) was laid out between 1745 and 1750, and that by 1785:-

> *'the whole square had been completed with commodious well-built houses. Originally there was no outlet on the north-east side; the locality was therefore quiet and retired; the pavement was grass-grown; and the whole had an aspect of dull respectability.'* [10]

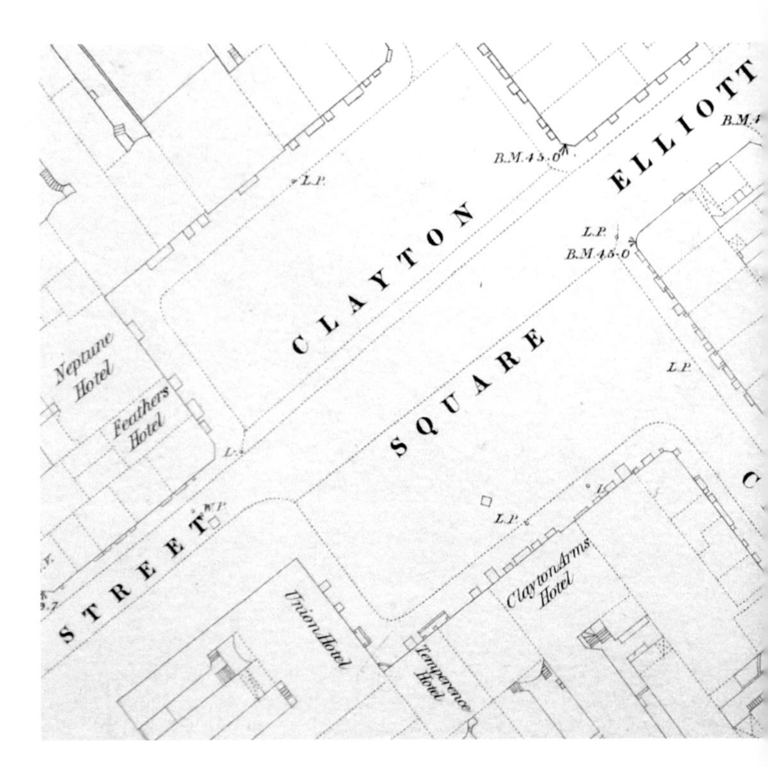

6,9. A detail from the 1848 O.S. map. Peter's office was next door clockwise to the Neptune Hotel. In 1847 James Picton took out a lease on the property between the Clayton Arms Hotel at no. 18 and the Temperance Hotel at no. 20 and converted it into his office.

The location of this area within the town is identified on the map on p. iv by the letter R.

Image courtesy of the Athenaeum.

The O.S. map for 1848 (fig. 6,9) shows the variety of hotels that had arrived in the Square since those early days of '*dull respectability*', and Peter's office at no. 3 was next door (clockwise) to the Neptune. Peter seems to have promoted Clayton Square as a haven for architects. In 1845 and 1847 one of the growing number of those appearing in the directories with the name Ellis – yet another Mary Ellis, although not necessarily a relation – is shown as running a commercial boarding house at 19 Clayton Square.

By 1848, *McCorquodale's Directory* for that year (fig. 6,10) shows that the boarding house had become the site for the office of James Picton – possibly the only occasion in his career that he took a lease on an ex-Ellis building! [11]

William Sherwood had also arrived at no. 5 and John Spencer at no. 7, and by the 1850s the directories show that they were joined or replaced by other architects including Thomas Shelmerdine, Christopher Ellison, William Joynson, Thomas Leyland and William Lloyd.

John Tiernan, in his account of Thomas Shelmerdine junior, notes that his father was:-

> *'an estate agent and valuer and Controller of the Leigh estate in Cheshire and, after moving to Liverpool, was advisor to the Liverpool estates of Lord Salisbury and those of the Watts of Speke Hall.'* [12]

Thomas Shelmerdine senior (ca. 1820-1895) was married at St Bride's Church in 1843 (LRO ref. 283 BRI 3/3) where Peter and Mary had been married, whilst *Gore's Directory* lists him as having joined Peter at 3 Clayton Square in 1845. However, for several years his name then disappeared from the directories, and John Tiernan's observation that Thomas Shelmerdine junior (1845-1921) was born in Manchester provides the explanation.

By the time the Shelmerdine family returned to Liverpool, Peter was sharing the premises at 3 Clayton Square with the son of Peter Robinson McQuie. Before Thomas Shelmerdine senior went to Manchester he evidently had taken a liking to the Square for, upon his return, the 1853 directory lists him as entering the office of William Sherwood at no. 5 where he remained for the rest of his life.

CLAYTON SQUARE,
Parker street to Elliott street.
1 *Feathers hotel*
— Henderson, John, hotel keeper
2 *Neptune hotel*
— Wilde, Frances, hotel keeper
3 Ellis, Peter, architect
— Wilford, Edward, attorney
— Morecroft, Thos. & Son, attorneys
— Bent, Edward Stanley, attorney
— Tapson, John, collector
— Yates, Edward, estate agent
4 Hughes, Chas. comercl. boarding hs
5 Whitley, George, attorney
— Sherwood, Wm. Staycey, architect
— Eaton, William, attorney
6 Yates, John, trimming establishmt
7 Cleaver, W. sup. of W. Derby Union
— Owen, William, solicitor
— Spencer, John, jun. architect
— Chapell, J. B. and Co. wine merchts
— Shaw, Richard and Co. printers
7A Bretherton, Francis, tailor
8 Thompson, Joseph, writing master
9 Byford, Ambrose, auctioneer
10, 11 Brooks, John and W. grocers
12 Cuthbert, James, seed merchant
13 Oldham, Charles, appraiser
14 Joseph and Creighton, impts. cigars
15 Quayle, John, tailor
16 Phipps, John Alex. paper hanger
17 Feeney, Joseph, hotel keeper
Clayton Chambers
— Mossop, Joseph, estate agent
19 Picton, James A. architect
White, John, house agent
20 Brown, William, temperance hotel
21 *Union hotel*
— Martin, John, hotel keeper

6,10. The Clayton Square listing in the numerical section of McCorquodale's 1848 directory showing the arrival of several other architects. Image courtesy of Sefton Local History Unit.

His obituary in the *Liverpool Mercury*, 28th September 1895, mentions that:-

> *'Among his contemporaries, and often associated with him in the giving of evidence as to the value of properties were the late Sir James Picton, Mr. Lewis Hornblower, Mr. Peter Ellis,... Mr Sumner* [sic]*,... Mr Culshaw,... and others.'*

Thomas Shelmerdine junior went on to become surveyor to the Corporation and, upon the death of James Picton in 1889, to embark upon an ambitious programme to build branch lending libraries. Father and son were involved in the purchase of much of the important land along the Mersey shore for the Mersey Docks and Harbour Board.

Just after Peter had arrived in Clayton Square he placed an advertisement in the *Liverpool Mercury* on 18th April 1845 regarding the sale of a '*compact residence*' near Cabbage Hall. It is the earliest that has been traced for Peter's involvement in property sales, a feature which continued throughout his life as an integral part of his office work alongside valuations. A decade later, in the edition of the *Mercury* for 29th August 1856, Peter advertised his brother's property which had been constructed following Robert's grant of a Corporation lease in 1824 (chapter 2, p. 29) and subsequently had been let out for rent:-

> *'To be sold, a large Yard and Workshops, together with Two Dwelling Houses, situate at 48, Finch-street. The property has a frontage to two streets, and is well calculated to suit any person requiring roomy premises.– Apply to Mr. Ellis, architect, Clayton-square.'*

James Picton records that in 1852 a general election took place. The Liberal candidates were Cardwell and Ewart, and the Conservatives brought out Messrs Turner and Mackenzie:-

> *'Mr Cardwell, who had excited considerable alarm in the minds of many who had previously supported him, by his Free Trade proclivities, and his abandonment of the principle of restriction in the navigation laws and differential duties, was again brought forward by the Liberal party... Each side accompanied its candidates to the hustings with a procession comprising party flags and colours, and bands of music... After the nomination, the Free Traders held an open air meeting in Clayton Square, where the assembly was addressed by the candidates.'* [13]

Trying to work in an office in Clayton Square that day might have been somewhat of a challenge, but at least the speeches of the Free Traders would have been welcome to Peter's ears because, the day after the election, the *Liverpool Mercury* published a list of how people had voted, showing that he had supported Cardwell and Ewart (*Mercury*, 7th July 1852). The result itself however would have been a disappointment to Peter, for James Picton went on to record that at the close of the poll the voting was Turner, 6693; Mackenzie, 6367; Cardwell, 5247; Ewart, 4910. It is interesting however that James Picton also noted (perhaps with satisfaction, for he also had voted for the Liberals) that:-

> *'In the ensuing session, a petition against the return of Messrs. Turner and Mackenzie on the plea of bribery by their agents was presented, and after parliamentary inquiry, the election was declared null and void.'*

In 1854 the *Liverpool Mercury* reported upon an action brought by Peter against a Mr Charles Hart for the sum of £20-10s for the preparation of plans and specifications in 1852 for a dwelling house in Upper Parliament Street (*Mercury* 9th June 1854). Hart claimed to have discovered that '*the cost of a building such as was projected by the architect would be more than he expected.*' Following a meeting at Peter's office, agreement had been reached for Peter to make another plan with which Hart was subsequently satisfied. However Charles Hart responded to Peter's bill for £52 by sending 30 guineas.

6,11. Peter's 1856 drawing of the proposed Canning Street elevation for phase 1 of the construction of St Saviour's National Schools. Image courtesy of the LRO, ref. 370 SCH 30/1.

The dispute over whether the price limit for the original property had included the price of the land (Hart's contention) or the building alone (Peter's understanding) occupied the attention of the court for a considerable time. The judge retired to consult with two advisers – one being James Picton – and returned to award £12-1s to Peter. There is no *Gore's Directory* evidence that the building was ever constructed for Charles Hart, but there is a hint that Peter may have made use of the plans many years later for another client. [14]

In the *Liverpool Mercury* for 8th December 1854 Peter is shown as supporting the:-

> *'Borough of Liverpool – Patriotic Fund – Royal Commission towards the Relief, Education, and Support of the Widows and Orphans of those Soldiers, Sailors and Marines of her Majesty's Armies and Fleets who may fall in battle or die in active service during the present War.'*

The war in question was the Crimean (1853-1856) and the Lime Street Ward collection was carried out by Messrs. Picton and Eden, to which Peter is shown as having donated £1 (ca. £50 - £100 today). On 6th March of the following year the *Mercury* records that Peter also donated £1 to the Liverpool District Provident Society (of which William Rathbone was a vice-president and which two decades earlier had aided Kitty Wilkinson in her work).

On 8th November 1856 the *Liverpool Mercury* reported the laying of the foundation stone for the new St Saviour's National Schools situated at the corner of Canning Street and Crown Street, only a few hundred yards from Peter's Falkner Square home. The report went on to mention that, following bible readings, prayers and hymn-singing:-

> *'Mr Ellis, the architect, then presented to the Rev. Mr. Warr a handsome silver trowel, with which he was to perform the interesting ceremony of laying the stone... In the stone were deposited several documents recording the origin of the schools and the names of its founders.'*

6,12. Peter's 1856 drawing of the proposed Molyneux Street elevation for phase 2 of St Saviour's National Schools ('Intended addition to Infants' School').
Image courtesy of the LRO, ref. 370 SCH 30/2.

The article noted that the proposed building was in the Gothic style and that besides boys', girls' and infants' schools (with room for 600 children), advantageously there would also be residences for the master and mistress:-

> *'The building is to be of brick, with stone cornices and facings, and, though a plain structure, nothing will be wanting in the shape of modern improvements and appliances to adapt it for the noble purpose to which it is to be devoted.'*

St Saviour's Church itself was on Huskisson Street and a few yards from Falkner Square. It was erected in 1840, and the Rev. Warr commented that when his ministry began in 1846, '*the district was, comparatively speaking, without a population, but it has since increased at least fourfold,*' thus necessitating the new schools.

The trustees of the Molyneux Charity were thanked for their grant of the land and the proceedings terminated with the national anthem, performed by the orphan boys' band. In 1856 Molyneux Street was still in the process of being laid out between Upper Canning Street and Upper Huskisson Street in preparation for the school. It was first listed in the 1857 directory and commemorated Mrs Molyneux.

The LRO has two books of Peter's plans and drawings for the school, of which fig. 6,11 is an example from phase 1 and fig. 6,12 from phase 2. Some of the firms to be involved in the construction were named in the *Mercury* article and all the signatures appear in the phase 1 book as verification of their having examined the plans. The building was modified several times during its life and also suffered air-raid damage in WWII, and the LRO has a photograph of the infants' school viewed from Molyneux Street (fig. 6,13) shortly before a new school was built in the 1970s. Both the street and the replacement school have long since disappeared and their site is now covered by the Liverpool Women's Hospital.

6,13. The infants' school viewed from Molyneux Street shortly before demolition in preparation for the 1970s replacement (compare Peter's drawing in fig. 6,12).
Image courtesy of the LRO, ref. 283 SAV 12/10/5.

Intriguingly, in amongst large bundles of papers concerning St Saviour's School which are stored at the LRO (ref. 283 SAV 12/10/1), there is an invoice from James Picton dated February 1856 presenting his bill for £25 for:-

> *'negotiating purchase of land from Mrs Molyneux's Charity Trustees, arranging terms, conditions and site, admeasurements & plans of land and various attendances & correspondences connected therewith. 2 $^{1}/_{2}$ percent on £1017.6.2.'*

The conveyance for the school, which is in the same bundle and is dated 27th October 1856, indicates that the management would be placed in the hands of a committee including *'twelve other persons'*, one of whom is named as Peter Ellis. James Picton's invoice shows that his clerk did not acknowledge it as paid until 6th November of that year, coincident with the occasion of the stone-laying ceremony. The remainder of the *'twelve other persons'* (various professional people) were all from Falkner Square and the immediate surrounding area. Thus, it seems, between the date that James Picton was invited to carry out his work (and as a result of which he perhaps anticipated designing the building) and the date of the conveyance, the local residents had united to promote Peter as their preferred architect.

Peter Howell Williams noted that:-

> *'Sir James Picton (1805-1889) was the son of a respectable builder, who nevertheless, was at one time, imprisoned for debt. He was a self-taught quantity surveyor,* [and] *was concerned with the construction of St. George's Hall.'* [15]

James Allanson Picton was thus a contemporary of Peter. Born into the Pickton family, the directory for 1835 shows him in the process of modifying his name. In the architects and surveyors section he is *'Pickton James A. 27 Warren street'*, whilst in the alphabetical section he has become *'Picton James A. architect and surveyor, 27, Warren street'*. His father, William Pickton, chose to preserve the original spelling for the whole of his life. [16]

In a curious parallel with Peter's start in life, James Picton wrote that:-

> *'on the 2nd December, 1805, I first drew breath. I was not the first child of the marriage. Another preceded me, called by the same name, who died in infancy.'* [17]

He moved from Clayton Square after his listing in the 1859 directory, and so his and Peter's offices faced each other a few yards apart for over a decade.

Above: 6,14. A photograph from the City Engineer's Department captures the last days of this part of Clayton Square in 1923.

Image courtesy of the LRO, ref. Photographs & Small Prints: Streets & Districts: Clayton Square.

6,15. Another photograph from the City Engineer's Department shows work commencing on the store for Owen Owen Ltd in 1924.

Image courtesy of the LRO, ref. as fig. 6,14.

Peter's office in Clayton Square survived until 1923 (fig. 6,14) when the north side of the Square was pulled down to make way for Owen Owen's department store (fig. 6,15). James Picton's office suffered an earlier fate; by the mid 1860s Michael Laurence had taken the lease on the office, and an enlarged *Temperance Hotel* was soon rubbing shoulders with the *Prince of Wales Theatre* (on the site shown on the 1848 map in fig. 6,9 as the Clayton Arms Hotel).

In later years Peter and Mary may well have visited the theatre for some light entertainment, and Peter would have been fascinated to watch the changes occurring to the Square after he had left his office there. The theatre survived until 1912 and was subsequently replaced by a picture house of the same name.

6,16. Clayton Square in 1922 by C Arthur Cox.
Image courtesy of the LRO, ref. Binns Coll. D384.

Michael O'Mahony, writing in 1931 shortly after the Owen Owen store was built, remarked that:-

> *'About 1822 Elliot Street was carried through to the square from Lime Street, and soon after the character of the district changed. The air of quiet decorum fled, and so did the old families, the once select houses were changed into offices or hotels, the Clayton mansions being gradually metamorphosed into the Prince of Wales Theatre... Old playgoers of the past would, if they returned today, find change piled on change. Where quiet hotels prospered in quiet corners, they would find stately emporiums; Houghton Street less than ever like a quiet by-street in a country town, and Leigh Street looking as if fretting for its lost seclusion. One feature of Clayton Square endows it with an interest which is not only as picturesque as it is pathetic, but which is unshared by any similar in the city – namely, the steady line of flower vendors who, unbroken by the rains and tempests of a harsh climate, heroically hold their ground from year to year.'* [18]

In 1922 the artist C Arthur Cox captured a nostalgic view of the flower sellers (fig. 6,16), and the doorway to the office that had been Peter's over 60 years earlier is at the centre of the scene and in the shadow of the Neptune Hotel which stands to its left.

In 1928 the flower vendors were rewarded for holding their ground by an invitation from Miss Margaret Beavan, the city's first woman Lord Mayor, to morning coffee at the Town Hall, as part of her determination to make the building accessible to a much wider range of people than hitherto:-

> *'This act not only won her the lasting devotion of the flower-girls themselves, but caught the imagination of the Liverpool public...* [and at her funeral in 1931] *...at the Cathedral steps, the flower girls of Clayton Square came forward as the cortège arrived and formally presented their own wreath.'* [19]

48 BANK-BUILDINGS.
Robinson Wm. J. attorney & notary
M'Quie P. B. accountant and agent
Healey Samuel R. & R. share brokers
Healey Samuel R. accountant
Marine Society, Samuel Moss, secretary
Salvage Association, Samuel Moss, secretary
M'Grotty Henry and Co. wine and spirit merchants
Hope William, merchant
Hope Thomas Arthur, gentleman
Hope William C. gentleman
Hope Samuel P. gentleman
Hope Thomas R. insurance agent
Jones William H. gentleman
Platt William P. lithographer

48 Ellis Peter, architect and surveyor
Cotton Edward, attorney
Todd James, corn merchant

6,17. From two adjacent columns of the 1862 directory showing Peter Ellis and Peter B McQuie sharing offices in the same building, as they had done in Clayton Square.

Image courtesy of the Athenaeum.

In 1857 Mary Helen's brother, William Harper Syers, died and the probate entry for the 13th February 1858 reads:-

> *'The will of William Harper Syers late of Liverpool in the County of Lancaster Appraiser and Auctioneer deceased who died 6 December 1857 at Liverpool aforesaid was proved at Liverpool by the oaths of Peter Ellis of Faulkner-square* [sic] *Liverpool aforesaid Architect and Francis* [sic] *Syers of Low-hill Liverpool aforesaid Widow the Relict (during Widowhood) two of the Executors.'*

According to William's family tree on the *ancestryinstitution.com* database his marriage pattern shows sad similarities to that of Robert Ellis, Peter's brother. William's first marriage to Eliza Weetman on 31st December 1834 ended when Eliza died in 1835 having born William a son (who survived). William then married Frances Bedford in 1836 and remained at Low Hill for the rest of his life.

Peter is last shown at Clayton Square in the 1860 directory, and whilst he was still there he designed the *Hahnemann Homoeopathic Dispensary* in Hardman Street (opened in November of that year and which will be covered in a later chapter).

The next directory was published in 1862 and by that time Peter had arrived for what turned out to be a brief period in an office at *Bank Buildings* in Castle Street, where he again met up with the son of Peter Robinson McQuie (fig. 6,17).

References and Notes to Chapter 6

1 James Stonehouse, *The Streets of Liverpool*, Edward Howell, 1869, p. 24. Reprinted 2002 by Liverpool Libraries and Information Services. One of the first occupants at Falkner Square, as shown in the 1847 numerical directory, was Rev. Frederick Parry who had relocated there from Falkner Terrace (where he is listed in the 1845 directory), having therefore bravely chosen to move from one Folly to another.

2 How the '*Mr Faulkner*' on a map of 1796 is consistent with the '*Mr Falkner*' who purchased land '*in later years*' is not clear. Variations in spelling were common (thus '*Blackburn*' and '*Blackburne*'), and the map is a late 1860s copy of an original which is apparently no longer in existence (mentioned again in chapter 9).

3 Peter was listed in *Gore's Directory* for 1847 and in *McCorquodale's Directory* for 1848 as living at number 46, whilst in *Gore's Directory* for 1849 he is shown at no. 38. Then, in the 1851 directory, although he is at no. 40 in the numerical he is still at no. 38 in the alphabetical, and it is not until 1853 that the directories suggest that he has stopped moving around and settled down at no. 40. To add to the apparent confusion, in 1847 Peter appears simultaneously in the numerical section at both 14 Sandon Street and 46 Falkner Square, presumably to accommodate the uncertainty of when their new home would be ready to move into.

That Mary and Peter only ever lived at one Falkner Square house is clear however from a comparison of directory entries for their next door neighbour. James Ryder is listed in 1847 and 1848 at number 45; in 1849 he apparently had moved to no. 37; and in 1851 he is shown at no. 39 where he was then permitted to remain.

This may seem inconsequential, but it appears to have been confusing to some previous researchers, and must have been an annual delight to local ironmongers.

4 J A Picton, *Memorials of Liverpool*, G G Walmsley (Liverpool), 2nd edn., 1875, vol. II, p. 260.

5 J A Picton, *op. cit.*, vol. II, p. 226.

6 C H Reilly, *Some Liverpool Streets and Buildings in 1921*, Daily Post and Mercury, 1921, p. 61.

7 M O'Mahony, *Ways and Byeways of Liverpool*, Daily Post, 1931, p. 67.

8 Joseph Sharples, *Liverpool. Pevsner Architectural Guides*, Yale University Press, 2004, p. 250.

9 Joseph Sharples (e-mail 29-08-12): '*Lessees who built individual houses were supposed to conform to an approved overall plan for the elevations, to ensure symmetry, unity of effect, etc. In practice, not all of them did conform, to the annoyance of their neighbours. If Ellis designed his own house, his input may have been limited to designing the layout of rooms behind the agreed façade.*'

10 J A Picton, *op. cit.*, vol. II, p. 172.

11 The Corporation Lease Register shows that James Picton obtained a lease on 29th June 1847 for '*All that piece or parcel of Land with the messuage or dwellinghouse thereon erected situate on the South side of Clayton Square and North side of Clayton Lane...*' and that it was re-granted to Michael Laurence in 1863 after James Picton had departed (LRO ref. 352 CLE/CON 3/9). Michael Laurence went on to construct what became known as *Laurence's Temperance Hotel*, and the LRO has a photograph of its demolition in 1921 in order to make way for an expansion of the department store *Brown's*.

12 John Tiernan, Messrs Cowell and Shelmerdine, and Dr Carnegie, *Journal of the Liverpool History Society*, 2009, p. 80. John also kindly supplied the reference to Thomas Shelmerdine's marriage at St Bride's.

13 J A Picton, *op. cit.*, vol. I, p. 512.

14 The case must have been difficult for Peter to bring. The directories for 1849 – 1853 show that Charles Hart had been Peter's neighbour, living two doors away.

A photograph of a building at the junction of Park Way and Upper Parliament Street is contained in the Quentin Hughes Archive at the Sydney Jones Library (ref. D71/22/57/17, kindly supplied by Iain Jackson at the School of Architecture, Liverpool University). Upon the photograph has been typed (all in lower case): '*house on parkway, liverpool, fenestration showing similar characteristics to that of oriel chambers*'. The map which accompanies the directory for 1878 shows that the house already existed by that date. The building has long since gone, but an undated LRO photo shows it as the '*Sir Joseph Cleary Community Centre*' (ref. Photographs & Small Prints: Streets & Districts: Upper Parliament Street).

15 Peter Howell Williams, *Liverpolitana*, Merseyside Civic Society, 1971, p. 51.

16 J Allanson Picton, *Sir James A Picton. A Biography*, G G Walmsley, 1891, p. 11, provides an account of the circumstances which caused the bankruptcy and imprisonment of William Pickton, and an explanation for James Picton's name change. '*It is a reasonable inference from tombstones and church registers that this particular family of Picktons took its name from the township of Picton,* near Chester, came thence to Warrington...* ,' and in the footnote: '** It will be observed that they inserted a "k" in the name. Sir James Picton regarded this as a corruption.*' In 1826 he joined the Warren Street practice of Daniel Stewart (the father of John Stewart who, with William Foster, is shown at Lawton Street on Michael Gage's map – chapter 3, fig. 3,4). Following Daniel Stewart's retirement, James Picton took over the business in 1835, the year in which the directory shows that, evidently already a keen historian, he felt the time had come to drop the corrupting '*k*'.

17 J Allanson Picton, *op. cit.*, p. 16.

18 M O'Mahony, *op. cit.*, p. 57.

19 Ivy A Ireland, *Margaret Beavan of Liverpool*, Henry Young & Sons, 1938, pp. 199 and 280.

LITHOGRAPHERS ENGRAVERS BY STEAM POWER
GORE'S ADVERTISER
ESTABLISHED
1766
MAWDSLEY & SON
ACCOUNT
BOOK
MANUFACTURER
WHOLESALE
STATIONERS
ENGRAVERS
WHOLESALE
STATIONERS
HARTLEY & TURNER
HATTERS
BENSON
HOLME
HARTLEY
LITHOGRAPHERS
GORES ADVERTISER
PRINTERS
JONES & SON
JEWELLERS

Chapter 7

Castle Street and Orange Court

With Peter being shown as having arrived at *Bank Buildings*, Castle Street, in the 1862 directory, an advertisement in the *Liverpool Mercury* in September 1863 indicates that he was about to move again, and James Picton's comment that '*The Bank Buildings of Messrs. Heywood were taken down in 1864*' provides an explanation as to why Peter's stay was so brief. [1]

Whilst Peter was there a case came to court in which a valuation of land of '*1 acre 3 roods and 35 perches, or 9226 superficial yards*' was required as a result of disagreement between John Gibbons of Mossley Vale ('*a gentleman engaged in the iron and nail trade*') and the London & North Western Railway Co (*Liverpool Mercury* 17th April 1863). The Company wished to obtain the land by compulsory purchase to drive through a cutting for their railway. Peter, Lewis Hornblower and several others acted on behalf of John Gibbons, whilst valuers for the Company included William Culshaw and James Picton.

> '*Mr. Peter Ellis, architect, valued the land at 2s. 9d. a yard, or £1268, the incidental damage by the railway cutting of about 8 feet deep at the sum of £1470 15s., and 20 per cent. for compulsory sale, viz., £547 5s., making a total of £3287. Mr Ellis urged many reasons for his valuations.*'

The other valuations on behalf of the plaintiff were £3474 (Lewis Hornblower), £3740, £3271, £3083 and £3496. The valuations on behalf of the Company were £2024 (William Culshaw), £2014 (James Picton), and £2041.

The jury awarded John Gibbons £1242 for the land, £1057 for depreciation (Peter's '*incidental damage*') but only £62 for the compulsory purchase. The eventual outcome was the railway line which exists today and passes through Mossley Hill Station.

The *Mercury* reveals further evidence of Peter's involvement as an agent for property sales and lettings. On 5th September 1863 he requested enquirers to '*Apply to Peter Ellis, 48, Castle-street, Liverpool, removing to 9, Orange-court, Castle-street*' regarding the letting of 59 Bold Street:-

> '*To be Let, Premises, Bold-street, corner of Heathfield-street. These extensive and commodious premises are nearly completed. They are so arranged that they may be occupied in one or several tenancies. Persons requiring such premises will now have the opportunity of adapting them, or having them adapted to their peculiar occasions.*'

The construction appears to have been a speculative enterprise rather than as a commission for a would-be occupant since, despite the premises being in the premier retail street in town, Peter was still advertising the property in April 1864. Whether he was the architect or merely the letting agent is unknown.

At that time the street was already home to several sewing machine companies and a variety of milliners, and by 1865 the directory was listing no. 59 as occupied by the *Grover and Baker Sewing Machine Company*.

An LRO photograph in the 1890s together with the directories between 1887 and 1903 show that by then it was home to '*Turner, Son and Walker, cabinet manufacturers, upholsterers and carpet warehousemen, late of 14&16 Islington.*' Fashionable Bold Street became the subject of many picture postcards. Two Edwardian cards include no. 59 in their views, and a detail from one of them shows it as occupied by Finnigan's Ltd (fig. 7,1) who, according to the directories between 1906 and 1925, were '*actual manufacturers of trunks, dressing bags and dressing cases.*' Peter's '*extensive and commodious premises*' stands out well above its smaller neighbours, and today it continues to provide accommodation where apparently size still matters (fig. 7,2). [2]

It may be recalled from chapter 6 that the son of Peter Robinson McQuie (mentioned in chapter 2 as living near to the Ellis family in Low Hill) shared an office with Peter Ellis in Clayton Square in the early 1850s. Peter B McQuie, an accountant and agent to the Scottish Amicable Assurance Society, was born in 1820 and was thus 15 years younger than Peter Ellis. Having first appeared in *Gore's Directory* in 1849 at an office in Dale Street, and after sharing the Clayton Square office with Peter (1851 & 1853 directories), he moved via Harrington Street and Exchange Alley to *Bank Buildings* (1860 directory). Thus by 1862, if not earlier, Peter Ellis and Peter B McQuie found themselves working in close proximity once more (p. 117, fig. 6,17), and in the following year it was whilst still at *Bank Buildings* that Peter Ellis became involved with developments at 14 Water Street where Peter B McQuie's father still had his office.

7,1. A detail from an Edwardian picture postcard showing 59 Bold Street.

Private collection.

7,2. 59 Bold Street in 2011. Construction taking place to the rear was for a building which has now severed the vehicular route through Heathfield Street which had led to Peter's first office on Renshaw Street.

7,3. A view by William Herdman (one of W G Herdman's sons) of the east side of Castle Street in 1864 with the Liverpool Branch of the Bank of England on the left and the Liverpool Commercial Bank on the right. Hardly noticeable between them is the narrow entrance to Cook Street.

Image courtesy of the LRO, ref. Hf 942.7214 HER 1864.

But before turning to the events that were to unfold in Water Street it is perhaps useful to deal first with a number of Peter's adventures at his next office, shown in the directories from 1864 as being at *Orange Court*, 35A Castle Street. The description by James Picton of William Herdman's view of Castle Street in his 1864 publication (fig. 7,3) mentions that:-

> *'A portion of the front* [of the Commercial Bank] *to Castle Street forms the Magnetic Telegraph Office, and in the rear are avenues with extensive ranges of offices forming Orange Court. At the time when Lillyman's Hotel flourished* [a building replaced by the Bank of England], *the narrow aperture of Cook Street was spanned by a large archway, and built over. When the rebuilding took place this was removed, and an attempt was made to induce the Corporation to purchase a portion of land to widen the street. Unfortunately this overture received a negative response; and at the present time, when a magnificent street* [Victoria Street] *is projected, to run parallel with Dale Street from Castle Street to the Old Haymarket, its usefulness will be nullified to a great extent by the narrow defile between the two Banks.'* [3]

Peter would stay at *Orange Court* for a further seven years, seeing through the completion of both Oriel Chambers in 1865 (*The Builder* of 4th November 1865 describing it as a *new* office building) and 16 Cook Street in 1867 (the first occupant announcing his *new* premises in the *Liverpool Mercury* in November 1867).

On 11th November 1863, soon after arriving at his new office, Peter placed a series of advertisements for the sale of:-

> *'a spacious and substantial Dwelling House in Great George-square, with good stables and coach-house in the rear, in Frederick-street. A suitable residence for a medical practitioner.'*

7,4. *The four odd-numbered properties, nos. 15-21 Great George Square, backing onto Frederick Street, in September 2012. In 1863 Peter advertised one of the original terrace of eight for sale in the Liverpool Mercury.*

He would have known that particular location well as a result of the houses he had constructed on the south east side of the Square in 1833-34, although whether this was also an Ellis-built house is uncertain since Frederick Street lay to the south west (p. 46, fig. 3,12). A terrace of four of the houses backing onto Frederick Street still exists today (fig. 7,4), the central pair having passed through a period of being the Norwegian Seamen's Mission (1941) and the Far East Restaurant (1968). [4]

On 29th February 1864 an advertisement in the *Mercury* placed by the Isle of Man Shipbuilding Co Ltd indicated that:-

> *'This Company is formed with the object of building, at Ramsey, in the Isle of Man, Iron Sailing Ships and Steamers,'* and that a *'conditional arrangement has been made for acquiring, at the amount of valuation made by Mr. Peter Ellis, the extensive Shipbuilding Yard, Patent Slip, Foundry, and Engineering Works of Mr. T. C. Gibson.'*

Is it a too-21st century thought that Peter and Mary perhaps had the opportunity for an all-expenses-paid short holiday on the Isle of Man whilst he was undertaking the valuation?

On the 13th June 1864 the *Mercury* reported on an appeal by the Castle Street printers and stationers, Mawdsley and Son, against their Poor Rate assessment. [5] It was one of several cases that were considered, the appeal court having obtained a valuation from Peter as an independent surveyor. He would no doubt have been pleased by the comments by one of the panel members at the end of the hearing:-

> *'The assessment of £315 was confirmed, Mr. Jeffrey remarking that it was gratifying to the magistrates to find that in the only case about which they had had any doubt – and in which it was said they had under assessed – they having referred the matter to Mr. Ellis found themselves upon his statement exact in their figures.'*

In 1868 James Mawdsley's son moved home from Smithdown Lane to Falkner Square. The Mawdsley family were successors to John Gore as publishers of the *Gore's Directories* (fig. 7,5), and it is therefore somewhat amusing to find that their compositors, whilst correctly showing the son, James Platt Mawdsley, as resident at 36 Falkner Square in the 1868 numerical section, cheekily squeezed him into Peter and Mary's home in the alphabetical section.

On 22nd May 1866 Peter began placing a series of advertisements in the *Mercury* for the sale of:-

> *'a good Place of Business, situate at the junction of Copperas-hill with the important new street leading to the railway station, and a Dwelling House adjoining in Gloucester-street, opposite St Simon's Church.'*

The church to which Peter referred was the one that had just been completed and which was due to be opened the following month rather than the church that had been demolished a year earlier (p. 17, fig. 2,4). Erection of this second St Simon's Church had been at the expense of some of the property of Peter's brother, John Ellis, and this sale was for John's other property that faced it in Gloucester Street and which by that date was being rented out by his eldest son.

The lease on the property makes no mention that it passed out of the hands of the family before being acquired by the L&NWR Company in 1882 for the expansion of Lime Street Station. Prospective purchasers may have anticipated that the site would eventually become a rather large and noisy hole in the ground (p. 20, fig. 2,12, in the triangle of land above the '*ERA*' of '*Copperas*'). [6]

7,5. A painting by J I Herdman (another of W G Herdman's sons) showing the premises of James Mawdsley and Son at 4 Castle Street in 1866, near the junction with Water Street. These shops and the banks on the opposite side of Castle Street (fig. 7,3) are exactly as Peter would have known them, and in the days before mechanised transport.

Image courtesy of the LRO, ref. 423/16 CAS 8.

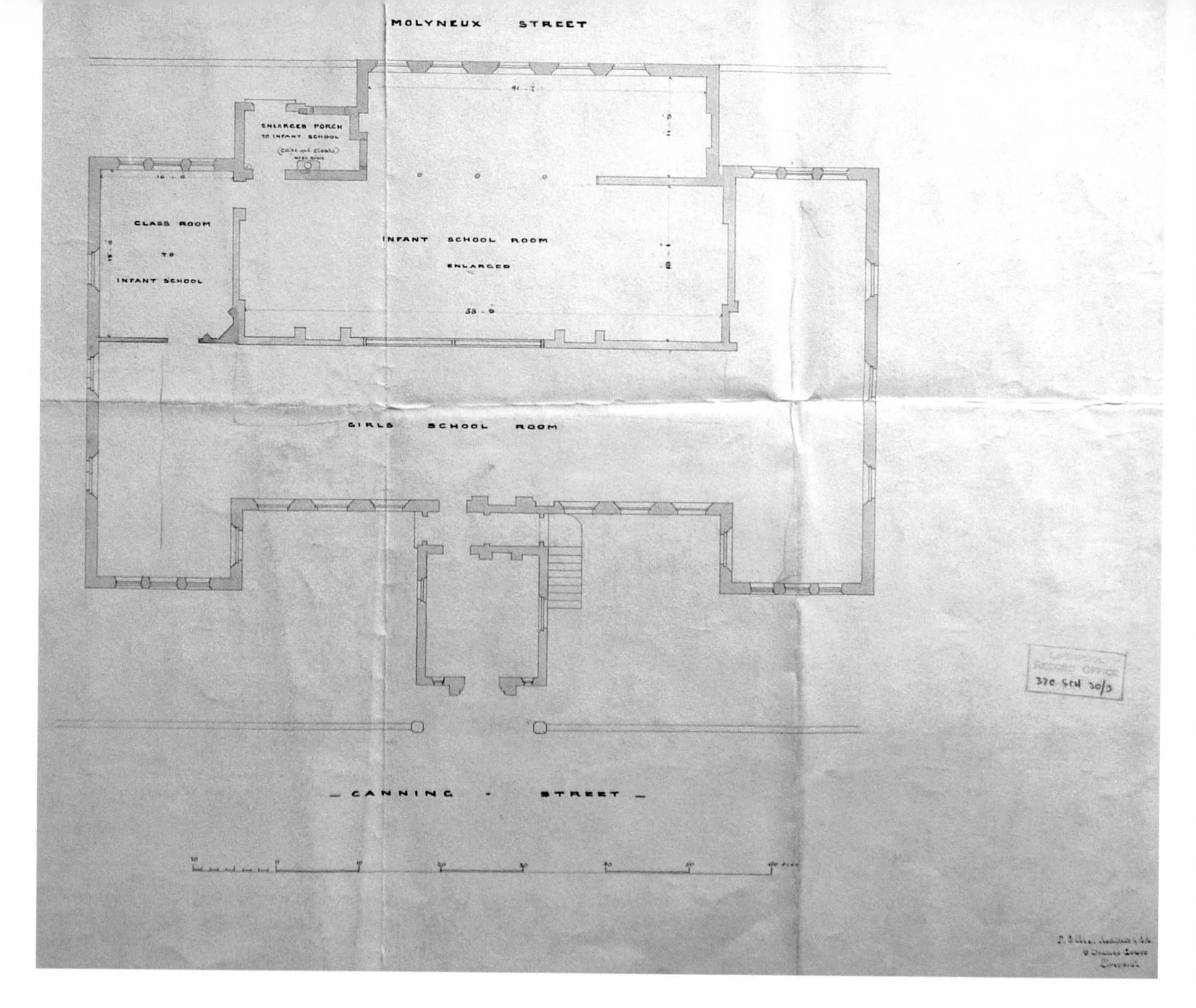

At an uncertain date in the 1860s Peter was requested to provide an additional drawing for phase 2 of the construction of St Saviour's National Schools for which he had been the architect whilst still at Clayton Square (chapter 6). Intriguingly the drawing (fig. 7,6) [7] is signed, '*P. Ellis. Architect & C. E. 9 Orange Court, Liverpool.*' Peter's description of himself on this plan for an alteration to the infants' school shows that he had begun to regard himself as both an architect and civil engineer during his period at Orange Court, and the significance of this will become apparent in a later chapter.

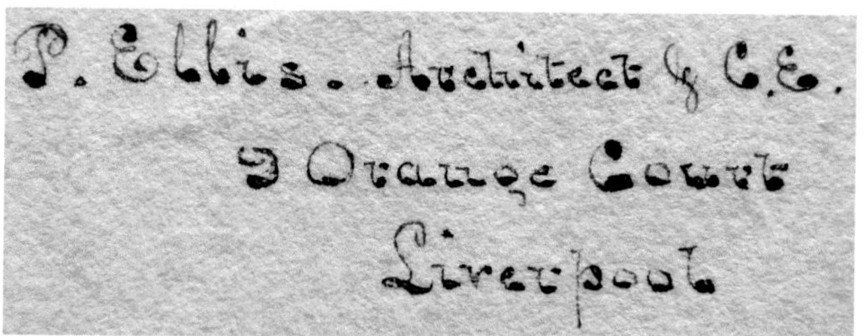

7,6. An undated plan for the 'Infant School Room Enlarged' of St Saviour's National Schools, and an enlargement of the bottom right hand corner showing Peter's description of himself as an architect and civil engineer sometime after September 1863 when he arrived at Orange Court.

Images courtesy of the LRO.

A detail from the 1848 O.S. map (fig. 7,7) shows '*the narrow defile between the two Banks*' about which James Picton had commented. The proximity of Peter's office to 16 Cook Street which he was commissioned to replace enabled him to reach it in a matter of a minute or so from Orange Court via the archway of the building marked with crossed lines (the sign for an archway; by the '*K*' of '*Cook*'). He would therefore have been immediately available on site for consultation on matters large or small whenever required. Comparison of the footprints for the premises at no. 16 prior to 1866 (as on the 1848 O.S. map) and after Peter's building was completed (later O.S. maps) indicates that he was constrained to design his replacement to continue to occupy a site which was irregularly shaped.

Measured drawings of Peter's building which were prepared in the 20th century by J Mackay-Lewis at the Liverpool School of Architecture show that the opposite walls in neither case are parallel (fig. 7,8). Peter was also required to maintain the narrow passageway that still runs between nos. 14 and 16 Cook Street in order to continue to permit access to buildings at the rear (fig. 7,10), a passageway which appears to have existed prior to 1827. [8]

Orange Court and the Commercial Bank vanished at the turn of the century and were replaced by *Castle Street Buildings* and its arcade along Cook Street, thus finally enabling the western end of the street to be widened.

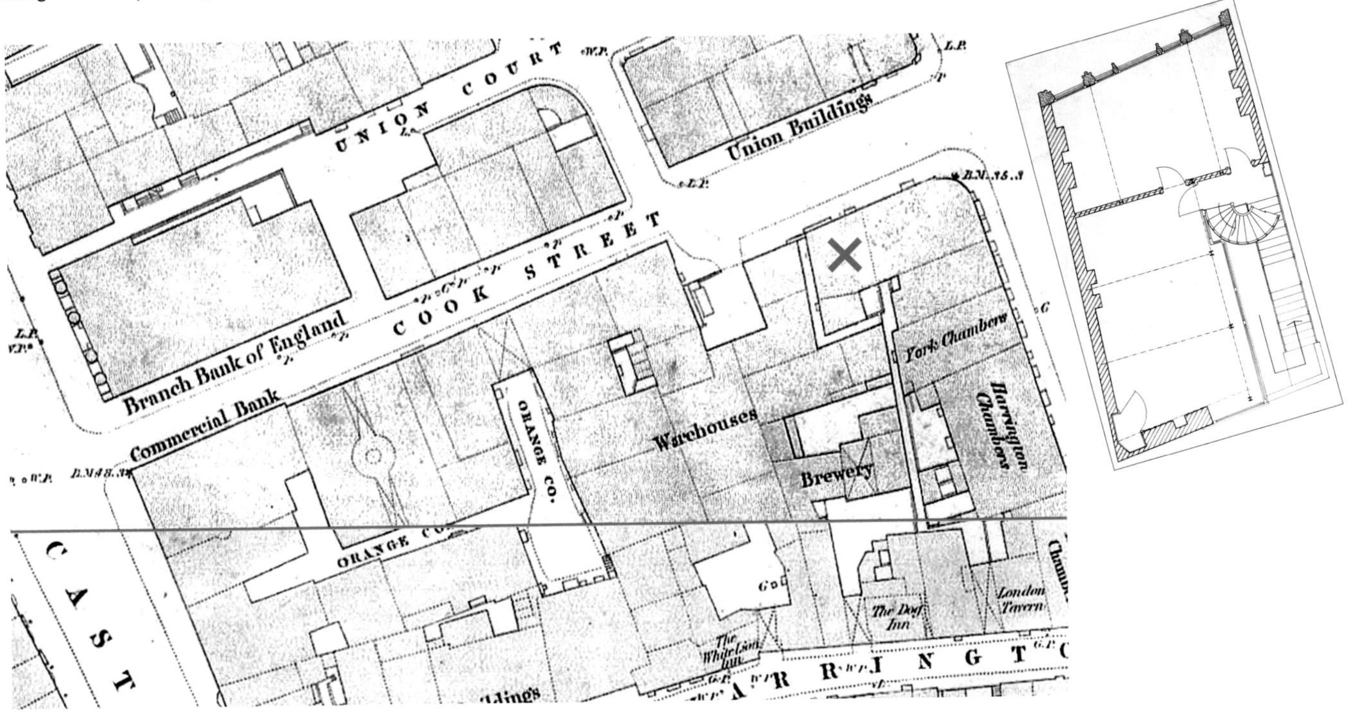

7,7. A detail from a combination of the southern edge of sheet 24 and the northern edge of sheet 29 of the 1848 O.S. map (from a version that had been revised in part to 1864, although not in Cook Street) showing Orange Court and the earlier 16 Cook Street (marked 'X'). Peter's building, which replaced the one shown here, was constrained to fit into exactly the same shape.

The location of this area within the town is identified on the map on p. iv by the letter S.

Image courtesy of Digital Archives.

7,8. A detail from one of the 16 Cook Street building plans drawn by J Mackay-Lewis. The plan is prior to late 20th century alterations which brought the start of the spiral staircase down to the upper ground floor.

Image courtesy of the LRO (which has the plans) and the University of Liverpool Library (which holds the copyright).

In 1864, soon after Peter had arrived at Orange Court, the *Post Office Directory* shows no less than four entries for '*John Ellis, veterinary surgeon*' (fig 7,11). The explanation can be found in the 1851 census records showing that John (Peter's brother) and his wife Mary had established a second home at Halewood where Mary was farming 120 acres and employing 10 labourers. By 1864 their central Liverpool home was now at Great George Square with the shoeing forge remaining at Upper Pitt Street. The fourth address at Hardy Street (originally St Vincent Street: see p. 46, fig. 3,12) was that of their 26 year old eldest son, John Ellis junior, who was in the process of establishing his own business.

7,9. Another of the drawings by J Mackay-Lewis, showing the original ground floor design (compare fig. 7.10).

Image courtesy of the LRO (which has the plans) and the University of Liverpool Library (which holds the copyright).

7,10. The narrow gated passageway between nos. 16 and 14 Cook St in September 2011.

Sadly, in the same year that Peter was busy with the construction of Oriel Chambers, John Ellis senior died at the age of 53, and his probate record reads:-

> *'Ellis John. Effects under £12,000. 31 December. The Will of John Ellis late of Upper-Pitt-street Liverpool in the County of Lancaster Veterinary Surgeon deceased who died 22 September 1864 at Halewood in the said County was proved at Liverpool by the oath of Peter Ellis of 40 Falkner-square Liverpool aforesaid Architect the Brother one of the Executors.'* [9]

In the following year the directory shows that John Ellis junior and his younger brother Peter (born 19th May 1842 and baptised at St Peter's) had entered into partnership at the surgery and shoeing forge at 15 Upper Pitt Street, that John had returned to the family home at 28 Great George Square, and that Peter was living at 38 Upper Pitt Street. The partnership however was short-lived, for in 1867 John and Peter gave notice that the firm had been dissolved by mutual consent (*The London Gazette*, 25th June 1867, p. 3573).

Peter went on to establish his own business at Williamson Street, but disappeared from the directories in 1872 where he is last listed at a home address in Mount Pleasant. The *Liverpool Mercury* suggests an apparently flourishing veterinary practice that often included the sale of horses, but a theft from his yard in 1871 and the subsequent failure to convict the men that were put on trial may have contributed adversely to his future business. [10]

Ellis John, veterinary surgeon, 28 Great George square
Ellis John, veterinary surgeon, Halewood
Ellis John, veterinary surgeon, 7 Hardy st. Gt. George st
Ellis John, veterinary surgeon, 15 Upper Pitt street

7,11. A section from the Post Office Directory for 1864 showing the homes of John Ellis senior at Great George Square and Halewood, his shoeing forge at Upper Pitt Street, and the home at Hardy Street to which his eldest son, John Ellis junior, had recently moved.

Image courtesy of Sefton Local History Unit.

John and Mary Longton (of Prescot) were married in 1863 at St Mary the Virgin, Prescot (Ann Appleton's baptismal church). They are recorded in the 1871 census with their three children, Jane, Mary and Edith, at Great George Square, and they remained there until 1876, with John's surgery continuing to be at Upper Pitt Street. In 1877 they moved their home to Sugnall Street, with John moving his surgery to Hope Street, and it is at Sugnall Street that the 1881 census shows them with a further three daughters, Gertrude, Mabel and Blanche, and at last a son and therefore – inevitably – John. They moved home once more, this time to Maryland Street, and it is at the premises on Hope Street that Peter would regularly have visited his nephew in later years for all matters concerned with the well-being of his horse.

When Peter arrived in Orange Court in 1863 he had only the office of one gunpowder company in uncomfortably close proximity. Later he found that he had become positively surrounded (fig. 7,12), and in 1871 he chose to move a few hundred yards to the greater safety of an office at Oriel Chambers. He would spend the remainder of his working life there, and so the time has come to turn back to the events that began to unfold on Water Street in July 1863.

35A ORANGE COURT.
7 Elliott Adam general merchant
8 Liverpool Philharmonic Society
Sudlow Henry secretary
9 Hargreaves George merchant
Wakefield W. H. & Co. gunpowder mnfctrs—Reginald Crooke agent
Robinson Joseph F. general broker
The Chillington Co. iron mrchts
Murcott John manager
The Asia Minor Cotton Company
Rees Thomas B. manager
Ellis Peter architect and surveyor
Gilmour, Neild & Co. merchants
Argentine Republic Consulate
Gilmour Wm. Rodger Esq. consul
10 Lowwood Gunpowder Co. Limited

7,12. Peter's listing at Orange Court in the 1871 directory, the year he departed to take up an office at Oriel Chambers.

Image courtesy of Sefton Local History Unit.

References and Notes to Chapter 7

1 J A Picton, *Memorials of Liverpool*, G G Walmsley (Liverpool), 2nd edn., 1875, vol. II, p. 17. This confirms that the 48 Castle Street of today is a replacement for the building in which Peter had an office. A view by W G Herdman shows the Bank Buildings of Messrs. Heywood under construction in 1786 as Castle Street was being widened (LRO ref. Herdman Coll. 1267A, and also reproduced in Kay Parrott, *Pictorial Liverpool. The Art of W G & William Herdman*, The Bluecoat Press, 2005, p. 53).

2 One of several other examples of advertisements comes from 20th March 1863, whilst Peter was still at Bank Buildings, concerning a considerable sale in 21 lots of '*Eligible Building Land at Waterloo, Select Residences and Profitable Investments at Hayman's-green, West Derby, St James's-road, Percy-street, Comus-street, Milton-street, Sawneypope-street, Burlington-street, Clifton-street, and Devon-street.*' Particulars of the lots were obtainable from six solicitors (being distributed between them), an accountant, and from Peter Ellis (the only architect, and from whom information on all 21 lots was available).

Another sale, of sufficient importance to warrant a large advertisement in *The Times*, took place whilst Peter was at Orange Court (*The Times*, 11th June 1870). Walton-lodge, a '*commodious suburban residence*' set in over 11 acres was put up for auction at the Law Association Rooms (next door to Peter's new building at 16 Cook Street). Particulars were obtainable from Peter and a London solicitor.

3 William Herdman, *Views in Modern Liverpool*, 1864, plate 35; text by James Picton, p. 46. LRO ref. Hf 942.7214 HER 1864.

4 The 1941 and 1968 photographs showing the *Norske Kirke* and the *Far East Restaurant* respectively are included in the LRO folder *Photographs & Small Prints: Streets & Districts: Great George Square.*

5 Another case of an appeal against the Poor Rate – with regard to Compton House (now Marks & Spencer's on Church Street) – in which Peter was called to provide a valuation was reported in the *Liverpool Mercury* on 15th July 1869.

6 The Corporation Lease Register, LRO ref. 352 CLE/CON 3/8, shows that on 15th May 1838 the Liverpool and Manchester Railway obtained leases on neighbouring property on Copperas Hill and Olive Street with regard to the tunnel that was required to link the railway to Lime Street. See p. 15, fig. 2,1 where the dotted lines crossing Copperas Hill, Olive Street and Back Russell Street mark the route for the intended tunnel, and see the eventual outcome in fig. 2,12 on p. 20.

7 LRO ref. 370 SCH 30/3, accompanying 370 SCH 30/1 (for phase 1) and 370 SCH 30/2 (for the originally planned phase 2). They are all indexed as '*Ellis, P., architect, 9 Orange Court, School Building Grant Plans by, n.d. [c. 1856]*'. The common date provisionally assigned by the LRO to all three documents of '*c. 1856*' is the date of laying the foundation stone for phase 1 (see p. 112). The plan in 30/3 must however have been prepared some time after Peter moved to Orange Court in September 1863.

8 The 20th century drawings for 16 Cook Street are part of collections at both the University of Liverpool (Quentin Hughes Archive, D71/22/13/1-6) and the LRO (ref. 7/8 Architect's Plans, Measured Drawings of 16 Cook St) and were also the subject of an article, 16 Cook Street, Liverpool, *Architectural History*, vol. 1, 1958, pp. 91-94 (obtainable from RIBA).

The site appears to be that which is identified in a Corporation lease of 14th July 1827 granted to '*Richard Brooke of Liverpool Gentleman,*' LRO ref. 352 CLE/CON 3/7. The lessee seems quite likely to have been the author of the 1853 account of '*Liverpool as it was during the Last Quarter of the Eighteenth Century.*'

The Quentin Hughes Archive also contains two photographs of the staircase connecting the first and second floors prior to the late 20th century alterations (covered in a future chapter).

9 When Mary Stockdale Ellis, the wife of John Ellis senior, died in 1875 her will was proved by '*Mary Helen Syers Ellis of 39 Catherine-street Liverpool Spinster the Daughter one of the Executrixes.*' Note the inclusion of the given name *Syers*. Another example of a connection between the Ellis and Syers families is mentioned in chapter 9.

10 The young vet, Peter Ellis junior, appears first to have found his way into the *Liverpool Mercury* on 24th May 1867 in an item entitled, '*The Dog with a Curly Tail*' which appeared in its correspondence columns. '*Mr. Peter Ellis, jun., of Derby-road, Bootle, requests us to state that it was his assistant, Mr. William Ellis, who is not a qualified veterinary surgeon, and no relation of his, who operated on the dog's tail. Mr P. Ellis adds, 'This was done without my knowledge, and I was in total ignorance of the matter until seeing it reported in your paper. I don't permit practical joking to be carried out in my establishment'.*'

With that incident safely behind him, by the following year Peter's veterinary business was well established in Williamson Street where, between 1868 and 1871, the *Liverpool Mercury* shows that he advertised a variety of horses for sale, of which the following are representative of the 16 advertisements detected by the on-line OCR search. '*On sale at Peter Ellis jun.'s Veterinary Establishment, 2, Williamson-street, a Chestnut Mare, 6 years old, steady to ride and drive, with good action*' (*Mercury*, 6th July 1868). '*For Sale, a Pair of handsome Bay Phaeton Horses, about 15 hands high, steady to ride or drive, with fine action. One of the pair has regularly carried a lady. – Apply, for particulars, to Mr. Peter Ellis, veterinary surgeon, 9, Williamson-street*' (*Mercury*, 17th July 1869).

In 1869 inhumanely treated oxen were taken by the police to Peter's surgery for examination, following which Peter was called to give evidence at a Liverpool Police Court hearing (*Mercury*, 28th May 1869). The 1871 Liverpool *Commercial Directory and Shippers' Guide* lists Peter as a member of the Royal College of Veterinary Surgeons, but sadly in September of that year he suffered theft from his Williamson Street premises. The case came to the Liverpool Police Court later that year (*Mercury*, 11th November 1871) but, despite apparently compelling evidence, the accused were acquitted at the subsequent Borough Session (*Mercury*, 2nd December 1871). The final report in the *Mercury* that has been traced concerning Peter appeared on 18th January 1877 regarding a dispute involving the estate of his father, John Ellis senior.

HENRY ST
WEST OF
FIRE STATION

Chapter 8

From an alarming fire to Oriel Chambers

And so it is time to look at the events of 3rd July 1863 at the western junction of Covent Garden and Water Street (fig. 8,1) as graphically recorded the following day in an article in the *Liverpool Mercury* (fig. 8,2) describing the fire that had consumed *Covent-buildings*,[1] the destruction of which would lead to the construction of Oriel Chambers.

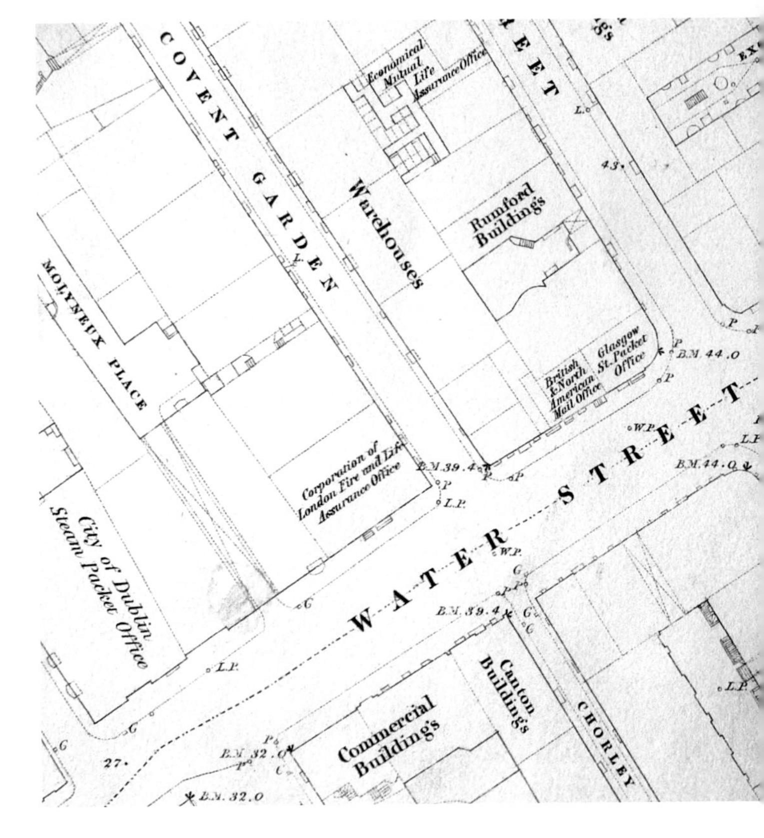

8,1. From the corner of sheet 24 of the 1848 O.S. map. The scene of the fire at 14 Water Street is where the 'Corporation of London Fire and Life Assurance Office' is erroneously marked.

The location of this area within the town is identified on the map on p. iv by the letter T.

Image courtesy of the Athenaeum.

ALARMING FIRE.

DESTRUCTION OF A WAREHOUSE, &c., AND A QUANTITY OF COTTON.

Yesterday morning, one of the most destructive fires which has occurred in Liverpool for some years took place, the scene of the conflagration being a large pile of offices and warehouses in Water-street, at the corner of Govent-garden. The building, which covers nearly 3000 yards of land, is known as Covent-buildings, and consists of cellars, with six stories above, the whole extending some distance backwards along the west side of Covent-garden. In the rear is a shed used as a store for tar and other materials. The offices were in the occupation of Messrs. C. D. Watson and Co., Chapple, Dutton, and Co., J. Bigham and Son, Mr. Bacon, J. Barber and Co., P. B. M'Quie, John Scott, Mr. Perrin, and J. G. Holden. The fire was discovered about half-past one o'clock, and on the alarm being given, the corporation fire brigade, and the brigade of the West of England Company, under the direction of Mr. Barrett, were in attendance with all possible despatch.

8,2. Liverpool Mercury, 4th July 1863.

Image courtesy of the British Library, from their 19th Century British Library Newspapers on-line archive, published by Gale Cengage.

© British Library Board.

The *Mercury* article describes the arrival of the Corporation fire brigade and the firemen of the West of England Company, and some indication of what fire-fighting equipment may have been available can be gauged from a drawing by John Isaac (fig. 8,3) [2] and an advertisement in *Gore's Directory* for 1862 (fig. 8,4).

8,3. The West of England fire engine setting off from the fire station in Henry Street. From a portfolio by John Raphael Isaac, Art-Union Rooms, 62 Castle Street.

Image courtesy of the LRO.

The *Liverpool Mercury* article continued:-

'Although there was a plentiful supply of water, for several hours the labours of the firemen appeared to have but little effect beyond the raising [of] *dense volumes of smoke, the height of the warehouse (which contained cotton), in which the fire seemed to have got the greatest hold, rendering it both difficult and dangerous to bring water to bear upon it with effect. About half-past seven o'clock the roof fell in with a tremendous crash, the fire at the time raging with undiminished fury.'* Subsequently, with floors giving way and walls collapsing, *'Bricks and other materials were continually falling, and great exertions were made in order to keep back the multitude assembled, with a view to prevent accidents.'*

For many years the building had provided office accommodation for Peter Robinson McQuie. In addition to his various pursuits as a merchant (p. 28, fig. 2,28) and antiquary,[3] he had also listed himself in the 1859 directory as an agent for fire-bricks, not knowing that bricks from a fire would literally be landing upon his desk in abundance only four years later. Although it became necessary to try to prevent an extension of the fire to neighbouring property, at about nine o'clock:-

'...one of the walls of the burning building fell with a loud crash, and did considerable damage to the offices on the east side of Covent-garden, known as the Borough-buildings. The roof was smashed, and several offices on that side of the street were more or less damaged.'

8,4. An advertisement in Gore's 1862 directory by Shand & Mason, 'manufacturers of steam and hand-worked fire engines & pumps' at their Blackfriar's Road works in London.

Image courtesy of the Athenaeum.

A whole army of Corporation officials had by this time assembled themselves to offer advice. Precautionary measures were adopted at the suggestion of John Weightman, the borough surveyor, and several tenants in Borough Buildings discontinued business and removed their books, papers and other property, some saving themselves with great difficulty. In the event Borough Buildings, only recemtly built, was reconstructed and would live on for over a century.[4] By about five o'clock in the afternoon the amount of water poured into the building had reduced the fire sufficiently for danger to the warehouse directly adjoining it to the west to have been averted (New Zealand House stands on this site today).

> *'Throughout the day, Water-street was crowded with spectators. His Worship the Mayor, the town-clerk, and several members of the town council visited the spot. The Mayor made numerous visits from time to time, and by his instructions the water was stopped in various districts of the town, in order that greater pressure might be secured for the purposes of the fire.'*

8,5. A detail from a view of Water Street looking east in the early 1860s prior to the fire, and published by William Herdman in 1864. Image courtesy of the LRO.

William Herdman, in his *Views in Modern Liverpool*, [5] captured the appearance of Water Street shortly before the fire. In the detail from Herdman's plate (fig. 8,5), the entrance to Tower Buildings (22 Water Street) is in the foreground whilst Covent Garden is shown entering Water Street where the horse-drawn omnibus is preparing to take the slight bend to the right. At the far corner of the junction can be seen the edge of Borough Buildings (10-12 Water Street), with red brickwork surrounding its upper windows and the Town Hall dome visible above it. Between Tower Buildings and Borough Buildings, and depicted by Herdman as being of the same uniform colour, are all the premises at 14-20 Water Street. On the nearside of the building that was destroyed is a warehouse at no. 16. Its two protruding catheads [6] at the roof line are seen more clearly in the 1880s view on p. 150. This later view therefore confirms that the warehouse did indeed survive the fire.

The following year the fire was judged to have been of sufficient note for a brief account of it to be included in the *Annals* that appeared at the back of the directory (fig. 8,6). It provides an indication of the financial significance of the fire and of the importance which was therefore attached to its replacement being fire-proof.

Destructive Fire in Covent-chambers, Water-street.—Besides the warehouses and offices, 2972 bales of Egyptian and Surat cotton were destroyed; the cotton was insured in the Liverpool and London, General, Royal, West of England, Royal Exchange, and Atlas offices, and a salvage of £39,500 was realized. The buildings were insured in the Yorkshire office for £4000. July 3.

8,6. A section from Gore's Annals in the 1864 directory, referring to the fire on July 3rd 1863. Image courtesy of the Athenaeum.

Covent-buildings was reported in the *Liverpool Mercury* account of the fire as the property of '*Rev. Mr. Anderson, of London*', and this detail will be seen later as significant in interpreting the decorative details with which Peter adorned the façade of Oriel Chambers (see inside back cover).

The fire having taken place on 3rd July, it was with remarkable speed that Peter's first advertisement appeared in the *Liverpool Mercury* on 14th July 1863 (fig. 8,7). Peter thus became involved with the Water Street site extremely quickly, and it seems possible that a combination of the destruction of the office of Peter Robinson McQuie and his son's contact with Peter Ellis at Bank Buildings may have played some part in facilitating the process (some internet references have suggested that Oriel Chambers was the result of a competition but none provide evidence for that claim).

Somewhat surprisingly, in December 1864, whilst Oriel Chambers was still being constructed, John Weightman (the borough surveyor who had offered advice during the fire) and G Fosbery Lyster, the Dock Engineer, [7] submitted a report to the City's Finance Committee outlining their plans for creating new '*Approaches to the River*'. [8] One of those plans shows that an option involved creating access to a proposed new street from '*A*' on the plan (Hargreaves Buildings on Chapel Street) to '*B*' on the plan (Oriel Chambers) and leading to a high level terrace and carriageway to the landing stage (fig. 8,8).

In the latter stages of preparing their report it seems that Weightman and Lyster had found it necessary to insert their '*In consequence*' note. The Hargreaves Buildings had been designed by James Picton and had only been completed in 1861, [9] and this threat to both buildings may have been one of the few occasions which united the two architects in common cause to fight the plans of a third party.

Thankfully for Oriel Chambers, Hargreaves Buildings, St Nicholas' Church and the Church Yard, these particular plans were not acted upon, and a less ambitious, purely pedestrian bridge was subsequently built from the Church Yard over the dock road (fig. 8,9).

FIRE IN WATER-STREET.—Excellent BRICKS and other BUILDING MATERIALS on Sale.—Apply to Peter Ellis, 48, Castle-street. 11jy14

8,7. From the For Sale columns of the Liverpool Mercury, 14th July 1863. Image courtesy of the British Library, from their 19th Century British Library Newspapers on-line archive, published by Gale Cengage. © British Library Board.

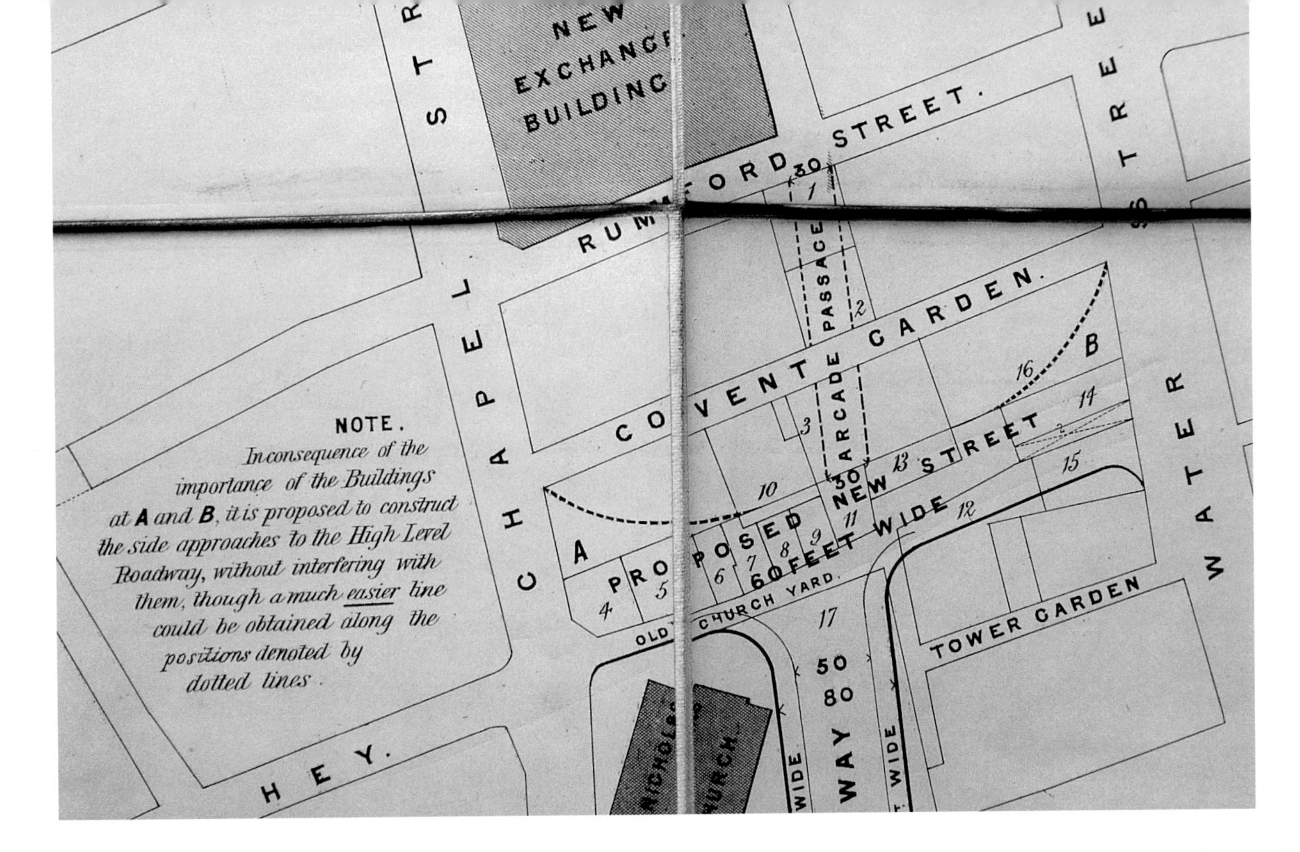

8,8. *A detail from G Fosbery Lyster's plan, dated 19th August 1864 and presented to the Finance Committee in December 1864, for a new approach to the landing stage. It indicates that 'a much easier line' to the proposed High Level Roadway was considered, whilst acknowledging the consequences to the buildings at A and B.*

Image courtesy of the LRO, ref. H 711 FIN (1864).

8,9. *The footbridge which was built a few years later in place of Lyster's more ambitious 1864 plan. It carried pedestrians from St Nicholas' Church Yard safely over the dock railway at George's Dock Gates. Image from The Graphic, 5th May 1877, p. 420.*

Private collection.

Completion of Oriel Chambers and Close found a first mention in an article entitled '*A Lounge in Liverpool*' which appeared in *The Builder* on 4th November 1865 where they are described along with a variety of other buildings recently completed or nearing completion in Liverpool.

> '*Of the many groups of blocks of new business-offices, we would especially mention a huge corner pile of building, called Oriel Close. This consists of a four storied building, every window in which is an oriel. Altogether there are more than fifty oriels in it, all of which are exactly alike, and arranged in straight tiers. Between each oriel there are moulded pilasters, or buttresses, reaching in one continuous line from basement to parapet, which are profusely decorated with Early English dog-tooth ornament. The principal rooms are lighted by three oriels, and their ceilings, owing to the exigence of the fireproof floors, are arched; each arch corresponding with an oriel, or three arches in each room. The fireproof floors are made of brick, each apartment being thus rendered independent of the accidents that may happen to others... Fire-proof flooring is much in esteem in Liverpool. It comes, perhaps, of a community of merchants that chances should be calculated to a nicety, and that all risk should be reduced to the minimum as far as expenditure can insure that desirability.*'

Two months later, and in contrast to this purely factual account in *The Builder*, a scornful Liverpool critic wrote an article suggesting that '*The plainest brick warehouse in the town is infinitely superior, as a building, to that large agglomeration of protruding plate-glass bubbles.*' This abuse is probably known off by heart by many of the people who have discovered the work of Peter Ellis since it was quoted with sadness by Quentin Hughes in 1964. [10]

The article was published anonymously in the 6th January 1866 edition of *The Porcupine*, a satirical Liverpool weekly which had recently commenced publication, was trying to establish circulation and was being published from an office in Lower Castle Street during the time that Oriel Chambers was being built a few yards away. The self-appointed guardian of good taste continued his invective at length:-

> '*Did we not see this vast abortion – which would be depressing were it not ludicrous – with our own eyes, we should have doubted the possibility of its existence. Where and in what are the beauties supposed to lie?... An oriel window is an inspiriting* [sic] *object; but a row of windows falsely so called, all bad to commence with, and all exactly alike, is the reverse. Did we say row? – we should have said a tier of rows – a sight to make the angels weep. If from the bubbles we pass our eye up to what is called a sky-line, it is perhaps, if anything, still more execrable. From the curved copings, which, in the meagrest versions of the debased Elizabethan, could not pass muster, up to the shapeless, spiritless pinnacles, all is bad.*' [11] (fig. 8,10)

So it continued, and had this denigration been confined to an obscure provincial publication, and as part of a highly idiosyncratic weekly series of 13 articles in which the author had poured scorn on much of the architecture of the city, [12] it could have passed into rightful oblivion.

However the writer was evidently so proud of his efforts that he immediately submitted the article to *The Builder*, and it was then published – again anonymously – in the edition for 20th January 1866.

8,10. Pointing heavenwards, the so-called 'sight to make the angels weep... shapeless, spiritless pinnacles, all is bad.'

Two years later similarly sarcastic comments found their way into another national publication, *The Building News*, this time actually naming Peter, together with a number of other architects in whose work the author also found fault:-

> *'The lover of the sublime in architecture, however, will be amply rewarded for previous disappointment if we turn down Water-street and contemplate the erection called Oriel-buildings, which the genius of Mr. Peter Ellis has called into existence. This is a kind of greenhouse architecture run mad... The style, in short, might be described as "lunar Gothic;" and no one who has not seen it would believe, we think, that such a thing could, in the present day, be erected in cold blood by any person calling himself a member of the architectural profession.'* [13]

Quentin Hughes, having praised both of Peter's buildings in *Seaport*, went on to reflect upon the adverse criticism that Oriel Chambers had received by adding that '*We can only guess what effect it may have had upon his architectural practice,*' and noting that Peter began to list himself in the *Gore's Directories* as both architect and civil engineer.

Subsequent commentators therefore drew their various conclusions, of which the following may be taken as representative of some of the beliefs that have grown up over the last half century: '*he was driven out of practice for his architectural eccentricity*' (1971); '*he ended up working as an obscure civil engineer*' (1995); '*destroyed by the criticism, and apparently built nothing else*' (2001); '*led to the disheartened Ellis abandoning architecture*' (2009). Chapters 10 and 11 will examine Peter's later career.

Recalling that a *'Rev. Mr. Anderson, of London'* was named by the *Liverpool Mercury* as the owner of the building that was burnt down, in 1956 Geoffrey Woodward provided evidence of a continuity of ownership for the building that replaced it. In an article – the first review to begin the process of rediscovering Peter Ellis – he noted that Oriel Chambers:-

> *'stands on the site of Covent Garden Chambers... The client was Rev. Thomas Anderson, whose initials and motto 'Stand Sure' appear on the façade.'* [14]

Thus the curvaceous first letter on the façade is a '*T*' for Thomas, and typing *'Anderson stand sure'* into Wikipedia is found to produce an article revealing the *Clan Anderson* crest badge and motto. That the connection between Peter Ellis and Thomas Anderson may have been closer than a mere business arrangement – and which might offer a further explanation as to why Peter's involvement with the sale of materials from the building that had been destroyed by fire had been so swift – is hinted at by the appearance of Rev. Anderson's name in 1885 as one of those standing surety in the Letters of Administration for Peter's will and also as an executor in Mary's will.[15] Peter would have discussed with Thomas Anderson the designs for the building, and this young curate – 27 years old when he gave Peter the commission in 1863, and eager to serve the God that he would follow faithfully for the rest of his life – may well have been a source of inspiration in the choice of the oriels which were designed to bring light into the world of the clerks, and also in the choice of roof-line. Far from a sight to make the angels weep, perhaps for Thomas the pinnacles were alighting places where the angels might sing. At the very least, the appearance of his name in both 1885 documents challenges any assumption that he was dissatisfied with the final result.

12 Electric and International Teleg. Co.
[*Covent-garden*]
14 Brebner Jas. merchant & insur. agt
M'Quie Peter R. and Son, merchants
Barbour John and Co. merchants
Bigham John, merchant
Hill John, metal broker
Bacon John, shipowner and steam-packet agent
Watson C. D. and Co. ship brokers
Persian Cosulate
Watson Caleb D. Esq. consul
Liverpool and Birkenhead Slate and Slab Co. W. B. Adamson, secretary
Perrin J., Son and Co. merchants
Chapple, Dutton and Co. merchants
Scott John, wine and spirit merchant
Truman, Hanbury, Buxton and Co. brewers
Griffith J. and A. and Co. brewers
16 Gordon John and Co. ship brokers

8,11. Occupants of 14 Water Street in Gore's 1862 directory, prior to the fire, together with neighbours in the basement of Borough Buildings at no. 12, and at the warehouse at no. 16.

Image courtesy of the Athenaeum.

Gore's Directory for 1862 lists the occupants in the year prior to the fire (fig. 8,11), and later directories show that they were scattered to offices all within a few hundred yards of no. 14. When Oriel Chambers and Close were completed, Caleb Watson the Persian Consulate returned. Into the 1870s John Gordon is shown as continuing to occupy the neighbouring warehouse, confirming that it had suffered sufficiently little damage to enable it to remain tenanted, whilst the Electric and International Telegraph office also survived whatever structural repairs were necessary to Borough Buildings.

In the mid-20th century Evelyn Saxton, a Liverpool librarian, regarded the discovery to be important enough to write in pencil at the foot of p. 40 of the LRO's copy of Charles Reilly's book *Liverpool Streets and Buildings* that

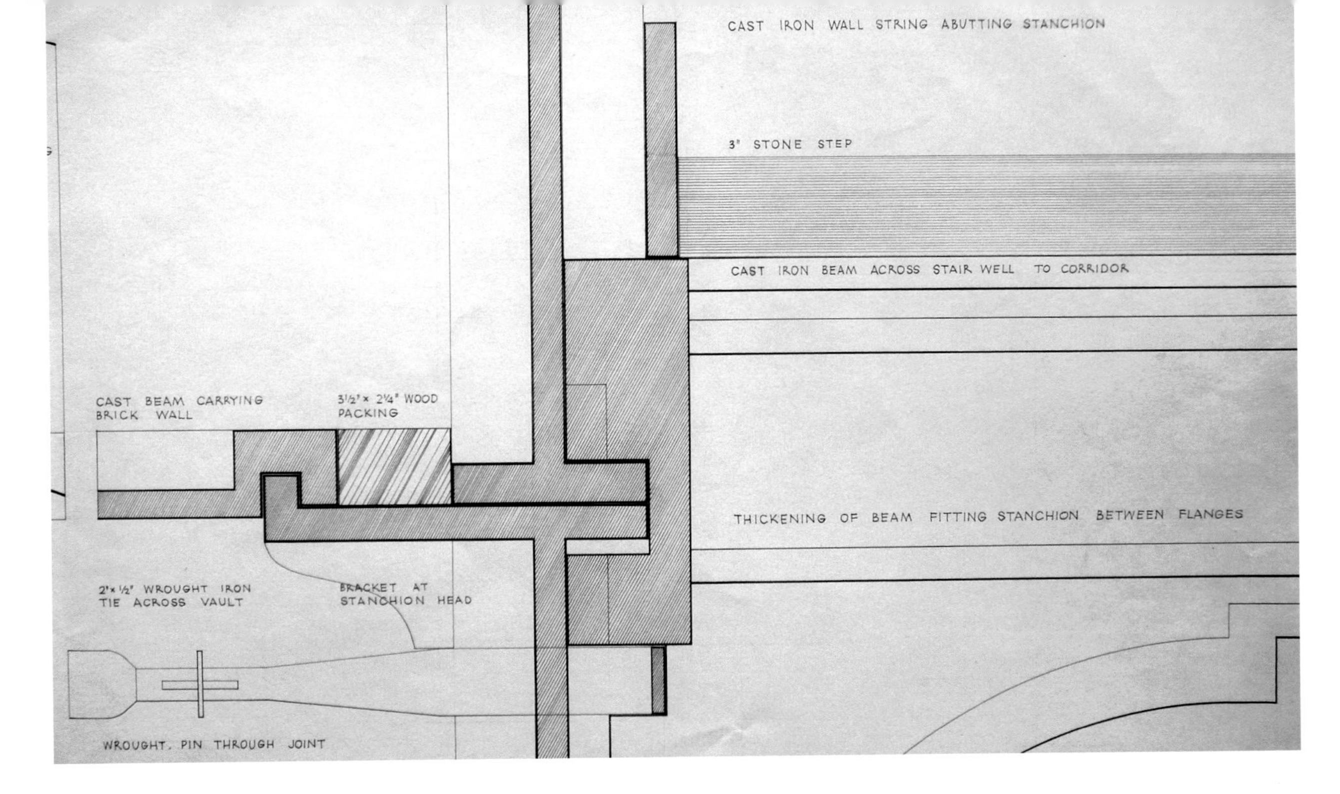

8,12. A detail from one of a number of measured drawings made by Roger Scarlett Clarke and colleagues, this one in 1956 showing how the cast-iron components locked together.

Image courtesy of the LRO (which has the plan) and the University of Liverpool Library (which holds the copyright).

'*Air-raid damage has revealed the framework to be definitely cast-iron,*' and a variety of measured drawings were produced by students at the Liverpool School of Architecture between 1955 and 1957 (fig. 8,12). [16] From where might Peter's idea of constructing Oriel Chambers around this cast-iron framework have originated, and from where might the castings have come? [17]

In 1836 Liverpool's railway terminus had arrived at the junction of Lime Street and Gloucester Street – where Peter had lived some years earlier – and had been built with a wooden roof. Subsequently redesigned by Richard Turner, when the new Lime Street Station was completed in 1851 it briefly had the largest single-span roof in the world.

> *'Here iron replaced timber to form a curved arch, symbolic of the great railway termini of the Western world. Turner pinpointed the objections to the old timber-trussed roof; the danger of fire, the necessity of a high-pitched roof to carry the slates and the wasteful depth of the trusses.'* [18]

Peter would also have known Cragg and Rickman's iron-framed churches that had been built between 1814 and 1816 – St George's in Everton, St Michael's in the Hamlet and St Philip's in Hardman Street. [19] He would have been familiar with St George's, constructed on the site of the famous Everton Beacon, from his courting days and perhaps from attendance at the funeral of Lewis Ellis, whilst in a later chapter we will see that St Philip's was next door to a building which he had designed a few years prior to Oriel Chambers. Quentin Hughes also notes several examples of visible cast-iron framed buildings in Liverpool such as the Export Carriage and Wheel Works of ca. 1859. [20] Might all these structures have acted as catalysts to Peter's creative thoughts, inspiring him to take the logic one stage further and also break with the tradition in office design?

Advertisements in the 1862 directory suggest that there were several local possibilities for sourcing the cast-iron including Henry Pooley & Son at the Albion Foundry in Dale Street (fig. 8,13), a firm that had been involved with Peter's 1856 St Saviour's National Schools. However, further afield, the Coalbrookdale Company in Shropshire is the one that R S Clarke of the Liverpool University Architectural Society pursued in 1956. The company is famous for its *Iron Bridge*, erected in 1779 and the first that was made completely of cast iron (fig. 8,14).

In carrying out his research Roger Clarke, apparently following up Geoffrey Woodward's earlier investigation in 1949, wrote letters to a number of firms regarding Oriel Chambers. They were to J&E Hall, London (known to have been makers of paternoster lifts), Melville Curlender (surveyor and valuer at Oriel Chambers), James & Bywaters, London (involved in preparing plans prior to reconstruction), and the Coalbrookdale Company Ltd. Unfortunately there seem to be no copies of the letters that Clarke sent, but the replies he received form part of the Quentin Hughes Archive at Liverpool University's Sydney Jones Library.[21]

In a reply to him on the 17th April 1956 from the Coalbrookdale Company he was no doubt disappointed to be told:-

> *'Oriel Chambers, Liverpool, 1864. In reply to your letter of the 14th inst., regarding the above we very much regret that we are unable to give you any information on this subject as unfortunately we now have no records whatever dating back to the period in question.'*

It has not been possible to determine whether Roger Clarke's decision to write to the Company was based on a reliable mid-20th century lead or merely on a hunch that the Company had provided the cast iron, but it was certainly a logical line of enquiry.

Although Coalbrookdale is perhaps best remembered today as being linked to Abraham Darby, in the latter half of the 18th century he had found it necessary to mortgage many of the shares in the firm with the Rathbone family. In the 1860s the firm of Rathbone Brothers & Co had offices at Drury Buildings in Water Street, a few yards from where Oriel Chambers was built, whilst the Coalbrookdale Iron Co had offices in neighbouring James Street.

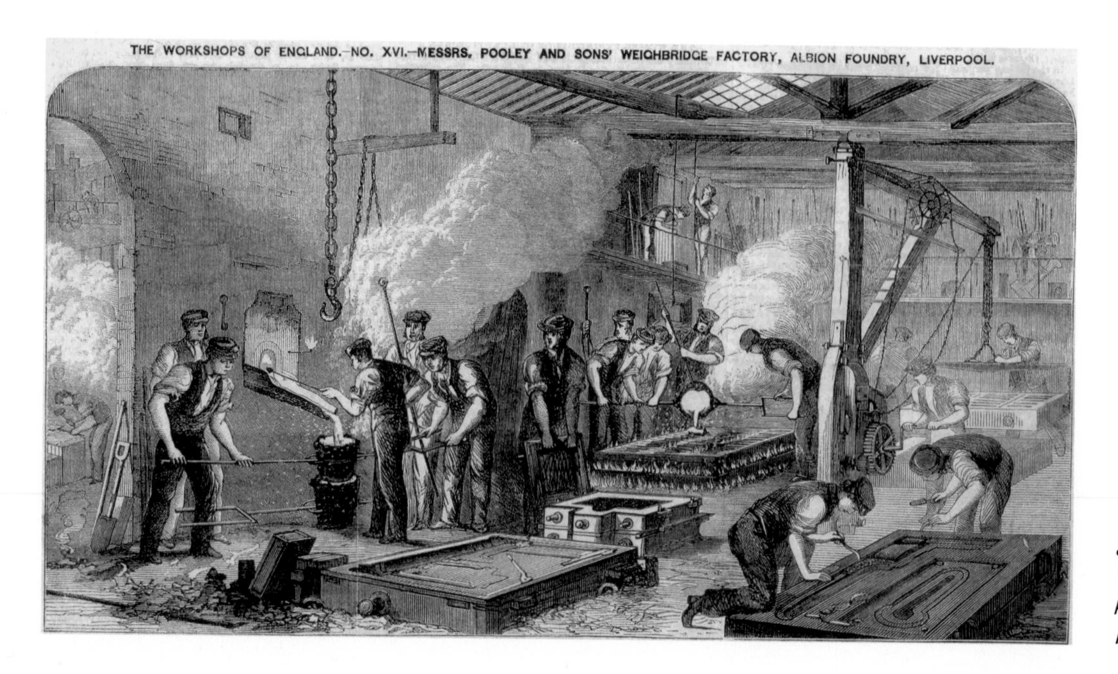

8,13. From the Illustrated Times, 8th November 1862, p. 456.

Private collection.

Of *Greenbank*, the Rathbone's country house in Toxteth Park, Lucie Nottingham comments that it had been rebuilt in the early 19th century with:-

> *'a fine cast-iron screen creating a verandah and first-floor balcony above. This screen was almost certainly manufactured at the family's Coalbrookdale foundry or, conceivably, at the Liverpool foundry of Joseph Rathbone and William Fawcitt* [sic], *which was closely connected with Coalbrookdale.'* [22]

In 1949 when Oriel Chambers was first measured after WWII bombing, '*the name of the architect seemed to have got lost,*' [14] and a comprehensive paper published in 1950 on '*The First Iron-Framed Buildings*' therefore perhaps came too early for the author to be aware of the significance of either of Peter's buildings. [23]

The Iron Bridge
& Tollhouse

Our forebears may have invented heavy industry, but in stark contrast to many of today's industrial projects, they never forgot the majesty of elegance or the importance of sheer beauty.

Absorb the sheer beauty of the Gorge and its historic Iron Bridge

Nowhere is this more artfully expressed than in the graceful lines and soaring arches of the world's first cast iron bridge. As the enduring symbol of our Industrial Revolution, it will stay in your memory forever. To the south side of the Iron Bridge you'll find the original Tollhouse, home to an exhibition revealing the secrets behind the Bridge.

The Tollhouse is open during the summer and at other times for pre-booked groups. Please check for details.

8,14. A detail from the 2012/13 Ironbridge tourist brochure (www.ironbridge.org.uk).
Image reproduced with kind permission.

Two other examples of the early use of cast iron in buildings and also claimed as forerunners of skyscrapers are recorded as being the Ditherington Flax Mill in 1797 and the Gardners Warehouse in Glasgow in 1856. The flax mill is located in a suburb of Shrewsbury, a dozen miles or so from Coalbrookdale, and is in the care of English Heritage. [24]

In a well illustrated website on Glasgow commercial buildings Gerald Blaikie writes that:-

> *'Glasgow was a European pioneer in the use of cast iron and steel for commercial buildings... rapid urbanisation of Glasgow in the early 1800's had created an unprecedented building boom which would eventually lead to the fabrication of cast iron buildings... in the mid-1800's, the industrial areas of the expanding city contained 122 furnaces... Gardners Warehouse in Jamaica Street, south of Argyle Street, dates from 1856 and is the oldest completely cast iron fronted commercial building in Britain... a structure of extraordinary elegance and lightness.'* [25]

Whatever the source of his cast iron, between December 1865 and March 1866 Peter arranged for a series of advertisements to be placed in the *Liverpool Mercury* for his fire-proof replacement to *Covent-buildings* (fig. 8,15), the first residents having already begun to arrive in October, immediately prior to the '*Lounge in Liverpool*' article.

To be Let.—Offices.

TO be Let, Fire-proof OFFICES, Oriel Chambers, Water-street.—Apply to Peter Ellis, Orange-court. 26fomh24

8,15. From the Liverpool Mercury for 1st March 1866, Peter's first advertisement having appeared on 20th December 1865.

Image courtesy of the British Library, from their 19th Century British Library Newspapers on-line archive, published by Gale Cengage. © British Library Board.

References and Notes to Chapter 8

1 The warehouse/office is reported in the *Mercury* article as *Covent-buildings*; in *Gore's Annals* for 1864 it is called *Covent-chambers* (fig. 8,5), whilst Geoffrey Woodward refers to it as *Covent Garden Chambers* (ref. 14); it is not given a name in the directories. It is shown on the 1848 O.S. map as occupied by the *Corporation of London Fire and Life Assurance Office* (fig. 8,1), although this company is absent from the alphabetical sections of the directories over the period and is not listed at no. 14 in the numerical sections. It would have been something of an embarrassment for the company if its offices had been there. The similarly named *Liverpool and London Fire & Life Assurance Co* is listed (and through which the *Annals* indicates that part of the insurance on the cotton was placed) but it had offices further up Water Street towards the Town Hall. By the time that Oriel Chambers was built on the site of the fire, the two buildings that are shown on the 1848 map as the *British & North American Mail Office* and the *Glasgow St. Packet Office* had become *Middleton Buildings* (the original home of the Cunard Line), whilst the building on the eastern junction of Covent Garden had become *Borough Buildings*. The *City of Dublin Steam Packet Office* remained that company's premises until 1874 when the site was redeveloped. The article inadvertently lists Peter Robinson McQuie with his son's initial '*B*'.

2 *Collection of drawings, lithographs, and engravings, principally views in Liverpool, Cheshire and North Wales, with portraits, &c. by John Raphael Isaac. c. 1851.* LRO ref. Hf 942.7214 ISA. The *Illustrated London News* of 14th March 1868 carried a sketch and an account of the Metropolitan Fire Brigade's practice on the Thames Embankment, where steam-operated appliances were apparently only just beginning to be introduced, and where it was said that '*A hand-worked engine, with its firemen, can be drawn by two horses at full gallop.*'

3 The Historic Society of Lancashire and Cheshire was founded in 1848 and, from the very beginning, their *Transactions* show that Peter Robinson McQuie played a prominent part. He was one of the Society's original auditors, a Member of Council for the Archaeology Section, and a frequent chairman of their meetings held at the Collegiate Institution on Shaw Street, a short distance from the Everton bridewell. Like Robert Syers some decades earlier, Peter McQuie was a collector with a keen interest in history. He is listed as donating gifts to the Society (including 14 volumes of the Liverpool Directory from 1805-1841 and a map of Manchester by James Wyatt), and as an exhibitor of a wide variety of other items (including copies of Leigh's *Natural History of Lancashire and Cheshire*, a 1769 edition of the *Liverpool Chronicle*, the 1799 *Liverpool Guide* by Moss, the 1807 *Stranger in Liverpool* by Kaye, and two views of Liverpool in 1797). He was also the custodian of material relating to his father, Captain Peter McQuie. Richard Brooke, in his book *Liverpool as it was during the Last Quarter of the Eighteenth Century*, pp. 236 and 462, recounts two stories communicated to him regarding Captain McQuie's successful sea battles against French and Spanish ships in 1797 and a third involving a mutiny by slaves in the same year which ended the captain's life.

Peter Brookshaw McQuie, the eldest son of Peter Robinson McQuie and Elizabeth Brookshaw and the office colleague of Peter Ellis, appears perhaps to have followed his father's interest in history for he is listed as an Athenaeum proprietor between 1865-1891 holding share number 234.

One of the Athenaeum's two copies of the 1805 directory contains a note signed '*McQuie, Lowhill*' which has been pasted inside the front cover and which mentions the directory and contains references up to 1859.

4 Graham Jones, Walking on Water Street. Part 3 – Borough Buildings, Water Street (1859 – ca. 1970), *Journal of the Liverpool History Society*, 2012, p. 82.

5 William Herdman, *Views in Modern Liverpool*, 1864, David Marples, plate 20. LRO ref. Hf 942.7214 HER.

6 Joseph Sharples, *Liverpool. Pevsner Architectural Guides*, Yale University Press, 2004, p. 205, explains the term *cathead* as the name for the cover over the pulley where it enters a warehouse on the top floor. The 1864 warehouse *Humyak House* at the bottom of Duke Street still exists today and provides a colourful comparison.

7 See Adrian Jarvis, *The Liverpool Dock Engineers*, Alan Sutton, 1996, for an account of Lyster's work.

8 John Weightman, *Approaches to the River*, December 1864. LRO ref. H 711 FIN (1864).

9 J A Picton, *Memorials of Liverpool*, G G Walmsley (Liverpool), 2nd edn., 1875, vol. II, p. 65.

10 Quentin Hughes, *Seaport. Architecture and Townscape in Liverpool*, Lund Humphries, 1964, p. 62. Reprinted with postscript by The Bluecoat Press, 1993.

11 Anon, The Architecture of Liverpool. Article VI, *The Porcupine: A Journal of Current Events – Social, Political, and Satirical*, 6th January 1866, p. 380. LRO microfilm ref. 050 POR. This article and the following one from 13th January were combined and appeared almost unedited in the 20th January 1866 edition of *The Builder* (it appears in *Seaport* mistakenly referenced as 22nd June, but correctly by Geoffrey Woodward (ref. 14 below)) with the authorship at the end of the article merely being given as '*Liverpool*'. Both articles in *The Builder* (4th November 1865 and 20th January 1866) are available from RIBA (www.architecture.com) from their online catalogue.

12 Over the first three articles (*Porcupine*, 2nd, 9th and 16th December 1865) the author concentrated his mean-spirited eye upon the work of John Foster junior. '*How Foster attained the reputation he did is a thing we could never fathom... One of the great advantages possessed by Foster, in addition to his local influence, was the halo shed over him by his travels and studies along with Cockerell in Greece. But how differently each used his opportunity! In Cockerell's work there is a lasting pleasure in the perfection and refinement of the details, and though he fails somewhat, at times, in breadth of effect – though sometimes guilty of grave errors of taste – though in the carving he is specially ineffective – even an ordinary observer cannot help feeling impressed with the conviction that his work is that of an educated mind... Every moulding bears the stamp of careful study; while, on the contrary, Foster, it is well-known, was of that indolent disposition which cannot abide the drudgery of work...* [he] *shows a wonderfully leaden dulness and want of imagination... the praise of Foster is usually qualified by a few touching words of pity for the ignorant influences which must have affected him.*'

Of Foster's principal buildings, he opened with the claim that, '*Take them as a whole, it would be difficult to find a more uninteresting group of edifices, either for the style which has been chosen or the manner in which it has been worked out,*' and, having proceeded to damn them one by one (for example, '*What can be a more unsatisfactory substitute for a real building than the present front of Lime-street Station?... It was intended to be a grandiose sham façade; but even in that proved a failure*' – see p. 93, fig. 5,10), he ended with the suggestion that, '*It would be both useless and tiresome to analyze more of Foster's buildings, for the same defect runs through all, and on no occasion that we know of has he risen to anything higher than the most slavish copyism.*'

In the fourth article (23rd Dec 1865) the author trained his malevolent gaze upon the Free Public Library. In the fifth (30th Dec 1865) he took a hatchet to the partially completed Corporation-buildings (the Municipal Offices on Dale Street). In the seventh (13th Jan 1866) he contrasted two buildings on Castle Street, on either side of the junction with Cook Street (see p. 123, fig. 7,3): '*...the Branch Bank of England is an exemplar of the application of Greek taste to modern wants, forming a style of which Cockerell was the introducer, as opposed to the vapid copying insipidities of the Foster school... It would be useless to waste many words on the Commercial Bank: the whole thing is a mistake.*'

In the tenth (3rd Feb 1866) his attention transferred to the Exchange: '*As a specimen of the bastard picturesque of the French Renaissance, which broke like a dirty flood upon us after the Foreign Office competition, the New Exchange Buildings, now in course of erection, offer as great a mark for satire and invective as anything done by native talent.*'

By the end of the thirteenth (3rd March 1866), although James Picton's buildings had escaped relatively lightly, the author had vented his spleen on much of the rest of Liverpool's architecture. '*How delightful it would be if, on first entering town of a morning, instead of having our optics assaulted with, say, such work as Gillham's shop, or even the Sailors' Home, some kind Murray would arise and besprinkle the town with designs...*' This writer's comments stand in contrast to those of the author of the *Lounge in Liverpool* article in the 4th November 1865 edition of *The Builder* who refers, for example, to the '*handsome Exchange*' and the '*considerable spirit and merit*' of the Corporation-buildings. Taking the 13 articles in their entirety, therefore, discerning *Porcupine* readers (if discerning townsfolk in fact read the *Porcupine*) would no doubt have been able to judge the relative merits of Oriel Chambers and the comments of the critic.

Although the identity of the writer is now known (for example in *Liverpool In Print*, search term: *Porcupine Oriel Architecture*), and may have been common knowledge within the Liverpool of Peter's day, Quentin Hughes chose not to name him in *Seaport*, and Joseph Sharples, *op. cit.*, p. 304, whilst listing him in the bibliography, charitably describes the articles as '*bracingly forthright in their criticisms.*' In 1839, and at the age of 34, Peter Ellis had been producing elegant designs for St George's Hall. In 1866 this *Porcupine* author, also aged 34, appears to have been disillusioned at the lack of rapid progress within his profession.

In the second of his articles he provides a glimpse of his frustration when he prefaces a lengthy '*digression*' with the belief that, '*Architecture is become a matter of seniority, and until a man be past his prime, used up, or bowed down with years, he has no chance*' (9th Dec 1865). In the tenth article he raises the hope that, '*Any young man, with a real love for his profession, – uneaten up by the desire for present money-getting, – if he work in faith and wait with patience, may be sure that some opportunity will occur...*' (3rd Feb 1866). His heroes were successful young architects: '*Now, mark this, – Waterhouse, Brodrick, Murray, are, or were, when they first achieved their position, very young men,*' and Murray was his favourite: '*We need only, in confirmation, point to James Murray, perhaps the only Liverpool architect really and justly distinguished, and he, poor fellow, to the eternal loss of his art, died when little over 30'* (9th Dec 1865). Whilst this 34 year old went on to have success with a number of architectural projects, he turned later in life to geology.

13 Anon, New Buildings in Liverpool (From Our Own Correspondent), *The Building News and Engineering Journal*, 7th February 1868, p. 90. The article was recovered from *Google Books* by typing (with the quotation marks as shown) "*Building News and Engineering Journal*" and *Peter Ellis Oriel* together into the search bar.

14 Geoffrey Woodward, Oriel Chambers, *The Architectural Review*, 119, 1956, p. 268 (a copy exists at the Athenaeum). A footnote reads, '*The above article was based on research carried out in 1949 by Richard Beattie, James Mount, Neil Prendergast and the author, who measured the building and produced a short historical report when students of the Liverpool School of Architecture.*'

15 The census records all show Thomas Anderson as being born in Liverpool in 1836, although a baptism record has not been traced. The 1851 census shows him at the age of 15 with his widowed mother, Anne Anderson, at North Meols, Southport. By 1861, at the age of 25, he had become the curate of St Gregory & St Peter, Sudbury in Suffolk. Although Anne was still living with him, by then he is shown as head of the household which includes a cook, a housemaid and a footman & groom. Having inherited Covent-buildings from his father he was thus already a man of some substance.

He remained a bachelor and stayed married to the church throughout his life. By 1871 he had moved to the parish of Pokesdown in Hampshire where he was the vicar, and it is there, on the day of the census, that he is shown as being visited by Henry W Syers. Henry, at that stage an undergraduate at London University, was one of the nephews of Peter and Mary (the son of Mary's brother John Aspinall Syers who had moved to Leamington in Warwickshire). The Letters of Administration on 7th January 1885 for Peter's will of 1840 names those standing surety as '*Henry Walter Syers of Clarendon Lodge Leamington in the County of Warwickshire Doctor of Medicine and The Reverend Thomas Anderson of Pokesdown Vicarage Bournemouth in the county of Southampton Clerk* [in Holy Orders].' Thomas is also named as one of the executors in Mary's will of 28th May 1885.

This pattern establishes a strong personal connection as having been maintained between Peter, Mary and Rev. Thomas Anderson subsequent to the commission for Oriel Chambers and which plausibly may therefore have extended back prior to that date.

What family members Thomas may have had in Liverpool is uncertain, though there are several possibilities. The directory for 1839 lists an Archibald Anderson and his sons Rev. David Anderson and Thomas Darnley Anderson, a merchant, at an address in Everton. The *Lancashire OnLine Parish Clerk Project* database shows that Rev. David Anderson was married in 1841 at St George's, Everton, and that he was the minister for the marriage of Thomas Darnley Anderson in 1847, also at St George's. The latter was one of the partners in the firm of Glen and Anderson whose offices are shown in the directories at the time of the fire at Covent-buildings as being directly across Water Street in India Buildings. If this merchant was a relative and had witnessed the fire, he may have been the first to mail a report to Thomas, and have then acted as an intermediary to expedite Peter's subsequent commission. Thomas Darnley Anderson was an Athenaeum proprietor from 1859-1879 holding share number 161, and James Picton (*op. cit.*, vol. II, p. 383) refers to '*Mr. T. D. Anderson, mayor in 1859*'. Prior to its demolition to make way for Peter's replacement building, the earlier 16 Cook Street included the solicitors Anderson & Collins amongst its occupants.

16 The drawings by Roger Clarke, W H G Housden, V H Cromie and David C Price are now held at the Liverpool Record Office, ref. 7/39 Architects plans: Oriel Chambers. Copyright of the University of Liverpool Library, they appear originally to have been part of the Quentin Hughes Archive, ref. D71/22/57/1-12. In this collection, along with a variety of photographs, there is a typescript by Roger Clarke, signed on 1st May 1957, describing what the students found during their measurement of the building with an introduction which reads, '*We are very fortunate in that through the demolition of the war damaged portion of the building we were enabled to examine closely the cast iron framed structure, which would not otherwise have been exposed to our scrutiny. Therefore we wish to record our gratitude to Mr Melville Curlender, who owns the building, and to the Crushed Brick and Stone Company Limited, demolition contractors, for the very kind way that we were given freedom to carry out the survey.*'

In a section regarding the beams, Roger Clarke noted that, '*An understanding of the potentialities of cast iron is revealed in the way that each beam is built up, being in fact, pretensioned. Running along the bottom of the beam, and tied to feet at the end is a wrought iron tie, of square and sometimes circular section, which was tensioned on the cast iron beam before it was erected. The tension in this tie must be considerable, as when the vaults were removed, and the columns pulled away, the beams broke laterally and not downwards.*' Quotations courtesy of the University of Liverpool Library. A number of drawings were subsequently reproduced in Oriel Chambers, Liverpool, *Architectural History*, vol. 1, 1958, pp. 84-90 (obtainable from RIBA).

17 As regards the origin of the protective facing for the cast-iron, Geoffrey Woodward refers to it loosely as '*York stone*' (*op. cit.*, p. 270), a term which is applied generally to the type of sandstone originally quarried in Yorkshire. Frank Green, a fellow member of the Liverpool History Society, in a short unpublished manuscript on 16 Cook Street (which was submitted as part of coursework for *Architecture of Liverpool*, conducted through the University of Liverpool, Centre for Lifelong Learning, in 2009), notes a reply he received from the Principal Conservation Officer at the Liverpool Planning Service, stating that '*it is known that the stone Ellis used for his other Liverpool building, 'Oriel Chambers', 1864, is of 'Storeton Stone' and was sourced from the Wirral. We don't know the precise location of this quarry, but understand that it has been closed for a long time. It's possible that he used the same quarry....*' [for 16 Cook St]. Frank's manuscript, a copy of which is held in the LHS Library, contains photographs and drawings of 16 Cook Street, an analysis of the internal and external features of the building, and a comparison with the construction of the Albert Dock warehouses.

18 Quentin Hughes, *op. cit.*, p. 163.

19 Regarding the Rickman and Cragg churches see, for example, Quentin Hughes, *op. cit.*, pp. 138-145, and James Picton, *op. cit.*, vol. II, pp. 74, 249 and 370. The ironwork for Rickman's churches had been supplied by John Cragg, owner of the Mersey Iron Foundry (shown at the junction of Tithebarn Street and Cheapside on Michael Gage's plan of 1835, a few yards from Peter's early home at Primrose Hill) and of the Old Mersey Forge (a neighbour of the Herculaneum Pottery; see Christopher Kerr's booklet on *St Michael's Hamlet, Liverpool*, 1984. LRO ref. 942.753 SAI). The bank of the Mersey between the Forge and the Dingle thus became known as the '*Cast Iron Shore*' and disappeared beneath Otterspool Promenade in the 20th century. St Michael's is still known as the '*Cast Iron Church*' and, like Oriel Chambers and St George's, is a Grade 1 listed building. John Cragg also arranged for his own house in St Michael's Road to contain a considerable amount of ironwork.

By the middle of the 19th century there was a flourishing export market for prefabricated buildings, and Quentin Hughes' account (*op. cit.*, p. 145) contains an advertisement for iron churches by Isaac Dixon at his Windsor Iron Works. On p. 109 of the 1849 *Illustrated London News* there is an enthusiastic commentary concerning an '*Iron Warehouse for California, constructed by Mr. Grantham, C.E., at Liverpool,*' with a sketch showing the warehouse being assembled on premises near the banks of the Mersey. John Grantham is listed in the directories as having an office at Orange Court until 1859.

It may be significant that, in an age when many business contracts arose from personal contact within a small community, Richard Rathbone and Richard Reynolds Rathbone were both listed in the 1849 directory as living in Falkner Square, shortly after Peter and Mary Ellis had moved there.

Quentin Hughes, in his book *Liverpool. City of Architecture, op. cit.*, p. 40, includes a colour photograph of the elegant verandah at *Greenbank*. The building was converted by him into a university club in 1964.

20 Quentin Hughes, *op cit.*, p. 57. See also Quentin Hughes, *Liverpool. City of Architecture*, The Bluecoat Press, 1999, p. 83, for a second view of the Export Carriage and Wheel Works and for his quoting of James Picton's comments on the use of iron in buildings.

21 Quentin Hughes Archive, ref. D71/22/57/16, at the University's Sydney Jones Library. The Coalbrookdale reply to Roger Clarke is quoted by courtesy of the University of Liverpool Library.

22 Lucie Nottingham, *Rathbone Brothers. From Merchant to Banker, 1742-1992*, Rathbone Brothers Plc, 1992, p. 28. The local foundry of Rathbone and Fawcett was on Lydia Ann Street, a few yards from where Peter's father had built property in Kent Square in the 1830s. It would have been an unlikely direct source of the ironwork for Oriel Chambers because the firm concentrated upon marine engineering and munitions and appears to have been well occupied in those fields during the American Civil War of 1861-1865 during the time that Oriel Chambers was being built (see Horace White, *'Fossets'. A record of two centuries of engineering*, Fawcett Preston & Co Ltd, 1958).

23 Turpin Bannister, The First Iron-Framed Buildings, *The Architectural Review*, 107, 1950, pp. 231-246. The article notes that St Anne's Church, Liverpool (1770-72) '*exhibited the earliest dated cast-iron columns in England,*' and also includes commentaries on the Coalbrookdale iron bridge, several mills including the one at Ditherington, the three Cragg and Rickman churches, and a variety of foreign examples of early uses of cast-iron in buildings.

24 Go to www.english-heritage.org.uk and enter '*ditherington*' into the search bar.

25 www.scotcities.com/warehouses.htm

Chapter 9

Open for business

Although the façade on Oriel Chambers bears the date 1864, the comment in the article in *The Builder* of 4th November 1865 regarding its being one of the '*many groups of blocks of new business-offices*' indicates why Oriel Chambers and Close did not receive a directory listing until 1867 (there being no directory in 1866). An advertisement in the *Liverpool Mercury* on 23rd June 1865 was placed by the solicitors Anderson & Collins and gives their address as being at the original 16 Cook Street. Demolition of those premises therefore started no earlier than the second half of that year, and it was not in fact until the 1868 directory that the new no. 16 was listed. The *Mercury* however provides some earlier indications of when the first occupants began to arrive in both of Peter's buildings.

From his saleroom in Oriel Close, the ship broker Henry Curry began placing regular advertisements from 25th October 1865 (fig. 9,1). Henry Curry's firm had long been established, and for several years it had been located at Walmer Buildings (at the eastern side of the junction of Water Street and Rumford Street, where Martins Bank Building now stands). In 1857 a young Charles Kellock entered the directories, being listed as a broker with *Curry & Co*, and by 1859 the firm had quickly become *Curry, Kellock & Co*. With Henry Curry now quite elderly, *Gore's* 1865 directory indicates a severing of the partnership, Curry being listed at Chapel Street and with Kellock continuing at Walmer Buildings. *C W Kellock & Co* became a prominent firm and continued into the 20th century and, by adding in the years of *Curry & Co*, proclaimed its '*100th anniversary*' in 1920.

H. F. CURRY & CO.,
BROKERS FOR THE SALE AND PURCHASE OF SHIPS AND STEAMERS, SHIP VALUERS, &c.,
ORIEL-CLOSE, WATER-STREET.

On Thursday, the 2nd November, at Twelve o'clock, at the Brokers' Saleroom, Oriel-close, Water-street, if not previously disposed of by private treaty,
The following Fishing Smacks:—

SIDWELL,
27 tons. Built at Dartmouth. Dimensions: Length, 40 5-10 feet; breadth, 13 3-10 feet; depth, 7 6-10 feet.

TURBOT,
30 tons. Built at Liverpool. Dimensions: Length, 43 7-10 feet; breadth, 12 8-10 feet; depth, 7 7-10 feet.

HERRING,
31 tons. Built at Douglas, Isle of Man. Dimensions: Length, 45 1-10 feet; breadth, 12 5-10 feet; depth, 7 6-10 feet.
The above boats are well fitted with nets, complete, and ready for work.—Apply to
H. F. CURRY & CO., Brokers.

9,1. Henry Curry's first advertisement in the Liverpool Mercury on 25th October 1865 having arrived at Oriel Close.
Image courtesy of the British Library, from their 19th Century British Library Newspapers on-line archive, published by Gale Cengage. © British Library Board.

Henry's office in 18 Chapel Street was a temporary one whilst he was waiting for his brand new office to become available. Sadly, as his life drew to a close, his time at Oriel Close proved equally short and his last advertisement was on 23rd August 1866.

In 1867 both Henry Curry's firm and his home address failed to appear in the directories, but the advertisements recognise his presence at Oriel Close and provide a fascinating glimpse of the life of a Water Street ship broker in the mid 19th century. [1]

Another early arrival, this time at Oriel Chambers, was the Commercial Union Assurance Co which began placing advertisements from 18th October 1865, noting that the Company was secured by '*Capital (fully subscribed)... £3,500,000*', and that it benefited from an annual income exceeding £250,000. By March 1866 it had extended its fire and life cover and was '*now prepared to accept Marine Insurance at current rates.*'

By 4th January 1866 the *Mercury* indicates that Henry Curry and the Commercial Union had been joined by the Birkenhead Amalgamated Brewery Co. Not previously listed in the directories, it was at the registered offices at Oriel Chambers that the Company held its general meeting on 8th May of that year, noted that '*the concern was working under a new name*', and declared a dividend rate of 10%. Delivering '*daily within a radius of three miles of the Liverpool Exchange*', by July they were advertising a range of brews including India Pale Ale from 10s.6d for a cask containing 9 gallons, '*strongly recommended during the summer months.*' At around 50p a pint in today's money, and delivered to the door, that sounds a good deal for publicans and townsfolk alike.

[*Covent garden*
14 ORIEL CHAMBERS.
Commercial Union Assu.Co
Lloyd's Register of Shipping
Mudge Robert E. secretary
Lockhart Robt.&Dempster mrchts
Scottish Widows' Life Assur. Socity
Ferguson Wm. resident secretary
London & Asiatic and American Company (limited)
Cardwell Thos. & Co. merchants
Russell, Coles & Co. merchants
Empire Assurance Corporation
Campbell Arthur F. T. manager
Preserved Provision Co
Eddowes Bros. & Co. prov. mrchts
Negroponte Constantine J. mrcht
Lucy Henry C. commis. merchant
Isborn Geo. R. surveyor
Spencely Castle solicitor
Petrie John sec. Scottish Imperial Assurance Company
14A ORIEL CLOSE.
1 Birkenhead Amalgamated Brewery Company (limited)
2 Rusden R. D. & Foster mrchts
3 Longton J. jun. & Co. shipownrs
4 Powell Duffryn Steam Coal Co
Davey Henry sole agent
5 Watson Caleb D. Esq. Persian Vice-consul
Watson C. D. & Co. merchants
6 Cheever, Pooley & Co. winemrchts
Bodiley William G. keeper
16 Gordon John & Co. ship & insu. brkrs

9,2. The entries for Oriel Chambers and Oriel Close in Gore's 1867 directory. Image courtesy of the Athenaeum.

Although Oriel Close was initially listed as 14A Water Street, this was altered to no. 16 in 1871, with the numbering further west (previously nos. 16 and 18) being imaginatively adjusted to nos. 18 and 18A. The listing of occupants in *Gore's Directory* for 1867 (fig. 9,2) and an examination of the directories for earlier years show how impressively Oriel Chambers and Close were able to attract firms from other buildings. The Commercial Union had arrived from Liverpool and London Chambers, Lloyd's Register from Tower Chambers, Robert Lockhart from Rumford Place, Thomas Cardwell from Borough Buildings, Russell, Coles & Co from Walmer Buildings, both the Preserved Provision Co and Eddowes Bros from Tower Buildings, both Negrepont and Powell-Duffryn from Brunswick Buildings, and Henry Lucy from Drury Buildings. From three buildings in Chapel Street came Caleb Watson (Richmond Buildings), Cheever and Pooley (Hargreaves Buildings) and John Petrie (no. 9). Scottish Widows, having expanded their presence at Exchange Buildings and Dale Street, now chose to list themselves at Oriel Chambers ahead of these earlier addresses. The solicitor Castle Spencely chose to begin his career there, and he and the architect George Isborn

9,3. The entrance passage to Oriel Close in February 2010 at the start of the external refurbishment to Oriel Chambers.

9,4. Oriel Close on the same day in February 2010, looking towards the entrance on Water Street that is shown in fig. 9,3.

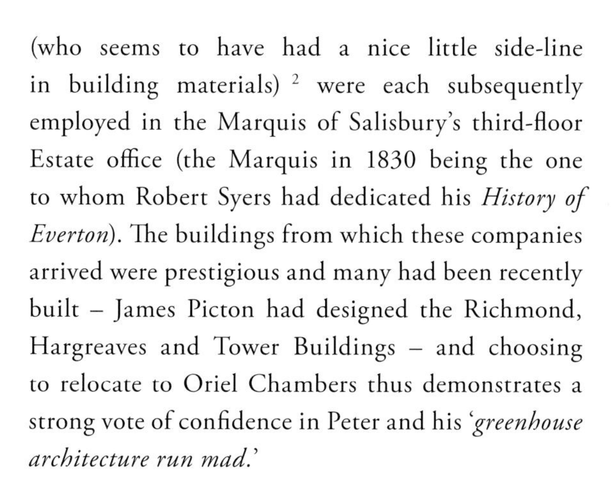

(who seems to have had a nice little side-line in building materials) [2] were each subsequently employed in the Marquis of Salisbury's third-floor Estate office (the Marquis in 1830 being the one to whom Robert Syers had dedicated his *History of Everton*). The buildings from which these companies arrived were prestigious and many had been recently built – James Picton had designed the Richmond, Hargreaves and Tower Buildings – and choosing to relocate to Oriel Chambers thus demonstrates a strong vote of confidence in Peter and his '*greenhouse architecture run mad*.'

Water Street's once-famous restaurant, *The Oriel*, is identified in the *Liverpool Mercury* as having arrived at Oriel Close in 1873 (in premises adjoining those of Llewellyn Syers at nos. 10 & 11 – see later), [3] and the mosaic tiling at the entrance to the Close has survived to this day (figs. 9,3 and 9,4). Like the businesses that had chosen to relocate, the townsfolk of Liverpool apparently also voted with their feet for, by the turn of the century *The Oriel* was occupying the whole of nos. 7-11 and, well into the 20th century, the restaurant was apparently the most fashionable place to be seen.

In May 1932 *The Liverpolitan* began its life in editorial offices at Oriel Chambers, proclaiming itself as '*A Monthly Review of Merseyside Affairs*' and with the aim of '*becoming a forum of responsible and well-informed opinion on all questions bearing on the prosperity and progress of a great maritime, mercantile and industrial community.*' In September 1932 it carried an article about the restaurant and its bar which was said to be '*of goodly size, being able at a rush hour to accommodate 300 men...*' What the women were supposed to do is not stated. Apparently at that stage of Liverpool's highly exotic life:-

> '*There can be bought and drunk on the premises a little-known drink called Pimm's Cup, which, in hot weather, has nearly all the properties of nectar...*' whilst the writer of the article went on to observe that, upon entering the bar, '*You are on hallowed ground. That the Oriel is spoken of in reverent voice and with bared head by sea-going men in every port in the world is more than a well-known fact. It is an authentic legend. With his hand on his heart, a second officer has told me that when Liverpool sailors meet in China or Peru, in the icy mountains or on the coral strands, the mention of the Oriel is a sheer inevitability.*'[4]

The Oriel was bombed out of existence in WWII, but the sign for no. 7 was still on the entrance wall when Quentin Hughes came to prepare his book, as p. 76 of *Seaport* indicates. Although the mosaic tiling still seeks to welcome visitors to the restaurant, the gate to the deserted courtyard is now routinely locked; but maybe the ghosts of the past don't mind.

In the mid 1870s Oriel Chambers became home to the *Brocklebank Line*, whilst the *Houlder Bros. Line* was resident there for several decades (both lines operating to Australia), and various other shipping lines and ship owners joined them.

The most enduring association however was with *Gracie Beazley and Co.* The Company, founded in 1864 by James Beazley as the *British Shipowners' Co Ltd* (fig. 9,5), arrived at Oriel Chambers in 1896 and stayed faithfully at the building throughout WWII and the reconstruction that followed. The Company was still there in 1970 when the last edition of Kelly's directory was published.

The British Shipowners' Company, Limited,

14, WATER STREET,
LIVERPOOL, *6th February, 1900.*

SIR,

In conformity with a Resolution passed at the Thirty-sixth Ordinary General Meeting of the Company, held this day, I have the pleasure to forward to you the subjoined Warrant for Dividend on the Shares held by you on the 27th January, the day on which the Transfer Books were closed.

I am, Sir,
Your obedient Servant,
T. W. WHITING,
Secretary.

DIVIDEND FOR YEAR ENDING DECEMBER 30TH, 1899,

THREE SHILLINGS AND NINEPENCE PER SHARE, FREE OF INCOME TAX.

Name of Proprietor Revd. T. W. Sale

Dividend on 15 *Shares,* £ 2 : 16 : 3

IMMEDIATE NOTICE SHOULD BE GIVEN OF ANY CHANGE OF ADDRESS.

I hereby certify that the Income Tax on the Amount of this Warrant will be paid by me to the proper Officer for the Receipt of Taxes.
T. W. WHITING, *Secretary.*

N.B.—Proprietors claiming exemption from Income Tax are informed that the Inland Revenue Department will receive this Statement as a Voucher.

This part may be retained by the Proprietor.

9,5. A dividend certificate issued in 1900 by the British Shipowners' Co Ltd which was founded in 1864 by James Beazley and subsequently managed by Gracie Beazley and Co at Oriel Chambers.

Private collection.

JOSEPH GOODACRE, Wine and Spirit Merchant (formerly of Church-alley), respectfully intimates that henceforth his business will be conducted at
THE NEW PREMISES,
No. 16, COOK-STREET,
Which have been erected with a special view to the peculiar requirements of the Trade.
The Stores are replete with a choice Stock of Wines and Spirits, which have been selected with great care, and are in the finest condition.
Hampers or Cases of assorted Wines or Spirits packed to suit the convenience of Customers.
All Goods delivered Carriage Free. 22node18

9,6. From the Liverpool Mercury for 26th November 1867 showing one of Joseph Goodacre's first advertisements for 'The New Premises'.

Image courtesy of the British Library, from their 19th Century British Library Newspapers on-line archive, published by Gale Cengage.

The earliest advertisement traced in the *Liverpool Mercury* to indicate completion of Peter's other new building at 16 Cook Street is for the wine and spirit merchant, Joseph Goodacre, who began to advertise '*The New Premises*' from November 1867 (fig. 9,6). The clients who commissioned Peter to build no. 16 were Paterson and Thomas,[5] and the earliest *Mercury* advertisement that has been traced for them is for 17th March 1868 where they were acting as house and land agents, whilst entering themselves in the directories as accountants. Paterson and Thomas together with Joseph Goodacre comprise the occupants listed there in the 1868 directory. Goodacre would have had the lower ground floor and basement for his wine and spirits, with the accountants on one of the upper floors. It is highly likely that Paterson encouraged Goodacre to relocate there, for the 1867 directory (printed before the move to Cook Street) shows them as neighbours in Church Alley (fig. 9,7). Joseph Goodacre may therefore have been given the opportunity to influence the design of the basement storage. [6]

Paterson and Thomas must have been pleased with what Peter produced, for the firm is shown as still at 16 Cook Street over a century later in the final edition of Kelly's directory. In addition to their permanent offices, the remainder of the 19th century saw no. 16 as home to a large variety of other occupants. By 1871 the Prudential Assurance Co, the Runcorn Smelting Co, the Weardale Iron & Coal Co, an architect and a consulting engineer had arrived. By 1880 the Lancashire and Yorkshire Railway Town Inquiry and Parcels Office, an agency of the Goole Steam Shipping Co, a wool merchant, a wool broker and a solicitor had joined the architect. 1894 saw it as a branch of the St Peter's Building Society (with Paterson and Thomas as managers), offices for a firm of solicitors, a stationers, a civil engineer, a shipping agent and a lithographic writer and – as a refreshing addition – the British Workman Public House Co Ltd cocoa rooms. In 1900 the building provided an office for the magnificently named *Up Up Patent Filling Paste Co Ltd* with an equally delightful E R Window as its secretary.

CHURCH ALLEY.—W [*Church st*
2 Tabley James beer house
3 Paterson Thos. Simpson estate agent
4 Goodacre Joseph wine & spirit mrcht
5 Wynne and Pinnington estate agents
6 Evans Barton victualler

9,7. The 1867 directory entry showing Paterson and Goodacre as neighbours in Church Alley prior to their arrival at 16 Cook Street. Today, the side of the building opposite the entrance to the Athenaeum defines the site of these offices.

Image courtesy of the Athenaeum.

Returning to developments at Water Street, the 1868 directory shows the arrival of an important new occupant at Oriel Close, that of the lithographer Llewellyn Syers, and to understand the significance it is necessary to go back a little in time. It may be remembered from chapter 5 that the two witnesses at Peter and Mary's wedding in 1836 had been Thomas Syers (Mary's brother) and Mary Ann Kelshall. Mary Syers (sister of the three brothers Robert, George and William Syers) had married John Kelshall, a Liverpool shipwright, on 11th September 1796 at St Thomas' Church (LRO microfilm ref. 283 THO 3/2), where Robert and George Syers' signatures appear as witnesses. On 13th March 1802 Mary gave birth to Mary Ann Kelshall, and she was baptised at St Nicholas' Church on 14th April of the same year. [7] Mary Ann Kelshall was thus a cousin of Mary Helen Ellis.

Born on the 17th February 1832, Llewellyn was the first child of Thomas Syers and Anna Maria Dickenson Syers, [8] but he was 11 years old before being baptised on 19th July 1843 at St Anne's, Richmond, on the same day that his younger brother, Thomas Daniel (born 12th January 1837), was also baptised (LRO microfilm 283 ANN 2/2). From 1829 to 1835 their father had been listed in the directories as having his shop in Clayton Square, but in 1835 *The London Gazette* (24th April, p. 811) recorded the dissolution by mutual consent of his partnership there with Joseph Jackson. Events seemingly took a turn for the worse, for in 1837 the *Gazette* (19th September, p. 2455) gave notice that the:-

> *'creditors who have proved their debts under a Fiat in Bankruptcy awarded and issued against Thomas Syers, late of Clayton-square, Liverpool, in the county of Lancaster, Tailor and Draper, Dealer and Chapman, are requested to meet the assignees of the estate and effects of the said bankrupt...'*

Further tragedy was to ensue for Llewellyn and his little brother before they were baptised, for the will of Peter Ellis (dated November 1840 and never revised) refers to a provision for the payment of '*Twenty pounds annually to the Trustees of the late Thomas Syers for the use of his Orphans...*' Did Anna Syers die giving birth to Llewellyn's brother in 1837, and did Thomas subsequently die of a broken heart and a shattered career? Both are uncertainties, but between 1837 and 1840 the little brothers would have needed a guardian angel to watch over them. And one duly arrived.

Mary Ann Kelshall received her first unambiguous directory listings in the 1839 and 1841 issues where she is shown at 29 Great Nelson Street, and the 1841 census shows that Llewellyn and his brother were already there with her.[9] Opposite them at 28 Great Nelson Street were living Thomas Henry Syers (one of the sons of Robert Syers, the writer of the *History of Everton*) and his wife Harriet. On the same baptism page and immediately above the 1843 records for Llewellyn and his brother appears the baptism of Thomas and Harriet's son, Henry Wadsworth Syers, which had taken place a week earlier at St Anne's. It thus appears likely that Thomas Henry, Harriet and Mary Ann had made arrangements to have Llewellyn and his brother baptised soon afterwards. [10]

The 1851 census shows that both Llewellyn (aged 19, by then an apprentice lithographer [11]) and his brother (aged 14, scholar) were still living with Mary Ann (unmarried, age 49, living on an annuity) at York Terrace, Everton, together with a servant and a daily governess. Llewellyn and his brother are listed as Mary Ann's cousins. In 1861 the census return shows that Llewellyn, lithographer and now 29, was still living with Mary Ann, age 59, together with a servant and a boarder, at Boundary Lane, West Derby Road.

Mary Ann's last directory entry was in 1865 at Towerlands Street, Edge Hill. Then, on 23rd January 1866 the records for Holy Trinity, Walton Breck, show that *'Llewellyn Syers, 34, bachelor, lithographer, 93 Woodville Terrace, Everton'* married *'Fanny Tyrer Nicholson, 26, spinster, 23 Nile Street'* (LRO microfilm 283 WBK 3/1). Llewellyn's father is given as *'Tailor Deceased'*, whilst Fanny's father, George Wilson Nicholson, is shown as *'Sail Maker Deceased'*. Woodville Terrace is listed in the directories as running off Breck Road, the name having originally been Breck Lane, the address to which the family of Mary Helen Syers had moved in 1834.

One of the witnesses signing the register at Llewellyn and Fanny's wedding is shown as Mary Ann Kelshall. By that date, however, Mary Ann had ceased to enter her name in the directories, and in 1870 she died. Her probate record on 6th May 1870 reads:-

> *'The Will of Mary Ann Kelshall late of Woodville-terrace Everton Liverpool in the County of Lancaster Spinster deceased who died 3 April 1870 at Woodville-terrace aforesaid was proved at Liverpool by the oath of Llewellyn Syers of 93 Woodville-terrace aforesaid Printer the sole Executor.'*

Tragedy had befallen Llewellyn and his brother as young boys, and they had been immensely fortunate to find care and protection with Mary Ann, who was thus destined to live out her life unmarried, a witness to the weddings of others. In the failing years of Mary Ann's life a grateful Fanny and Llewellyn Syers, in the midst of bringing up their young son Alfred, faithfully in their turn had looked after her. Just how important a part she played in the lives of some of the other people in this story will probably never be known.

New Mode of Reckoning Cab Fares.—The mode of determining cab fares in such towns as Liverpool and Manchester has always been found a perplexity, and he would be deemed a clever man who could solvé this difficult problem. Mr. L. Syers, of Oriel Close, Water-street, in this town, has just published what he terms a ready reference and cab-fare plan, which at least possesses the qualifications of simplicity and clearness. The map of the parliamentary limits of the town are covered with hexagons each representing a quarter of a mile in diameter, so that the precise distance may be ascertained from place to place at a glance. Should the authorities adopt this plan after its accuracy has been thoroughly tested, it will tend very much to simplify an extremely difficult question.

9,8. A report in the Liverpool Mercury for 13th November 1868. Image courtesy of the British Library, from their 19th Century British Library Newspapers on-line archive, published by Gale Cengage. © British Library Board.

Llewellyn Syers first appears in the directories in 1867 as a lithographer at the age of 35, shown at his home address at Woodville Terrace. From 1868 to 1879 the numerical sections of the directories list him as a lithographer at premises in 11 Oriel Close (and later also at no. 10), whilst the alphabetical sections additionally note him as being an engraver and printer. The *Liverpool Mercury* for 13th November 1868 (fig. 9,8) indicates that he had put a map of Liverpool to ingenious use, and his interest in maps will be mentioned again later.

The 1871 census record shows that Llewellyn and Fanny by then had a four-year old son Alfred and that, on the day that the census collector called, Ann Ellen Ellis, a 67 year old widow, was a visitor. The census collector was sufficiently impressed to note that Llewellyn was a *'Master Lithographer employing 4 men & 6 boys.'*

Within the small number of census records examined during this research, this collector deserves particular praise for his admirable handwriting and his attention to spelling – thus providing one of the very few occasions that Llewellyn Syers managed to have both first name and surname entered correctly into records.

The priest at his baptism in 1843 registered him as *Llewllyn*. The census collector in 1851 recorded him as *Llanelly*, and the collector in 1861 managed an impressive double with *Llewlyn Syres*. The priest at Llewellyn's marriage got it right, but the transcriber for the online database managed to spoil the result with *Llewelly*.

Perhaps, inevitably, the final insult for Llewellyn was to be recorded as dying six years before the directories and the *Liverpool Mercury* suggest that he stopped working. The online probate record for 1873 reads:-

'Syers Llewellyn. Effects under £3,000. 3 April. The Will of Llewellyn Syers late of Woodville-terrace Everton Liverpool in the County of Lancaster who died 17 March 1873 at Woodville-terrace was proved at Liverpool by Fanny Tyrer Syers of 93 Woodville-terrace Widow the Relict the sole Executrix.'

This is, to say the least, a little puzzling, for within a fortnight Llewellyn seems to have thought better about departing from this life and placed a series of advertisements in the *Liverpool Mercury*, beginning on the 29th March 1873, suggesting that by then he may have been looking forward to moving in a more earth-bound direction:-

'Wanted, by June or July next, a comfortable, roomy House in the suburbs; not less than three entertaining rooms and eight bedrooms, with usual offices and good drainage. West Derby or Tuebrook preferred. Rent about £100.– Address "House," care of L. Syers, printer, Oriel-close, Water-street.'

If this was a desired move for himself rather than for one of his clients then the advertisement came to nothing, for in 1875 and 1876 Fanny and Llewellyn are each recorded in the alphabetical section of *Gore's Directory* as still living at Woodville Terrace. Then in 1877 they are both listed as having moved to Gladstone Terrace, Oakfield Road, Anfield (fig. 9,9), whilst on 2nd January of that same year Llewellyn placed an advertisement in the *Mercury*:-

'Found in the Philharmonic Hall, on Saturday Evening, Dec. 23rd, a Purse containing money. Owner may have it by paying for this advertisement.– Apply to L. Syers, lithographer and printer, Oriel-close, Water-street.'

Syers Mrs. Fanny 9 Gladstone terrace Oakfield road, N
—— Mrs. Frances 148 Crown st. E
—— Henry W. tea dealer (*T. H. S. & Son*) Springbank, Sefton road Litherland, W
—— James 51 Warwick st. S
—— Joseph porter 30 Lovat st. E
—— Llewellyn lithographer engraver and printer Gladstone terrace 9 Oakfield road Anfield, N—office Oriel close 16 Water st. W

9,9. Gore's 1877 directory entry for Fanny and Llewellyn Syers showing their having moved to Oakfield Road. The Henry W Syers who is also shown was another nephew of Mary Helen Ellis, the Henry Wadsworth Syers who had been baptised a week before Llewellyn at St Anne's.

Image courtesy of the Athenaeum.

In 1878 and 1879 the *Gore's* alphabetical sections list Fanny as now living at Osborne Terrace, Egerton Street, New Brighton, with Llewellyn, by then well established in business, choosing to be entered solely at his business address at Oriel Close.

It is only in 1880 that Llewellyn's name finally disappeared from the directories, and it would therefore appear that up to that period Llewellyn was still enjoying life as a lithographer, stubbornly defying his 1873 probate entry. In the 1880 directory his premises are listed as having been taken over by another lithographer and stationer, William Lowe, who subsequently advertised, '*On Sale, 24 Views in St. Helena, India, Abyssinia, &c.*' (*Mercury*, 14th October 1881).

The 1881 census confirms that Fanny, at the age of 40, had become a widow, that she was still living at Osborne Terrace with Alfred, now her 14 year old son, and that an Ann Ellis, a widow aged 78, had been visiting them that day. Whether this was the Ann Ellen Ellis who had been a visitor in the 1871 census is uncertain, but it indicates a well-established and continuing closeness within the Ellis and Syers wider families.

The history and science of the development of lithography is an interesting one. The word means '*written on stone*' (Greek – lithos, '*stone*'; graphein, '*to write*'). It remains to this day as one of a variety of specialist techniques for printing, and is said to have been invented near the end of the 18th century by a Bavarian. The prints in Herdman's 1843 and 1856 collections of his '*Pictorial Relics*', for example, bear the statement, '*Drawn on Stone by W G Herdman*', or '*On Stone by W G Herdman*', of which a number have been used in earlier chapters (for example fig. 9,10).

9,10. A detail from W G Herdman's depiction of Low Hill in 1790 (see p. 21, fig. 2,13). The lithographer was Greenwood. Private collection.

Use has been made earlier, with reference to the fields upon which Primrose Hill (p. 7, fig. 1,14) and Falkner Square (p. 104, fig. 6,2) were each built, of sections of a 1796 map by Charles Eyes. Copies of this map exist at both the Athenaeum and the Liverpool Record Office, and although it states in the decorative title that it is the result of '*an Actual Survey by Chas: Eyes 1796*', along the bottom margin run the words:-

> '*Published according to Act of Parliament, June, 1796, by Chas. Eyes. - Sold by Adam Bowker, 17, Stanley St. Dale St. Liverpool. Lithographed by L. Syers, 14a Water St. Liverpool.*'

The map also includes a table '*Showing Increase of the Town and Port of Liverpool*' in various categories, with comparison columns headed with the dates 1570, 1710 and 1851. This final date therefore makes it clear that the map was being offered for sale (as a limited edition of 250 copies) on the understanding that it was a reproduction of a 1796 original.

9,11. The shop of Edward Bowker at 27 Renshaw Street in 1901, where Edward was still listed in 1900 as a fine art dealer and bookseller, at premises proudly displaying, 'Patronised by HRH the Prince of Wales'. It stood a few doors away from where Peter's office had been in the 1830s and early 1840s.

Image courtesy of the LRO, ref. WG30, Renshaw Street, March 1901 (one of several with the same watercolour gallery number).

The directories indicate that through much of the 1850s and 1860s Adam Bowker had listed himself as a furniture broker, then between 1867 and 1870 as a '*furniture broker & map seller*', and then in 1871 as a bookseller (with his son, Edward, having joined him). In 1872 Adam and Edward moved from Stanley Street to 27 Renshaw Street and by 1886, when Adam's name disappears from the directories, his son is shown as taking over the business as '*bookseller and fine art dealer.*' Edward continued at this address until the turn of the century when his delightful '*Old Curiosity Shop*' (fig. 9,11) fell victim to a comprehensive Corporation Improvements Scheme (see chapter 3, figs. 3,21 and 3,22).

Thus between 1868 (when Llewellyn is first listed as a lithographer at Oriel Close, 14A Water Street) and 1870 (the last year that Oriel Close was no. 14A before becoming 16 Water Street), Llewellyn reproduced a Charles Eyes' map of Liverpool from three quarters of a century earlier. [12] Once completed, the reproduction was perhaps offered for sale in Adam's shop alongside the book '*Liverpool Table Talk a Hundred Years Ago*', published in 1871, the year in which he had first listed himself in *Gore's Directory* as a bookseller. [13] Neither the Athenaeum nor the LRO possesses a copy of the original Eyes' map and it may be that we have Llewellyn's family connection with Robert Syers to thank for having made this reproduction possible. Robert had known where to put his hands on at least one early map (the inset at the foot of fig. 4,2, chapter 4, is titled '*Copied from an Old Map in the Town Chest*') and may therefore have possessed others and left them to his family.

Whatever the explanation for the record of his Mark Twain-like departure from this life in 1873, in fact for most of the 1870s Llewellyn Syers enjoyed working in close proximity to his uncle, because in 1872 Peter is shown in *Gore's Directory* as having arrived to occupy the ground floor premises of 10 Oriel Chambers, whilst advertisements in the *Liverpool Mercury* indicate that he had in fact already moved there during 1871. One advertisement (19th May) was with regard to the sale of the Woolton Hall Estate, and another (8th July) was for the sale of a safe.

> *'TREASURE SAFE, BY MILNER. - To be Sold, a large Safe, of recent make and of the highest class, appropriate for bankers, bullion merchants, and jewellers. Will be sold for little more than half the cost. - Apply to Peter Ellis, Oriel-chambers, Water-street.'*

9,12. A view of the north side of Water Street around 1880. Compare the magnificent array of chimney pots on Oriel Chambers with the situation today (fig. 9,13).

Image courtesy of Colin Wilkinson at The Bluecoat Press (see http://streetsofliverpool.co.uk)

The earliest known photograph of Water Street (fig. 9,12), kindly made available by Colin Wilkinson at The Bluecoat Press who dates it at roughly 1880, shows what the neighbouring buildings looked like as Peter Ellis would have passed them on his daily journey to and from his office at Oriel Chambers from 1871 onwards. In the foreground at the junction with Rumford Street is Middleton Buildings, the home of the Cunard Line, and between that and Covent Garden is Borough Buildings, [14] the home of the Liverpool Steam Ship Owners' Association, of the American Chamber of Commerce, and of Ismay and Imrie's White Star Line. Both buildings have long since vanished and an office block, 8 Water Street (Norwich House), now occupies the site. On the left of Oriel Chambers can be seen the warehouse/office which had survived the 1863 fire (see the comment on p. 135). Its archway entrance led to a courtyard called Molyneux Place (p. 133, fig. 8,1) and, beyond that, to the Old Church Yard of St Nicholas.

Both the office and courtyard were teeming with ship brokers, merchants and agents at that period. When the building was replaced around 1893, the entrance from Water Street to Molyneux Place was lost. In 1922 this replacement was given the name New Zealand House (being largely occupied by the New Zealand shipping companies of James Dowie & Co and Marwood & Robertson) and the building still exists today. On the extreme left of the picture is a building which had been constructed in the mid 1870s and which became the home of the African Steam-ship Company and of the ship owners John Glynn & Son. It had a short life, being replaced in the early 20th century by Colonial House, built as the headquarters for the empire of Alfred Lewis Jones and which was destroyed in WWII.

9,13. The north side of Water Street in July 2012, from the edge of Norwich House (8 Water Street) to the River Mersey.

Thus, of the five buildings with which Peter was familiar, only his own Oriel Chambers has survived, despite the Blitz, and a photograph in 2012 (fig. 9,13) shows just how much Water Street has changed and extended itself towards the river Mersey since Peter arrived at his office each day. The photograph shows, right to left, the merest edge of Norwich House (with its protruding 1970s windows), the junction with '*Cove t Garden*' (the missing '*n*' having escaped long ago), Oriel Chambers and the entrance to Oriel Close, New Zealand House (with its restaurant awning), Reliance House (the replacement for Colonial House), and Tower Building (the site of the ancient Tower of Liverpool, and where the river Mersey at high tide many centuries ago had lashed its walls). Beyond the dual carriageway, the Royal Liver Building stands on part of the site of George's Dock, closed around 1900.

9,14. Cook Street in 1941 after the May bombing, photographed by Marsh & Son, Hoylake.
Image courtesy of the LRO, ref. Photographs & Small Prints: Streets and Districts: Cook Street.

Had Peter still been alive when the Royal Liver was being built he would no doubt have been fascinated by the construction methods (and might have recommended a paternoster lift). When, once a year, Water Street used to provide one of the extended venues for the Mathew Street festival and the street was temporarily closed to traffic for the erection of a stage, how many of those thousands of fans who came to the city to enjoy the concerts had any idea of the world-wide significance of Oriel Chambers, the building outside which they happily danced and sang?

Unlike Oriel Chambers and Close which suffered considerable damage during the May Blitz of 1941, 16 Cook Street had a very narrow escape during WWII bombing. The 1941 photograph (fig. 9,14) shows the remains of the arcade on Cook Street shortly after the air-raid of 3rd-4th May, looking towards Castle Street and with nos. 14 and 16 just off camera to the left. Following the blitz the basement of the bombed out arcade was converted into an emergency reservoir for fire-fighting.

9,15. The scene at the junction of Cook Street and North John Street in 1948 by a photographer from the City Engineer's office.

Image courtesy of the LRO, ref. Photographs & Small Prints: Streets and Districts: Cook Street.

9,17. A view in September 2011 of the lower ground floor premises of the carpet specialists Morris Jones and Son and the upper ground floor office of the contemporary art gallery Editions. Compare the modern frontage with the situation in fig. 9,16 below, left (and p. 179, fig. 10,12) when there was a panel carrying the occupant's sign. This was removed some years ago and a right hand doorway constructed to match that on the left.

9,16. A detail from a photograph in a 1965 edition of The Architectural Forum. [16]

Image courtesy of the University of Liverpool Library.

A busy 1948 scene (fig. 9,15) shows the junction with North John Street with the tailor's shop of John Marley on the ground floor of no. 18, then no. 16 and one of the cafés of J Lyons at no. 14, and finally the cleared area further to the right which had become one of a large number of post-war bomb-site car parks. [15] This vacant ground later became the home for 43 Castle Street, the modern office block that exists today.

In the 1960s the lower ground floor and basement of 16 Cook Street were occupied by a branch of Cash and Carry (fig. 9,16, where a *Daily Post* vendor can be seen taking advantage of the little-used passageway between nos. 14 and 16), whilst today they are home to Morris Jones & Son, carpet specialists (fig. 9,17). Intriguingly, from the early 1950s and until at least 1970 a certain G Raymond Ellis, chartered architect, also had his office in Peter's building.

References and Notes to Chapter 9

1 From October 1865 Henry Curry placed advertisements several times a week in the *Mercury*, on occasion with up to five advertisements within the same edition. His first at Oriel Close was for the sale of three fishing smacks of between 27 and 31 tons, '*fitted with nets, complete, and ready for work*' (fig. 9,1). In November his advertisements included the sale of a schooner of 72 tons, '*carries 130 tons dead weight on a light draft, shifts without ballast, and will take the ground with any cargo.*' By December he had added a 155 ton brig, '*classed twelve years A1 at Lloyd's... fitted with patent reefing topsails*', whilst in January 1866 the '*Brigantine Catherine Hughes*' and the '*handsome Barque Selina*' were up for auction. His last advertisement was 23rd August 1866.

2 *Liverpool Mercury*, 11th August 1866: '*To Builders and Contractors. – Sand for Sale, Alfred-street, Wavertree-road. – Apply to Mr George R. Isborn, architect and surveyor, Oriel-chambers, Water-street.*' 27th October 1866: '*Brick Earth for Sale, on moderate terms, Rose-lane, Wavertree. – Apply to Mr. Geo. R. Isborn, architect and surveyor, Oriel-chambers, Water-street, Liverpool.*'

3 The *Mercury* indicates that *The Oriel* had predecessors. In the 20th April 1869 edition an advertisement was placed, '*Wanted, immediately, a good Broiler. – Apply at S. Walsh's Dining Rooms, 14A, Oriel-close, Water-street*', whilst the edition for 1st September 1869 noted that '*Abraham Abrahams applied for a license to Nos. 7, 8, and 9, Oriel-close, and 14A, Water Street. Rent, £300; assessment, £270. Mr. Worship supported, and stated that the premises were used purely for a refreshment house, which would not be open on Sundays. Granted by 9 to 3.*' (A Abrahams is listed at 7-10 Oriel Close in the 1870 directory and is shown as succeeded by Frederick Thomas in 1871; the directory for 1872 shows 7-9 as empty, and that Llewellyn Syers had expanded into no. 10). Then, finally, the advertisement columns of the edition for 8th November 1873 contained the notification that '*Oriel Restaurant, Oriel-Close, 16, Water-Street, Liverpool. Under entirely New Proprietorship. Breakfasts, Luncheons, Dinners, and Teas, from Nine a.m. Till Eight p.m.*'

4 'There is a Tavern in the Town. IV. - The Oriel. By Tankard', *The Liverpolitan*, September 1932, p. 23. LRO ref. Hq 052.721 LIV, 1932.

5 16 Cook Street, Liverpool, *Architectural History*, vol. 1, 1958, p. 91 (available from RIBA), cites Paterson and Thomas as the clients who commissioned 16 Cook Street. The writer of the article had access to '*Office papers written by Patterson* [sic] *in 1911*' (which gave the cost of the building as £7,052) and '*Drawings and Report: prepared by David Barlow and J. Mackay-Lewis and kept at the Liverpool School of Architecture.*' After the introduction, pp. 92-94 consist of three pages of drawings, the originals of which are now held at the LRO.

Joseph Sharples (e-mail 31-03-13) has kindly provided two further pieces of evidence which suggest that 16 Cook Street was still internally unfinished on its upper floors in late 1867, and was not available to be occupied by other tenants until well into 1868 (thus missing the deadline for *Gore's Directory* for 1868). The first is an advertisement in the *Liverpool Mercury*, 22nd April 1868, '*16 Cook Street, To be Let, the offices on first, second and third floors of this building. Apply to Paterson and Thomas, house and land agents, 16 Cook Street.*' The second is from the *Liverpool Journal*, 30th May 1868, '*16 Cook-street – The offices in this newly erected building being now ready for occupation...*'

6 The current owners of 16 Cook Street are a husband and wife partnership, Olwen McLaughlin (an Athenaeum proprietor) and Stephen Edgar. They purchased the building for their contemporary arts gallery and framing business *Editions* (fig. 9,17). Stephen is an enthusiastic guide for periodic tours of the premises and, ever since they arrived, he suspected that the design of the basement indicated that it had been purposely constructed for the correct storage of wine and spirits, noting that it was cool and relatively dry unlike the cellars of neighbouring buildings.

7 The record of Mary Ann Kelshall's birth can be found on the *Lancashire OnLine Parish Clerk Project* website, but what happened to Mary and John Kelshall after the birth of Mary Ann is uncertain.

The family tree for Robert Syers that has been posted on ancestryinstitution.com lists a Mary Syers who died in 1830, age 51, as his sister, but this cannot be the same sister that married John Kelshall unless she reverted to her maiden name (the family tree does not know of her marriage, possibly because she is listed on the database as *Syres*, this being a consequence of a mistaken entry by the priest). There is a one-line probate record for the death of a John Kelshall in 1807, describing him as a mariner (a shipwright that was required on voyages and had perished as a result?).

In contrast to ancestry records, the Kelshall name in the directories (except for one isolated instance in 1867) is unique to Mary Ann. In those days information was still often communicated only verbally, since many people could not read or write, and the potential for names to be recorded incorrectly was high if they sounded very similar. A comparison of ancestry records and directory listings shows that there are several instances where it is clear that the same people appear in the former as *Kelshall* and in the latter as *Kelshaw*, whilst there are even occasional overlaps with *Kilshaw*. A Mary Ann Kelshaw appears in the 1821 directory as a milliner and in the 1824 directory as a dressmaker but then vanishes.

8 The marriage record for Thomas Syers and Anna Maria Dickenson has not been traced, but the date of the marriage would have been between 1829 (when Thomas is listed at home with his parents at 15 Everton Village) and the birth of Llewellyn in 1832. Only one Anna Maria Dickenson is listed on ancestryinstitution.com, born on 21st May 1805 and baptised at All Hallows, Tottenham, London on 20th June. If this is the correct record (and assuming *Dickenson* was her maiden name), she was almost exactly 2 years older than Thomas Syers (born 27th May 1807).

9 The 1841 census record appears to have been poorly completed. The collector entered the Great Nelson Street address as being occupied by a Mary Kelshall, independent, age 25, Llewellyn Syers, age 9, and Thomas Syers, age 4. The absence of Mary's middle name is not too much of a problem – many census collectors made incomplete entries, including the 1841 one for Mary Helen Ellis – but by 1841 Mary Ann Kelshall was 39 years old. The *Lancashire OnLine Parish Clerk Project* website does not know of a Mary Kelshall born around 1816.

10 Thomas Syers is listed at Great Nelson Street in the numerical section of the 1841 directory, but he is not listed in the alphabetical section, perhaps suggesting that he died in 1840 after the numerical for 1841 had been compiled but before the alphabetical was completed.

Why he did not have his children baptised soon after their births is not known. The 1843 baptism records show his profession as '*Draper*' without mention that he was '*deceased*'. This omission was however apparently not uncommon since, for example, there is no mention on the certificate for the second marriage of Robert Ellis in 1840 that his father was also dead (chapter 3). In addition the address on both Llewellyn and his brother's certificates is given as Great Homer Street, although this was not their address in 1843 at the time of the baptisms but was the address of Thomas Syers in 1832 when Llewellyn was born.

11 With whom Llewellyn had become apprenticed as a lithographer by 1851 is unknown but, given that Peter Ellis had chosen John McGahey as the lithographer for his St George's Hall competition designs in 1839, it was perhaps with John that Llewellyn received his training. The LRO has several examples of John McGahey's work.

12 James Picton (*Memorials*, vol. II, p. 311) refers to '*Charles Eyes's map of 1796*' but gives no indication as to whether he believed he was examining an original or Llewellyn's copy, and subsequent historians appear to be split as to whether an original ever existed.

In the typed index of maps held at the Athenaeum, the entry for the map that Adam Bowker offered for sale carries the suggestion that it is '*Apparently a compound of Eyes's map of 1785 and Gore's map of 1796.*' Comparison of Llewellyn's lithograph and the 1785 Eyes map does indeed show them to be essentially identical in outline and, according to this theory, the changes required to update the 1785 map could have been made by using Gore's map as a reference.

An alternative view was held by Ronald Stewart-Brown in his account, Maps and Plans of Liverpool and District by the Eyes Family of Surveyors (*Transactions of the Historic Society of Lancashire and Cheshire*, 62, 1910). He wrote (p. 155) that '*In 1796 Charles Eyes seems to have published another plan of Liverpool.*[3] *I have not seen the original survey or any original issue of this plan, but there is a reprint by Bowker in which the plan is said to be "from an actual survey by Chas. Eyes, 1796."* [4] ', with his footnote no. 4 suggesting that '*Gore's smaller plan of 1796 is no doubt based on Eyes' survey of that year.*'

Thus it could be argued either that Adam and Llewellyn constructed their map from various sources (and perhaps decided that putting the name of Charles Eyes on it would make it more attractive to purchasers), or that Charles Eyes did indeed produce a 1796 map based on his personal survey and bearing his name, that a copy had survived and had come into the possession of Llewellyn Syers (or Adam Bowker), but that the original has since vanished.

Stewart-Brown makes the additional observation, this time regarding John Eyes' map of 1765 (the original of which does survive), that '*In 1865 a reprint, in colour, of the original plan was published by Dr. Dawson.*[3] ', with his footnote no. 3 reading '*Lithographed by McGahey, and sold by A. Bowker.*' Thus John McGahey (with Llewellyn working alongside?) produced a lithograph copy of the 1765 map, Llewellyn Syers produced a lithograph copy of the 1796 map, and both were sold by an enterprising Adam Bowker from his premises in Stanley Street.

For many years a conjectural aerial view of '*Liverpool as it appeared in 1650*' hung in the Liszt Room of the Philharmonic Hotel in Hope Street. The original is to be found in the Binns Collection, vol. 9, LRO ref. 942.7204, and the Philharmonic copy was inscribed '*Taken from a model designed & made by Augustus Harding, July 1853, and Published by A. Bowker & Son, Booksellers, 27, Renshaw St, Liverpool.*' It was a great disappointment to discover that when the Philharmonic Hotel was recently redecorated this view was apparently discarded. George Chandler's book *Liverpool* (Batsford, 1960, p. 274) illustrates yet another Bowker map from '*Bowker's Views of Old Liverpool*'.

13 In the second chapter of *Liverpool Table Talk a Hundred Years Ago* (LRO reference 942.721073 BOA) there appears the comment that '*John Eyes, whose maps of Liverpool in 1765 and 1796 have rendered his name famous, was an architect and surveyor*' (mistakenly attributing the 1796 map to John Eyes who died in 1773). On the final page of the book a comment is made concerning '*a very curious Map of Liverpool published in 1796, by Charles Eyes, surveyor of the town.*'

The *Table Talk* book was the result of a combination of the work of two authors. The first chapter, with a preface date of 1856, was by James Boardman and was based on contributions which had originally appeared in the *Liverpool Mercury*. The second chapter, '*Being a Continuation of Mr. James Boardman's Work Upon the Same Subject*', provides neither an author nor a date of writing.

However, the book was published in 1871 and one of the publishers was Adam Bowker at his address in Stanley Street. Since the second chapter opens with the words, '*In Stanley-street...,*' the chances are that the author was Adam Bowker himself.

14 Graham Jones, Walking on Water Street. Part 3 – Borough Buildings, Water Street (1859 – ca. 1970), *Journal of the Liverpool History Society*, 2012, p. 82.

15 Another photograph of the devastated Cook Street Arcade, viewed from Castle Street, appears in the 70th Anniversary booklet, *Mersey Blitz. Liverpool Under Siege*, Liverpool Daily Post and Echo, 2011, p. 17, whilst a photograph of it in use as an emergency reservoir '*as it appears today*' (1943) is on p. 21 of *Bombers over Merseyside*, Liverpool Daily Post and Echo. After the war the artist Allan Tankard was commissioned to capture views of the city, and a scene looking west from Victoria Street in 1949 shows a less busy Cook Street than that in fig. 9,16, perhaps on a leisurely Sunday afternoon (LRO, ref. Binns Coll. C241, also reproduced by Kay Parrott, *A Portrait of Liverpool, The Paintings of Allan P Tankard*, The Bluecoat Press, 2006, p. 39).

16 Quentin Hughes, *The Architectural Forum*, Nov. 1965, p. 49. The text for this article, entitled *The Perils of Vision*, was a slight variation of the 1964 *Seaport* narrative. The paper is included as part of the Quentin Hughes Archive at the Sydney Jones Library, ref. D71/22/57/17.

No. 3.

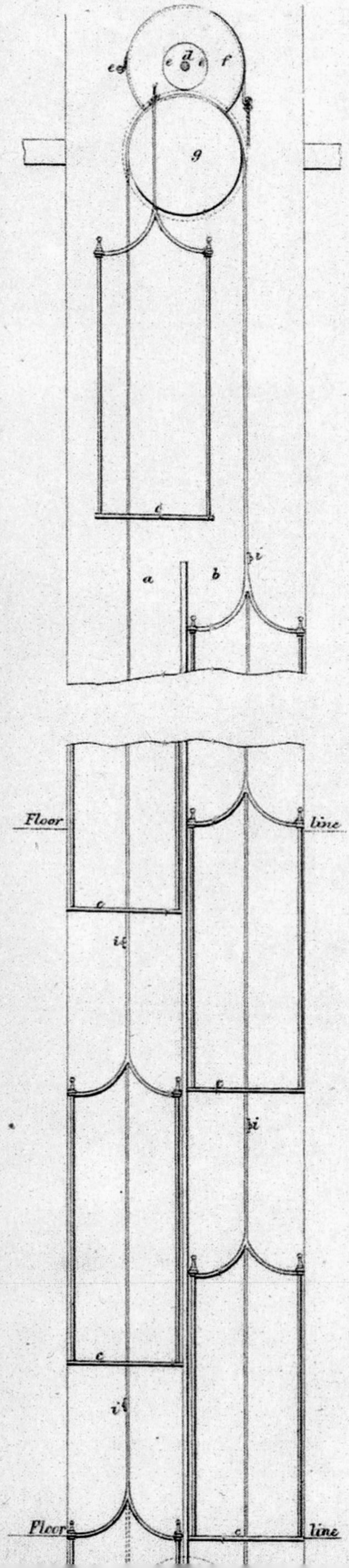

No. 2.

No. 4.

Floor line

Floor line

Floor line

Floor line

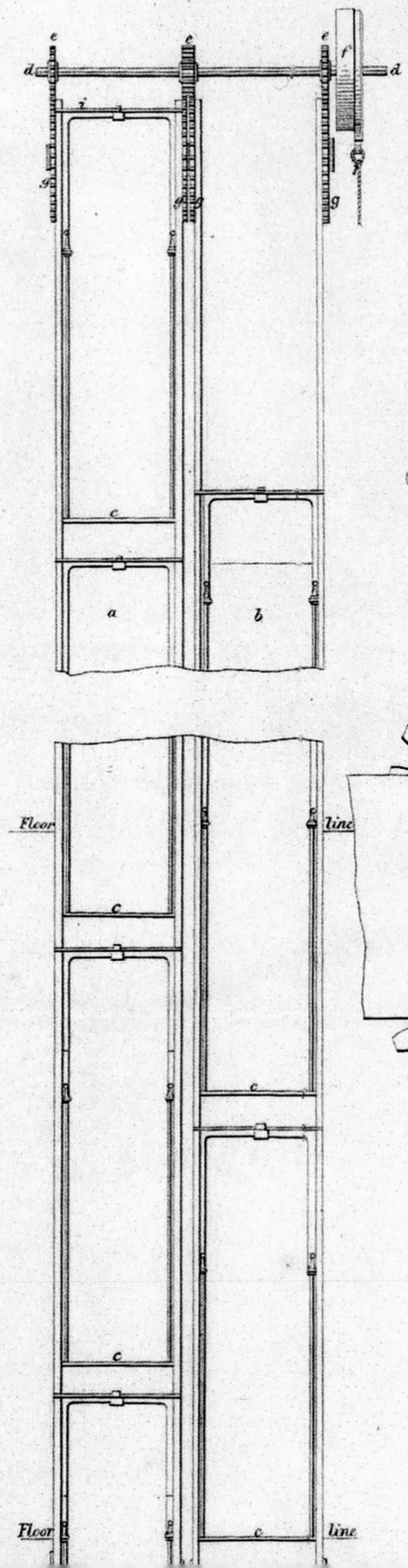

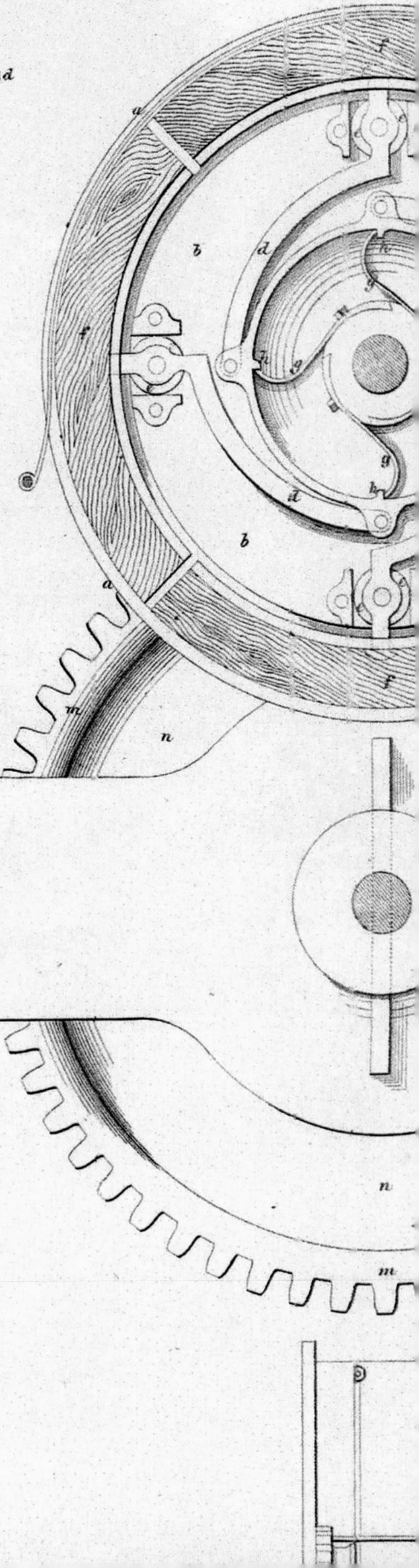

Chapter 10

Onwards and upwards

We have seen that Peter had begun to think of himself as both an architect and a civil engineer by the time he produced an undated revision to the St Saviour's National Schools infants' classroom whilst at Orange Court (p. 126, fig. 7,6).

Quentin Hughes drew attention to Peter's choice of directory descriptions after the completion of 16 Cook Street:-

> *'although he practised for another eighteen years, it will be noticed that by 1867 the entry in Gore's Directory has been changed to include 'Civil Engineer' and by 1884 (the next entry) the words Civil Engineer precede Architect suggesting that the bulk of the firm's work was in that field and that Ellis's talent was directed away from architecture after the completion of No.16 Cook Street.'* [1]

He did not elaborate upon where within civil engineering he thought Peter's talents might have been leading him, but Quentin Hughes was certainly accurate in the suggestion that the area had attracted Peter's attention.

However, it is interesting how many subsequent commentators leapt upon the phrase '*was directed away from architecture*' (as though by an external force) and drew the conclusion that this aspect (if not the whole) of Peter's career had been destroyed by the damning article concerning Oriel Chambers.

That he never designed another building became (and remains) a commonly held assumption, and it is significant therefore to note that on 10th August 1866, six months after the denigratory *Porcupine* article, an advertisement was placed by a committee secretary requesting tenders for the erection of a Welsh Baptist Chapel in Hall Lane, indicating that information was obtainable from Peter (fig. 10,1).

Readers of the advertisement would have anticipated that the person from whom particulars could be obtained was the architect himself, and in a letter to Gillian Moore in 1997 Quentin Hughes confirmed that Peter did indeed design the chapel. [2] Clearly the Welsh Baptists had maintained their faith in Peter.

Contracts.

TO BUILDERS.—TENDERS are desired for the ERECTION of a WELSH BAPTIST CHAPEL in Hall-lane. The necessary information and particulars may be had of Peter Ellis, 8, Orange-court, Castle-street.—By order of the committee,
R. WILLIAMS, Secretary.

10,1. An advertisement in the Liverpool Mercury, 10th August 1866, regarding a chapel for which Peter was the architect.

Image courtesy of the British Library, from their 19th Century British Library Newspapers on-line archive, published by Gale Cengage. © British Library Board.

The southern end of Low Hill was at the junction with Prescot Street and Kensington (p. 69, fig. 4,12). Hall Lane was its continuation south, a few yards from Peter's earlier home at Gloucester Place. The lane was last shown by its earlier name of Mount Vernon on Mawdsley's map of 1864 which accompanied their *Gore's Directory* of that year (fig. 10,2), and James Picton wrote of the area that:-

> *'The land on the east side of Mount Vernon Street, extending to Hall Lane (originally Mount Vernon), was for several years the Volunteer parade-ground, and witnessed many a gay display of martial ardour in the early days of Volunteering. In 1864 it fell into the hands of the Welsh builders, and was soon covered with neat rows of cottages.'* [3]

The chapel is first listed in the 1870 directory at the corner of Hall Lane and Doddridge Street, and Mawdsley's map of 1872 (fig. 10,3) shows the streets that the builders had constructed. The map is marked '*14a*' at the junction, and in the accompanying legend the building is confirmed as an addition to the list of Liverpool's several Welsh chapels. James Picton continued his commentary on the area with the observation that:-

> *'The only building of a public character in this block is the Welsh Baptist Chapel, Hall Lane, built in 1869. It is a brick building, in the pointed style. The front has a three-light window, the mullions of which are neatly moulded in brick.'*

Whether he unwittingly bracketed Peter with the Welsh builders into whose hands the Volunteer ground had fallen, perhaps unaware that he had been the architect of the chapel, is not known, and this appears to be the only occasion in which one of Peter's buildings received a favourable comment in James Picton's *Memorials.*

10,2. A detail from Mawdsley's map of 1864 showing the triangle of land which had been the Volunteer parade-ground. Mount Vernon was a continuation south of Low Hill Road, whilst Mount Vernon Street was a continuation of Harper Street.

Image courtesy of the Athenaeum.

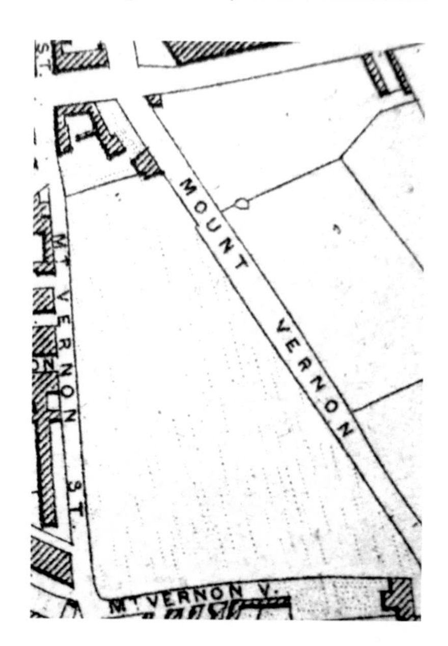

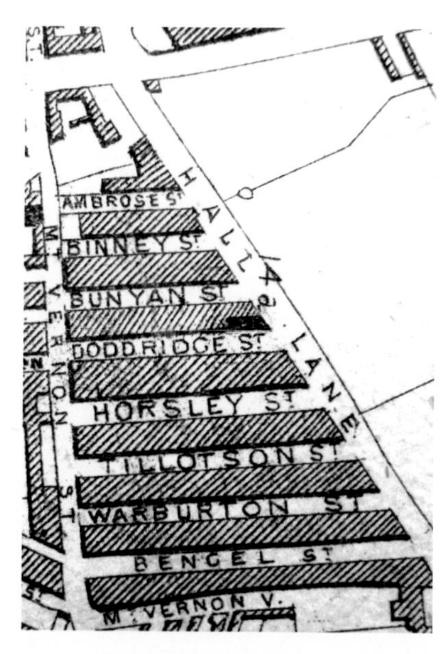

10,3. A detail from Mawdsley's map of 1872 showing the renaming of Mount Vernon to Hall Lane and the streets that the Welsh Builders had constructed.

Peter's Welsh Baptist Chapel is marked as '14a' at the eastern end of Doddridge Street.

Image courtesy of the Athenaeum.

In 1877 the chapel (fig. 10,4) [4] became a Reformed Presbyterian Church, a description it maintained until WWII when it appeared in the directories as the *Reformed Presbyterian Church of Ireland*. After the war it became home to *St Stephen's Evangelical Church*, and was last listed as *St Stephen's Evangelical Church and Barbican Bible Institute* in 1962. From the very beginning of its life in Hall Lane the chapel had been outnumbered by six hotels and public houses, and the 1827 O.S. map (fig. 10,5) marks where one of them, *The Star*, stood on the opposite corner of Doddridge Street. [5] The street was at an acute angle to Hall Lane, and the map also shows how Peter designed the building to maximise the use of the plot of land.

10,4. The Hall Lane Welsh Baptist Chapel (1868 – 1876), subsequently a Reformed Presbyterian Church and which ended its life in the 1960s as the St Stephen's Evangelical Church and Barbican Bible Institute.

Image courtesy of the LRO.

10,5. The Hall Lane area on the 1927 O.S. map ('Resurveyed in 1890-1. Revised in 1925') showing the Church at the junction with Doddridge Street, the Sacred Heart Church at the junction with Prescot Street, and some of the several public houses which were destined briefly to outlive Peter's building.

Image courtesy of the LRO.

The whole western side of Hall Lane was eventually cleared and today the site of the chapel is occupied by the *Kensington Fields Community Centre*, whilst Mount Vernon Street has vanished having been replaced by an extension of Low Hill to the junction with West Derby Street and Grove Street. With '*Gateway*' being a currently fashionable planners' designation, the whole area is now part of the '*Hall Lane Gateway Scheme*', part-funded by the European Union.

On 7th April 1874, the *Liverpool Mercury* reported upon a social gathering of employees of the Parcels and Luggage Delivery Company Ltd which had taken place the night before. The gathering had been:-

> *'in commemoration of the opening of the new premises, 20, School-lane... suitable provision being made in the warehouse for the reunion... The new premises are large and commodious, and seem to be well adapted for the purposes of the company. They were built by Messrs. Campbell Brothers, Mr. Peter Ellis being the architect.'*

In the decade after the construction of Oriel Chambers and 16 Cook Street, Peter thus designed another building although, sadly, the warehouse seems to have had a surprisingly short life. The company had listings at that address in 1875 and 1876, during which time it observed the bankruptcy of a similarly named rival, [6] but later directories show that it then moved to nearby Wood Street.

The building provided a home for glass merchants for most of its remaining time, following which the whole of the western side of the junction of School Lane and Hanover Street was redeveloped, and a large block called Abney Buildings seems to have swallowed up the Parcels and Luggage Delivery Company's site. Confirmation can be seen in the similarly designed gables on the School Lane and Hanover Street sections both of which bear the date 1883. [7]

From these chapel and warehouse commissions, from evidence in chapter 11 of advertisements and reports of proceedings in the *Liverpool Mercury* right up to his death, and from Peter's obituaries in the *Daily Post* indicating that he was *'generally and deservedly respected'* and had continued to be *'held in high esteem by the members of his own profession,'* it will become clear that, despite the *Porcupine* article, Peter maintained his practice as a highly regarded architect, surveyor and valuer, *'ever ready with his kindly advice.'*

If the buildings that he created were unpretentious – modest terraces of houses, a school of *'plain structure'*, a simple chapel, a warehouse and, as we shall see later, a homoeopathic dispensary *'free from architectural extravagance'* – and not on the James Picton scale of magnificence, then that was Peter's appropriate response to what the townsfolk and his clients required; as Nikolaus Pevsner remarked, even of Oriel Chambers itself, *'He wanted functionalism obviously, not grandeur.'* [8] That Peter was capable of grandeur is, of course, clear from his designs for St George's Hall.

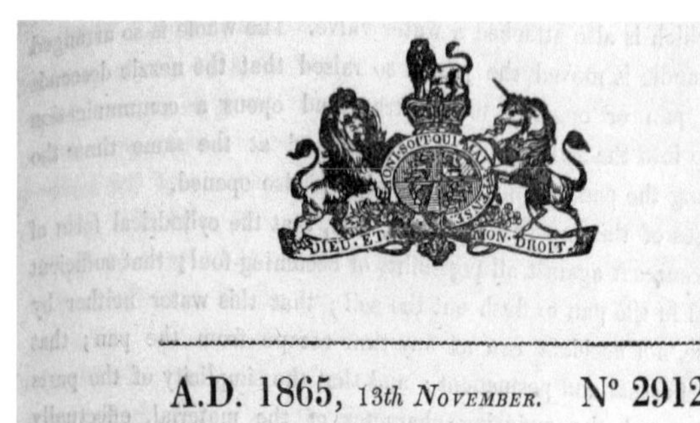

A.D. 1865, 13th November. N° 2912.

Watercloset.

LETTERS PATENT to Peter Ellis, of No. 9, Orange Court, Liverpool, in the County of Lancaster, Architect, for the Invention of "AN IMPROVED DESCRIPTION OF WATERCLOSET."

Sealed the 1st May 1866, and dated the 13th November 1865.

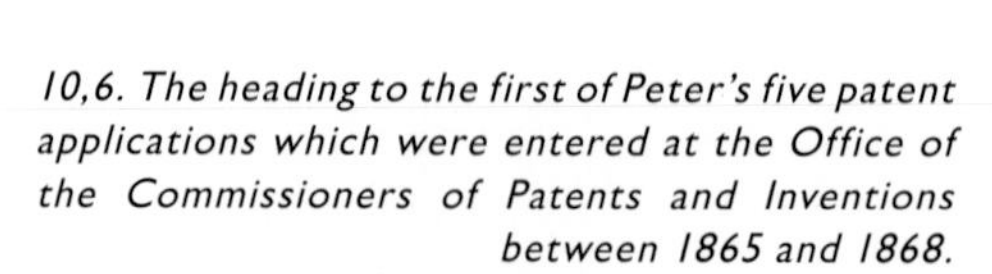

10,6. The heading to the first of Peter's five patent applications which were entered at the Office of the Commissioners of Patents and Inventions between 1865 and 1868.

Image courtesy of Sheffield Central Library, Reference and Information Section.

In addition, however, as Quentin Hughes had observed, in the mid-1860s Peter's interests had already begun to move in a new direction, and it is this aspect which perhaps adds most to our understanding of the sheer breadth of his creativity. James Picton chose to retire at the age of 60 to concentrate upon writing his *Memorials* whereas, at the same age, Peter decided to enjoy life as an inventor, having discovered that there were many other things which were firing his imagination.

Between 1865 and 1868 Peter applied for provisional cover for several patents on a surprising range of ideas. In 1865 the provisional was for the invention of '*an improved description of watercloset*' (fig. 10,6), in 1866 for '*an improved lift, hoist, or mechanical elevator*', in 1867 for '*an improved description of breech loaded and needle exploding fire arms, and cartridges appropriate thereto*', in 1868 for '*improvements in letter boxes and bags for receiving letters*' and also in 1868 for '*an improved conveyance or omnibus parts of which invention are applicable to other carriages.*'[9]

The patent applications make fascinating reading and only samples of text from the first and the last will be covered here since they are all obtainable from Sheffield Central Library.

The timing of Peter's first provisional is interesting in that it follows soon after the decision by Liverpool in 1863, as a result of the Sanitary Amendment Act of 1854, to convert the pail closets in the town's courts to water closets. The opening description of provisional 2912 on 13th November 1865 stated:-

> *'That my said improved watercloset consists of an enamelled cast or wrought iron pan. That part of the bottom of the pan is in an inclined elevation, so that water in good quantity is retained therein. This pan is moveable on axles, and sustained in position by a counterpoise; that connected with the said pan is a capacious nozzle descending to a near contact with an equally poised or balanced pan closing the mouth of the customary trap connected with the soil pipe. Within the said first-described pan, but supported independent of it, is an enamelled oval or circular rim, also of cast or wrought iron. Attached to the first pan is the handle of movement, to which is also attached a water valve. The whole is so arranged that when the handle is moved the pan is so raised that the nozzle descends upon the under pan or opening to the trap, and opens a communication through the trap into the soil pipe to the sewer, and at the same time the valve for cleansing the pan and flushing the pipe is also opened.'*

The subsequent full specification, with no less than 11 accompanying figures, indicated that in its various modifications it was:-

> *'appropriate for schools, hospitals, prisons, and second-class uses, in places of business and dwelling houses; it is also applicable as a sink for housemaids' use...*[and to]*... guard against improper matters being put down the closet, particularly when used in schools...'*

A counterpoise under the pan and a tin attached to the valve spindle, each containing lead shot, were to be employed to '*facilitate exact adjustment*' and to '*regulate the speed of operation*'.

Peter's signature was witnessed at Orange Court by his clerk, John E Belcher of Seacombe Villa, Cheshire. John's name appears on all the applications, and the name of Samuel Belcher – possibly his son – will appear in chapter 11.

A main concern in the last of his five patent applications, 3663 on 2nd December 1868, was to provide a means of preventing omnibus crew from pocketing some of the fares. Peter's provisional was outlined as involving:-

'A carriage of equal or greater than usual width for internal accommodation, but occupying less width of the public roads; the interior floor to be but about eight or nine inches above the road; the roof to be easily, safely, and decorously accessible and well guarded, and with means of rapid covering in the event of inclement weather or rain; with precise, certain, and commodious means of recording the number of persons or passengers using the same, and with a sure system of break [sic] *for preventing undue acceleration on declining roads; and the whole from the character of the construction stronger, safer, easier of traction, and from a better system of ventilation more agreeable of use.'*

The full specification included nine diagrams, two of which are shown in figs. 10,7 and 10,8, and the provisional continued with a detailed description of the carriage and included an explanation that:-

'a passenger going into the omnibus enters the passage and approaches the barrier; the conductor by his lever opens the barrier, less trouble than opening a door, and at the same time the access to the passage closes, and this process connected with appropriate wheelwork records the fact of the opening; the same process is used on a passenger leaving the omnibus, and the opening of the barrier is again recorded; thus by dividing the numbers indicated by two the exact number of passengers is known. The barrier cannot be moved without the recording or registration, and as the passage will not contain two persons then there can be no apprehension of fraud. I also propose means of communication between the conductor and driver by a speaking tube.'

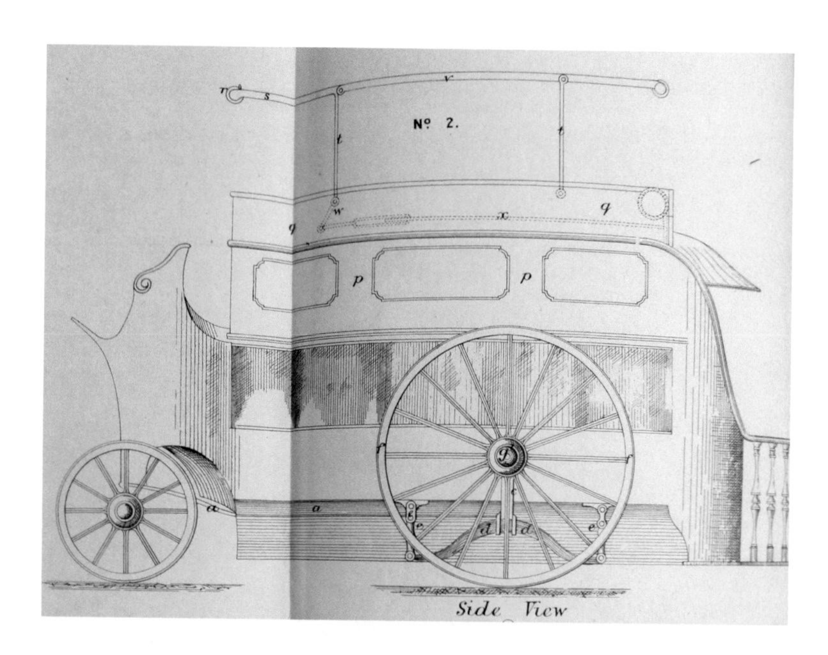

10,7. A side view in the December 1868 application 3663 of Peter's proposed omnibus. Until electrification of the tramway system from 1898, omnibuses and tramcars were drawn by horses. See the horse-drawn omnibuses in Water Street in the early 1860s on p. 135, fig. 8,5.

Image courtesy of Sheffield Central Library, Reference and Information Section.

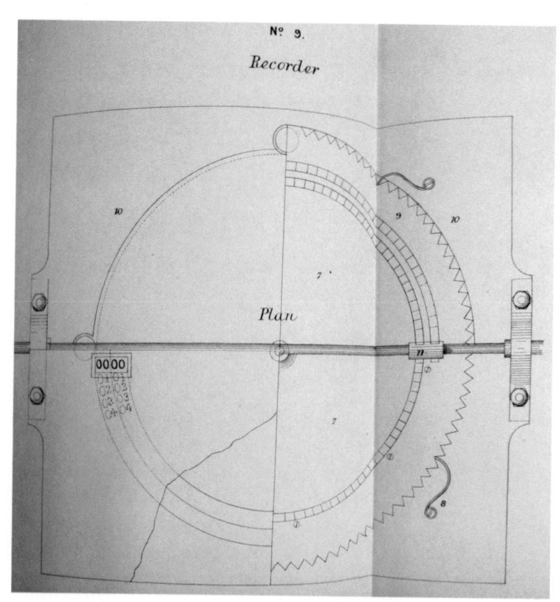

10,8. The mechanism for recording the number of rotations of the turnstile for passengers entering and leaving the omnibus in application 3663.

Image courtesy of Sheffield Central Library, Reference and Information Section.

Just as the town's decision to change to water closets seems to have prompted the first of Peter's ingenious inventions, so it appears that problems on the town's omnibus services had led Peter to produce a creative solution to it in the last of his applications. In their fascinating history, J B Horne and T B Maund mention that the *Liverpool Road and Railway Omnibus Co Ltd* was registered in 1860 and in their book they provide a selection of abstracts of the company's meetings at their Clayton Square offices. They indicate that on 8th February 1868 the minute book recorded that:-

> *'There is much fraud among the bus guards, as there is with all bus companies. Two directors went to Paris to study bus operation in that city, and to look into different methods of fare collection. As a result counting dials are now used by the guards on one of the company's routes and an Automatic Checker, out of the guard's control, is on trial on one of the Dock Omnibuses.'* [10]

Horne and Maund include an example (for 1870) of a list of horse-drawn omnibus routes, of which one was from the Pier Head to Falkner Square for 3d (see p. 135, fig. 8,5). As an alternative to walking or riding to work, Peter may therefore have made use of this omnibus service to travel to and from his office at Orange Court, and might thus have become aware at first hand of a fraud which apparently was common. Peter would have been working on his ideas well in advance of filing the provisional on 2nd December 1868 and probably prior to the company's visit to Paris earlier that year. His invention may also have seen the light of day on an experimental basis. [11]

If theft of fares on omnibuses was a problem in the 1860s, the description which Peter provided in his ingenious application regarding letter boxes suggests that a way of making mail secure against theft once delivered (both external theft via the letter box flap and by servants from the letter bag) was also a concern, whilst his proximity at Orange Court to agents for both the Wakefield and the Low-wood gunpowder manufacturers may have resulted in a casual conversation which prompted him to sense an opportunity regarding improvements to the mechanisms of firearms.

These five patents are a joy to read for their sheer imaginative detail. However, in the 1870s Peter allowed all of them to lapse through a decision not to pay the third-year £50 renewal fees or the seventh-year £100 fees (several thousand pounds today).

This adventure into patenting might therefore be seen as little more than a side-line to Peter's story (*'working as an obscure civil engineer'* as one commentator has speculated) were it not for the fact that the 1866 application no. 1845 subsequently led to the construction of Peter's lift in Oriel Chambers. The announcement in *The London Gazette*, 27th July 1866, p. 4250, reads:-

> *'Patent Law Amendment Act, 1852. Office of the Commissioners of Patents for Inventions. Notice is hereby given, that provisional protection has been allowed... to Peter Ellis, of No. 9, Orange-court, Liverpool, in the county of Lancaster, Architect, for the invention of "an improved lift, hoist, or mechanical elevator, adapted for hotels, warehouses, railway stations, and other places, and intended to facilitate and render easy the ascent of persons and goods"... recorded in the Office of the Commissioners on the 13th day of July, 1866.'*

Three years later *'A New Description of Lift'* was the title of an article in *The Architect* (fig. 10,9), a journal that had begun publication that year.

A NEW DESCRIPTION OF LIFT.

A LIFT has been invented and patented by Mr. Peter Ellis, architect, of Liverpool, which we may class as a *person lift*, but which differs from any other in the fact of its having *two* shafts instead of *one, with several cages or chairs in each shaft*, and in moving continuously up one shaft and down the other (reminding us somewhat of the movement of the buckets to a dredging machine), the passengers entering or leaving without stoppage, although having the power to stop it in case of necessity. We consider this invention so important in relation to large sets of offices, hotels, and the adoption of living in flats by the middle classes, that we give a description of the first completed specimen, which has been in use for some months in Oriel Chambers, a large block of offices erected by Mr. Ellis in the busiest part of Liverpool.

The shafts or recesses are about two feet square, placed side by side (they might be back to back, if circumstances required), and owing to the condition of continuity, are of somewhat greater length at top and bottom than the mere floor levels would require. Over the diaphragm and in the head-stall is a single-axled pinion carrying a belt-flange, the periphery of which is immediately over the centres of the shafts. A similar flanged disc occurs at the bottom on a lever-moved compensating slide for extension and uniform pressure. On these is placed an endless belt fitted with chair axles at distances of about eight feet. The whole of these arrangements are concealed by casing, leaving only the channel for the travelling axles.

Motion is communicated by a pulley-driven pinion geared into the flanged spur wheel; the driving pulley is dished, runs free on the shaft, and contains a very peculiar break arrangement, consisting of a combination of springs and arms shackled upon a free centre. The outer rim of the disc presses on the inner rim of the driving pulley, and projects some two or three inches beyond the edge. On this projection the suspending break operates by means of a strong wire carrying handles to every storey. By the use of this break a suspension of motion can be accomplished without any shock, and with absolute certainty. There is also an arrangement for permanently suspending the motion of the lift without arresting the action of the break.

The chairs consist of a light iron framework, about 7½ feet high, carrying at the top a step or bush. The floor is of wood, made double, and contains friction-wheels some 12 inches in diameter, fitted with friction-rollers round the edges. As the chairs are suspended freely, and, after passing the diaphragm at the top, their motion is changed from ascent to descent, it is evident that some important contrivance is indispensable, not only to do this, but to give the necessary regularity and precision of movement. This has been cleverly effected by a strong grip or clutch suspending over the shafts and depending considerably below the axle of the spur-wheel. Bearing the belt into this clutch (which is brought into position by the motion of the ascending carriages), the slide of the chair-frame enters, and the chair is rigidly and securely carried over, and delivered into the descent below the diaphragm, before leaving the clutch.

Supposing all the chairs in each shaft were always full, or equiponderant, hand-power would amply suffice to work this double-action lift. As it is, a small two-horse engine (probably not worked higher than one), placed at the top of the building, does the work. The engineer not only attends to the engine, but acts as office-keeper. No attendant is required, either to go up and down with passengers or to control the chairs.

We were informed that, although there is an arrangement for producing a brief pause in the progress of the lift at each storey if required, it had not been found necessary. Probably, in case of its adoption, where most of the passengers would be ladies, as, for instance, to the showrooms above large shops, such an arrangement might be found useful.

The total height of the lift is about 40 feet, and the time required for ascending from the lowest to the highest storey, or *vice versâ*, is about half a minute. Above 420 persons may ascend and descend within an hour. And, in the case of very large buildings, another pair of shafts might be added, thus doubling the capacity without much increase of expense.

From personal inspection of this lift, we can certainly speak most highly of the ingenuity displayed in its arrangements.

Even with the aid of Peter's diagram (fig. 10,10) the accompanying text of his invention is complicated to interpret, and the report in *The Architect* would have made it more accessible to those who were interested technically but not *'skilled in the art.'* Peter would have been delighted with the report, for the author wrote that:-

> *'We consider this invention so important in relation to large sets of offices...*
> *that we give a description of the first completed specimen, which has been in use for some months in Oriel Chambers, a large block of offices erected by Mr. Ellis in the busiest part of Liverpool...*
> *From personal inspection of this lift, we can certainly speak most highly of the ingenuity displayed in its arrangements.'*

Fig. 10,9. From The Architect, vol. 2, 4th December, 1869, p. 278.

How Rob Ainsworth discovered this immensely important reference shortly before he died is unknown, but the article was subsequently retrieved from Google Books by searching with the four words 'Architect Lift Ellis Oriel'.

Fig. 10,10. The diagram accompanying Peter's provisional 1866 specification no. 1845. Its bottom right hand corner indicates that it was 'Drawn on Stone' (i.e. a lithograph: compare p. 159, fig. 9,10).

Image courtesy of the Mitchell Library, Glasgow Libraries.

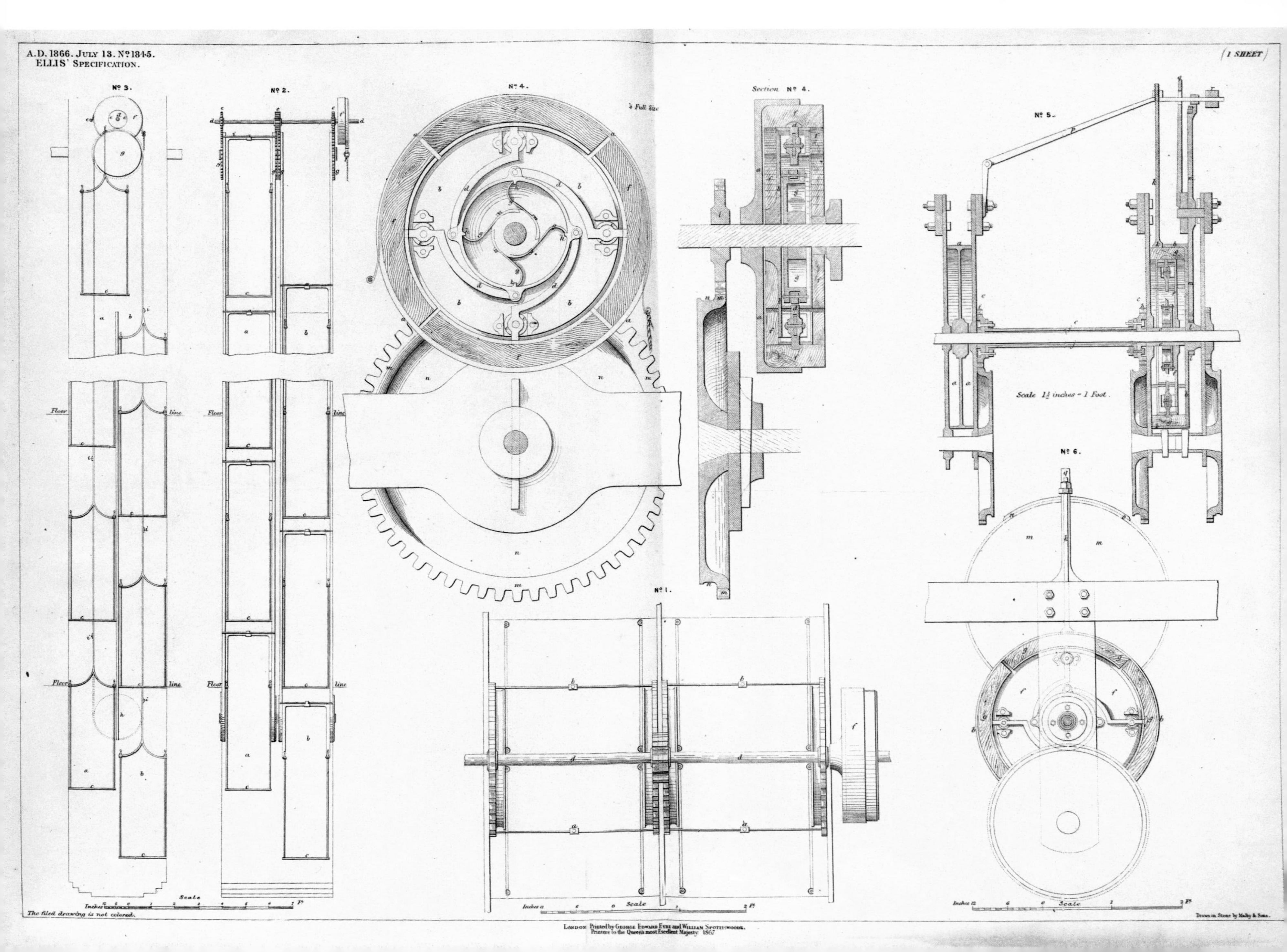

A.D. 1866. July 13. No 1845.
ELLIS' Specification.
(1 SHEET)
No 3.
No 2.
No 4.
¼ Full Size
Section No 4.
No 5.
Scale 1½ inches = 1 Foot.
No 6.
No 1.
Floor
line
Scale
Inches 12 6 0 1 2 Ft
The filed drawing is not colored.
London: Printed by George Edward Eyre and William Spottiswoode,
Printers to the Queen's most Excellent Majesty. 1867.
Drawn on Stone by Malby & Sons.

Thus described was the world's first *paternoster lift*, [12] and the report offers us the tantalising possibility that Peter's patent application was examined by American architects who, historians argue, had some years earlier also shown interest in the construction of Oriel Chambers and 16 Cook Street. Lifts, both of the paternoster and the conventional Otis type, quickly transformed the commercial value of the upper floors of the skyscrapers that soon arose, and why Peter chose not to maintain patent cover for this remarkable invention is a puzzle (void 19th July 1873 for non-payment of stamp duty). After Peter's death his probate record shows that he left an estate which in today's money would be valued at over one million pounds. Is that sufficiently large to suggest that the application was purchased from him and then quietly allowed to lapse?

A provisional for an apparent variant of Peter's design was applied for in 1878 and subsequently became known as '*Hart's Cyclic Elevator*', and the firm of J&E Hall is now typically cited as the company first involved in the construction of paternoster lifts – a decade after the pioneering installation at Oriel Chambers. [13] It may be recalled from chapter 8 that Roger Clarke wrote to J&E Hall in 1956. Roger presumably had seen in the wartime wreckage something that had set his heart racing, but he would have been disappointed by J&E Hall's reply that:-

> *'It may well be that a "Paternoster" type lift was installed in this building during the period you mention but we are afraid we have no actual record of this.'* [14]

As a result Quentin Hughes perhaps felt that whatever Roger Clarke had discovered did not have the necessary confirmation to warrant inclusion of a comment in *Seaport.*

10,11. A detail from the display banner which stands inside the entrance to 16 Cook Street and which was designed by Stephen Edgar.

To become a competent civil engineer at the age of 60 with the capacity to invent and then organise the construction of a lift that revolutionised high-rise building design whilst continuing to work as an architect, surveyor and valuer is extraordinary.

The problem of how to provide Oriel Chambers and 16 Cook Street with the maximum amount of natural light could also be considered more as an engineering challenge than an architectural one, and the choice of quotation on the 16 Cook Street display reflects the point (fig. 10,11). Stephen Edgar, one half of the husband and wife team who are the current owners of 16 Cook Street, indicates that there is no evidence that the building ever had gas lighting.[15]

10,12. Left to right, 18 to 14 Cook Street, ca. 1950, with the buildings still wearing their wartime grime.[17]
Image courtesy of Ron Jones.

Quentin Hughes, writing of Charles Cockerell's 1849 Bank Chambers (which stood almost opposite 16 Cook Street), noted that:-

> *'With the short northern days in winter, Liverpool streets can be dark, and architects* [of that period] *found it difficult to adapt classical designs to provide adequate lighting conditions in the offices. Proportions and relationships of window opening to wall surface established for generations in warmer climates could not be easily terminated. Bank Chambers was one of the first attempts made to solve this problem.'* [16]

Cockerell's building was able to retain classical proportions, but it had the distinct advantage of facing south. 16 Cook Street which faces north required Peter's more radical engineering solution (fig. 10,12). Bank Chambers was demolished in 1959 whereas no. 16, now a Grade II* listed building, quietly and confidently lives on. Comparing the three north-facing buildings of nos. 14, 16 and 18, the upper floors of nos. 14 and 18 each have a window opening to wall surface area of a little over 20%, whereas for the central floors of no. 16 the figure is a little over 50%.

References and Notes to Chapter 10

1 Quentin Hughes, *Seaport. Architecture and Townscape in Liverpool*, Lund Humphries, 1964, p. 63. Reprinted with postscript by The Bluecoat Press, 1993.

In fact the alphabetical section of the directories shows a variety of listings following the customary '*architect and surveyor*' description which had accompanied Peter's entries from 1849 to 1865.

The description for 1867 reads
'*architect and surveyor and valuer*'.
Between 1868-1872 it was
'*architect and civil engineer*'.
Between 1873-1875 it reverted to
'*architect surveyor and valuer*',
and settled down from 1876 to
'*C.E. architect surveyor and valuer*'.

The descriptions in the numerical section when Peter was at Orange Court were more brief:
'*architect*' (1864-70) and
'*architect and surveyor*' (1871).

The listings in the numerical section for Oriel Chambers varied between:
'*architect and C.E.*' (1872),
'*architect and valuer*' (1873-74),
'*architect and surveyor*' (1875-76),
'*civil engineer &c*' (1877),
'*architect and valuer*' (1878-80),
'*architect and surveyor*' (1881), and
'*architect and valuer*' (1882-84).

Thus, with the exception of the 1877 entry for Oriel Chambers, it is only the alphabetical listings from 1876 in which Peter chose to put Civil Engineer first.

2 Letter from Quentin Hughes to Gillian Moore, 22nd March 1997, as Appendix 5 of her undergraduate thesis, *Peter Ellis (1804-1884), A Study of the Life and Work of a Nineteenth Century Provincial Architect*, University of Teesside: Institute of Design. BA (Hons) History of Design & Architecture, April 1997.

Part of the letter reads, '*The only other building besides Oriel Chambers and 16 Cook Street that I know he designed is a non-conformist church, now destroyed and replaced by a Roman Catholic one, on Hall Lane, just behind the Royal Liverpool University Hospital. I have seen a photograph of the interior and a print of the façade but the building seemed very uninteresting and, in no way, foreshadowing his revolutionary work on the office buildings.*'

The '*foreshadowing*' comment suggests that Quentin Hughes was perhaps relying on information from memory and may not have recollected (or known) the date of the chapel's construction (1868/69, ref. 4). The '*Roman Catholic one*' appears to be a reference to the 1886 Sacred Heart Church (which still exists), although fig. 10,5 indicates that this was on a neighbouring site to Peter's chapel and did not replace it. There will be further mention of Gillian's interesting thesis in chapter 12 with regard to John Wellborn Root. Quotations here, in ref. 14 and in chapter 12 are courtesy of the University of Teesside.

3 J A Picton, *Memorials of Liverpool*, G G Walmsley (Liverpool), 2nd edn., 1875, vol. II, p. 436.

4 The photograph (which bears the caption '*Hall Lane*'), is listed on the *Liverpool In Print* website under the title '*St. Stephen's Evangelical Church,*

Hall Lane: Views: 1870: General view, c. 1970,' and is contained in a pamphlet by D J Bassett concerning another church and entitled *'Eglwys y Bedyddwyr, Edge Lane'* (ref. 286.1 EDG). The website lists the building as existing from 1868, James Picton (ref. 3) having suggested 1869.

I am immensely grateful to Roger Hull at the Liverpool Record Office who, despite the closure of the service in November 2012 in order to commence repacking the archive for the move back to William Brown Street, kindly retrieved this pamphlet from storage in December and e-mailed me a copy of the photograph.

5 From north to south the hotels and pubs were the *Wellington*, *Albert* (later *Majestic*), *Star*, *Admiral*, *Apollo* and *Alexandra*. Freddy O'Connor, *Liverpool. Our City. Our Heritage*, The Bluecoat Press, 1990, p. 144, shows the *Star* shortly before its demolition in the early 1970s. In another of his valuable records of areas now long vanished (*Liverpool. It All Came Tumbling Down*, Brunswick Printing & Publishing, 1986) Freddy O'Connor's photo on p. 52 shows the remnants of the houses that had been built on Ambrose Street. They were very compact dwellings (James Picton's *'neat rows of cottages'*) and, together with the glimpse of Doddridge Street houses in fig. 10,4, provide an indication of what were typical of the properties in that triangle of land in which the chapel congregation had lived and died.

6 Two companies with very similar names appear in *Gore's Directory* for 1875, the *'Parcels and Luggage Co. limited (James Shield sec.)'* at Unity Buildings, Lord Street, and the *'Parcels and Luggage Delivery Co. limited (T. Curtis manager)'* at 20 School Lane. The *Mercury* article noted that *'Mr. T Curtis, the manager of the company'* presided at the 1874 social gathering, but incorrectly entitled the piece *'The Parcels and Luggage Company, Limited.'* No doubt the staff at 20 School Lane would have been somewhat relieved to see that on 18th May 1875 *The London Gazette* (p. 2685) reported that an order had been made for the voluntary winding up of the rival *Parcels and Luggage Company Limited*, thus avoiding further confusion for their customers and continued anxiety for the parcels and luggage.

7 Joseph Sharples, *Liverpool. Pevsner Architectural Guides*, Yale University Press, 2004, p. 200, mentions the Hanover Street section of the Abney Buildings, and has kindly provided e-mail confirmation (29th August 2012): *'Parcels & Luggage Office: I am aware that Ellis designed this building, which is mentioned briefly in the British Architect as well as the Mercury. When I first read about it, I investigated and satisfied myself that it no longer exists. I also looked for illustrations of it, but without success. The building in School Lane between the new Quaker Meeting house and the so-called Bling building on the corner of Hanover Street is part of Abney Buildings, which was probably designed by Henry Hartley and which has its main entrance in Hanover Street.'*

8 Nikolaus Pevsner, *The Buildings of England. Lancashire. I. The Industrial and Commercial South*, Penguin Books, 1969, p. 36 (the dustcover is entitled *The Buildings of England. South Lancashire*). Regarding this quotation and those in chapters 11 (ref. 3) and 12 (refs. 7, 9 & 17), because Penguin Books have been unable to trace the original contract or rights information for this title they are unable to give formal permission to quote.

9 *The London Gazette.*

29th December 1865, p. 6980, provisional 2912, water closet (petition recorded 13th November 1865, sealed 1st May 1866).

27th July 1866, p. 4250, provisional 1845, lift, hoist or mechanical elevator (petition recorded 13th July 1866, sealed 5th January 1867).

22nd February 1867, p. 97, provisional 251, fire arms & cartridges (petition recorded 30th January 1867, sealed 26th July 1867).

25th December 1868, p. 6836, provisional 3662, letter boxes (petition recorded 2nd December 1868, sealed 11th May 1869).

1st January 1869, p. 9, provisional 3663, public conveyance (petition recorded 2nd December 1868, sealed 11th May 1869).

The quotations from the patents are courtesy of Sheffield Central Library, Reference and Information Section.

10 J B Horne and T B Maund, *Liverpool Transport, Volume One, 1830-1900*, Senior Publications, second edition, 1995, p. 15.

11 Horne and Maund, *op. cit.*, p. 146. Although the authors do not name the inventor, and the reference may not be to Peter's patent application, they mention that turnstiles were experimented with on a number of tramcars (date not given), and that the system was considered to be foolproof. However it apparently did not meet with success because '*the ladies of that period were so dressed as to object to passing through a limited space!*'

12 An article on Wikipedia notes that '*the name paternoster ('Our Father', the first two words of the Lord's Prayer in Latin) was originally applied to the device because the elevator is in the form of a loop and is thus similar to rosary beads used as an aid in reciting prayers.*' The author of the article – like those for several related references – appears unaware of Peter's invention (as of April 2013).

13 *The London Gazette.* 25th January 1878, p. 411, provisional 81 (petition recorded 5th January 1878) to '*Frederick Hart, of 59, Tavistock-road, Westbourne Park, W., Consulting Engineer, for the invention of "improvements in elevators".*'

Although Hart does not cite Peter's application, the opening paragraph ('*especially to that class...*') indicates that he was basing the invention on an awareness of prior art. '*This invention has for its object improvements in elevators, and relates especially to that class of elevators in which a series of cages suitable for receiving passengers or goods are kept in continuous motion ascending on one side and descending on the other side.*' The application includes 12 diagrams. The patent and the quotation is courtesy of Sheffield Central Library, Reference and Information Section.

The patent was sealed on 13th June 1878, the specification was published on 5th July, and J&E Hall went into immediate production, with their advertising commencing in November of that year.

Dr Lee Gray's recent article (Hart's Cyclic Elevator, Part One, *Elevator World*, April 2012, p. 100) provides an analysis of Hart's patent, and Dr Gray also does not refer to Peter's invention.

I am grateful to staff at the Liverpool Central Library for obtaining a copy of this article via the British Library Inter Library Loan scheme.

14 Quentin Hughes Archive, D71/22/57/16, at the University's Sydney Jones Library. Quotation courtesy of the University of Liverpool Library.

In his letter to Gillian Moore (in a continuation of the quotation in ref. 2) Quentin Hughes mentions that '*I returned to Liverpool in about 1950, began to collect material for Seaport and set some of my students the task of making measured drawings of both office buildings.*'

Two of the drawings of the upper ground floor of Oriel Chambers (LRO ref. 7/39 Architect's plans) were produced by David C Price in 1956. The first shows the position of a conventional lift with a note stating that '*The south stair and the lift are alterations from the original.*' The second drawing (a reconstruction of the section of the building that was bombed in WWII) shows the position of what had been a staircase at the northern end wrapped around a closed rectangular enclosure which appears wide enough to have been capable of originally accommodating a paternoster lift.

15 In his occasional tours of the building, Stephen also draws visitors' attention to the fact that the middle three floors of the building are identical in construction and that, in principle, the modular process of adding floors in this manner could have been continued upwards indefinitely. All that would have been required, he says, to tempt clients to occupy such a high-rise building was a lift...

16 Quentin Hughes, *Seaport*, *op. cit.*, p. 44.

17 Left to right in the view are the premises of John Marley the tailor at no. 18, H T Woodrow & Co, printers and manufacturing stationers, on the lower ground floor of no. 16, and J Lyons restaurant at no. 14. The directory for 1949 is the last to list John Marley and the next directory in 1952 indicates that Jackson the tailor had arrived at no. 18. The photograph is therefore contemporary with that on p. 163, fig. 9,15.

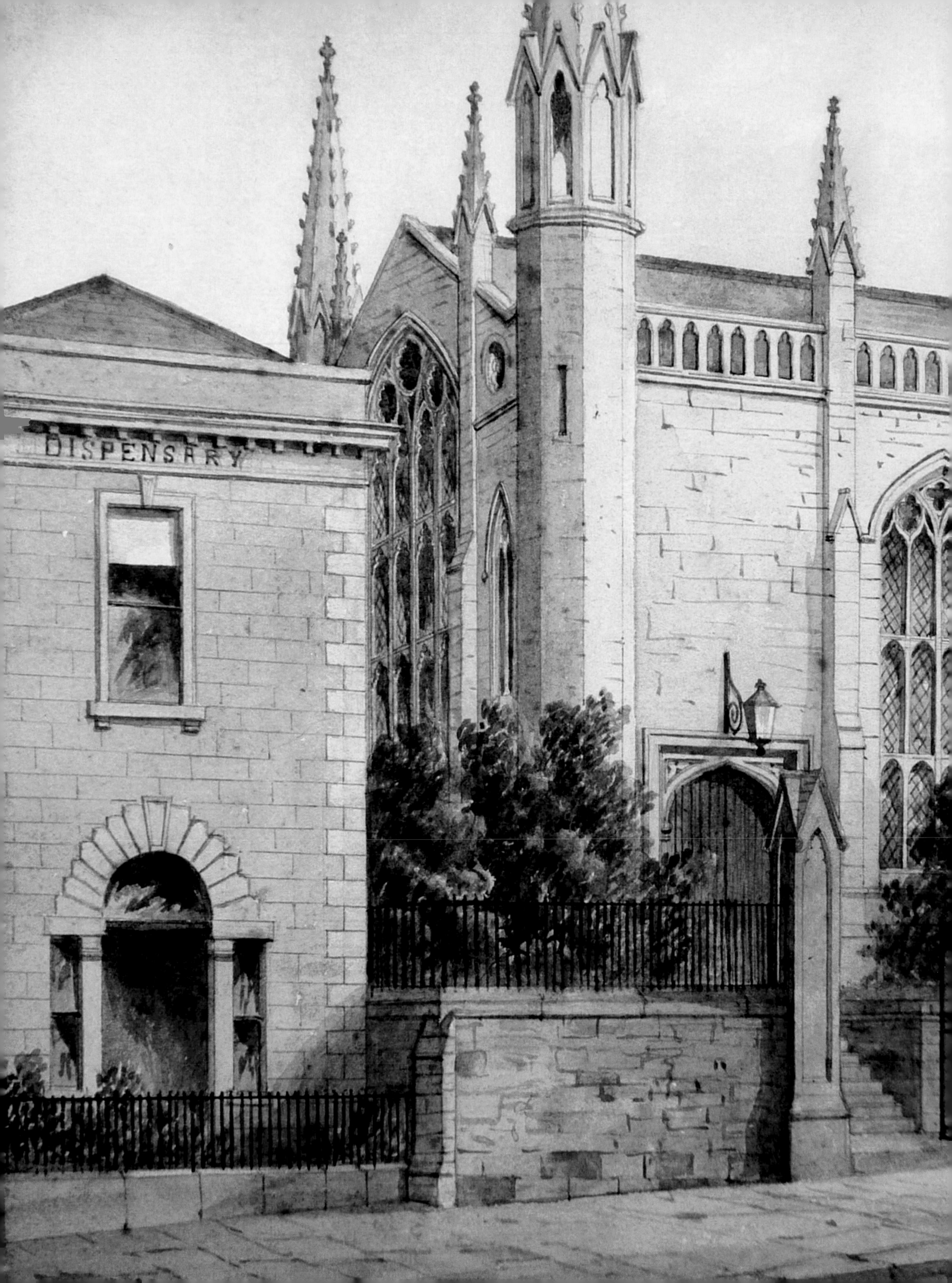
DISPENSARY

Chapter 11

The Final Years

Peter never entered himself in the directories as having retired, being listed as occupying his ground floor office right up to his death. [1] He continued regularly to be asked to provide valuations for official purposes in addition to those for private clients. On 6th January 1876 the *Mercury* reported that Peter was called upon to assess, at a sheriff's jury sitting at St George's Hall:-

> *'the compensation to be paid to the owner of a public house situate at the corner of William Brown-street and Mill-lane, which was required by the corporation for the purpose of improvement in connection with the Free Library and the Walker Art Gallery.'*

This case would perhaps have been of particular interest to him as he recollected being told by his parents of his early childhood on what was then Shaw's Brow and how they had marvelled at the beauty of the smock mills, by 1876 long since gone. Of the valuations submitted by several people mentioned in the account, Peter's was one of the most generous.

Two years later, a complicated case in the High Court involving a four day hearing, reported in great length and entitled *'Judgment in the Liverpool Property Case'*, also required Peter's expert opinion (*Liverpool Mercury*, 1st April 1878). The plaintiff, a Liverpool journeyman wheelwright previously living on about 30 shillings a week, some years earlier had come into an unexpected inheritance valued at many thousands of pounds. In the *Mercury* account, he was described as *'an ignorant artisan who had submitted himself and property to the care and protection of another'* (and to other professionals who subsequently became involved), that he had been taken advantage of, and that finally, after much of his inheritance had disappeared in fees and legal charges, he had been:-

> *'left the owner of £24. Fortune's frolic was played out; the fairy gifts had fled; plaintiff was awakened from his dream.'*

Part of the case had involved the sale of property on his behalf (including some at Mill Lane) for a total of £3750. The *Mercury* reported that the judge, finding in favour of the unfortunate wheelwright, included in his summing up that:-

> *'The evidence given on behalf of the plaintiff was that the property was sold at very much less than its true value. Mr. Hornblower was of opinion it was worth £6600 in 1872, and that its present value is £7600. Mr. Peter Ellis, a gentleman of similar high standing to Mr. Hornblower, valued it at present at £7159, and was of opinion that its value in 1872 was not much less.'*

Given Peter's own background as the son of an artisan who had started out in life making a living as a joiner, he would no doubt have been delighted that the judge relied upon his and Lewis Hornblower's valuations in reaching a conclusion that the conveyance of the properties should be set aside and that costs be awarded to the wheelwright.

Peter appears to have enjoyed continuing to work at Oriel Chambers, for advertisements in the *Liverpool Mercury* show him as still offering property for sale and to rent and providing valuations as late as May 1884.[2] In the *Mercury* on 13th March 1882 Peter advertised one of two adjoining houses in Upper Pitt Street which he had built at the junction with Cookson Street in the early 1830s and both of which he still owned:-

> *'25, Upper Pitt-street, Great George-square. - This Dwelling House to be Let; possession may be taken at once. Very centrally situated to stations, stage, and trams. Key at 27.- Peter Ellis, 10, Oriel-chambers, Water-street.'*

11,1. Canning Street looking east from Bedford Street (chapter 5, fig. 5,2) towards Falkner Square and its trees. A view in August 2011, but very much as Peter would have known it on his journeys to and from work or during visits to his nephew's home in Maryland Street and the homoeopathic dispensary on Hardman Street. During 1880/81 he would have passed the home of an architect colleague, Thomas Haigh, at 4 Canning Street.

Oposite right: 11,2. St James's Cemetery looking west from the junction of Canning Street and Hope Street (p. 105, fig. 6,3; location V on the map on p. iv), in the days long before the town was a city or its folk had dreamed of an Anglican cathedral. Private collection.

The fact that Peter chose to transfer his business office from Orange Court to Oriel Chambers for his last thirteen years suggests both that he remained proud of the building that he and Thomas Anderson had designed and that the other occupants held him in high regard and welcomed him amongst them. Whatever the pompous critics had said, the legion of clerks, sitting on their stools with their desks pushed into the oriel windows, would have been hugely grateful. Peter's paternoster lift would have been a great talking point for visitors, and his on-site presence for such visits may also have played a part in his choice of office there.

But let us now take an imaginary walk with Peter in his later years to visit his nephew. You may recall that his brother John had died in 1864, and that John Ellis junior had continued the practice as a veterinary surgeon. In 1877 John and his family moved to Sugnall Street and simultaneously he moved his practice to Hope Street. By 1882 the family had moved again, this time to Maryland Street, just around the corner from the veterinary practice.

Leaving his home in Falkner Square, a pleasant few minutes walk along Canning Street (fig. 11,1) would have brought Peter to its junction with Hope Street. Pausing to stand with his back to Gambier Terrace and looking west, he would have had a splendid view of St James's Cemetery (fig. 11,2) (now obscured by trees and a rather large 20th century cathedral). The cemetery was laid out in a disused quarry between 1826 and 1829, the quarry being shown on Charles Eyes' map of 1796 (chapter 6, fig. 6,2). For Nikolaus Pevsner the choice of the quarry was *'a stroke of genius. It makes the cemetery the most romantic in England.'*[3]

In the view, a prominent feature to the right of centre is John Foster junior's Oratory, originally the chapel for the cemetery and begun in 1827, whilst the building to the left of centre is the Chaplain's House. In the centre is a distant view of the spire of St Michael's Church in Upper Pitt Street, and Peter might have smiled upon seeing that, recollecting the baptism there in 1838 of the nephew he was on his way to visit.

Today a stroll from the entrance to the cathedral that was built many years later, past a view of the Oratory (fig. 11,3) and into the peaceful cemetery gardens, brings visitors to the Huskisson Monument (fig. 11,4), also designed by John Foster junior, which stands as a memorial to the first person in the world to be killed by a steam passenger engine.

11,3. The Oratory in August 2012 in a view looking north (approximately at right angles to fig. 11,2).

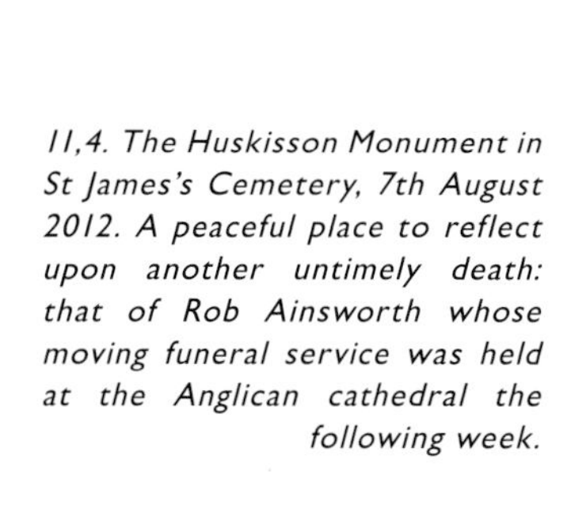

11,4. The Huskisson Monument in St James's Cemetery, 7th August 2012. A peaceful place to reflect upon another untimely death: that of Rob Ainsworth whose moving funeral service was held at the Anglican cathedral the following week.

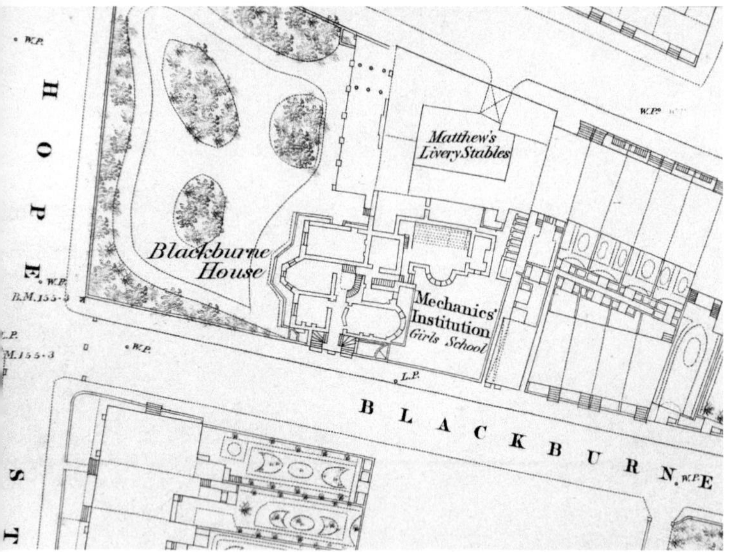

11,5. From the 1848 O.S. map showing Blackburne House and the Mechanics Institution.

Image courtesy of the Athenaeum.

Turning north along Hope Street, Peter would have passed a detached mansion on his right, set back in its grounds between Blackburne Place and Falkner Street. It was completed around 1790, and in 1844 George Holt, who was keen on women's education, purchased it when the female branch of the Liverpool Institute was established in premises previously that of the Mechanics' Institution (fig. 11,5). After becoming a gift to the Institute upon George Holt's death, in 1874 it was rebuilt as the Liverpool Institute High School for Girls, and this is how Peter would have known it. Blackburne House is now a grade II listed building and is home to the Women's Technology and Education Centre.

Continuing his journey northwards, Peter's view would have been that recorded by William Herdman (fig. 11,6). It shows the Unitarian Church in the foreground (first stone laid in May 1848) and, further on, the original Philharmonic Hall (first stone laid in September 1846; opened 1849). [4] James Picton had much to say in praise of both buildings. [5] Beyond the Hall there is a glimpse of the Myrtle Street Baptist Chapel. The original Philharmonic Hall was destroyed by fire in 1933 (fig. 11,7) and out of its ruins arose the Hall which is home to the internationally famous Royal Liverpool Philharmonic Orchestra.

11,6. The east side of Hope Street in 1864, looking north.

Image courtesy of the LRO, from 'Views in Modern Liverpool', 1864, plate 11, ref. Hf 942.7214 HER.

11,7. The destruction of the original Philharmonic Hall on the night of 5th July 1933. On the nearside of the junction can be seen The School for the Blind.

Image courtesy of the LRO, ref. Photographs & Small Prints.

11,8. A watercolour by H Magenis in 1882 with a glimpse of the Hahnemann Homoeopathic Dispensary (opened 1860) for which Peter was the architect, shown adjacent to St Philip's Church on Hardman Street.

Image courtesy of the LRO, ref. LIC 333.

Of the early history of Hope Street, James Picton noted that its northern end had remained blocked off until about 1835 by the tavern in which William Roscoe had been born (the Athenaeum possesses a painting of '*Bowling Green House*' based on a 1765 drawing, and the site is shown on Horwood's map of 1803). The same view today is dominated not by a tavern but by the Metropolitan Cathedral, an appropriate northern terminus to this street called Hope which, at its southern end, rubs shoulders with the Anglican Cathedral.

As he reached the junction with Hardman Street and Myrtle Street, Peter would have glanced to his left to check on the well-being of the homoeopathic dispensary (opened 1860 and for which he had been the architect, fig. 11,8). It had been built adjacent to St Philip's Church on the small plot of land shown on the 1848 O.S. map (fig. 11,9).

11,9. From the 1848 O.S. map showing the vacant plot adjacent to St Philip's Church (location X on the map on p. iv) upon which a decade later the Homoeopathic Dispensary was built.

Image courtesy of the Athenaeum.

St Philip's was another Cragg and Rickman church and, having observed it frequently as he supervised the construction of the dispensary in the late 1850s, it may well have played a part in influencing Peter's use of cast-iron in the designs of Oriel Chambers and 16 Cook Street. Peter would undoubtedly have smiled and remembered with delight the description of the dispensary which had appeared in a long article in the *Liverpool Mercury* (Monday 26th November 1860) on the occasion of its opening the previous Saturday:-

> *'The new dispensary has been erected from the designs by Mr. Ellis, architect, of this town, who also superintended the work. The style is Italian, and the general features of the front elevations are both appropriate and unpretending, and free from architectural extravagance, convenience and accommodation having been studied in the planning of the structure rather than ornamental effect. It is built of stone, the walling being partially wrought, with dressed quoins, architrave, and cornice. The frieze bears the inscription "Homoeopathic Dispensary" in large characters, and in the centre of the Hardman-street front is a granite tablet, on which is inscribed "Founded 1841. Supported by voluntary contributions. Erected on this site 1860." This inscription is encircled by handsome mouldings. The principal entrance for subscribers, physicians, and visitors is in Hardman-street. A very neat porch communicates with a spacious square entrance hall. Opposite the door is an heroic-sized statue of Hahnemann, the distinguished founder of the homoeopathic system, standing upon a massive pedestal of polished Aberdeen granite... The patients are admitted by an entrance from Baltimore-street, the rooms appropriated to them being spacious, lofty, well ventilated, and warmed.'* [6]

The choice of Peter as architect for the dispensary appears to have been not only because he was an excellent designer who focused upon what his clients needed and was not driven by the need for '*ornamental effect*', but also because he was a keen supporter of homoeopathic medicine. From the earliest days of the dispensary the annual reports begin with the statement that:-

> *'All persons who are benefactors of Ten Pounds and upwards at one time... shall be Governors for life... The Annual Subscribers of One Guinea or more... shall be Governors for the time being.'*

The reports show that Peter donated £20 at the outset (over £1000 today) and that throughout his life he was an annual subscriber of one guinea. [7]

In the early 1880s Peter would have had good cause to be concerned for the continued existence of the dispensary. Richard Livesey described the sad end to the church next door, brought about by the arrival of a priest who systematically destroyed its life and then, remarkably, set about selling it. In June 1882 an advertisement appeared for a '*valuable freehold site for shops*'; in the auction in July the site '*was eventually knocked down at £5 3s. 6d. a yard... for the Palmerston Land and Building Company*'; and in the 20th December 1882 edition of the *Liverpool Courier* the writer suggested that, with regard to the apparent uncertain future of the fabric of the church following the sale, '*the whole procedure is simply a scandal.*' [8]

With the tragic loss of the church, the future of the dispensary was bound to be uncertain. Thankfully for Peter, the building outlived him by three years until it was demolished and replaced (fig. 11,10) when the much larger Hahnemann Homoeopathic Hospital was opened on Hope Street.

11,10. Kirkland's Bakery (opening announced in the Mercury, 10th December 1888), on the site where the homoeopathic dispensary had once stood. Now the 'Fly in the Loaf', viewed in September 2012.

Returning to Peter's journey, and glancing right at the Hardman Street junction, he would have noticed the Myrtle Street Baptist Chapel, the site of which is now a car park. The first Baptist Chapel near Liverpool had been erected in Everton Road at the end of the 17th century when it was a quiet rural lane (the burial ground that remained long after is shown on p. 70, fig. 4,16), and James Picton, in William Herdman's '*Views in Modern Liverpool*', 1864, p. 16, traced out the successive moves which led the Baptists from Everton Road to Myrtle Street. Further to the right Peter would have seen the Myrtle Street Gymnasium, opened in 1865 as a result of the pioneering work of John Hulley who introduced a *Velocipede Club* there. [9]

Having satisfied himself that the dispensary had not been demolished whilst his back was turned, a few paces further, and on the northern side of the junction of Hope Street and Hardman Street, Peter would have reached the premises of his nephew's veterinary practice at 34 Hope Street.

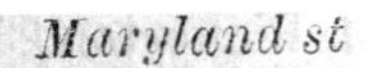

Maryland st
28 Beard Mrs. Eleanor
30 Hakes James surgeon
32 Farrell Joseph George manager
32 Wilson John job master
34 Ellis John veterinary surgeon
36 Gore Robert T. victualler
Hardman st

11,11. Gore's Directory for 1883 showing the practice of Peter's nephew at 34 Hope Street. Image courtesy of Sefton Local History Unit.

The practice was next door to the original and much smaller Philharmonic Hotel at no. 36 (fig. 11,11) (also listed as 51 Hardman Street).

In 1889, five years after Peter's death, John Ellis moved from 34 Hope Street, and his shoeing forge was taken over until 1899, first by John Wilson at no. 32, and then by another veterinary surgeon, Thomas Lloyd. In 1900 34 Hope Street vanished forever from the directories, the premises having been demolished and the site absorbed for a much grander establishment, described by Joseph Sharples as '*the most richly decorated of Liverpool's Victorian pubs... The decorative richness even extends to the lavatories.*' [10] The site of the veterinary practice of Peter's nephew now lies beneath part of this famous hotel (fig. 11,12).

11,12. The Philharmonic Hotel in September 2011. The site of the premises of John Ellis, Peter's nephew, lies beneath the rooms on the right hand side of the hotel. On the extreme left is the building that once was The School for the Blind (see fig. 11,7).

11,13. A copy of Peter's death certificate. Liverpool registration district, sub-district Mount Pleasant, volume 8b, page 108, entry 380.

Image courtesy of the Liverpool Register Office.

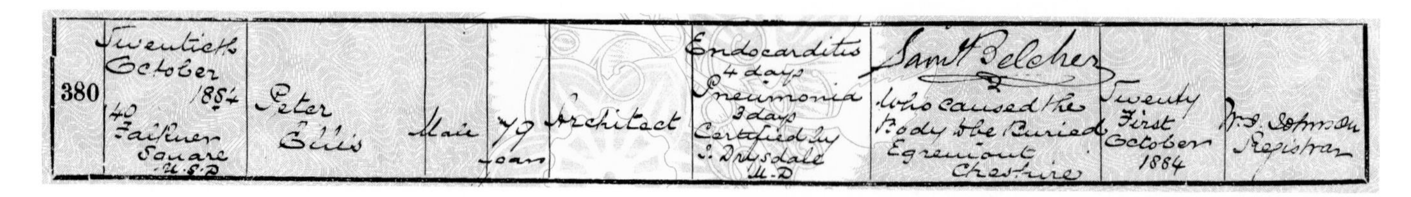

380	Twentieth October 1884 40 Falkner Square U.S.D.	Peter Ellis	Male	79 years	Architect	Endocarditis 4 days Pneumonia 3 days Certified by J. Drysdale M.D	Saml Belcher who caused the Body to be Buried Egremont Cheshire	Twenty First October 1884	J.S. Johnson Registrar

Having been an executor for the estate of Mary's brother William Harper Syers in 1858, Peter's services were called upon again when the last of her brothers died in 1882. The probate for 10th January 1883 reads:-

> *'The Will of John Aspinall Syers formerly of Everton near Liverpool in the County of Lancaster but late of 38 Leam-terrace Leamington in the County of Warwick who died 8 September 1882 at 38 Leam-terrace was proved at the Principal Registry by Peter Ellis of 40 Falkner-square Liverpool Architect the surviving Executor.'*

John's wife, Lavinia, lived a further 10 years and died at Worthing. One of their sons, Henry Walter Syers (born 1853), graduated from London University, became a medical practitioner, and will be mentioned again shortly.

Then, on Monday 20th October 1884, Peter's own time had come. He was born into a town of approximately 100,000 inhabitants and lived long enough to see it become a city in 1880 with over six times as many residents.[11] The places where he had grown up – Shaw's Brow, Primrose Hill, Gloucester Street and Low Hill – had all been transformed before his death, and would be transformed once again long after he had gone. The buildings that had provided his offices at Renshaw Street, Clayton Square and Orange Court outlived him, but they too would vanish in the 20th century as the city changed.

Peter died at home, and the certificate recorded death as a result of endocarditis (inflammation of the lining membrane of the heart) followed by (or concurrently with) pneumonia (fig. 11,13; by a curious twist of fate the Liverpool Register Office for obtaining a copy of the death certificate is now situated at St George's Hall, the building for which Peter had so hopefully submitted his designs in 1839).

Two things of note are revealed by the certificate. The first is that it was Dr John James Drysdale of Rodney Street who certified Peter's death. He had settled in Liverpool in 1841, was the first practitioner of homoeopathy in the town and a member of the first meeting of the Society, and is listed in the 1884 Annual Report of the Dispensary as their leading physician.[12] It is thus clear that right up to his death Peter had remained a firm believer in the homoeopathic system of treatment. He had thus not only been a pioneering architect, prepared to experiment with new engineering ideas for old problems, but had also been a practising supporter of alternative medicine.

The second point of interest is that the signature and residence of the informant of Peter's death is shown as '*Samuel Belcher who caused the body to be Buried,*' who was living at Egremont. Why should a distressed Mary have entrusted this man with the task of informing the registrar, and why should Samuel have been one of those who also attended Peter's burial at Toxteth Cemetery?

The answer is found in entries in the Liverpool directories between 1887 and 1889 where Samuel is listed as an architect and surveyor in office no. 5 on the top floor at Oriel Chambers. It may be remembered that the witness to Peter's patent applications had been his clerk at Orange Court, John E Belcher of Seacombe Villa (chapter 10), and later of Green Lawn, Rock Ferry, and Samuel was perhaps his son. Just as Cornelius Sherlock and Edward Davies had been articled to Peter early in his career (chapter 5), so it appears almost certain that Samuel had begun his training at Peter's office in the 1880s, that he had become a close friend, and had therefore offered assistance to Mary as Peter departed this world.

Following Peter's death, Samuel would have been obliged to complete his training with another architect, but had then chosen to return to Oriel Chambers to begin his independent practice. This is perhaps another indication that Peter's life as an architect had still been thriving to the very end of his career and that Oriel Chambers, with all its memories, had beckoned a grateful Samuel back.

The day after Peter died the *Liverpool Daily Post* carried the notification of his death together with a brief obituary:-

> *'Ellis – October 20, at his residence, 40, Falkner-square, Peter Ellis, architect and surveyor, of this city.'*

> *'DEATH OF A LIVERPOOL ARCHITECT – Our obituary column announces the death of Mr. Peter Ellis architect and surveyor, of Falkner-square. Mr. Ellis had long been in practice in Liverpool; he was well known in his profession and among the public, and was generally and deservedly respected.'* [13]

The funeral took place on 23rd October and the following day the *Daily Post* carried its account of the event. It provides a valuable glimpse into Peter's life and personality which would otherwise have remained unknown, together with a record of some of the *'numerous assembly of friends'* who attended his burial:-

> *'The Late Mr. Peter Ellis. – Yesterday morning the remains of the late Mr. Peter Ellis, architect and surveyor, were interred at Smithdown-road Cemetery in the presence of a numerous assembly of friends. The deceased gentleman was held in high esteem by the members of his own profession and solicitors and others with whom he had business relations. A varied knowledge of the value of property in Liverpool made his opinion of great importance in arbitrations, and he was frequently associated with the late Mr. William Culshaw and with Sir James Picton in settling the disputed claims which came before the tribunals. Mr. Ellis, for more than half a century, was at the head of the leading practice in his way of business in Liverpool, and was ever ready with his kindly advice to those who sought it. Being of a retiring disposition public affairs had little attraction for him, though his sympathies were ever with the Conservatives. At the funeral there were present in the cortège which left deceased's late residence, 40, Falkner-square, soon after eleven o'clock, Mr. John Ellis, Dr. Syers, Mr. C Sherlock, Mr. Thos. Haigh, Mr. Belcher, and the Ven. Archdeacon Bardsley, who officiated at the funeral. A few private carriages joined in the procession to the cemetery. The coffin was of polished oak with brass mountings, and bore the inscription: "Peter Ellis. Died 20th October 1884. Aged 80 years." Messrs. Woollright and Co., Bold-street, carried out the funeral arrangements.'* [14]

This warm tribute to a man who had continued *'at the head of the leading practice in his way of business in Liverpool'* is hardly a summary of someone whose career had been destroyed by denigratory articles by the architectural press nearly 20 years earlier. Unfortunately the reporter filed his account incorrectly on two points.

The first is less important, and perhaps no more than wishful thinking by the reporter or the person who provided him with his copy, in its assertion that Peter's *'sympathies were ever with the Conservatives.'* The account of the 1852 election in chapter 6 makes it clear that he voted for the Liberals on that occasion, whilst the Athenaeum has poll books for the parliamentary elections of 1833, 1835 and 1841 showing that he had also voted for the Whigs and not the Tories on each of those occasions. However, the second error – that the coffin inscription included the words, *'Aged 80 years'* – is more important. Both Peter's death certificate and his gravestone record his age as 79, and his baptism record (chapter 1, fig. 1,6) confirms an 1805 birth. This funeral account, which was known within the Liverpool School of Architecture when Geoffrey Woodward wrote his article in 1956, [15] perhaps provides the clue as to why Quentin Hughes recorded Peter's dates as *'1804-1884'* and why the birth date has not subsequently been corrected.

Peter's entry in the Probate Calendar appeared on 7th January 1885:-

> *'Administration (with the Will) of the Personal Estate of Peter Ellis late of Falkner-square in the City of Liverpool Architect who died 20 October 1884 at Falkner-square was granted at Liverpool to Mary Helen Ellis of 40 Falkner-square Widow the Relict the Residuary Legatee for life if she remains a Widow.'*

The probate reveals a personal estate initially recorded at a very precise £16,430-8-10d (gross) and later, when re-sworn in August of the same year, at £17,931 (over one million pounds today). [16] By way of comparison James Picton, by then *'Sir James Allanson Picton Knt'*, died in 1889 leaving £90,000 and with a Reading Room named after him (albeit nicknamed *'Picton's Gasometer'* by the local wits). [17] The architect of the Reading Room, built 1875-79, was none other than Cornelius Sherlock, and Peter would no doubt have been proud that one of his early trainees had gone on to produce such fine work. Dying in 1888, Cornelius left a personal estate of just over £6,000.

The date of Peter's will (3rd November 1840, and thus never revised), explains the statement *'if she remains a Widow'* with regard to Mary (who was 73 years old in 1884 but only 29 in 1840). Peter had bequeathed *'the whole of my property of whatsoever kind unto John A. Syers of Liverpool Cotton Broker and John Ellis of Liverpool Veterinary Surgeon upon trust...,'* with the requirement that they look after Mary's needs and wishes if she survived him. However, because both Mary's brother John Aspinall Syers and Peter's brother John Ellis had died after 1840 but before 1884, it was Mary Ellis herself to whom the grant was made. Under *'Sureties'* in the Letters of Administration were named Henry Walter Syers (Mary's nephew, the son of John Aspinall Syers, and the *'Dr. Syers'* mentioned as attending the funeral) and the Rev. Thomas Anderson (see chapter 8).

Following the grant of administration, Harvey, Alsop and Stevens, solicitors of 9 Fenwick Street, acting on behalf of Mary, placed a Statutory Notice to Creditors in both the *Mercury* (23rd January 1885, in which it incorrectly gave Peter's address as Falkner Street) and *The Times* (2nd February 1885, by which time the address had been corrected).

11,14. Henry Sumners' 1854 design for 'St George's Place' (today called St John's Gardens).

Image courtesy of the Athenaeum (which also possesses a lithograph of an interior view of St George's Hall from a drawing by Henry Sumners which appeared as a supplement to the Liverpool Standard in 1854).

Notices for the sale of Peter's property subsequently appeared in the 30th June and 14th July 1885 columns of the *Liverpool Mercury*. A description of lot 1 (40 Falkner Square) has been covered in chapter 6. Lot 2 comprised six leasehold dwelling houses in White Street which Peter had assisted his father to build, leased from 28th January 1832 at a peppercorn rent, and with a gross annual rental of £78. Lot 3 was for two dwelling houses at the corner of Upper Pitt Street and Cookson Street which Peter had built, leased from 20th April 1833 also at a peppercorn rent, and with a gross annual rental of £56 (including one of the properties which Peter had advertised to rent in 1882 – see earlier in this chapter). The annual rentals suggest that the two properties which Peter built were somewhat more substantial than the six in White Street.

The sale was advertised as taking place at the Law Association Rooms at 14 Cook Street (currently the restaurant *Piccolino*, see p. 128, fig. 7,10).

Although the notice indicated that '*Vacant possession can be given,*' and in the 1885 directory 40 Falkner Square is shown as empty, in the 1886 directory Mary is entered as still living there. By 1887 however she had moved to 2 Croxteth Grove, and Henry and Emma Sumners had taken up residence at 40 Falkner Square.

Henry Sumners (ca. 1826-1895) was also an architect and surveyor, and Joseph Sharples notes several examples of his work including (with William Culshaw) the Midland Railway goods warehouse on Whitechapel (which was converted a few years ago for use as the National Museums Liverpool Conservation Centre, although closed to the public in 2010 as a result of sweeping budget cuts). In 1854 Henry Sumners had also offered a design for the complete redevelopment of the area to the sides and west of St George's Hall (fig. 11,14). This involved a Museum and Library on William Brown Street, but these were eventually built 1857-60 from designs by John Weightman (who a few years later in 1864, it may be recalled from chapter 8, considered slicing through Oriel Chambers). Henry's plan also involved an immense salt-water bath (underneath the large dome visible in the distance) and the removal of St John's Church to a new site. None of this took place but, perhaps most intriguingly, Joseph Sharples, after comments regarding Peter Ellis's 16 Cook Street, mentions that:-

> *'No. 14, almost contemporary, could not be more different. It was built as the National Bank. The drawings, dated 1863, are signed by William Culshaw, but the designer was probably Henry Sumners.'* [18]

Peter and Henry would undoubtedly have known each other well professionally. However, prior to moving to Peter and Mary's home in 1887, the directories from 1868 show Henry as living at 98 Upper Canning Street (the property being on the eastern side of Grove Street, now the site of the Liverpool Women's Hospital). The route to his office in Dale Street would thus have taken him past Peter's home, and he and Emma would almost certainly also have known Peter and Mary socially.

Over dinner together they may perhaps have occasionally recalled the excitement and subsequent disappointment that had accompanied the submission and rejection of Peter's St George's Hall designs and of Henry's St George's Place scheme. Henry also had known what it was like to suffer at the hands of *The Builder* which had described the round-arched apse windows of his Greek Orthodox Church (which still stands on the corner of Berkley Street) as *'an ugly and disproportioned feature to which no considerations of archaeology can reconcile us.'* [19] Was it the result of a special friendship with Peter and Mary that prompted Henry and Emma to move to a house which had such fond memories for them? The Corporation Lease Register shows that Emma was re-granted the lease on 28th June 1889, and probate records indicate that the house remained with the Sumners family until the death of their daughter in 1912.

Mary was born six years after Peter and she lived four years beyond him. She died at Croxteth Grove on 10th May 1888 and was buried in Peter's grave. On 7th August of the same year the Probate Calendar shows the entry:-

> *'The Will of Mary Helen Ellis formerly of Falkner-square but late of Croxteth-grove both in Liverpool in the County of Lancaster Widow who died 10 May 1888 at Croxteth-grove was proved at Liverpool by Henry Walter Syers of Clarendon Lodge Leamington in the County of Warwick M.D. the nephew one of the Executors.'*

This will refers to Mary's own estate (valued at less than £1000, even after being re-sworn) rather than the residue of Peter's. Mary appointed *'Reverend Thomas Anderson of Pokesdown Vicarage Bournemouth in the County of Hampshire Clerk in Holy Orders and my Nephew Henry Walter Syers'* as executors and trustees.

Provision was made for Thomas Anderson to receive a legacy of £100, for Henry Walter Syers to receive £50 and for Jane Unsworth (Mary's faithful maid for over a decade and who perhaps transferred with her to Croxteth Grove) to receive £40.

The executors were instructed to share the residue of Mary's estate between the children of her deceased brother John Aspinall Syers (of whom Henry was one) and the grandson of her deceased brother Thomas Syers (Alfred Syers, the son of Llewellyn and Fanny Syers).

In the event, the copy of the will made by the solicitors shows that Thomas Anderson, perhaps feeling impracticably far away in Bournemouth, '*renounced the Probate and Execution thereof,*' and so the task fell to Henry Syers alone.

The explanation for the absence of a mention of either a son or daughter, and why it was a nephew on the Syers side of the family that proved her will, is revealed in a third document. Mary never acted upon the Letters of Administration that had been granted to her in January 1885, and on 22nd June 1888, shortly after Mary died, John Ellis (the nephew with premises at 34 Hope Street and who had by then moved the family home to 166 Chatham Street, the continuation north of Sandon Street) was granted a fresh administration of Peter's will.

The document includes the sad statement that:-

> *'Letters of Administration with the Will... of Peter Ellis late of Falkner Square in the City of Liverpool Architect deceased, who died on the 20th day of October 1884, at Falkner Square aforesaid, without ever having had a child... were granted... to John Ellis...'* [20]

Peter had outlived all his siblings and, without children of their own, he and Mary would have maintained a particular interest in their nephew's rapidly growing family at their earlier homes in Sugnall Street and Maryland Street, as well as loving contacts with the various branches of the Syers family.

And it is perhaps appropriate therefore to introduce at this point two other young people in whom Peter and Mary had taken a caring interest. The numerical section of the 1884 directory shows the delightful appearance of the names of the Misses Johnson in the listing at 40 Falkner Square (fig. 11,15) where, with Peter and Mary's blessing and the collusion of James Platt Mawdsley at no. 36, Elise and Hannah could be contacted with regard to their academy.

36 Mawdsley James Platt stationer
Sandon st
Huskisson st
37 Elliston Mrs. Emma A
38 Wallace Mrs. Mary
39 Marshall Mrs. Helen
4C Ellis Peter, C.E. and architect
Johnson The Misses teachers of dancing and music
Canning st

11,15. The entry in the numerical section of the 1884 Gore's Directory showing Elise and Hannah Johnson at 40 Falkner Square, and James Platt Mawdsley, the publisher of the directory, living a few doors away.
Image courtesy of the Athenaeum.

In 1882 these talented young ladies, with gifts for drawing, dancing and music, had set out hesitantly upon their careers from the family home in Berkley Street, a few hundred yards from Falkner Square, in what was to be the final year of their father's life.

Attempts to open a drawing academy at 47a Hope Street having proved short-lived, Elise and Hannah were encouraged to move to 17 Sandon Street, diagonally opposite Peter and Mary's home, to see if their switch to a dancing academy might be more successful (fig. 11,16; invitingly named the *Ecole danse*).

The listing in the academies section of the directory was *'Johnson, The Misses (dancing) Falkner house Falkner square'*. Thus potential clients could only discover the precise location of the academy by examining the Falkner Square numerical section, calling at the prestigious home of a well-known architect, and then being redirected to 17 Sandon Street a few yards away (which was not strictly in Falkner Square) with Peter and Mary's commendation.

Johnson, The Misses teachers of dancing Ecole danse Falkner house Falkner square,E

11,16. Elise and Hannah's listing (confidently entered in bold type) in the alphabetical section of the 1884 Gore's Directory. Image courtesy of the Athenaeum.

11,17 – 11,20. From Rob and Graham's visit to Toxteth Cemetery in October 2011 to plant primroses.

The inscription reads:- 'In loving remembrance of Peter Ellis who died 20th October 1884 aged 79 years. Also of Mary Helen his wife who died 10th May 1888 aged 77 years.'

However, how these nightingales from Berkley Street came to sing for Peter and Mary at 40 Falkner Square (and it is unique to that numerical directory listing that they chose to reveal their talents for music) is a tale perhaps best kept for an evening around the fireside. Later directories indicate that the Misses Johnson prospered at 17 Sandon Street and that, in 1886 and 1887, aided and abetted by another twinkle-eyed Falkner Square resident, they continued the earlier deception by arranging to be contacted at another prestigious address prior to being redirected to their academy. [21]

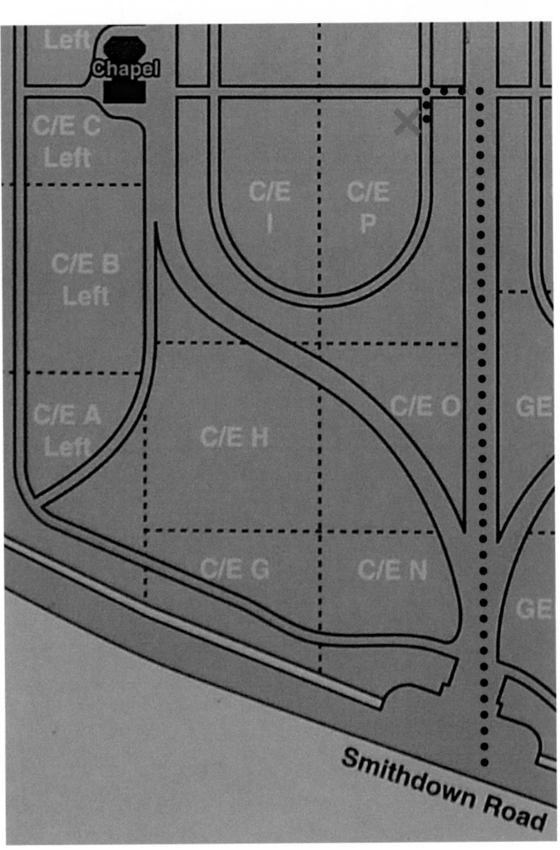

Never having shared the joy of bringing up their own daughter or son, and finally reunited in Toxteth Park Cemetery after a separation of four years, Peter and Mary have lain peacefully together for over a century. They would perhaps be pleased to know that Oriel Chambers, 16 Cook Street and their home at Falkner Square have all survived the ravages of bulldozers and bombs and have preserved a memory of their existence.

Their grave can be found by entering the cemetery through the main entrance on Smithdown Road and walking along the principal path for about 150 yards. To the left will then be seen a wide grassy path leading to the derelict chapel and, upon taking that path, within about 15 yards and just to the left, their cross and resting place will be reached.

References and Notes to Chapter 11

1 Although the numerical sections of the 1885 directory show 40 Falkner Square and Peter's office at Oriel Chambers as empty, there is an entry for him in the alphabetical section (*'Ellis Peter, C.E. architect surveyor and valuer 40 Falkner square, E – office 10 Oriel chambers 14 Water st. W'*), this part of the directory presumably having been compiled before Peter's death in October 1884.

2 *'£5000 Wanted, on Mortgage, on three blocks of Semi-detached Houses in Liverpool, valued by Mr. Peter Ellis. Principals only dealt with. – Address B 155, Mercury-office.'* (10th January 1884). *'Wanted, £5000 at 4 percent on good Freehold Villa Houses in Liverpool, valued by Mr. Peter Ellis. Principals only dealt with. – Address K 143, Mercury-office.'* (15th and 20th May 1884).

On 14th June 1873 Peter placed an advertisement in the *Mercury* regarding *'Workshops and Yard to be Let, suitable for a cabinet-maker, a joiner, or other trade, in Fontenoy-street, close to Dale-street.'* This would have brought back distant recollections of life in neighbouring Primrose Hill, and his father's early occupation there as a joiner.

Other examples of advertisements concerning valuations carried out by Peter include those in 1878 (17th May), 1881 (30th May), and 1882 (13th June and 27th June).

Peter's name also appears in a case concerning forgery by a collector in the Liverpool Gas Fittings Company (8th and 9th July 1878), and a Town Council meeting in which reference was made to a valuation that Peter had previously carried out (3rd October 1878).

3 Nikolaus Pevsner, *The Buildings of England. Lancashire. I. The Industrial and Commercial South*, Penguin Books, 1969, p. 181.

4 Notification of the opening of the original Philharmonic Hall was carried in a long and enthusiastic report *'from our own correspondent'*, together with two views (internal and external), in the 1st September 1849 edition of the *Illustrated London News*, p. 153.

5 J A Picton, *Memorials of Liverpool*, G G Walmsley (Liverpool), 1875, 2nd edn., vol. II, p. 254 for the Church, p. 251 for the Hall.

6 Opening of the New Homoeopathic Dispensary, *Liverpool Mercury*, Monday 26th November 1860. The article also gave extensive coverage to the circumstances which had necessitated the construction of the dispensary and provided a description of the building's internal arrangements. To the selective eyesight of James Picton the dispensary was invisible. In his tour of the area he wrote of walking north along Rodney Street, emerging at its junction with Leece Street and turning right into Hardman Street. *'Ascending the street, the first object which strikes the eye is St Philip's Church, a Gothic building of rather peculiar construction...'* (*op. cit.*, p. 248).

7 The records of the Hahnemann Homoeopathic Dispensaries on Hardman Street and elsewhere, and subsequently the 1887 hospital on Hope Street, are contained in a series of archives at the LRO, listed under references which all begin 614 HAH.

There is also *'A Brief History of the Liverpool Hahnemann (Homoeopathic) Hospital 1887-1972'* by Clifford Brewer under ref. Hq 362.116 BRE.

The handwritten minute books from 1857, ref. 614 HAH 20/1/1, show that *'The first meeting of this Society was convened at the house of Dr Drysdale, 44, Rodney Street, Liverpool, on the 6th May, 1857,'* and, for example, that the third meeting was held at Dr Roche's home at 79 Canning Street, and the sixth meeting at Dr Stoke's house at 13 Bedford Street North.

At the 15th meeting on 5th December 1860 it was decided that *'members residing in Liverpool shall contribute an annual subscription of £1-1-0, country members 10/6, towards the formation of a medical library at the Homoeopathic Dispensary in Hardman Street, and also the nucleus of a museum or collection of specimens of medicines &c.'* Following the opening of the dispensary, subsequent meetings were held there, beginning on the evening of 2nd January 1861.

An agreement had been reached some years earlier that absentees would be fined for non-attendance, and the minutes of the meeting of 4th December 1861 record: *'Dr. Hayward absent, fine 2/6.'* At the meeting on 5th February 1862 a resolution was presented suggesting *'the propriety of placing this Dispensary on a similar basis* [to others]*, and requiring payment from all patients at the rate of one penny for each prescription, and one shilling, or half a crown, per week or month, for visits to be paid to their own homes.'* Dr Hayward's fine for non-attendance at one of their clinical meetings thus equated to the monthly cost to a patient for securing home visits, and it is perhaps doubtful that modern private health practitioners have maintained this charming aspect of self-regulation.

The *'Sundry Reports, Liverpool Homoeopathic Dispensaries, 1872 – 1884'* are filed under ref. 614 HAH 8/2/1. Amongst the list of donors (where Peter's contribution of £20 is mentioned) there appears *'Mr Henry Tate'* (of Tate and Lyle sugar fame and the founder of the Tate Gallery) who donated £25 and who would later be the inspiration for the Hahnemann hospital in Hope Street.

In the report for January 1884 it was noted that the previous year had seen 27,646 in-door attendances and 12,628 out-door attendances at Hardman Street, and that (added to those at the dispensary at Roscommon Street in Everton) *'the numbers for the past year are greater than those of any preceding one,'* frequently between 100 and 200 each morning.

Homoeopathic medicine was by then on such a well established basis that the annual meeting of the subscribers in 1884 is recorded as taking place at the Town Hall with the Mayor occupying the chair. The Mayor donated £10 at the meeting, and his speech in support of the dispensaries was received with frequent outbursts of *'hear, hear.'*

However, the 1860 *Mercury* report (ref. 6) had also noted that *'homoeopathy has had to encounter no small amount of prejudice and opposition... prejudice on the part of the community... and opposition from the professors of allopathy,'* and a quarter of a century later the correspondence columns of the 1887 *Liverpool Review* (LRO microfilm; 26th February, 19th and 26th March) reveal a heated exchange between Dr John Hayward (a founder member of the Hardman Street Homoeopathic Medical Board - see adjacent paragraph) and a supporter of allopathy (conventional medicine) who saw fit to caricature and ridicule homoeopathy.

8 The events are recorded by a parishioner and for many years the organist, Richard E Livesey, in *Reminiscences of Saint Philip's Church. Hardman Street, Liverpool. 1867-1882*, G G Walmsley, 1882 (LRO ref. 283.1 PHI). The 1883 directory lists no property between Baltimore Street and South Hunter Street, suggesting that the loss of the church had generated some uncertainty as to the future of the dispensary. In the event, it was re-listed in the 1884 edition together with eight (and eventually ten) shops which had appeared alongside it, and was last listed in 1887. The LRO has further information on St Philip's (ref. 283 PLP) including reference to a report in the *Liverpool Post and Mercury*, 15th December 1925, p. 5, indicating that the church had in fact survived behind the newly erected shops and became a dance hall.

9 John Hulley, the founder of the modern Olympic movement, has already been mentioned in chapter 2, ref. 2. See the *Illustrated London News*, 1st May 1869, p. 449 for a sketch of a bicycle tournament in his gymnasium, and p. 445 for an account of the tournament in which competitors, each riding a '*two-wheeled velocipede*', attempted to remove rings suspended from a beam using lances.

10 Joseph Sharples, *Liverpool. Pevsner Architectural Guides*, Yale University Press, 2004, p. 234.

11 Peter lived in an age before the arrival of the motor car, the electrified tram and the overhead railway. Everywhere that he is known to have lived and worked on a regular basis lay roughly within a radius of a mile of his birthplace on Shaw's Brow and was therefore easily accessible by horse or on foot. However, advertisements in the *Liverpool Mercury* during May 1878 indicate that he did occasionally travel further afield, in this case to Garston to carry out a valuation for a client wishing to sell a group of eight houses and a shop. Peter may have chosen to travel there by paying 6d to take the horse-drawn omnibus from Castle Street, and no doubt would have watched with interest to see what the conductor did with his fare.

12 For references to Dr Drysdale in the Hahnemann Minute Books, see LRO ref. 614 HAH 20/1/1. For mention of him in the Annual Report dated January 1884, see LRO ref. Hahnemann Annual Reports, 614 HAH 8/2/1. Drysdale was a fairly unusual name and, although it may be mere coincidence, the firm of John and Joseph Drysdale, South American merchants, is shown as having an office at Oriel Chambers from 1887.

13 *Liverpool Daily Post*, 21st October 1884. Notification: p. 7, column 1. Comment: p. 5, column 4 (LRO microfilm). The notification of Peter's death also appeared in *The Times*, 29th October 1884, p. 1.

14 *Liverpool Daily Post*, 24th October 1884. LRO microfilm Eq 330, Obituary Notices, Vol. 4, 1884, item 6. Women did not usually attend funerals in those days, instead sending their carriages as a mark of respect. Mary's would have been one of the carriages mentioned.

The '*Mr. Thos. Haigh*' mentioned in the funeral party was a fellow architect; amongst other buildings, he designed Compton House in Church Street (now Marks and Spencer's; see Joseph Sharples, *op. cit.*, pp. 175-6). Like Cornelius Sherlock and Samuel Belcher, Thomas clearly had regarded it as important to attend the burial. The same age as Peter, and although having moved in 1882 from 4 Canning Street to retirement in a house at Speke, Thomas had made the journey back to offer his farewell to a colleague, and is further proof that Peter remained highly respected in the community.

15 Geoffrey Woodward, Oriel Chambers, *The Architectural Review*, 119, 1956, p. 268, quoted from the Daily Post account of the funeral. Quentin Hughes, who would also have had access to the report, would have seen the *'Aged 80 years'* statement, and might therefore have made the calculation of 1884 - 80 = 1804 birth.

16 Copies of Peter and Mary's wills and the associated Letters of Administration can be obtained from Leeds Probate Registry, York House, York Place, Leeds LS1 2BA. For historical currency conversions see: www.nationalarchives.gov.uk/currency

17 Obituary. Mr. Cornelius Sherlock, *Liverpool Citizen*, 28th January 1888. Also quoted by Hugh Hollinghurst, *Classical Liverpool, language, sculpture and architecture*, Liverpool History Society, 2008, p. 88.

18 Joseph Sharples, *op. cit.*, p. 144. See fig. 10,12 (p. 179) for a 1950s comparison of the two buildings.

19 Quoted by Joseph Sharples, *op. cit.*, p. 245.

20 Geoffrey Woodward, *op. cit.*, commented, with regard to Oriel Chambers, that *'In 1949, when the building was first measured, the name of the architect seemed to have been lost. However, as the result of a short article in the Liverpool Daily Post describing the research, a letter was received from the architect's grand-daughter revealing his identity.'* Since Peter and Mary had no children, who this *'grand-daughter'* actually was is an intriguing puzzle.

21 For many years 17 Sandon Street had been run as a boys' school. On p. 80 of the advertisements section of *Gore's Directory* for 1862, for example, it is shown as the *'Falkner Square Academy. A Select Day and Boarding School for Young Gentlemen,'* run by Andrew Wilson. The academy was maintained later by Joseph Collins, and then in 1883 the address is shown as empty.

In 1884 the Misses Johnson, accompanied by their mother, were correctly entered at that address in the Sandon Street numerical, but with the three other listings all leading to the impression that *Falkner house* was at 40 Falkner Square. The 1886 and 1887 directories show the same pattern, with Hannah and Elise being listed at 16 Falkner Square in the numerical, the same address as that of William Wilson.

Chapter 12

20th century acclaim

History, to be accurate, must be thick enough to include the various levels of taste, to explain, or at least to expound, survivals as well as innovations, for frequently it is the conflict between tradition and novelty which produces the total culture of a time.

George Boas, quoted by Henry-Russell Hitchcock in *Early Victorian Architecture in Britain*, Vol. 1

That an appreciation of the importance of Oriel Chambers did not come until a very considerable period after Peter's death is evident from Charles Reilly's adverse comments as late as 1921:-

> *'After the empty site where the old Cunard Building was, comes the oddest building in Liverpool – Oriel Chambers. It is a sort of honeycomb of numberless plate-glass oriel windows held together by a stonework skeleton frame designed to look like cast-iron. One feels sure it obeys in every detail Mr Ruskin's lamp of truth – it is at once so logical and so disagreeable. But I hope it won't be destroyed for many years to come. Its humour as a cellular habitation for the human insect is a distinct asset to its town'.* [1]

Whether the German High Command pencilled a '*note for action*' in their own copy of Reilly's book is unknown, but the May Blitz of 1941 did indeed destroy a substantial part of the Covent Garden section of Oriel Chambers (facing page and fig. 12,1).

Facing page. A photograph taken in 1942 by W H Tomkinson showing the bomb damage to the Covent Garden face of Oriel Chambers in May 1941.

Image courtesy of the LRO, ref. Photographs & Small Prints: Commerce & Industry: Firms: Oriel Chambers.

12,1. A detail from a view along Covent Garden in 1949 showing what had been lost through wartime damage.

Image courtesy of the LRO, ref. as for facing page.

12,2. A photograph taken in 1942 by W H Tomkinson showing the entrance to the Covent Garden face of Oriel Chambers following wartime damage in May 1941. Having survived the bombing it failed to survive the bulldozers.

Image courtesy of the LRO, ref. Photographs & Small Prints: Commerce & Industry: Firms: Oriel Chambers.

For Peter's critics, that bomb damage would have provided a golden opportunity to pull the whole building down, but by then the tide was at last turning in his favour, and it was an article in *The Architectural Review* in 1956 that led the way:-

> *'The list of Victorian framed buildings that can now be seen to forecast modern architecture is steadily growing; few show such a mixture of boldness and assurance as this rediscovered pair in Liverpool by Peter Ellis.'* [2]

So began Geoffrey Woodward's short account of the research which he and his colleagues had carried out in 1949 whilst students at the Liverpool School of Architecture. He looked back sadly on the fact that:-

> *'Further demolition was carried out in the interest of public safety, with a complete lack of sympathy for the unique character of the building.'*

Oriel Chambers lost its attractive Covent Garden entrance which had survived the war (fig. 12,2) and which was replaced during the subsequent rebuilding programme by the doorway which exists today (fig. 12,3). Geoffrey Woodward's review provided an enthusiastic analysis of both Oriel Chambers and 16 Cook Street:-

> *'Having survived almost ninety years of hostility and derision, the building, now partially in ruins, became the object of serious investigation and humble appraisal,'* and, for 16 Cook Street, *'The mastery and confidence shown in the treatment of these elevations makes it difficult to realise that they were designed over 90 years ago and that their architect remains unrecognized and unacclaimed both by his own generation and by ours.'*

12,3. The doorway to 5 Covent Garden which replaced the original side entrance to Oriel Chambers; photographed in May 2010 together with part of the adjacent window of Mersey Chambers.

12,4. The old and the new on the Covent Garden façade, photographed in August 2011, showing the original elevation alongside the new building by James & Bywaters (the doorway in fig. 12,3 is to the right of this photograph).

Although Geoffrey Woodward had lamented the demolition of the damaged parts of Oriel Chambers, in 1964 Quentin Hughes provided a generously worded caption to a photograph in *Seaport*. '*War damage on the Covent Garden façade made good and the demolished portion rebuilt sympathetically by James and Bywaters, 1963.*' [3] Subsequently an article outlining the reconstruction appeared in *Architecture: North West* with the comment that:-

> *'The new building was planned on an identical structural grid to the old building to keep the street rhythm going and to maintain the same scale. A strong vertical emphasis was provided which is planned off-centre to the structure to achieve direction towards Water Street and an attentive feeling towards the old building.'* [4]

Along with the reconstruction of this Covent Garden façade (fig. 12,4) changes were also made to the Water Street frontage. The lower ground floor level in 1949 (fig. 12,5) may be compared with the alterations as they look today (fig. 12,6), two doorways having replaced the windows on either side of the entrance. The plaque below the '*14*' to the right of the main entrance reads:-

> *'Oriel Chambers 1960. David Brock, Architect. War damaged in May 1941. Reinstated by Melville Curlender.'*

In 1964 Quentin Hughes had also written, perhaps with a side-swipe at Charles Reilly's cheap '*Ruskin*' sarcasm, that Peter was:-

> *'of national importance for he carried a stage further the logical aesthetic of iron frame construction foreseen by Ruskin and initiated in such buildings as the Crystal Palace... Few buildings foreshadow the Modern Movement so strikingly as his courtyard designs for Oriel Chambers and No. 16 Cook Street, built at a time when cast iron was tending elsewhere to deteriorate into an abundance of elaborate and florid decoration'.* [5]

Peter was soon to become seen as being of even greater than national importance. Hofmann and Kultermann in their survey of world architecture from 1850 to the date of their publication (1969 in Germany; 1970 in the English translation) chose just seven buildings throughout the world to illustrate the 1850-1870 period: one in France, one in Italy, one in the USA and four in Britain (the Red House, Bexley Heath; the Corn Exchange, Leeds; St Pancras Station, London; and Oriel Chambers).

12,5. A view of the lower ground floor offices at Oriel Chambers in 1949, showing the premises of the cigar merchant Turmeau's and the stationers Beale and Hillier. On the upper ground floor can be seen the agency offices of the P&O Line.

Image courtesy of the LRO, ref. Photographs & Small Prints: Commerce & Industry: Firms: Oriel Chambers.

12,6. A view in March 2012 of the changes which were made to the lower ground floor frontage of Oriel Chambers half a century ago. On the right is the office of Copy Stop. The premises on the left (previously the tailor's Berkley Bowen) had become empty when the photograph was taken.

Hofmann and Kultermann used Geoffrey Woodward's account as their starting point and provided what is perhaps the earliest published full-page colour photograph of Oriel Chambers together with an admiring commentary:-

> *'The building is an early example of the type of commercial architecture which is usually thought to have begun around the end of the century in Chicago, and which is normally associated with the steel skeleton technique. The epoch-making importance of this building has only recently been recognised... its large protruding windows designed to admit the maximum amount of light into the interior (an idea which W. L. Jenney, in particular, adopted in his Chicago skyscrapers)... The building is a masterpiece of early commercial architecture... The importance of the work of Peter Ellis, which may have been seen by Louis Sullivan when he travelled to Paris via Liverpool, lies in the fact that he took account of the requirements of the work which would be done inside the building (by providing a glass façade), and still managed to produce a solution which is both formally and stylistically convincing... It is a starting point for modern architecture...'* [6]

This is a remarkable and quite moving account from two German architects who no doubt were immensely grateful that the Luftwaffe had managed to damage the building only sufficiently for the secret of its construction to be revealed. Joseph Sharples has noted of Liverpool in general that:-

> *'With hindsight, wartime bomb damage was less destructive than the subsequent efforts of architects and planners... Reconstruction received further encouragement in 1965 when the Liverpool City Centre Plan was published... this headily up-beat document was intended to provide a framework for comprehensive redevelopment. Its authors declared that two-thirds of the centre was obsolete...'* [7]

Fortunately the programme was scaled back greatly and a significant number of buildings that had survived the war also survived the Shankland Plan, though other areas of the city such as Everton were destined to be comprehensively obliterated by the City Planners. [8]

The commentaries by Geoffrey Woodward, Quentin Hughes, and Hofmann and Kultermann together with their accompanying photographs provide excellent technical insights into why 16 Cook Street and Oriel Chambers are now treasured features of Liverpool's heritage.

By 1969 Nikolaus Pevsner was citing Oriel Chambers as '*one of the most remarkable buildings of its date in Europe*', a view echoed in 1983 by D K Stenhouse, in his paper on Liverpool's Office District, [9] and praise for Peter's work has continued into the 21st century.

In an article in an on-line publication, a photocopy of which can be seen in the entrance to 16 Cook Street, the architect Adam Caruso wrote:-

> *'I am particularly interested in why Peter Ellis chose to clad his cast-iron structures in stone, organised according to a Gothic language – something that prefigured what John Wellborn Root and Louis Sullivan would later do in Chicago. He was developing an expression for his building that was in addition to, and was autonomous of, their technology.'* [10]

The website *Engineering Timelines* notes of Oriel Chambers that it:-

> *'had considerable influence on the design of tall office buildings, particularly in America through the American architect John Root's early Chicago skyscrapers. For these he drew heavily on Ellis's work, which he studied first hand while in England to avoid the American Civil War.'* [11]

The comment that John Wellborn Root saw Oriel Chambers and 16 Cook Street, either complete or under construction, and was influenced by them is now a feature of almost every modern commentary. Following her approach to the Chicago Public Library for information, Gillian Ward has done more than many to consider in detail Root's connection with Liverpool as a result of his father's partnership in the company *Beach, Root and Co* with premises in Hackins Hey (a few hundred yards from Oriel Chambers and 16 Cook Street). With convincing photographic comparisons, she comments that:-

> *'the feature employed by Root which is most reminiscent of Ellis's work is the oriel stair tower of the Rookery, of which 16 Cook St* <u>*must*</u> *be the precursor.'* [12, 13]

12,7. The Mersey Ferries' own on-board tribute to Peter Ellis, from a poster photographed on the Royal Daffodil in May 2010. Image used courtesy of Mersey Ferries.

In a fascinating article on Glasgow warehouses and office blocks, Gerald Blaikie writes of James Salmon's stunning 1902 Hatrack Building that, *'I suspect that Salmon was inspired by Oriel Chambers in Liverpool...'* [14] This Glasgow building also bears some striking similarities to 16 Cook Street.

In 2006 Oriel Chambers was the subject of a field trip by students from the Manchester School of Architecture which was followed up by the production of an historically valuable video. [15]

Such is the esteem in which Peter's work is now held that an excursion on the Royal Daffodil in 2010 would have provided an opportunity for visitors to Liverpool to read a Mersey Ferries' poster with its own tribute to him (fig. 12,7), whilst a six year old with an interest in knowing the location of the smallest skyscraper in the world found that the reply made passing reference to Oriel Chambers. [16]

12,8. Oriel Chambers on 14th February 2010: scaffolding completed and with shrouding underway in preparation for renovation.

12,9. 25th March 2010. 'Businesses open as usual', it says, merely follow the arrows...

Oriel Chambers passed into new ownership in 2006 and plans were put in hand for internal modernisation and an external facelift. Scaffolding began in January 2010 with shrouding following on in February (fig. 12,8) and the renovation took much longer than the occupants of the basement shops had anticipated. For eight months many potential customers passing the hidden doorways, and despite the notices (fig. 12,9), may have assumed that the two shops had temporarily closed down.

In October 2010 work on the exterior of the building was finally completed (see Introduction, p. xi). By December Berkley Bowen's premises had become empty, but Copy Stop continues to provide a valuable local service. If you visit it when the owner, Tony Connell, is there you may be fortunate to learn quite a lot about the building's more recent history.

12,10. Oriel's remaining chimney stacks, the chimney pots having been removed in the late 20th century.

Peter's design included a fireplace in every office, an architectural consideration that was apparently far from commonplace at the time. The wonderful original tall chimney pots (see p. 150) had been replaced by taller chimney stacks and smaller pots by the turn of the century (see, for example, the 1960s view on p. 58 of Quentin Hughes' *Seaport*), and the pots were removed completely some years ago leaving only the stacks today as a reminder (fig. 12,10).

The entrance to Oriel Close is now normally locked, its ground floor premises currently sad and empty, and access to Oriel Chambers itself is via the apparently inevitable 21st century intercom and key-pad. How changed from the days when Peter would have walked unhindered into his office, and '*The Oriel*' was *the* restaurant in Liverpool!

Whereas casual access to Oriel Chambers and Oriel Close is far from straightforward for Peter Ellis enthusiasts, the situation at 16 Cook Street could hardly be more different (fig. 12,11). Liverpool is extremely fortunate that the second of Peter's two famous buildings is owned by Olwen McLaughlin and Stephen Edgar who display a sensitive love for the building and its history.

12,11. April 2012. The open doorway greets the visitor to 16 Cook Street, from where there is already a tempting glimpse of the display panel designed by Stephen Edgar, one of the building's owners.

12,13. The 16 Cook Street staircase in April 2012 as typically photographed from the tiny courtyard. One of Quentin Hughes' photographers (Graham Smith or David Wrightson) also managed to obtain a view from an upper floor at the rear of a building in Harrington Street which shows the relationship of the conical top to the neighbouring buildings (ref. 3, p. 64).

If you step through its open doorway during weekday business hours you will be greeted with an attractive floor mounted display reminding you that, '*Peter Ellis's iconic buildings shocked Victorians with his bold use of modern methods and materials*' (fig. 12,12).

Booking on one of the guided tours which Stephen holds at regular intervals can be made via the office of their Contemporary Arts Gallery, *Editions* (0151 236 4236).

The office has a doorway through which entrance to the rear of the building may be gained, and thus an exterior view of the staircase (fig. 12,13). For Nikolaus Pevsner, '*The courtyard is from the point of view of the Modern Movement even more amazing*', and for Quentin Hughes the staircase was '*the most remarkable feature.*' [17] Together they illustrate Peter's ingenuity in making full use of the confined space into which the building had to be constructed.

No wonder Peter chose to introduce '*civil engineer*' into his self-description: a beautiful cast-iron staircase cantilevered from the main floors in one building; the world's first paternoster lift in the other!

12,12. A close-up of the display panel at 16 Cook Street. Behind it, the exquisite cast iron staircase begins its ascent (see back cover).

The staircase that Peter originally designed began conventionally (fig. 12,14) and only became spiral from first floor level, and that is how the firm of Paterson and Thomas would always have known it. Following late 20th century modifications the spiral was extended one floor lower by carefully reproducing the design of the upper section. Ascending the staircase today (fig. 12,15) provides a series of fascinating glimpses of the surrounding buildings and delightful views across rooftops (figs. 12,16 and 12,17).

12,16. A view looking south from the top of the staircase.

12,14. A mid-20th century view of the first rise of the original cast-iron staircase leading to the spiral staircase (which now extends to the floor below). The 'PA' and 'TH' of the firm of Paterson and Thomas can just be seen in reverse on the front window.

Image courtesy of the University of Liverpool Library (ref. Quentin Hughes Archive D71/22/13/6).

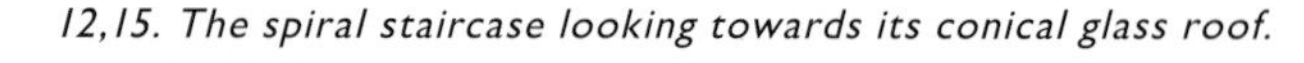

12,15. The spiral staircase looking towards its conical glass roof.

12,17. A view looking east, with the Municipal Building clock to the left and the tower of the Clayton Square Shopping Centre to the right.

It seems very appropriate that a firm of architects has its practice in this building, and the office of ABW contains Peter's interesting but now unusable safe which, to casual inspection, appears to be nothing more than a doorway to another room. The heavy iron door however is two and a half inches thick and eight feet six inches high. It is secured with four large bolts operated by an octagonal door-knob, but the key for the tiny half-inch keyhole was lost in the dim and distant past and the safe is now of curiosity value and as useful additional storage.

The building is described as having '*a cast-iron frame with 6 in. by 6 in. members and flat brick arches.*' [18] The arched ceilings at the rear of each floor of the building (fig. 12,18) are at right angles to those nearest the street. The plan on p. 127 (fig. 7,8), shows this method of construction, together with the position of the original safe in the bottom left hand corner of the plan.

12,18. The graceful arched ceiling in the office of the architects ABW, with a glimpse of the door to the original safe, now unused, in the corner of the room.
Image used with kind permission.

12,19. 40 Falkner Square from the entrance to the gardens in June 2011.

12,20. The English Heritage plaque.

It is very fitting that an English Heritage plaque now marks Peter's presence at 40 Falkner Square (figs. 12,19 and 12,20), and the Blue Plaques Team kindly provided a copy of the final report of their 1999 Merseyside Plaques Panel Meeting endorsing the suggestion of erecting the plaque. In support of the proposal it is evident that the committee drew heavily upon the commentary in *Seaport* by Quentin Hughes, and the report also recorded that Henry-Russell Hitchcock in his *Architecture Nineteenth and Twentieth Centuries* (1958) *'gives proper notice to Ellis'* (and in which Hitchcock acknowledges Geoffrey Woodward's important original account).

Simon Harratt, historian and author of the report, [19] remarked that Peter Ellis:-

> *'was the most remarkable Liverpool architect of the mid-nineteenth century... now praised for the radically functional aspects of his designs which are regarded as portents of the later emergence of the skyscraper in 1880s Chicago.'*

However, he perhaps provides most delight for Peter Ellis admirers when he also noted that Peter:-

> *'is accorded a full entry in the International Dictionary of Architects and Architecture (1993). By contrast, the Liverpool and Merseyside architects, Sir Patrick Abercrombie and Sir Charles Reilly are not deemed worthy of inclusion in this volume.'*

12,21. February 2013. Some of the many fallen and damaged gravestones close to that of Peter and Mary.

Despite wartime bombing, Oriel Chambers was destined to '*Stand Sure*', as the façade continues to proclaim (see inside back cover). Providence has also protected Peter and Mary's cross in a part of the cemetery where quite a number of gravestones are now lying broken and forlorn (fig. 12,21).

In October 2011, Rob and I planted primroses at their grave, and also in one of the beds of shrubs at Primrose Hill, exactly 200 years after Peter had moved from his home there at the age of six to his third home in Gloucester Street, and fresh plants were added in March 2012 and February 2013.

It would be good to think that some aspiring architects on one of the city's university courses might like to adopt the site in Primrose Hill, to tend the beds occasionally and keep them tidy.

Between the tree and the flyover (fig. 12,22) is where Ellis Court once existed and is as close as can be identified to the home at 19 Primrose Hill where Peter learned to walk, and from where he stepped forth into the life that would lead to Oriel Chambers, 16 Cook Street, 40 Falkner Square, the world's first paternoster lift – and much else.

12,22. The tree in Primrose Hill which locates the entrance to Ellis Court. Somewhere nearby, at what was 19 Primrose Hill, had been Peter's home between 1807 and 1811.

References and Notes to Chapter 12

1 C H Reilly, *Some Liverpool Streets and Buildings in 1921*, Liverpool Daily Post and Mercury, 1921, p. 40. LRO ref. 720 REI. Professor Reilly was equally enchanted with other buildings on Water Street. '*One would think it would be impossible to achieve a more clumsily-detailed building than the Liver Building, yet the same architect has beaten his own record with the Tower Building. To do so, in addition to the same coarse classical detail as the Liver, though in this case with an incongruous admixture of equally bad Gothic, he has had resource to a veneer of white glazed ware...*'

9-0 p.m. FIREWORKS (provided by the LORD MAYOR) in Newsham Park.

9-20 p.m.—10-10 p.m. — Broadcast debate from 6LV.: "Is Civic Week Worth While?" Proposed by Mr. MATTHEW ANDERSON, Civic Week Secretary; opposed by Professor C. H. REILLY. In the chair: Sir ARNOLD RUSHTON, J.P.

In 1927 a debate, '*Is Civic Week Worth While?*', was announced in that year's '*Liverpool Civic Week*' booklet (reproduced above) and was broadcast on Merseyside's first local radio station 6LV from a café in Lord Street during the crystal set era. It was proposed by Matthew Anderson and opposed by Charles Reilly. If Matthew was a descendant of a relative of the Thomas Anderson for whom Peter designed Oriel Chambers, it would be interesting to know who won the debate.

Having made his dismissive remarks about Oriel Chambers in 1921, it is significant that by the age of 60 Charles Reilly had become a convert to the modernist movement. In his '*semi-architectural autobiography*' (*Scaffolding in the Sky*, George Routledge & Sons, 1938, p. 287) he remarked that '*my conviction that we live to-day in a new world requiring a new architecture, and that we have the materials for it at hand, has grown stronger.*' He was thus sufficiently proud to have been the consulting architect for London's 1930s Peter Jones Store ('*The new building in steel and glass, facing Sloane Square and King's Road in Chelsea*') to include a view of it in his book.

2 Geoffrey Woodward, Oriel Chambers, *The Architectural Review*, 119, 1956, p. 268.

3 Quentin Hughes, *Seaport. Architecture and Townscape in Liverpool*, Lund Humphries, 1964, p. 59. Reprinted with postscript by The Bluecoat Press, 1993.

4 Extension. Oriel Chambers Liverpool, *Architecture: North West*, June-July 1965, p. 11. LRO ref. 720.5 ARC.

5 Quentin Hughes, *op. cit.*, p. 57.

6 Werner Hofmann and Udo Kultermann, *Modern Architecture in Colour*, p. 64. English translation by Peter Usborne, 1970, Thames & Hudson, London.

The decorative brackets which can be seen on each side of the Covent Garden doorway prior to demolition (fig. 12,2) were still present on the Oriel Close entrance in Hofmann & Kultermann's view in plate 6 of their book. Sadly these were removed during refurbishment of the Water Street face.

7 Joseph Sharples, *Liverpool. Pevsner Architectural Guides*, Yale University Press, 2004, p. 35. When Nikolaus Pevsner wrote his original commentary (*The Buildings of England. Lancashire. I. The Industrial and Commercial South*, Penguin Books, 1969) he was aghast at what had happened and was continuing to happen to Liverpool's architectural history.

He viewed the demolition of many of the city's churches as '*a disgraceful record... Foster's St Catherine Abercromby Square of 1829-31, and Rickman's St Jude Hardwick Street of 1831 have been allowed to disappear – the last named only in 1966 and St Catherine just as recently and especially scandalously*' (p. 144). Demolition of the front of the Cotton Exchange in 1967 was '*yet another act of civic vandalism*' (p. 162), '*The magnificent, classical warehouse of 1811* [at the Duke's Dock], *one of the oldest preserved examples of the type in Liverpool, was senselessly destroyed in 1966*' (p. 164), whilst one of James Picton's fine designs, '*Richmond Buildings, to the disgrace of Liverpool, was demolished in 1967*' (p. 171).

He regarded the Sailors' Home in Canning Place as '*an amazing sight*' (p. 169) and would have been outraged when it too was demolished a few years later (now commemorated by the *Pooley Gates* - see Stephen McKay's article in the 2013 *Journal of the Liverpool History Society*).

Peter Howell-Williams (*Liverpolitana*, Merseyside Civic Society, 1971, p. 16) clearly had reservations about the quality of the city's rebuilding programme. '*Criticism of post-war office blocks by the Civic Society is acknowledged to have been right... Will any new city building be as well regarded in a century's time as that, say, of Peter Ellis' Oriel Chambers?*'

8 Ken Rogers, *The Lost Tribe of Everton & Scottie Road*, Trinity Mirror Media, 2010.

9 Nikolaus Pevsner, *op. cit.*, p. 177. D K Stenhouse, Liverpool's Office District, 1875-1905, *Transactions of the Historic Society of Lancashire and Cheshire*, 133, 1983, p. 80.

10 Adam Caruso, Inspiration: Ellis Buildings, Liverpool, *Building Design*, London, 8th January 2010, Issue 1898, pp. 14-15. See also Adam Caruso, The autonomy of artistic expression in the cast iron buildings of Peter Ellis, in Mario Rinke (ed) and Joseph Schwartz (ed), *Before Steel. The introduction of structural iron and its consequences*, Zurich, 2010, pp. 115-124.

11 From the Engineering Timelines website: www.engineering-timelines.com/scripts/engineeringItem.asp?id=713

12 Gillian Moore, *Peter Ellis (1804-1884), A Study of the Life and Work of a Nineteenth Century Provincial Architect*, University of Teesside: Institute of Design. BA (Hons) History of Design & Architecture, April 1997, p. 58. See her chapter 5, '*The American Connection*' for comments regarding *Beach, Root & Co* at Hackins Hey. The underlining of '*must*' is Gillian's, and her text is accompanied with a reproduction on p. 59 of an external view of the Rookery, and on p. 60 with photographs of the interiors of the staircases of the Rookery and 16 Cook Street. The letter from Quentin Hughes that Gillian received (her appendix 5) includes his comment, '*I agree there is a connection between Root's work and that of Ellis.*'

A copy of Gillian's typescript is held at the Walker Art Gallery. It was brought to my attention by Joseph Sharples in part of his valuable e-mail of 29th August 2012, and kindly made available for inspection by Janette Moran at the Walker.

13 Websites are largely repetitive in the sparse information on Root's connection with Liverpool. Wikipedia and elsewhere variously indicate that (a) he was born on 10th January 1850 in Georgia and raised in Atlanta, and that when this Confederate State fell to the Union in 1864 he was sent to Liverpool where his father Sidney Root had a shipping business; (b) whilst there he studied at the Clare Mount (or Claremont) School (location unidentified), went later to Oxford to begin to study drawing, and returned to America in 1866 when the civil war had ended; (c) he graduated in civil engineering at New York in 1869, became an influential American architect, and died on 15th January 1891 at the age of only 41.

The directories indicate that Sidney Root's business partnership had been established in Liverpool by 1864. *Gore's Directory* for that year lists '*Beach, Root & Co., merchants, Apsley buildings, 4 Old Hall st*', whilst the *Post Office Directory* for the same year (compiled later than *Gore's*) lists '*Beach, Root & Co. merchants & shipowners, Batavia buildings, Hackins hey.*' The 1865 and 1867 *Gore's Directories* list the company at this latter address, with the business becoming '*J. N. Beach and Co*' from 1868.

The name Root is highly unusual and first appears in the Liverpool directories in 1859 for a John Root, mariner. In 1860 this mariner is listed at '*45 Egerton Street, Sandon Street*'. Then from 1862 to 1864 Julia Root, presumably his widow, is shown at the same address and, in 1865, at 2 Bloom Street (also close to Falkner Square). Whether John Root, mariner, and Sidney Root were related is unknown but, if they were, John the mariner may have sailed on Sidney Root's ships which were employed in blockade running.

14 From Gerald Blakie's well-illustrated commentary in: *www.scotcities.com/warehouses.htm*

15 Sean Michael Furlong and Matthew Frost, *Manchester School of Architecture Fieldtrip Film Year 3, 2006-07.* This four minute video tour of Oriel Chambers and 16 Cook Street was prior to the former's internal renovation. It has a background accompaniment, *The Liverpool Waltzes*, a delightfully appropriate 1862 piano piece by Edward Hime. See: *www.youtube.com/watch?v=S_pQPhVWNTY*

16 Contained in architecture writer Owen Hatherley's reply to '*Edmund, 6*' in the *Ask a grown-up* column, *Guardian Weekend*, 26th Jan 2013, p. 6, and in which he continued by citing Louis Sullivan's 1891 10-storey Wainwright building in St Louis as the world's smallest skyscraper (see comments by Hofmann & Kultermann and by Adam Caruso regarding Louis Sullivan).

17 Nikolaus Pevsner, *op. cit.*, p. 171. Quentin Hughes, *op. cit.*, p. 65.

18 16 Cook Street, Liverpool, *Architectural History*, vol. 1, 1958, pp. 91-94 (obtainable from RIBA).

19 Simon Harratt, *Final Report: Peter Ellis*, for English Heritage National Blue Plaques Scheme, Merseyside Plaques Panel Meeting: 19th April 1999. Courtesy of the Blue Plaques Team, English Heritage, London, in a personal communication, 8th August 2011. Quotations from the report are with kind permission.

Members of the team have been made aware of Peter's date of birth and the decision has been made to leave the plaque with the dates shown, being based on the information that was available in 1999.

Appendix I

Chronology

		Chapter	
1805	1st August	1	Birth of Peter and baptism 1st September at St John, Haymarket.
1820	18th May	2	Corporation lease on building land in Gloucester Street (for Peter's father).
1824	24th February	2	Corporation lease on building land in Finch Street (for Robert Ellis, Peter's brother).
1824	7th December	2	Corporation lease on building land in Audley Street (for Peter's father).
1830	6th November	3	Corporation lease on building land in Kent Square (for Peter's father).
1832	7th January	3	Corporation lease on building land in Great George Square, Upper Pitt Street and White Street (for Peter's father).
1833	20th April	3	Corporation lease on building land in Great George Square, Upper Pitt Street and Cookson Street for the construction of up to 15 houses (for Peter; Peter Ellis senior has retired).
1835	4th March	5	Corporation lease on three properties in Chatham Street (later Sandon Street, one of which was Peter's first home) and neighbouring building land for the construction of two more houses (eventually 18 and 20 Sandon Street).
1836	28th April	5	Marriage to Mary Helen Syers.
1843	1st April	5	Corporation lease on building land in Falkner Square upon which Peter built 78 Canning Street.
1844	2nd November	6	Corporation lease on building land in Falkner Square upon which Peter built 40 Falkner Square.
1852	undated	6	Design of a house in Upper Parliament Street, the subject of a court case in 1854. Design and location possibly used for another client some years later.
1856	8th November	6	First stone laid for St Saviour's National Schools for which Peter was architect.

		Chapter	
1860	24th November	11	Hardman Street Homoeopathic Dispensary opened for which Peter was architect.
1863	5th September	7	First of a long series of advertisements placed by Peter for the letting of 59 Bold Street. Whether Peter was architect or merely letting agent is unknown.
1865	18th October	9	Commercial Union began to advertise its arrival at Oriel Chambers.
1865	25th October	9	Henry Curry began to advertise his arrival at Oriel Close.
1866	20th January	8	Criticism of Oriel Chambers in *The Builder*.
1866	10th August	10	*Liverpool Mercury* advertisement requesting tenders for construction of Hall Lane Baptist Church, with details obtainable from Peter. Peter subsequently confirmed by Quentin Hughes as being architect.
1867	26th November	9	Joseph Goodacre began to advertise his arrival at 16 Cook Street.
1870	undated	10	Hall Lane Baptist Church first listed in *Gore's Directory.*
1874	7th April	10	Parcels & Luggage Delivery Co Ltd celebrated the opening of their office at 20 School Lane for which Peter was architect.
1884	20th October	11	Peter died at home at 40 Falkner Square.
1941	4th May	12	Part of Covent Garden side of Oriel Chambers bombed.
1956	May	12	Geoffrey Woodward commenced process of 20th century acclaim.

After the Corporation leases which were issued to Peter early in his career (1833 – 1844), it appears that he subsequently was commissioned to design buildings for construction on clients' land. Some of these buildings have been identified because they happened to receive a report in the *Liverpool Mercury* and mentioned him by name. Buildings such as the Hall Lane Chapel, however, did not receive a *Mercury* report, and it is almost certain that other buildings which Peter designed also fall into this category (possibly 59 Bold Street) and would require evidence from other sources in order to be positively identified.

Appendix 2

Genealogies

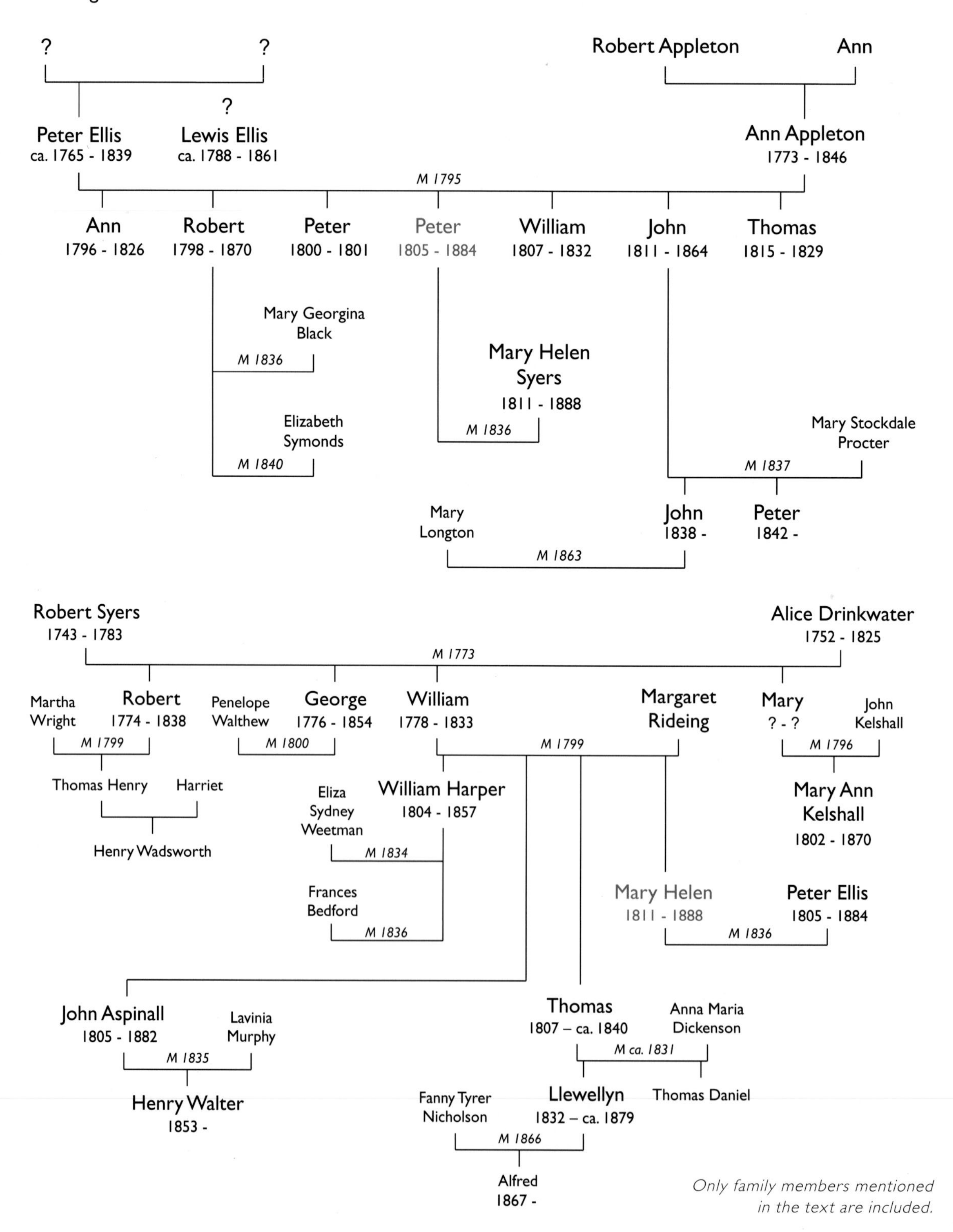

Only family members mentioned in the text are included.

Postscript

Arriving off the TransPennine Express at platform nine on Lime Street station, passengers are greeted by a glass panel separating the platform from the station car park. Etched into the panel are T S Eliot's famous lines:-

We shall not cease from exploration
And the end of all our exploring
Will be to arrive where we started
And know the place for the first time.

Walking around the city and revisiting the places where Peter grew up and later worked, fell in love and got married, and discovering some of the people he knew, has been an extraordinarily moving and transforming experience. Researching his story has helped me to discover many things about our wonderful city and its history that I would never otherwise have known. Eliot's *Four Quartets* opens with the lines:-

Time present and time past
Are both perhaps present in time future,
And time future contained in time past

and, retracing Peter's footsteps, so often I found myself transported to an earlier age as Peter's story unfolded itself before me.

There are so many tantalising questions that remain unanswered, and inevitably Rob and I may have drawn a few conclusions which future research will indicate require correction. However I hope you have enjoyed the journey that we have created for you, and that we have provided a few things of interest which will help you to know a little more than hitherto of the man whose office buildings are now so widely celebrated.

On a night when the wind is not gusting up Water Street from a chilly Mersey, when the restaurant revellers have departed, and when all earthly noise is hushed, if you shut your eyes and listen carefully outside the building, perhaps you will find that it is still possible to hear Peter's footsteps as he enters Oriel Chambers and the occasional movement of a chair as he sits thoughtfully at his desk.

Graham Jones
Water Street
2013

Index

People (excluding Peter and Mary)

Buildings (churches grouped first)

Additions and corrections

Additions

Page 2 (fig. 1,3), page 4 (fig. 1,8) and elsewhere.
Approximately 90 of James Brierley's late 1820s – early 1830s pen-and-ink views of Liverpool are kept at the Athenaeum. The publication of *Brierley's Liverpool* by Liverpool historian David Brazendale, in which he presents the collection along with detailed background information, remains eagerly awaited. Contact sales@carnegiepublishing.com to reserve a copy of this limited edition book (due October 2013).

Pages 54-55.
John Kilshaw was buried at St George, Everton (LRO microfilm ref. 283 GEV/4/1) and the monument to him and his family stands in the churchyard. The plaque on the left in the photograph reads:-

> *'In memory of John Kilshaw of Everton who departed this life on the 12th day of July 1848 aged 64 years also Jane relict of the above who departed this life on the 25th day of October 1848 aged 61 years.'*

The 1847 and 1848 directories show that John had retired to 1 Church Street (Heyworth Street today) in what were to prove to be both his and Jane's final years. The 1841 census did not include their eldest daughter Agnes (shown on the monument as born in 1810) as being with the family at Gloucester Street because she had been married in 1839 at St Bride's Church (where Peter Ellis and Mary Helen Syers had been married) (LRO ref. 283 BRI/3/2). However, although she had been about three years old when John Kilshaw obtained his 1813 Corporation lease, she was not included in the *'three lives and 21 years'* (and the children of John's three chosen joiners were all sons).

Pages 92-93.
Regarding Peter's introductory sentence to his *'Rejected Designs'* and the background to the competition. *The Civil Engineers and Architect's Journal*, 1840, p. 158, contains a critical letter by *'Q'* of 27th April concerning the conduct of the Assize Courts competition (and by implication that of the Concert Hall) in which *'the same egregious blunder has been here committed, -or if not blunder, the same crooked and perverse policy has been pursued'*. The writer concludes, with regard to Elmes' success, that *'it is rather singular that that gentleman should have chosen to enter a second competition immediately after succeeding in a previous one, unless he had particularly good reasons for anticipating success.'* My thanks to James O'Keeffe for this reference which can be read on Google Books.

Page 130, ref. 1.
Regarding Peter's office at Bank Buildings, 48 Castle Street in 1862. The view of *'Heywood's Bank, Castle Street, 1787'* (i.e. when the building had just been completed) appears in John Hughes' account of *Liverpool Banks and Bankers, 1760-1837*, Henry Young and Sons, 1906 (LRO ref. H 332.1 HUG), and a footnote on p. 98 of the book indicates that this was the building that was taken down in 1864.

HEYWOOD'S BANK, CASTLE STREET, 1787

Page 145, ref. 11.
Biographical details of the author of *The Porcupine* and *The Builder* articles appear in *The Mellards & Their Descendants* (LRO ref. H 920 REA; my thanks to Joseph Sharples for this reference) and in the 2003 *Journal of the Liverpool History Society* ('A Lover of Stone and Clay' by Florence Gersten, pp. 44-51). The former account records him in the late 1850s as being at his father's home in Lowther Street (off Sandon Street and a few yards from Falkner Square), and indicates that the articles that he had contributed to *The Builder* prior to 1866 had usually been signed. The latter account lists the many buildings for which he was the architect and concludes with the suggestion that '*It is time that Liverpool's debt, to this amiable and gifted man, was acknowledged.*'

Page 148, ref. 17.
Regarding the use of Storeton Stone for Oriel Chambers. On page 37 of *A Guide to Merseyside's Industrial Past* (published jointly by the North Western Society for Industrial Archaeology and History and Countyvise Ltd, 1984) Paul Rees indicates that Storeton Quarry was off Mount Road, Higher Bebbington and that it was:- '*Probably worked from Roman times. Provided stone for Hamilton Square (1830-40), the original Philharmonic Hall, Liverpool (1845) and many other buildings on both sides of the Mersey. Closed 1907.*' Quoted with kind permission of the Merseyside Industrial Heritage Society (www.mihs.org.uk) being the successor to the North Western Society.

Page 182, ref. 13.
Dr Lee Gray at the University of North Carolina at Charlotte has kindly e-mailed a copy of his May 2012 Part Two article which the British Library was unable to provide. It contains interesting descriptions of the first J&E Hall Cyclic Elevators in England and Scotland, and Dr Gray intends to provide a technical comparison of Peter's patent and Fred Hart's design. A disused 20th century paternoster lift exists at M&S on Church Street (the 1867 Compton House for which Thomas Haigh, who attended Peter's funeral, was the architect). Although now boarded up, it remains intact and was in use until the late 1990s. Whether it replaced a much earlier version is not known. My thanks to Ged O'Shea at M&S for the opportunity to inspect it.

Main corrections

Page 1, 2nd column, 3rd paragraph, 3rd line (and page 185).
The flour mills on Shaw's Brow were tower mills not smock mills. Having begun his career as a flour dealer as well as a joiner, Peter Ellis senior would certainly have known the difference.

Page 61, fig. 4,1.
The caption refers to the date of Mary's birth. The entry in the register was of course on the date of her baptism.

Page 171, 10th line.
Alter 1827 to 1927 (as correct in fig. 10,5).

Page 210, 14th line.
Amend 'Gillian Ward' to read 'Gillian Moore' (as correctly named in ref. 12, page 220, and in chapter 10).

Page 215, fig. 12,17.
The tower (Radio City Tower, formerly St John's Beacon) is adjacent to St John's Shopping Centre not the nearby Clayton Square Shopping Centre.

Page 227, 1st column.
Delete p. 219 from the entry listing for the Sailors' Home.

Graham Jones

Locations

Biographies

Robert Ainsworth (1955 - 2012)

Rob was born on 17th February 1955 and brought up in the Dingle, one of six siblings. The son of Amy and Robert, a brewery-man at Higson's Brewery in Liverpool's Stanhope Street, Rob was educated at Matthew Arnold Primary and Dingle Vale Secondary Modern, becoming head boy in his final year. He qualified as an Electrical Technician with Liverpool City Council, working for the LCC until 1993 when he branched out into contract work. In 1998 he moved into training and employment with the Civil Service, becoming an Executive Officer. Prior to early retirement in 2007 he qualified as a Yacht Master and gained an HND in Marine Operations from Liverpool John Moores University. From the early 1990s Rob was involved with a variety of heritage campaigns, including rescuing Galkoff's from demolition, and assisted the Liverpool Carters Association in fundraising to erect the carthorse statue '*Waiting*', located outside the Museum of Liverpool. Deeply concerned with conservation, he helped set up the Liverpool Cultural Heritage Forum. He became a formidable champion of just causes, gained recognition throughout the city for his efforts, and was the resident historian on Citytalk Radio. Rob held pivotal roles within the Liverpool History Society including, most recently, treasurer and webmaster. Greatly missed by family and friends, he died on 4th August 2012 following major vascular surgery.

(Adapted, with kind permission of Cynthia Stonall, LHS Hon. Librarian and friend, from her tribute in the Society's newsletter 34).

Graham Jones (1946 -)

Graham was born and brought up in Aigburth in the parish of St Michael's in the Hamlet where he was a member of the 46th Liverpool Company of the Boys' Brigade. He was educated at St Michael's Primary, the Blue Coat in Wavertree, and King's College, London. At King's he gained a BSc and PhD in Chemistry and then returned to Merseyside to take up a career as a research scientist with ICI at their Corporate Laboratory at Runcorn Heath. He later transferred to ICI's Petrochemicals Division on Teesside to lead a team working on one of the processes involved in polyester production. Taking early retirement in 1998 in order to retrain, he gained a C&G 730 Further & Adult Education Teachers' Certificate at York College and the Relate Certificate in Marital and Couple Counselling, and worked with Relate at Scarborough as a counsellor on a voluntary basis until 2008. Since then he has split his time between conducting historical research in Liverpool and enjoying rural life at the family home which he and his wife, Martha, retain in North Yorkshire. They have two grown up sons who have successfully flown the nest. Graham is an only child, left-handed, plays the piano badly (but not quite as badly as he cooks) and, in Myers-Briggs terms, is an INTJ. He knows absolutely nothing about architecture.

Matthew Duddington (1988 -)

Matthew trained at Staffordshire University, gaining a 1st with honours in Animation in 2010. He lives in Stoke on Trent and has established a freelance career as a Digital Creative and Storyteller: *www.matthewduddington.com*
This is his first commission as a book designer.